Listening to Rap

Over the past four decades, rap and hip hop have taken a central place in popular music both in the United States and around the world. *Listening to Rap: An Introduction* enables students to understand the historical context, cultural impact, and unique musical characteristics of this essential genre. Each chapter explores a key topic in the study of rap music from the 1970s to today, covering themes such as race, gender, commercialization, politics, and authenticity. Synthesizing the approaches of scholars from a variety of disciplines—including music, cultural studies, African-American studies, gender studies, literary criticism, and philosophy—*Listening to Rap* tracks the evolution of rap and hip hop while illustrating its vast cultural significance.

The text features more than 60 detailed listening guides that analyze the musical elements of songs by a wide array of artists, from Afrika Bambaataa and Grandmaster Flash to Nicki Minaj, Jay-Z, Kanye West, and more. A companion website showcases playlists of the music discussed in each chapter. Rooted in the understanding that cultural context, music, and lyrics combine to shape rap's meaning, the text assumes no prior knowledge. For students of all backgrounds, *Listening to Rap* offers a clear and accessible introduction to this vital and influential music.

Michael Berry is Lecturer in Music Theory at the University of Washington.

Listening to Rap

An Introduction

Michael Berry

University of Washington

Routledge
Taylor & Francis Group

NEW YORK AND LONDON

First published 2018
by Routledge
711 Third Avenue, New York, NY 10017

and by Routledge
2 Park Square, Milton Park, Abingdon, Oxon, OX14 4RN

Routledge is an imprint of the Taylor & Francis Group, an informa business

Library of Congress Cataloging-in-Publication Data
Names: Berry, Michael (Musicologist), author.
Title: Listening to rap : an introduction / Michael Berry.
Description: New York : Routledge, 2018. | Includes bibliographical
    references and index.
Identifiers: LCCN 2017060398 (print) | LCCN 2018000649 (ebook) |
    ISBN 9781315315881 (ebook) | ISBN 9781138231146 (hardback) |
    ISBN 9781138231153 (pbk.)
Subjects: LCSH: Rap (Music)—History and criticism. | Rap (Music)—
    Analysis, appreciation.
Classification: LCC ML3531 (ebook) | LCC ML3531 .B47 2018 (print) |
    DDC 782.421649/117—dc23
LC record available at https://lccn.loc.gov/2017060398

ISBN: 978-1-138-23114-6 (hbk)
ISBN: 978-1-138-23115-3 (pbk)
ISBN: 978-1-315-31588-1 (ebk)

Typeset in ITC Stone Serif
by Apex CoVantage, LLC

Visit the companion website: www.routledge.com/cw/berry

Contents

Listening Guides

Preface

In his book *Decoded*, Jay-Z writes:

> [Rap] music is meant to be provocative—which doesn't mean it's necessarily obnoxious, but it is (mostly) confrontational, and more than that, it's dense with multiple meanings. Great rap should have all kinds of unresolved layers that you don't necessarily figure out the first time you listen to it. Instead it plants dissonance in your head. You can enjoy a song that knocks in the club or has witty punch lines the first time you hear it. But great rap retains mystery. It leaves shit rattling around in your head that won't make sense till the fifth or sixth time through. It challenges you.
>
> Which is the other reason hip hop is controversial: people don't bother trying to get it. The problem isn't in the rap or the rapper or the culture. The problem is that so many people don't even know how to listen to the music.[1]

This book is about how to listen to rap music, about decoding all of those layers and trying to get it. Most people are initially attracted to the beat, while others are drawn in by the rhyme and wordplay. The music and the poetry work together to articulate aspects of a rich and varied culture that can be traced back through its origins in the South Bronx to its precursors in street gangs, discos, the Black Power movement, the Caribbean, and West Africa. An understanding of the circumstances that gave rise to hip-hop culture provide a context for understanding the current state of rap, which has been shaped by the influence of both technology and commercialization. As hip-hop culture spread throughout the globe, local and regional scenes sprung up, which were in turn reinforced and recreated as they then spread around the country and around the world. As it spread, rap music would influence (and be influenced by) place, politics, and religion.

Listening to Rap synthesizes approaches taken by scholars from a variety of disciplines, including music, cultural studies, African-American studies, gender studies, literary criticism, and philosophy. While this is not intended to be a history of rap, per se, each chapter is loosely chronological so that, when taken together, a history of the genre emerges. Each chapter is accompanied by a timeline that organizes the main events in the chapter, and a master timeline appears in the appendix. The main strength of the book comes from its analyses of dozens of rap songs, with discussions of lyrical and poetic content, musical form, cultural markers, and video. These analyses, which take the form of listening guides, are situated in broader discussions of a dozen topics. Many of the most well-known and significant artists—those who have enjoyed commercial and critical success—from rap's history are included, as well as some artists who may be less well known, but whose work nonetheless merits the kind of consideration found in this book. This book is not meant to be an exhaustive list of every rapper who has released a recording: I have opted for depth over breadth, which meant excluding some of my favorite rappers, and probably some of yours, too.

The book is effectively in two parts. The first part comprises Chapters 1–5 and explores what might be called the structural features of rap: music, poetry, influences, and early history. The second part, Chapters 6–12, deals with cultural and social aspects and how they are projected through the music. While the layout of the chapters suggests that topics like gender and race are distinct, it is impossible to discuss one without discussing the other. Where possible, I try to present an intersectional perspective on the issue at hand, which sometimes leads to privileging one topic over the others for the sake of pedagogical ease. Again, the book is by no means comprehensive: I have chosen to include some topics and to exclude others to highlight the most prominent approaches to hip-hop research. Other topics, such as disability and film studies, have been covered in the scholarly literature, and, where appropriate, I have made an effort to direct interested readers to relevant resources.

In the early days of the culture, Afrika Bambaataa—one of the "founding fathers" of hip hop—proposed **four pillars** of the culture: DJing, MCing, graffiti writing, and break dancing or b-boying. Bambaataa later added a fifth pillar, knowledge of the culture. For the purposes of this book, "hip hop" refers to the broad cultural movement that encompasses all of these art forms. "Rap" refers to the musical component of this culture, typically a combination of MCing and DJing. Not everyone uses these terms in the same way: many people, for instance, use "hip hop" to refer to socially conscious or underground music and "rap" to refer to "gangsta" or commercial music; others use "hip hop" to refer to music from the early years of the genre—roughly pre-1990—while "rap" refers to more recent music (after 1990). Rap music is but one part of hip-hop culture, and it is impossible to talk about the music without considering graffiti and break dancing alongside it. Both art forms receive some treatment in this book.

The culture of hip hop has, of course, evolved considerably in the last forty years, and we could now say it encompasses film, fashion, and other media as well. These areas are addressed where appropriate, but the primary focus of the text is the music. We could also argue that the original four elements have ceased to be interdependent as they were in the beginning, with each element now being practiced by specialists. Rap music has also evolved—the producer has taken over the role of the DJ, the MC has eclipsed the DJ in popularity, rappers are more likely to be solo artists than members of a crew, and much of the lyrical content has become commercialized and homogenized. This evolution is one of the main themes of this book.

Another theme that pervades this book is the influence of technology on the music. In rap's early days, the music consisted of long (as in several hours) mostly improvised sets by DJs, with MCs serving to move the crowd: the music was intended for dancing. It was not until rap made its way onto recordings that anything like a rap "song" really came into existence, and as a consequence, an MC's lyrics became increasingly important and DJs were relegated to a supporting role. Recording also eroded the improvisatory nature of early hip hop. Samplers, drum machines, and synthesizers fundamentally altered the sound of rap while nevertheless trying to preserve the aesthetic created by DJs using vinyl on their turntables. In the 1990s, *Billboard* magazine's adoption of SoundScan set into motion a chain of events that slowly homogenized rap and ultimately led to a musical landscape flooded with artists whose only job was to sell records—artistry and innovation came second. Laptop computers, the internet, and social media have begun to democratize the industry again to some extent, affordably bringing the means of production and distribution into the hands of the creators, revitalizing the underground.

TO THE STUDENT

This book assumes no prior knowledge of rap music, nor any kind of musical training. My hope is that whether you grew up on hip hop or this is your first encounter with the genre, this book has something to offer you. In order for you to get the most out of this book, I have offered some suggestions below that have emerged as the result of nearly ten years of working with students of all backgrounds and skill levels.

Each chapter begins with a few learning objectives and a summary, as well as a time line to provide a general chronological frame for the events in the chapter. These time lines are combined into a master time line that appears at the end of the book. Throughout the chapter, key words are presented in boldface type and are defined in the glossary. Text boxes offer brief overviews of terms unique to hip hop, important "behind the scenes" personalities, record labels, and other topics of interest. The core of each chapter is the listening guides, which provide strategies for listening to the music and making connections with the material presented in the text.

When you listen to the examples in this book, I would encourage you to set aside time to listen thoughtfully. There is nothing wrong with putting on music while you work out, drive, or wash dishes; however, the kind of mindful listening that this book asks of you is best done in an environment free from distractions. Read the chapter, listen to the music, and follow along with the listening guides. I would encourage you to listen to the songs repeatedly until they become familiar, and, if possible, to watch the videos that go along with them. Treat listening to music and watching music videos with the same kind of mind-set as when you read your textbooks or watch a documentary for class.

While the book includes listening guides for dozens of songs, many of the listening guides only have brief excerpts of lyrics that serve as cues, or no lyrics at all. The lyrics for many of these songs can easily be found online: two sites that I would recommend are The Original Hip-hop Lyrics Archive (ohhla.com) and Genius (genius.com). OHHLA has a much cleaner layout than many lyric sites, and it contains a vast catalog of music. Genius (formerly Rap Genius) may be particularly useful to you if you do not have a strong background in rap. In addition to the lyrics, the site offers some information about each song (i.e., the album, producer, and other trivia), and in many cases the lyrics are annotated—sometimes by the artists themselves. These annotations are useful for learning the meanings of some slang terms that are unique to rap (or a particular artist or region) that may be unfamiliar to you. As with anything on the internet, take the lyric transcriptions and annotations with a grain of salt. Both sites have transcription errors—always compare what you see with what you hear—and anyone, regardless of their level of expertise, can add annotations to Genius (much like Wikipedia). The annotations more often than not treat the lyrics at a very superficial level, and you should be well qualified to improve on the annotations after working through this book.

Most of the music discussed in the book is widely available for purchase or to stream, and the website that accompanies the book has Spotify and YouTube playlists that include all the songs with listening guides. The "additional listening" selections and other music can also be found on Spotify, Apple Music, TIDAL, or other sites. Many of the songs have music videos, adding a whole new layer of meaning to be considered, and most are available on YouTube. Make sure that what you watch is an "official" video for the song: check the name of the channel on which the song appears. Videos with the VEVO tag, or the record label, are official: rapfiend1984's video is probably not. Depending on the platform, the timings on the listening guides in the book might not line up exactly with what you are listening to or watching, but they should be reasonably close. Be sure to compare the recording information given on each listening guide with the recording you find online.

I have made no effort to censor any of the material in this book: I believe that the songs should be heard as the artists intended them to be heard. Some of the material covered in rap music generally and this book in particular can be difficult to talk about. Below are some suggestions for approaching classroom discussion or writing about these topics:

- Recognize and respect that each person in the class comes from a different background and may have perspectives or lived experiences that differ from yours. This does not make them any more or less valid than your experiences.
- Use "I" statements when talking, and avoid generalizations that use "you," "we," or "they."
- Avoid interrupting, talking over, minimizing or making fun of someone else's contribution.
- Let your instructor know if you are having difficulties with the conversations: they can point you toward additional resources if need be.

TO THE INSTRUCTOR

This book is designed for an undergraduate class on rap music. It makes no assumptions about the students' prior knowledge of music in general or rap music specifically. It came into being as the result of nearly ten years of teaching hip-hop classes to students of diverse backgrounds: first-year and upper-level students; first-generation college students, honors students, music majors, and non-music majors. My intention is that, whatever a student's background may be, this book will offer everyone a way in to listening to, talking about, and writing about rap music.

I designed the book to be self-contained and usable by novice or experienced teachers who may or may not have rap or musical backgrounds. My hope is that a graduate teaching assistant in a music program, a gender studies program, or an African-American studies program could hit the ground running with this book and that experienced teachers will find new ways to approach rap through the diversity of topics presented. This book could easily be paired with any number of histories of hip hop—like Jeff Chang's *Can't Stop Won't Stop* or *Yes Yes Y'All*, a volume of oral histories compiled by the Experience Music Project—or it could be paired with an anthology of source readings, like Murray Forman and Mark Anthony Neal's *That's the Joint!* Tim Strode and Tim Wood's *Hip Hop Reader*, or Justin Williams' *Cambridge Companion to Hip Hop*, to name a few. I have tried to make the chapters as self-contained as possible, so that they may be reordered or certain ones omitted without much loss of continuity or so that each may be used independently of the book as a whole. Having said that, Chapters 1 and 2 lay out some fundamental musical and poetic terminology and analytical techniques that the rest of the book relies on. Groups with strong musical or poetic backgrounds might skip those chapters (respectively) or gloss over them as review. I have also tried to include as many cross-references to other chapters as possible, as a means of highlighting the interrelationships among the topics or the different ways in which a single song can be studied.

Each chapter contains relevant background information on the topic at hand. Important words are highlighted and defined both within the chapter and in the glossary at the end of the book. While the book is not chronological—it is not a history of rap—each chapter is loosely chronological and includes a time line of pertinent events at the beginning. A master time line that compiles these individual timelines appears in an appendix at the end of the book. The songs in each chapter have been carefully chosen to illustrate specific points.

Listening guides call attention to specific features of music and lyrics and draw connections to the topic at hand. Listening prompts encourage students to apply their newfound knowledge to the interpretation of songs and may be used as the basis for student-created listening guides. Each chapter ends with a list of important names and terms, as well as a few questions for discussion, which call on students to summarize, synthesize, and apply the material in the chapter. "Additional listening/viewing" suggests some songs that deal with the themes presented in the chapter and, in some cases, relevant documentaries. These songs could serve as the basis for classroom discussion or writing assignments. In addition to the works cited in the notes to each chapter, there is a bibliography of what I consider to be the most important books on rap music for those interested in studying the topics in this book in more detail. In short, the end matter of each chapter is my attempt to address the needs of students who are asked to do research on rap music, as well as the needs of instructors who are looking for additional materials for classroom use.

Because some of the topics covered in this book can be challenging to discuss, here are a few suggestions for facilitating these conversations:

- Consider creating a community agreement that covers classroom discussion on the first day of class. Such an agreement lays down ground rules for discussion and takes into account the different backgrounds and lived experiences of each student.
- Give students adequate advance notice when a difficult conversation is coming up or when you intend to play a particularly challenging song or video.
- Thank students who offer controversial or less popular opinions or who constructively disagree with your point of view.
- Ask students to reframe personal criticisms in a more neutral way.
- Provide alternate means of contributing to the discussion: anonymous index cards, e-mail, office-hour visits, online discussion boards, or Twitter, for instance.

There are a number of resources online for facilitating difficult conversations: many are hosted by the faculty resource center at universities across the country. The faculty resource center at your institution could also point you in the direction of resources.

Acknowledgments

My editor at Routledge, Genevieve Aoki, was excited about this project from the initial e-mail that I sent her. Peter Sheehy answered all of my questions promptly and was very helpful. I am also grateful to the three anonymous reviewers for their thoughtful critiques. The careful eyes of my copyeditor (and hip-hop fan), Will DeRooy, saved me from a good deal of embarrassment, and I thank him for recommending some examples that were unfamiliar to me.

Matthew Santa and Wes Flinn are colleagues and friends who were supportive and enthusiastic about this project from the start and offered me feedback at every step along the way. Wes class-tested some of the material at a very early stage, and I am grateful for Matt's keen eye and pedagogical acumen. Kyle Adams read the chapters on beats and voice: they are much improved as a result. Thank you to Ryler Dustin for comments on the poetry section. Ian Condry and Noriko Manabe offered valuable input on the Japanese rap section. Kelly Nowicki helped with the American Sign Language interpretation in Chapter 2. Devin Naar and I had a long and fascinating discussion about Judaism and Jewish culture.

In 2012 and 2013, I had the great pleasure of team-teaching a hip-hop class with Georgia Roberts at the University of Washington at Bothell. Georgia, who comes at hip hop from English and ethnic-studies perspectives, opened my eyes to new ways of thinking about rap. My initial encounters with the Black Panthers, cultural Marxism, M. K. Asante, and Saul Williams are the result of our work together.

Special shout-out to the hundreds of students over the years who have taught me as much as I hope to have taught them. This material originated in classes in the Honors College at Texas Tech University and has been refined through my experiences at University of Washington–Bothell and UW Tacoma. In particular, I have had lengthy discussions on hip hop with Lance Davis, Lisa Fleming, Steve Glenn, Michaelea Lemons, Lesley-Rose Ng'endo Gutter, Jason Nam, Rashida Robbins, Richard Ung, and Corey Young.

My parents, John and Mary Berry, have been supportive of all of my musical endeavors, from waiting patiently in the car while I had my first double-bass lessons through graduate school and moves around the country. My father—an outstanding teacher in his own right who knew practically nothing of rap until I started writing this book—read most of it, offered thoughtful suggestions, and even spent a weekend listening to New Jack Swing. My sister Diane has been supportive in ways too numerous to list. Rufus and Spencer encouraged me to get away from the computer every now and again to take them outside or throw a bone around the house for them to chase.

Finally, Star Murray has been a tremendous companion through the writing process, offering emotional support, feedback on the manuscript, enthusiastic encouragement, a willingness to have difficult conversations, and patience beyond what I deserve. My daughter Edith was asleep while I wrote most of this book: she is the reason I wrote it, and it is to her that I affectionately dedicate it.

NOTE

1 Jay-Z and dream hampton, *Decoded* (New York: Virgin Books, 2011), 54.

TIME LINE

1973	At a party in the South Bronx, DJ Kool Herc uncovers the power of the break.
1980	Electronic-instrument manufacturer Roland introduces the TR-808 drum machine.
1986	Uptown Records, the label that gave rise to New Jack Swing, is founded.
1988	Public Enemy releases *It Takes a Nation of Millions to Hold Us Back*.
1991	Gilbert O'Sullivan sues rapper Biz Markie for copyright infringement and wins in a landmark case for sampling.
1994	The US Supreme Court rules in favor of 2 Live Crew, whose "Pretty Woman" is deemed a parody of Roy Orbison's classic song.
2001	The first CD "turntables" by American Audio and Pioneer hit the market.
2002	Eminem releases the movie *8 Mile*, featuring the hit "Lose Yourself."

IN THIS CHAPTER, YOU WILL LEARN ABOUT

- Basics of musical form and song structure
- How DJs and producers create tracks
- Vocabulary for discussing the sound of a beat

CHAPTER 1

Listening to Beats

OVERVIEW

Rap music was first and foremost dance music; more often than not, when you ask someone what they like about rap, "the beat" is their response. In this chapter, we'll survey some of the musical features of rap, focusing mainly on the beats: the music that supports the lyrics. The chapter begins with some preliminary musical concepts, which will provide us with a common language for talking about how we experience the music. We will then examine the history and techniques of the DJ and their evolution into sampling, one of the hallmarks of rap music. Four fundamental elements of musical sound—pitch, intensity, duration, and sound color—provide us with some general strategies for talking about how producers craft a distinct "sonic signature."

BUILDING BLOCKS OF MUSICAL FORM

The word **beat** has two distinct meanings in hip hop. First, a beat is the musical track that supports a rapper's rhyming. As Joseph Schloss defines it, it is a "musical collage composed of brief segments of recorded sound."[1] Another definition of beat is a regularly recurring pulse; more casually, it's what we tap our foot to or nod our head along with as we listen to music. It is this second definition that will concern us over the course of this section. Typically, the beat is most easily heard in the lower-pitched instruments, such as the bass or kick drum. Beats can be closely spaced (fast) or widely spaced (slow). The **tempo** of the song describes the relative speed of the beats. Tempo can be discussed in a very general sense—OutKast's "B.O.B." has a very fast tempo; UGK's "One Day" has a rather slow tempo—or it can be given more precisely in beats per minute (bpm). Beats tend to organize themselves into **meter**, which is the grouping of beats into regularly recurring patterns of strong and weak. For the moment, beats will be indicated with x's: capital X's will indicate strong beats and lowercase x's will indicate weak beats. Figure 1.1 illustrates what does and does not constitute a beat:

Beat (the x's are evenly spaced):														
X		X		X		X		X		X		X		X	

Not a beat (the x's are not evenly spaced):											
X	X		X			X		X		X	X	X		X	

Figure 1.1 Understanding beats

Duple meter (the "X x" pattern repeats at regular intervals):															
X	x	X	x	X	x	X	x	X	x	X	x	X	x	X	x
1	2	1	2	1	2	1	2	1	2	1	2	1	2	1	2
Triple meter (the "X x x" pattern repeats at regular intervals):															
X	x	x	X	x	x	X	x	x	X	x	x	X	x	x	X
1	2	3	1	2	3	1	2	3	1	2	3	1	2	3	1
Quadruple meter (the "X x x x" pattern repeats at regular intervals):															
X	x	x	x	X	x	x	x	X	x	x	x	X	x	x	x
1	2	3	4	1	2	3	4	1	2	3	4	1	2	3	4
Not a meter (there is no regularly recurring pattern):															
X	x	X	x	x	X	x	X	X	x	x	x	X	x	x	X
1	2	1	2	3	1	2	1	1	2	3	4	1	2	3	1

Figure 1.2 Duple, triple, and quadruple meter

For most rap songs (and popular music in general), the meter is **quadruple**; that is, the beats are organized in a pattern of X x x x. Meter can also be duple (X x) or triple (X x x). Each occurrence of the metric pattern is called a measure or a **bar**, and beats are labeled by number for ease of reference. Figure 1.2 illustrates duple, triple, and quadruple meter. Rap's origins in **funk** result in a strong emphasis on the first beat of the bar; however, in many songs, the second and fourth beats of the bar feel accented. This feel does not change the strength of the first beat of the bar; rather, these accents serve to propel the music forward, back to "the one."

Meter can be **simple** or **compound**. In a simple meter, the beats are evenly divisible by two: with respect to the diagram below, count "one-and, two-and." In compound meter, the beats are evenly divisible by three: count "one-la-li, two-la-li." The majority of the songs discussed in this book are in simple meter; few are solely in compound meter, although occasionally rappers will slip into and out of compound meter over the course of a song. Sometimes rappers will superimpose a compound meter in their rhyme over a simple meter in the background track (or vice versa) to create a sense of musical tension or friction. A number of recent rap tracks do this effectively: tracks by Hopsin ("Bout the Business"), Desiigner ("Panda"), and Big Sean ("Blessings") use simple meter to contrast with the prevailing compound meter (a rhythmic technique called "hemiola"). Figure 1.3 illustrates simple and compound meters, as well as hemiola. In "Bring the Noise" (see below), Chuck D raps the second verse in compound meter. This contrasts with his simple-meter rapping in verses one and three, but also clashes with the prevailing simple-meter beat underneath his vocals. To determine whether a song is in simple or compound meter, start tapping along with the beat, then try tapping twice as fast. If what you're tapping makes sense with the music you're hearing, then chances are the music is in simple meter. If it sounds or feels strange, try tapping three times as fast: if that works, it's in compound meter.

Keeping Time

A useful way to keep track of beats in a bar involves clapping on the first beat of the measure and counting the remaining beats by touching your thumb to your pinky, ring finger, and middle finger, respectively. Physical activity like this is a useful way to start internalizing beat and meter.

Simple meter:

X	-	x	-	X	-	x	-	X	-	x	-	X	-	x	-
1	&	2	&	1	&	2	&	1	&	2	&	1	&	2	&

Compound meter:

X	-	-	x	-	-	X	-	-	x	-	-	X	-	-	
1	la	li	2	la	li	1	la	li	2	la	li	1	la	li	

Hemiola:

X	-	-	x	-	-	X	-	x	-	x	-	X	-	-	
1	la	li	2	la	li	1	la	li	2	la	li	1	la	li	

Figure 1.3 Simple meter, compound meter, and hemiola

Much of the preceding material has focused on a rather small level of detail, as if we're zooming in on the music. From here on, we start to zoom out and look at larger components of songs. A **verse** is a large unit of music consisting of multiple bars. A song can have any number of verses. Some songs, like The Sugar Hill Gang's "Rapper's Delight" or Tupac's "Brenda's Got a Baby" consist of one long verse; others, like "The Message" by Grandmaster Flash & The Furious Five or "Juicy" by The Notorious B.I.G. include multiple verses. The defining characteristic of the verse is that each appearance of it tends to have the same music but different lyrics. In contrast to more melodic popular music, it's important to note that rappers might vary their flow in each verse: the background music is what stays the same each time. Over the course of rap's history, 16 bars has emerged as a standard verse length. Sixteen is an ideal number because it can be understood as eight pairs of bars, four groups of four bars, or a pair of eight-bar sections. Some—but not all—raps are written such that a line of text lasts for a bar; thus a pair of bars might be grouped according to the rhyme at the end of each line. Rhyme scheme, line breaks, and other aspects of poetry are covered in more detail in the next chapter.

The chorus or **hook** of a song is typically what listeners remember, what they find themselves singing or reciting after the song is over: hooks are designed to be catchy. They can be rapped, but they are often sung. Hooks are also several bars long (usually four or eight) but typically shorter than the verses. A hook's first appearance in a song may be before the first verse (that is, it starts the song) or after the first verse. The distinguishing characteristic of a hook is that it features the same music and the same lyrics each time it recurs. The music underneath the hook can be the same as or different from the music that supports the verses. The hook's music is typically intensified in some way, especially if it uses the same music as the verses. It may be louder, or it may feature additional (or fewer) instruments.

The arrangement of verses and hooks (along with other less significant musical components) gives us a way of talking about the **form** of a song. Certain forms have become almost standard: three 16-bar verses with a sung hook, for instance, characterize much mainstream rap after about 1995. Others are more unusual and require careful listening. A song may begin with an **intro**, which is typically short, might have spoken (not rapped) text over it, and may or may not be musically related to what follows. An **outro** is like an intro, but at the end of a song. A **bridge** is neither a verse nor a hook, but might be used near the middle of a song for contrast or to transition to something new.

Eminem's hit song "Lose Yourself," from the semi-autobiographical movie *8 Mile*, illustrates most of the concepts presented so far in this chapter. Notice that, in this listening guide, the focus is not on the lyrics, but on the musical features of the beat.

LISTENING GUIDE 1.1

Artist: Eminem
Song: "Lose Yourself"
Album: Soundtrack to *8 Mile*
Record label: Shady/Aftermath
Year released: 2002
DJ or Producer: Eminem
Samples used: (none)

TIME	MUSICAL CHARACTERISTICS	DESCRIPTION
0:00	Non-thematic introduction	Piano: this music does not resemble any other music that we hear in the remainder of the song.
0:31	**Thematic introduction** with spoken text (8 bars)	Try counting "1-2-3-4, 2-2-3-4, etc." along with the beat to keep track of the bars. Guitar plays two notes for each beat: this is *simple* meter (try clapping twice as fast—on each guitar note) Pitch level changes every four beats/every bar: this indicates *quadruple* meter. The guitar chord falls on beats two and four, accenting them. This musical material repeats throughout the rest of the song.
0:55	**Verse 1** (16 bars; 8 + 8)	The music intensifies at the start of the second eight bars as the drums become more prominent. The low drum sound is on beats 1 & 3; the high drum on beats 2 & 4.
1:39	**Hook** (8 bars; 4 + 4)	The music in the chorus is strengthened with the addition of the synthesizer playing on strong beats (1 & 3). The hook consists of four lines of text repeated once.
2:01	Verse 2 (16 bars)	The second verse sounds like one continuous 16-bar stretch because the instrumentation remains more or less constant throughout.
2:45	Hook (8 bars; 4 + 4)	Synthesizer punctuation returns.
3:09	Verse 3 (24 bars; 8+8+8)	Eminem extends the typical 16-bar verse by adding another 8 bars.
4:15	Hook (8 bars; 4 + 4)	Synthesizer punctuation returns.
4:37	Hook (?)	Here, Eminem starts to recite the hook again but cuts it off after the first two words. What sounded like the hook now becomes an **outro**.

DJING

The looped (that is, repeated) break beat, or **break**, has been the cornerstone of rap's aesthetic from the beginning. The break is the part of a song in which nearly all the instruments drop out except for the percussion. It can appear at the beginning, middle, or end of the song, and it's typically only a few bars long. DJ Kool Herc was the first to recognize the "power" of the break—it was the part of the song the dancers waited for—and realized that repeating the break would keep the party rocking. Since then, breaks have been looped on turntables by

DJs; producers have crafted breaks from samples or synthesized new breaks; and the looping aesthetic is occasionally recreated by live bands like The Roots.

A standard DJ setup consists of a pair of turntables, a mixer, and speakers (including headphones). Figure 1.4 illustrates a basic DJ rig. The most important parts of any turntable are (a) the platter, (b) the tonearm (which holds the needle), and (c) the pitch control. This two-turntable setup was not new in the early 1970s—it was used in radio stations and by disco DJs to keep the music going continuously—but the ways in which hip-hop DJs *used* it were new. As playing break beats and, later, scratching became commonplace, DJs realized that not just any turntables would do. Many turntables were belt-driven and, as a result, were slow to start spinning. Belt-driven turntables were also not powerful enough to rebound quickly from scratching techniques. Grandmaster Flash eventually settled on a set of Technics SL1200 turntables because they were solidly built and, more importantly, their direct-drive motors provided the power and responsiveness he needed. The Technics SL1200 series became the most popular turntable among hip-hop DJs, until the line was retired in 2010 (they remain popular; they are just harder to get). A slipmat is a record-shaped piece of felt that comes between the record and the platter: it allows the DJ to cue the record and hold it in place while the platter is spinning and facilitates the back-and-forth motions of scratching without stressing the motor or damaging the record.

The mixer serves several important functions. Its main controls include (d) two vertical faders that control the output volume of the left and right turntables, (e) a **crossfader** that mixes the input from the left and right turntables, (f) a cue switch that allows the DJ to listen to either (or both) turntables in the headphones, and (g) line-in and line-out jacks. On the simplest mixers, other controls allow the DJ to manage the gain (the strength of the signal incoming from each turntable), treble, and bass. More sophisticated mixers have graphic

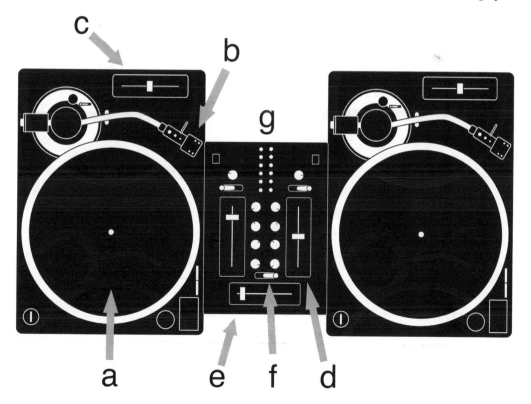

Figure 1.4 A typical hip-hop DJ setup with two turntables and a mixer (center)
Source: jmercdermottillo/Shutterstock.com

equalizers, computer interfaces, and controls for more than two channels. Vertical faders are volume controls: moving them away from you increases the volume; moving them toward you decreases the volume. The cue switch allows the DJ to listen to one turntable "privately" while the other one plays "publicly." This makes it easier for them to cue the next record up accurately without the crowd hearing it. Line-in jacks allow the DJ to connect a microphone, a drum machine, a keyboard, or any number of other electrical sound sources to the mixer; line-out jacks send the sound to amplifiers, speakers, and headphones.

The crossfader is perhaps the most important control on the mixer. If the crossfader is all the way to the left, then 100% of the left turntable's sound and none of the right turntable's sound is sent to the speakers; if it's all the way to the right, then 100% of the right turntable's sound and none of the left is sent to the speakers. If it's in the middle, both records can be heard simultaneously. Here is a basic set of instructions for looping a break beat on a pair of turntables:

- Set crossfader all the way to the left.
- Start the record on the left turntable.
- While that break plays, cue up the break on the right turntable.
- Once the left turntable's break concludes, move the crossfader all the way to the right and start the record on the right turntable.
- While the right turntable plays, change the record on the left turntable (if need be); cue up the next break.
- When the right turntable's break concludes, move the crossfader all the way to the left and start the record on the left turntable.[2]

These steps are repeated dozens, if not hundreds, of times a night by skilled DJs. What makes this even more challenging is that many breaks last only a few seconds: repeating this process becomes a carefully choreographed juggling act. It's worth mentioning that the audience will not hear the music being cued in steps 3 and 5—the DJ can hear it through the headphones by using the cue switch, though. A DJ can also move the crossfader quickly to the opposite side and back to **punch phrase** a short segment of the other record into the mix.

Classic Hip-Hop Breaks

In his book *Groove Music*, Mark Katz offers a list of twenty classic breaks:

"Amen Brother" by the Winstons (1969)
"Apache" by The Incredible Bongo Band (1973)
"Ashley's Roachclip" by The Soul Searchers (1974)
"Assembly Line" by The Commodores (1974)
"The Big Beat" by Billy Squier (1980)
"Dance to the Drummer's Beat" by Herman Kelly (1978)
"Funky Drummer" by James Brown (1970)
"Funky President" by James Brown (1974)
"Get Out of My Life, Woman" by Lee Dorsey (1966)
"I Just Want to Celebrate" by Rare Earth (1971)
"Impeach the President" by The Honey Drippers (1973)
"It's Just Begun" by The Jimmy Castor Bunch (1972)
"Johnny the Fox Meets Jimmy the Weed" by Thin Lizzy (1976)

"Mary Mary" by The Monkees (1967)
"Rock Steady" by Aretha Franklin (1971)
"Super Sporm" by Captain Sky (1978)
"Synthetic Substitution" by Melvin Bliss (1974)
"Take Me to the Mardi Gras" by Bob James (1975)
"Walk This Way" by Aerosmith (1975)
"You'll Like It Too" by Funkadelic (1981)

These records all come from a period of roughly fifteen years (1965–1980) and represent a variety of genres. There are rock songs (Aerosmith, Billy Squier), soul (Aretha Franklin), and funk (James Brown, Funkadelic). Many of these songs are still sampled today: such sampling can be seen as a way of connecting to hip hop's past. Some of these songs are included in Joseph Schloss' "b-boy canon," a collection of classic songs that forms the backbone of learning to b-boy or break-dance.[3]

It can be problematic to talk about the idea of a "canon"—that is, a list of the most important and/or influential tracks—in hip hop, given that the genre is still rather young, but as early as the mid-1980s, such a canon began to emerge. Lenny Roberts, an avid record collector, worked with Afrika Bambaataa and others to compile a collection of the most popular beats onto a single album, called *Ultimate Breaks and Beats*. This compilation made even the most obscure breaks available to anyone by eliminating the need to seek out and buy a lot of rare recordings. The compilation, which eventually ran to 25 volumes, met with mixed reviews in the hip-hop community. Some believed that using the compilation was a form of cheating, while others got their start in DJing thanks to the records.

In the earliest battles, DJs would compete to see whose system was the loudest. DJs would set up their systems on opposite sides of a community room, school gym, or park. One DJ would play for thirty minutes to an hour, and then the next would play. The cheers of the crowd decided the winner. Occasionally, a battle was won when one DJ simply drowned out the other's system. DJ Baron recounts the first time he and his crew battled Afrika Bambaataa:

> Afrika Bambaataa was on one side of the gym, and we was on the other. The place was jam-packed. But Bambaataa had one up his sleeve: Disco King Mario had loaned Bam a power amp. We were going back and forth, and all of a sudden you couldn't hear us no more [laughs], 'cause Bam borrowed this amp from Mario and blew us out of the water, just drowns us out totally. We lost the battle, but we made our money, 'cause it was our party. So the next day, we went out and bought a BGW power amp, and we couldn't be touched then.[4]

Once scratching became a critical part of DJing, battles were no longer about who was the loudest, but about who had the best technique.[5] Scratching was invented by Grand Wizard Theodore but was brought into the public eye (and honed) by Grandmaster Flash, another pioneer of hip hop. With respect to the diagram above (Figure 1.4), typically the left turntable plays continuously and the DJ scratches on the right turntable with their right hand, controlling the crossfader as need be with the left hand. In the setup diagrammed above, the turntables are rotated so that the tonearms are at the top (farthest from the DJ) rather than on the sides: this keeps them out of the way of the DJ's scratching hand. DJs often search a record for a sound suitable for scratching—not just any random spot on a record will work—and they may mark it with a sticker. Sharp, percussive sounds work well—things like drum beats, horn hits, or shouts.

The baby scratch is the most straightforward: it was the original scratch and is typically taught first.

1. Set the crossfader to the middle position (50% L/R).

2. Start the left turntable playing (the right one remains "off," but the sound of the scratches will be picked up and transmitted).

3. Push the record on the right turntable forward and pull it back rhythmically using the right-hand fingertips. If you imagine the record as a clockface, start the scratch with the record at 12:00, push it forward to about 10:00, and then return it to 12:00. Scratches can be of any length, duration, or speed.

There are a few other scratches for which the right turntable isn't moving (the "tear," for instance); more sophisticated scratches (such as the "crab" and the "transformer") involve both turntables spinning, with the DJ using the crossfader to "punch" in the scratches over the music playing from the left turntable.

As CDs began to outsell records and tapes, audio-equipment manufacturers began to develop CD players with scratching capabilities: the first of these devices appeared in 2001. The DJ could load CDs into the device and use miniature turntable scratch pads—roughly 4 to 8 inches in diameter, and much smaller than a 12-inch record—to manipulate the digital audio signal (the CD isn't physically scratched). The devices offered improved accuracy in terms of cueing and dropping, but the lag between action and sound was often problematic.[6]

With laptops and digital audio files like MP3s becoming more affordable and common, it didn't take long for those technologies to make inroads into the world of the DJ. Programs like Serato and Traktor allow DJs to use their iTunes library and in some cases even streaming services in place of records, thereby saving a lot of physical space (not to mention the exertion involved in lugging crates of records from gig to gig). These programs use a specially designed record (called "control vinyl") that sends a signal to the computer, telling it how to manipulate the digital file. The software offers a high degree of precision and control through the laptop interface—timings, beats per minute, pitch, and other parameters can be easily manipulated—and the control vinyl provides a more "natural" feel than the CD-turntable devices. Some DJs dislike the invasion of digital technology, arguing for the purity of the vinyl experience, but for many, the convenience of the transition to digital (especially when traveling) outweighs those objections. Katz relates that many artists lament the shift from DJing as an aural skill to more of a visual skill, enabled by the incursion of the digital.[7]

As sample-based rap grew in popularity in the mid-1980s, some DJs transitioned into the role of producers. Others went in a different direction, honing their craft to an exceptionally high level of skill. A DJ in Southern California who called himself Babu recognized that what he and his peers were doing was something distinct from what early hip-hop DJs had done. Babu popularized the label **turntablist** to describe DJs who made music to be *listened* to rather than danced to.

SAMPLING

Looping the break quickly became the core of the DJ's aesthetic; however, turntables had their limitations. Practically, DJs could only work with two records at a time, and the ability to speed up, slow down, or otherwise alter a record was also limited. Grandmaster Flash and others began incorporating drum machines into their DJ setups, allowing them to have a constant, looping drum track (albeit a synthesized one) along with the turntables' output. Albums by Run-D.M.C., Slick Rick, and DMX, among others, all featured beats created on the Oberheim DMX drum machine in conjunction with turntables and scratch techniques.

Tools of the Trade

As DJs began searching for ways to augment their capabilities, three electronic musical instruments became important parts of their arsenal. A **sequencer** is used to arrange different sounds—sampled and synthesized—into a particular order and then loop that sequence. A **drum machine** is a specific kind of sequencer that allows the artist to choose from a palette of synthesized or sampled drum sounds. Typically, these sequences are about a bar (four beats) long, much like the break beats they attempt to replicate. The Oberheim DMX (which sold for about $3,000) and the much more affordable Roland TR-808 (which sold for about $1,200) were the most popular drum machines in hip hop during the 1980s. A **synthesizer** uses analog or digital technology to mimic other sounds, most often musical instruments. Most synthesizers take simple sound-wave forms (like a sine wave) and manipulate them into more complex wave forms that resemble those of the sound being mimicked. A **sampler** is a digital musical instrument capable of recording, storing, and altering the sampled sound. The E-mu Emulator and the Akai MPC 2000 were the most commonly used samplers in early hip hop. Different artists prefer different technologies, since each has its own unique sounds and capabilities. These tools can take the form of an actual device or a software application, and are sometimes combined into digital audio workstations (or DAWs for short). Programs like ProTools, Logic, and GarageBand integrate many of these features and can run on a standard laptop.

The interface of drum machines like the Roland TR-808 provides us with an easy way to visualize rhythm. **Rhythm** comprises any combination or division of beats. If we use terms like "strong" and "weak" to talk about meter, we might think of rhythm in terms of "long" and "short" (with many possibilities in between). When we listen to a rapper, a DJ, or a beat, the rhythm is most often what catches and keeps our interest. Implicit in the definition is that any meter can be rhythmic (or can have rhythm), but rhythm does not require or imply a meter: some freestyle (improvised) or **a cappella** (that is, voice alone with no musical accompaniment) raps fall into this category, since they do not have a beat to support them (although the rapper may be "hearing" one internally).

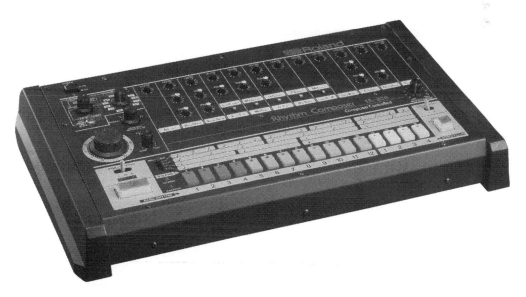

Figure 1.5 A Roland TR-808 drum machine
Source: Image courtesy of Roland Corp.

The TR-808 has a series of 16 numbered buttons along the bottom, and they are grouped by color in sets of four: 1–4 are red; 5–8 are orange; 9–12 are yellow; and 13–16 are white. Each color corresponds to a beat, and each button, to a subdivision of that beat. Figure 1.6 represents this visually as a table: a few instruments are listed in the first column. According to the diagram, the kick drum sounds on beats 1, 3, and the "&" of 3; the snare sounds on beats 2 and 4; and the the hi-hat articulates a simple meter, dividing each beat evenly in half. We could use this diagram to program an 808 by assigning the kick drum to buttons 1, 9, and 11; the snare to buttons 5 and 13, and the hi-hat to all the odd-numbered buttons. The diagram above represents a very common drum pattern heard in many songs from the mid-1980s. Sir Mix-A-Lot's "Posse on Broadway" uses this pattern almost exactly, except the hi-hat is assigned to every button.

Diagrams like this provide us with a useful way of talking about text delivery as well and its relationship with the beat. Figure 1.7 shows how the delivery of the text correlates to the synthesizer part in the refrain in Grandmaster's Flash & The Furious Five's hit "The Message" (discussed in more detail in Chapter 10). Melle Mel's text lines up almost note for note with the synthesizer part, which has a note in positions 1 through 8 (or on every subdivision of beats 1 and 2). We will return to these diagrams throughout the book as a means of illustrating important musical points about beats and text delivery.[8]

The appearance of new, more readily available digital technology provided artists with a more precise way to do what they were already doing with turntables; namely, isolating specific portions of a record and repeating them. **Sampling** is the act of digitally extracting a sound or a component of a sound. Once the sound is removed from a record, it can be manipulated in any number of ways: slowed down, sped up, trimmed, or combined with sounds from other records. If a drum and a horn sound at the same time on a record, the DJ can filter out the horn, for instance, so that only the drum sound remains. Where we might think of breaks in the turntable era as vertical slices of music lasting a few seconds, we can think of sampling as not only vertical slices of increasing detail (i.e., a single drum hit lasting fractions of a second) but as horizontal slices as well (i.e., removing the higher-pitched instruments to keep only the low-pitched instruments).

Hi hat:	X		x		x		x		x		x		x		x	
Snare:					x								x			
Kick drum:	X								x		x					
Button:	1	2	3	4	5	6	7	8	9	10	11	12	13	14	15	16
Beat count:	1	e	&	a	2	e	&	a	3	e	&	a	4	e	&	a

Figure 1.6 A simple beat programmed into a TR-808 drum machine

Melle Mel:		It's	like	a	jun-	gle	some-	times		it	makes	me	won-	der	how	I
Synthesizer:	x	x	x	x	x	x	x	x								
Kick drum:	x	x					x		x							
Button:	1	2	3	4	5	6	7	8	9	10	11	12	13	14	15	16
Beat count:	1	e	&	a	2	e	&	a	3	e	&	a	4	e	&	a

Figure 1.7 Interaction of lyrics and beats, "The Message"

Two websites make it easy to find out who sampled what: whosampled.com allows you to look up a song and find out what samples it uses. The-breaks.com does the reverse: you can enter an artist's name and find out which songs sample their work.

While they may be viewed as two very different activities—or as the end of one era and the dawn of another—sampling grew rather organically out of DJing in the mid-1980s. As sampling became more common, and as rap became less of a live event and more of a recorded product, DJs increasingly became known as **producers**. Even today, many of the best-known and most highly regarded producers are also skilled, knowledgeable DJs. The roles are basically the same: to create music to support the rapper and move the crowd. The producer rose to prominence in the 1960s with people like Phil Spector, who was responsible for a number of "girl-group" hits, and George Martin, who produced the Beatles. In the past, producers typically worked with a finished (or mostly finished) product: they might write the arrangements and select instruments, adjust the volume of the instruments so that they blend, or add effects after the recording is done. Many of these producers even developed a characteristic "sound" by which their records could be identified. Today, producers have greater say in the creative and compositional process than they did previously: it's one of the reasons that some producers are as well-known as the artists they produce.

Sampling was not new to the music world: producers had been using samplers to "patch" holes in records for some time. If, for instance, a saxophone solo was missing from a recording, a producer could cut and paste a saxophone solo from one recording into another. DJ Marley Marl had been working in the studio creating beats with records and a drum machine and had been experimenting with samplers in the early 1980s. While trying to isolate a vocal sample for a remix he was working on, he inadvertently sampled a snare hit as well. Marl realized the possibilities that his mistake offered: "I could take any drum sound from any old record, put it in here and get that old drummer sound on some shit."[9] In essence, sampling offered producers a way to construct audio collages, clipping their favorite bits and pieces from different sources, altering them, and rearranging them into something new.

The well-known West Coast producer and former N.W.A. member Dr. Dre would often hire musicians to recreate parts of the recording he was interested in, record them playing it, and then transform that recording as he would a sample. Loren Kajikawa points out that such an approach had several advantages: first, it gave Dre greater control over the source material. Second, it enabled him to manipulate individual lines (i.e., a guitar part) with much more precision than if he had sampled the part and filtered it. Third, paying a musician a one-time fee to record a few short riffs absolved Dre of having to pay increasingly steep fees for licensing a sample.[10]

Dre's approach points to an interesting paradox with respect to the use of live instruments in hip hop. Many critics of rap music contend that its practitioners do not actually play instruments. At its origins, rap music was made with turntables; one could easily argue that a DJ is an instrumentalist, manipulating the turntables in front of an audience in real time. Drum machines and samplers followed not long after, as DJs became producers and moved from the stage to the studio. Early rap records, like The Sugar Hill Gang's "Rapper's Delight" and Kurtis Blow's "The Breaks" (discussed in Chapter 6) used a band in the studio to lay down the backing tracks. The Roots are a well-known example of a rap group that recreates the aesthetic of the looped break beat while playing "conventional" instruments. Dre's sampling of live musicians is almost like a compromise between these two approaches. The bottom line is that all of these approaches function to isolate and loop a break, whether that break is a cut from a single record, a riff played by a band, or a beat composed of samples from different records.

Just as Bambaataa and others would go to great lengths to disguise the records they were playing, sometimes producers also mask the source of the sample. They may change its speed, or take a particularly thin slice of a record, or disguise it with electronic effects like distortion or delay.[11] They may choose a particularly obscure or unusual record to sample from, perhaps as a challenge to other producers, as Schloss suggests.[12] Hiding the identity of a sample in this way raises an important question: is knowing the source of the sampled material a prerequisite for understanding the meaning of the song? Sometimes the choice of sample seems to be more than coincidental: Ice-T's song "I'm Your Pusher" samples Curtis Mayfield's song "Pusherman." The sample seems to support Ice-T's lyrics, which use the drug trade as a metaphor for the music industry. Kanye West's song "Gold Digger" is supported by Ray Charles' hit "I've Got a Woman," the lyrics of which form an ironic counterpart to Kanye's rhymes. The sample Kanye uses is not actually Ray Charles, but Jamie Foxx reprising his role as Charles in the 2004 biopic *Ray*. As with Dr. Dre, this strategy may have ended up saving Kanye money in terms of sample-clearance fees. Instances like this seem to indicate that knowing the source of the sample is important: that the sample somehow imparts additional meaning(s) to the song; however, Schloss argues that most producers choose samples simply because they sound good and will get the crowd moving.[13]

Sample-based rap music peaked in the late 1980s and began to wane as the 1990s unfolded. Two main factors contributed to its decline. First, increasing legal judgments led to rising sample-clearance fees, making it difficult for all but the wealthiest artists to sample extensively. Journalist Nelson George suggests that as long as producers were sampling black artists, everything was fine, but once more progressive acts like Public Enemy and De La Soul started sampling white music, the practice started to come under scrutiny.[14] Second, the rise of affordable personal computing technology—desktops and laptops that could support sampling, synthesis, and recording software—led to an influx of "uninitiated" producers creating and sharing music.[15]

Copyright and Sampling

Two high-profile lawsuits in the early 1990s challenged rap music's use of sampling. In both cases, the creators of the original work sued the rap artists, arguing that use of the original constituted copyright infringement. Prior to the lawsuits, the relationship between copyright and sampling was murky at best: these rulings set important precedents that would alter the composition of rap music for years to come. Record labels now employ people whose job it is to clear samples, while some producers continue to sample outside of the law, choosing obscure tracks and substantially altering more familiar ones to escape detection.

In copyright law, fair use is determined by considering four basic criteria:

1. The purpose and character of the use, including whether such use is of a commercial nature or is for nonprofit educational purposes;
2. The nature of the copyrighted work;
3. The amount and substantiality of the portion used in relation to the copyrighted work as a whole; and
4. The effect of the use upon the potential market for or value of the copyrighted work.

In short, any use that would prevent the original authors or artists from earning revenue they rightly deserved for their work would *not* be considered fair use.

Biz Markie, a member of the Juice Crew (along with Marley Marl, MC Shan, and Big Daddy Kane), sampled a piano sound from Gilbert O'Sullivan's 1972 song "Alone Again (Naturally)" for use in his song with the same title. Markie even sings some of O'Sullivan's lyrics in the hook. In 1991, Markie was found guilty of copyright infringement and was required to pay damages to O'Sullivan. His record label was also required to stop selling the album unless and until the song was removed. The judge even referred the case to criminal court, arguing that Markie should be charged with theft, but that case never materialized.

A version of Roy Orbison's hit "Pretty Woman" on 2 Live Crew's 1989 album *As Nasty as They Wanna Be* became the target of a copyright infringement lawsuit initiated by Acuff-Rose Music, Orbison's publishing company. Prior to recording the song, the group approached Acuff-Rose in an effort to obtain the rights legally, but they were denied. The group recorded and released the song anyway, arguing that their version was a parody of the original, which would fall under the provisions of fair use (which is to say they had no obligation to pay for the rights in the first place). About a year after the album's release, as record sales surpassed the quarter-million mark, Acuff-Rose sued the group, presumably because they felt they were entitled to a share of the profits. The case made its way to the US Supreme Court (as *Campbell vs. Acuff-Rose*), which ultimately ruled in favor of the rap group in 1994.

LAYERING

The image in Figure 1.8 is a New York City subway car painted by an artist nicknamed Blade. It is two-dimensional but suggests several dynamic layers—three dimensions—in different ways. The large black letters are slanted and lack straight lines, imbuing them with a sense of motion. The sides of the letters are painted gray, implying a third dimension, thickness,

Figure 1.8 "Blade," South Bronx, 1980 © Martha Cooper

and causing the letters to pop off the surface of the train. A yellow streak starts behind the letter "A," shoots over the top of "A" and "L," and disappears underneath the car, or perhaps it continues on a path toward the viewer. The streak also affirms the depth of the black letters and suggests space in front of and behind them. All the art added by Blade is framed by the physical construction of the subway car: its shape and size, the doors and the windows add another layer—perhaps a layer of "realness" in contrast to the fantasy of art—and force viewers to reconcile the three-dimensional illusion that has been added to a two-dimensional canvas. And it's entirely possible that Blade's work was painted over another artist's work on the same car (or that another eventually painted over Blade's work).

In music, as in graffiti, layering is an illusion—more accurately, a metaphor. When we talk about layering in music, we can visualize it in three dimensions: height (which is dictated by pitch), width (which is dictated by pulse and rhythm), and depth (which is typically dictated by intensity or volume). We can visualize musical layers in a few ways. Musicologist Robert Walser published one of the earliest efforts to grapple with rap's musical material, as opposed to its lyrical content or cultural backdrop.[16] Walser suggests that discussions of rap's musical content may have been slow to emerge due to the contention of many critics that rap was not music but noise and, therefore, not worthy of musical analysis.[17] As part of an effort to demonstrate that rap is, in fact, music and worthy of musical analysis, Walser transcribes (that is, converts sound into notation) portions of Public Enemy's "Fight the Power": his Figure 1 is reproduced here as Figure 1.9 and includes two bars (indicated by the vertical lines) of quadruple meter (indicated by the 4/4 at the beginning).[18]

In Walser's transcription, each instrument is given its own line, and we might think of each of these eleven lines as a distinct layer. We could group each of these individual strands into three layers according to the kind of instrument: the first four lines are all voices ("J.B." On the fourth line stands for "James Brown," whose grunts are sampled here); the next four lines—guitar, synth, noises, and bass—comprise a second family; and the last three lines—cymbal, snare, and kick drum—constitute a third family.

Another way to visualize layering is by examining music-production software like Pro-Tools or Logic. Figure 1.10 is a screenshot of a project composed in Logic. Each different shaded horizontal band represents a distinct layer of the musical texture and basically corresponds to an instrument, much like the musical notation example above. There are places where some layers drop out (i.e., don't sound), which is indicated by the black space. The silence represents a rupture in the flow not only in that particular layer, but also in the track as a whole. We can think about layering in terms of density: songs like Grandmaster Flash's "The Message," E-40's "Tell Me When to Go," or Kanye West's "New Slaves" have few layers: they are relatively "thin" songs. This might have been intended to let the content of the text shine through with minimal distraction. Public Enemy's "Bring the Noise" and DJ Khaled's "All I Do Is Win" have thick textures.

Public Enemy's production team, called the Bomb Squad, is legendary for their very dense, layered production style, which projects an aural impression of chaos, a busy city street, or any number of other noisy environments. Adam Krims says these densely layered, often very dissonant (i.e., not pleasing to the ear) tracks represent the "hip-hop sublime," where "massive, virtually immobile and incompatible layers of sound are selectively and dramatically brought into conflict with one another."[19] The "hip-hop sublime" characterized much gangsta rap from 1986 to roughly 1996, after which the preferred style began to change.[20] Krims stresses that the dissonance—the sense that they don't "belong" together—of these layers is what sets them apart from other contemporaneous production styles like **G-Funk** or the music produced by Puff Daddy. In all of these styles, the sampling reinforces the sense of beat and meter; the hip-hop sublime does not suggest a particular key, scale, or

Figure 1.9 Walser's transcription of the opening of Public Enemy's "Fight the Power"

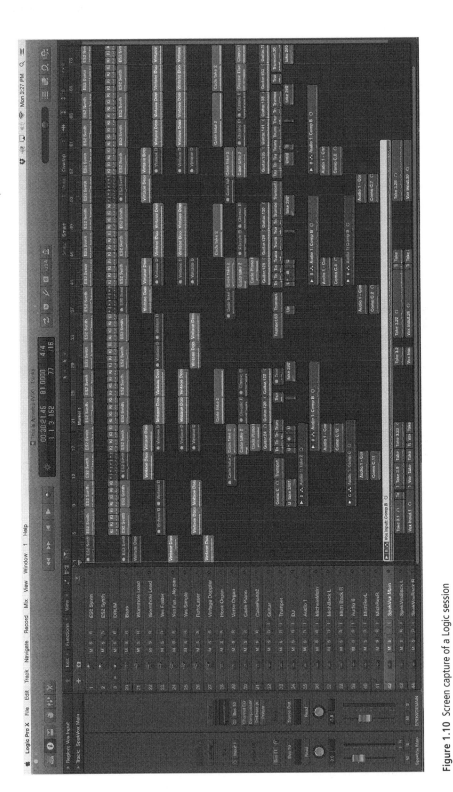

Figure 1.10 Screen capture of a Logic session

Source: Image courtesy of Speculation

note (it suggests multiple, conflicting keys, scales, or notes) while G-Funk or Puff Daddy's typically *does* reinforce or project a particular key, scale, or note.

LISTENING GUIDE 1.2

Artist: Public Enemy
Song: "Bring the Noise"
Album: *It Takes a Nation of Millions to Hold Us Back*
Record label: Def Jam
Year released: 1988 (Deluxe Edition: 2014)
DJ or Producer: The Bomb Squad
Samples used: "Message to the Grassroots" speech, Malcolm X; "Get Off Your Ass and Jam," Funkadelic; "Funky Drummer," James Brown

The bonus materials that accompany the deluxe edition of *It Takes a Nation of Millions to Hold Us Back* provide an opportunity to examine layering in one of Public Enemy's most well-known songs, "Bring the Noise." The title of the song alone suggests the dissonance that Krims describes. There are four versions of "Bring the Noise" on the playlist: the album version, a "no noise" version, a no-noise instrumental version, and the unaccompanied vocal track. The album version starts off with the repeated "too black, too strong." Loren Kajikawa writes that the two clauses come from a recording of Malcolm X's 1963 speech, "Message to the Grassroots." In the original speech, the two phrases do not appear next to one another—in fact, they are part of a metaphor about adding cream to coffee: "It's just like when you've got some coffee that's too black, which means it's too strong." Kajikawa notes that this cutting and rearranging on a relatively small scale is emblematic of Public Enemy's approach to sampling.[21] Malcolm X's voice opening the song situates Public Enemy in a long line of black activists as well, a point that Kajikawa takes up in depth.

After listening to the album version, listen to the no-noise version next. The album version can be thought of as the instrumental plus the vocal plus "the noise," which is sampled from the first ten seconds of Funkadelic's 1975 single "Get Off Your Ass and Jam" (also on the playlist). The no-noise version leaves off the Malcolm X samples and starts immediately with the music. The mix on this version is slightly different from the album version: the bass is more prominent throughout, and the drums sound a little brighter and softer. In contrast to the album version, the beat continues to flow through the beginning of the second verse: on the album version, it drops out and the rupture is filled with James Brown's "Funky Drummer" break.

The alternate mix makes it a bit easier to hear the patchwork nature of the beat in the no-noise instrumental version. Some of the samples are slightly louder than others, and in some cases, the "edges" of the samples are audible. Public Enemy producer Hank Shocklee told *Keyboard* magazine that he prefers the E-mu SP-1200 for production because it "allows you to do everything with a sample. You can cut it off you can truncate it really tight, you can run a loop in it, you can cut off certain drum pads. The limitation is that it sounds white, because it's rigid."[22]

When Chuck D first heard the beat, he was not sure what to do with it: the tempo was much faster than many of their other records (in fact, Public Enemy was known to speed up the finished tracks in the studio to make them sound even more chaotic). Inspired by Rakim, Chuck tried a varied flow characterized by rapid-fire bursts of lyrics punctuated by sudden stops.[23] In the a cappella version, it is easy to hear just how Chuck varied his flow. The first verse includes more simple divisions of the beat; the second verse relies on compound divisions of the beat. The compound divisions in his flow clash a bit with the prevailing simple divisions in the instrumental tracks. (Note that this a cappella track includes lyrics for only the first two verses.) Chuck's voice has a mild digital echo added to it, to add depth and create the illusion of space. Flavor Flav's interjections are layered on top of Chuck's lines.

In an interview with Tricia Rose, the Bomb Squad's Eric "Vietnam" Sadler relates that pushing the instruments and recording devices to their limits (or beyond) helped give Public Enemy its trademark noisy sound: "Now, engineers . . . they live by certain rules. They're like, 'You can't do that. You don't want a distorted sound, it's not right, it's not correct.' With Hank [Shocklee; also of the Bomb Squad] and Chuck [D, who also helped with PE's production] it's like, 'Fuck that it's not correct, just do this shit.'" Sadler continues, saying that he and his peers learned to engineer so that they could chase the sound that they wanted, "correct" or not.[24] Rose regards the desire of these producers to work "in the red" (that is, pushing the limits of the technology, which often results in cautionary red lights on the mixing board) as another way in which rap music is transgressive.

Public Enemy's influence extended well beyond the East Coast. After Ice Cube parted ways with N.W.A., the Bomb Squad produced his first solo album, *AmeriKKKa's Most Wanted*. In the documentary *The Art of Rap*, Cypress Hill's B-Real tells Ice-T that they aimed to replicate the densely layered style of Public Enemy.[25] The Bomb Squad's unique approach to sampling produces a sonic signature that sets their music apart from that of their peers.

SONIC SIGNATURES

The DJ's importance to early hip hop is apparent when considering the names of many hip-hop duos: the DJ's name typically appears before the rapper's name (e.g. Eric B & Rakim; DJ Jazzy Jeff & The Fresh Prince). Producers, as well, occupy an important place in the realm of rap music: many of them, such as Sean "Puffy" Combs, Pharrell Williams, and Dr. Dre, are as well-known as the artists they produce. The work of many high-profile DJs and producers can be identified solely on the basis of the distinct sounds that comprise their beats; Mark Gillespie refers to this as a **sonic signature**. A producer's sonic signature emerges from a combination of the instruments ("real" or digital) that the producer uses, the kinds of samples preferred, the overall sound quality of the final product, and—in some cases—even a name shout-out.[26] In this section, we will examine the sonic signatures of three different producers from three different eras in an effort to identify the unique characteristics of each. The sonic signatures reveal elements of regional style, era, available technology, and, of course, prevailing tastes.

Every musical sound has four primary characteristics: pitch, intensity, duration, and sound color. Pitch refers to the relative highness or lowness of a sound. Intensity deals with volume, and it applies not just to the relative softness or loudness, but also to things like attack, decay, and apparent placement in the mix (i.e., foreground and background, which are in essence functions of volume). Duration encompasses tempo, meter, and rhythm and can also refer to the articulation of a note—is it separated from the notes around it, or are they connected smoothly? Sound color (also known as timbre, pronounced "TAM-ber") is perhaps the most elusive term here: it refers not only to the sound of specific instruments, but also to things like the warmth of a sound, reverb or distortion effects, and some elements of texture. At the end of each section, there is a breakdown of the pitch (P), intensity (I), duration (D) and sound color (S) characteristics of each style. It is important to note that these are generalizations and might not apply equally well to all songs by a given producer.

Teddy Riley and New Jack Swing

Teddy Riley was a musical prodigy from Harlem who was steeped in gospel traditions from a very young age. New Jack Swing, the production style he pioneered, was responsible for bringing rap music back in touch with R&B: Riley produced tracks not only for rap artists like Kool Moe Dee ("How Ya Like Me Now?"), Doug E. Fresh, and Heavy D & The Boyz (*Livin Large*), but also R&B stars like Keith Sweat, Al B. Sure! and Bobby Brown. The style laid the groundwork for artists like TLC and Mary J. Blige (sometimes referred to as "New Jill Swing"), Jodeci, D'Angelo, and R. Kelly.

Barry Michael Cooper, a journalist and screenwriter for the 1991 film *New Jack City*, christened the style in a 1987 *Village Voice* cover story. In the story, he described the style as "RoboCop funk in full effect; go-go music gunned down by rap and electronics, then rebuilt with more vicious beats and an incharge, large attitude."[27] Producer Kyle West, who worked with Riley, observed that, in contrast to other club music in the 1980s: "there was more rhythm, percussion, and movements within the drum tracks [in New Jack Swing]. Keyboard-wise, it was very busy and we would call it organized noise. It was like chaos, but organized. It showcased the backbeat in music and a lot of the percussion shuffles."[28]

Pitch: Densely layered synthesizer harmonies in the high and middle registers are anchored by funky, syncopated synth bass notes.

Intensity: As relayed by the excerpts above, New Jack Swing is "vicious," "in charge," "busy," and "chaotic." The percussion leads the charge, with a sharp snare front and center.

Duration: New Jack Swing features faster tempos than most rap or R&B from the same era: many songs clock in around 110 beats per minute, up from a typical 80-to-90 beats per minute. The percussion drives the tempo through a strong backbeat (that is, beats 2 and 4). Riley favored the Linn drum machine, and the "swing" button not only gave the music its characteristic sound, but also lent the style its name.

Sound color: The sound is very synth-driven, featuring both keyboard synthesizers and electronic drums. Vocally, the music is sung in an R&B style as opposed to rapped. For the most part, this style does not rely on samples. The production is generally polished and clean-sounding.

Swing refers to an uneven division of the beat—a long-short feel—that results from grouping the first two subdivisions in a compound meter. If we count the beats as "1, 2, 3, 4," and the divisions of the beat as "1-la-li, 2-la-li, 3-la-li, 4-la-li," the swing feel emerges when we silence the "middle x": "1—li, 2—li, 3—li, 4—li." Swing feel is common in jazz and early rock and roll (circa the 1950s) but started to disappear in favor of the even divisions of the beat favored in later rock and pop music.

Uptown Records

Uptown Records, a subsidiary of MCA, was launched in 1986 by Andre Harrell, a former member of the rap duo Dr. Jeckyll & Mr. Hyde. The label owes much of its early success to Riley and his pioneering fusion of rap and R&B. Uptown's roster included Riley's own band, Guy; R&B singers Al B. Sure! Johnny Kemp, and Bobby Brown; and rappers Heavy D & The Boyz and Father MC. The label peaked with releases by Mary J. Blige and Jodeci, two artists who set the template for the future of hip hop–infused R&B.

The label influenced not only music, but film, television, and fashion as well. Movies like *New Jack City* and *Boyz n the Hood* (both 1991), television shows like *In Living Color*, *Living Single*, and *New York*

Undercover—as well as Arsenio Hall's late-night talk show (and comedy rap album)—all shared the sensibilities of the style pioneered by Uptown. High-top fade haircuts, designer clothes, and conspicuous jewelry provided the distinct look cultivated by these artists. A young Sean Combs got his start as an intern at Uptown Records while he was attending Howard University. After being dismissed from Uptown in 1993, he struck out on his own and started Bad Boy Records, which came to embody its own unique style of East Coast hip hop. Uptown struggled through the mid-1990s and ultimately dissolved by 1999.

DJ Premier and the Boom-Bap

DJ Premier's name appears at the top of many "best producer" lists. He got his start with Guru in the group Gang Starr in the late 1980s, has worked with KRS-One, Mos Def, Nas, Biggie, Jay-Z, and many other top names, and he remains active even today. His sonic signature is closely linked with the "golden era" of East Coast rap, which samples funk, jazz, and soul records liberally: the style is sometimes referred to as "boom-bap," an onomatopoetic description of the drum sounds. Premier uses Akai sequencer/samplers, turntables, guitars, pianos, and drums to create his dirty, heavy-hitting signature sound. Despite their heaviness, his beats have the warmth of vinyl, no doubt a result of his background as a DJ.

Pitch: Premier's beats tend toward dissonant pitch combinations—Krims' "hip-hop sublime"—often heard in the piano and keyboard parts.

Intensity: The boom-bap (boom-BAP, ba-boom-boom-BAP) between the bass and snare drum is the most prominent element in many of Premier's beats, and it supports the bass line.

Duration: Premier's beats clock in around 90 beats per minute.

Sound color: In contrast to Riley's beats, which are newly composed for instruments, Premier's beats are sample-based. Premier takes pride in masking the source of his samples: "Even if I played it to the person who made the original sample, I'd like them to go 'Oh man, I like what you did.' "[29] Many of his beats feature turntable scratches and short vocal samples reassembled into a chorus.

Metro Boomin and Trap

The sound of Atlanta-based Metro Boomin's productions loomed large over the airwaves during the mid-2010s. His sound is characteristic of **trap** music, which emerged from Atlanta's drug trade in the 2000s, and which we will consider in more detail in Chapter 11. Metro Boomin has worked with Drake, Nicki Minaj ("Want Some More"), Gucci Mane, and—perhaps most notably—Future. In addition, he has released a few of his own mixtapes: *19 and Boomin* is the one that catapulted him to stardom. Metro Boomin composes his beats using a sequencing program called Fruity Loops Studio. Aside from their distinct sound, his beats typically feature one of two name-drops: Gucci Mane saying "Metro Boomin want some more" or, more recently, Future saying "If young Metro don't trust you, they gonna shoot you."

Pitch: Like most trap music, Metro Boomin's beats feature a really low, deep, booming bass line at the bottom and a rapid-fire, synthesized hi-hat. This results in a wide space in the mid range, which is sometimes filled in with synth string or choir sounds.

Intensity: The bass and hi-hat frame the sound. Most of the mid-range sounds are pushed to the back of the mix.

Duration: Of the three styles surveyed here, Metro's beats are slowest, averaging about 70 beats per minute. The bass line changes very slowly, in sharp contrast to the rapid articulation in the hi-hat.

Sound color: Metro's hi-hats sound very bright and tinny; the bass is very low and almost distorted as a result. Overall, the production sounds very thick, full, and dark.

The three production styles described above are among many that have contributed to hip hop's evolution. As vanguards of new styles, each producer was also responsible for inspiring many imitators. Gillespie argues that new producers will sometimes borrow aspects of a popular producer's signature in an effort to capitalize on the success of that producer.[30] Those borrowed elements are key to defining the new producer's sonic signature; that is, to some extent a producer's signature emerges only in reference to other producers' signatures, resulting in a web of interconnections among them. The goal of this strategy is typically financial gain and, as such, can result in similar-sounding songs at the top of the sales charts. Justin Williams expands on Gillespie's work and suggests that producers' sonic signatures can reveal their musical influences and, in some cases, even their mentors. He traces the origins of Eminem's signature style (which is evident in "Lose Yourself," as discussed earlier in this chapter) through songs of his mentor Dr. Dre and the broader influence of heavy-metal riffs by bands like Megadeth, Blue Öyster Cult, and Black Sabbath that inform his style. Furthermore, the influence of Eminem's production can be heard in tracks by his protégés 50 Cent and The Game.[31]

It's worth noting that not all producers have a sonic signature: some are shape-shifters, altering their sound over time or to complement a particular artist. J Dilla is one such artist. Dilla was a legendary producer who worked in the realm of sample-based rap and produced tracks for A Tribe Called Quest, The Roots, De La Soul, Janet Jackson, and Busta Rhymes.

 ## OUTRO

Names you should know:

- Eminem
- Public Enemy
- Teddy Riley
- DJ Premier
- Metro Boomin

Terms you should know:

- Beat
- Tempo
- Meter (duple, triple, and quadruple; simple and compound)
- Bar (or measure)
- Form
- Intro/Outro
- Verse
- Hook (or chorus)
- Bridge
- Turntable
- Mixer
- Crossfader
- Break
- Punch phrase
- Scratching
- Turntablist
- Sequencer/Drum machine
- Synthesizer
- Sampler/sampling
- Rhythm
- A cappella

- Producer
- Layering
- Sonic signature

- New Jack Swing
- Boom Bap
- Trap

Questions for discussion/writing prompts:

1. Compare and contrast DJing and turntablism. It might help to watch videos of classic DJs (Kool Herc, Grandmaster Flash, DJ Jazzy Jeff, for instance) and turntablists (DJ Qbert, DJ Kuttin Kandi, and others).

2. Many have argued that copyright restrictions inhibit an artist's creativity. Others counter by saying the original artists deserve fair compensation for their work. Choose one side and defend your position.

3. Find a rap song that you like and identify the producer. Find two or three other songs by the same producer and try to describe their sonic signature. Does the producer use live instruments, turntables, samplers, or some combination thereof? Use terms like "pitch," "intensity," "duration," and "sound color."

Additional listening/viewing:

Musical form (three 16-bar verses with a hook):

- Spirer, Peter. *The Art of 16 Bars*. Chatsworth, CA: QD3 Entertainment, Inc., 2005
- "Juicy," The Notorious B.I.G.
- "I Used to Love H.E.R.," Common (see Chapter 5)
- "December 4th," Jay-Z

DJ tracks:

- "The Adventures of Grandmaster Flash on the Wheels of Steel," Grandmaster Flash
- "Eric B Is on the Cut," Eric B
- "DJ on the Wheels," DJ Jazzy Jeff
- "DJ Premier in Deep Concentration," Gang Starr

Turntablist albums:

- Pray, Doug. *Scratch* [documentary]. New York: Palm Pictures, 2001.
- *The Audience's Listening*, Cut Chemist
- *The World Famous Beat Junkies*, The Beat Junkies
- *X-Pressions*, X-Ecutioners
- *Wave-Twisters—Episode 7 Million*, QBert

New Jack Swing:

- *Make It Last Forever*, Keith Sweat
- "My Prerogative," Bobby Brown
- "Poison," Bell Biv DeVoe
- "MotownPhilly," Boyz II Men's "MotownPhilly"
- "You Remind Me," Mary J. Blige

- Wreckx-N-Effect, "New Jack Swing"

DJ Premier:
- "Just to Get a Rep" and "Mass Appeal," Gang Starr
- "Mathematics," Mos Def
- "Unbelievable," The Notorious B.I.G.
- "New York State of Mind," Nas

Metro Boomin:
- "X," 21 Savage
- "Karate Chop" and "Maison Margiela," Future
- "Be Me See Me," Young Thug
- "Want Some More," Nicki Minaj

NOTES

1 Joseph Schloss, *Making Beats: The Art of Sample-Based Hip Hop* (Hanover, NH: Wesleyan University Press, 2004), 2.
2 See also Mark Katz, *Groove Music: The Art and Culture of the Hip Hop DJ* (New York: Oxford University Press, 2012), 56.
3 Katz 256–7. See also Schloss, *Making Beats*, 37–8, and idem., *Foundation: B-Boys, B-Girls, and Hip-Hop Culture in New York* (New York: Oxford University Press, 2009), chapter 2.
4 Jim Fricke, *Yes Yes Y'all: The Experience Music Project Oral History of Hip-Hop's First Decade*. Ed. Charlie Ahearn and Experience Music Project (Cambridge, MA: Da Capo Press, 2002), 99.
5 Katz 46–9.
6 Katz 215–19.
7 Katz 226.
8 These diagrams are similar to those pioneered by Adam Krims, *Rap Music and the Poetics of Identity* (Cambridge: Cambridge University Press, 2000) and adapted by Felicia Miyakawa, *Five Percenter Rap: God Hop's Music, Message, and Black Muslim Mission* (Bloomington: Indiana University Press, 2005), Kyle Adams, "Aspects of the Music/Text Relationship in Rap" *Music Theory Online* 14 no. 2 (2008): www.mtosmt.org/issues/mto.08.14.2/toc.14.2.html, "On the Metrical Techniques of Flow in Rap Music" *Music Theory Online* 15 no. 5 (2009): www.mtosmt.org/issues/mto09.15.5/toc.15.5.html, Loren Kajikawa, *Sounding Race in Rap Songs* (Berkeley: University of California Press, 2015), and others.
9 Quoted in Nelson George, *Hip Hop America* (New York: Viking, 1998), 92.
10 Kajikawa 94.
11 The 2005 lawsuit *Bridgeport Music, Inc. vs. Dimension Films* brought charges against N.W.A. for sampling Funkadelic's "Get Off Your Ass and Jam" without permission in their "100 Miles and Running." A court of appeals ruled that any use of a sample, regardless of length or transformation, required permission: the copyright owner alone has permission to duplicate the work.
12 Schloss, *Making Beats*, 155–7.
13 Schloss, *Making Beats*, 146–8.
14 George 94.
15 Schloss, *Making Beats*, 6.
16 Robert Walser, "Rhythm, Rhyme, and Rhetoric in the Music of Public Enemy" *Ethnomusicology* 39 no. 2 (Spring/Summer 1995): 193–217.
17 Walser 193.
18 Walser 201.
19 Krims 54.
20 Adam Krims, *Music and Urban Geography* (New York: Routledge, 2007), 106–24.

21 Kajikawa 71–2.

22 Mark Dery, "Public Enemy Confrontation," *Keyboard* (September 1990): 81–96. Reprinted in *That's the Joint! The Hip-Hop Studies Reader*. Ed. Murray Forman and Mark Anthony Neal (New York: Routledge, 2004), 419.

23 Christopher Weingarten, *It Takes a Nation of Millions to Hold Us Back* (New York: Continuum, 2010), 68.

24 Tricia Rose, *Black Noise: Rap Music and Black Culture in Contemporary America* (Hanover, NH: Wesleyan University Press, 1994), 74–5.

25 Paul Toogood and Ice-T, *Something from Nothing: The Art of Rap* [documentary] (Universal City, CA: Vivendi Entertainment, 2012).

26 Mark Gillespie, "'Another Darkchild Classic': Phonographic Forgery and Producer Rodney Jerkins' Sonic Signature" (MMus dissertation. Université Laval, Quebec), chapter 1.

27 Quoted in George 115.

28 C. L. Williams, "New Jack Swing Forever: How a Movement Redefined an Era" *Pop Matters* (October 6, 2011): www.popmatters.com/feature/148896-new-jack-swing-forever-how-a-movement-redefined-an-era.

29 Paul Tingen, "DJ Premier: Hip-Hop Producer" *Sound on Sound* (July 2007): www.soundonsound.com/people/dj-premier.

30 Gillespie chapter 2.

31 Justin A. Williams, *Rhymin' and Stealin': Musical Borrowing in Hip Hop* (Ann Arbor: University of Michigan Press, 2013), chapter 5.

IN THIS CHAPTER, YOU WILL LEARN ABOUT

- Common poetic devices and how they are used in rap
- Modes of storytelling
- How texts (lyrical and musical) make meaning
- Poetic aspects of rap in languages other than English

Listening to Poetry

OVERVIEW

In "Follow the Leader," Rakim states "Rap is rhythm and poetry." Having covered musical aspects of rap in the previous chapter, we will examine its poetic aspects in this chapter. The chapter begins with a summary of some common poetic techniques—devices like rhyme, alliteration, and metaphor. The middle of the chapter examines questions of subjectivity and narrative in order to ask, who is telling the story and how are they telling it? Intertextuality is the belief that texts have no inherent meaning, but that their meaning emerges through comparisons with other texts. This is an important strategy for listening to rap, given its heavy reliance on borrowing. The chapter closes with an overview of how different languages—Spanish, Japanese, and American Sign Language—reflect the transformations that language undergoes in the process of crafting rhymes.

INTRO

Rakim's ability to paint vivid, fantastic pictures with dense, poetic rhymes has remained virtually unmatched. His song "Follow the Leader" is a tour de force of poetic techniques: we will use it here to illustrate some of the most common poetic devices found in rap lyrics. The song opens with the lines: "Fol*low* me into a so*lo* get in the f*low*/And you can picture like a ph*oto*." In the first line, the words "fol-*low*" and "so-*lo*" rhyme with "flow": when words within a line rhyme, we call this **internal rhyme**. Rhyme relies on a comparison between syllables that include a consonant (here, "-l") and the following vowels ("-ow"). Not only does rhyme force us to compare the sound of the rhyming words, it also forces us to compare the possible meanings of the words. The combination of rhythm and rhyme is also a powerful memory aid and helps listeners predict what word or syllable is likely to come next. A good MC will avoid the obvious rhymes in favor of new and surprising pairings. The desire to avoid perfect rhymes, coupled with the fact that there are many words that lack perfect rhymes, has led MCs to investigate the creative possibilities of **slant rhyme**. Slant rhyme, which is sometimes called "near" or "half" rhyme, occurs when the consonants but not the vowels, or the vowels but not the consonants, sound similar. The relationship between the words at the end of the lines, "flow" and "photo," is a *near* rhyme ("-low" and "-to"). Here, the "oh" sound is common to both words, but the "-l" and "-t" sound make it not a perfect rhyme.

In the next few lines, we hear a repetition of the "m" sound:

Music *m*ixed *m*ellow *m*aintains to *m*ake
Melodies for MCs *m*otivate the br*ea*ks
I'm everlasting, I can go on for d*ays* and d*ays*
With rhyme displ*ays* that engr*a*ve deep as X-r*ays*

This repetition of a sound (consonant or vowel) at the beginning of words is known as **alliteration**. If the consonant sound appears within the words, the technique is called **consonance**. The transition from the "m" alliteration to the long "a" internal rhyme is helped by the word "motivate," which contains both sounds. Both alliteration and internal rhyme often serve to blur the line breaks implied by **end rhymes**. In the next couple of lines, Rakim raps: "I can get iller than 'Nam, a killin' bomb/But no alarm: Rakim will remain calm." If you listen to the track, you'll hear Rakim force the words "'Nam," "bomb," "alarm," and "calm" to rhyme by the way he pronounces them. This technique is an example of what Adam Bradley calls **transformative rhyme**: words that do not rhyme at all are pronounced in such a way that they do.[1]

In the third verse, Rakim's rhymes get increasingly more complex as they move toward **multisyllabic rhymes**. The rhyme schemes above involve only one syllable ("-low," for example). In multisyllabic rhymes, the rapper tries to rap combinations of syllables, as in the following lines:

> You're just a rent-a-rapper, your rhymes are *Minute-Maid*
> I'll be here *when it fade*, I'll watch you flip like a *renegade*
> I'm *Rakim*, the fiend of a *microphone*
> I'm *not him*, so leave my *mike alone*

In the first pair of lines, Rakim rhymes "Minute-Maid" and "when you fade" with "renegade": "when" and "ren-" rhyme, and "fade" and "-gade" rhyme (note also the play on "Maid/Made," which becomes apparent when you hear the line). In the second pair of lines, Rakim uses slant rhyme to rhyme "Rakim" and "not him" early in the lines and "microphone" and "mic alone" at the end of each line. The difficulty inherent in crafting multisyllabic rhymes often necessitates the use of slant rhyme.

Homonyms are words that sound the same and are spelled the same, but have different meanings: "fair" can mean light or just, for example. Homophones are related to homonyms: they are words that sound the same but are spelled differently (and likely have different meanings). In the line "You're just a rent-a-rapper/Your rhymes are Minute-Maid" the word "made" is an example of a homophone: Rakim plays on the sound shared by "made" (the rhymes were hastily assembled) and "Maid" (a brand of juice, often seen as concentrate to be mixed with water). Taken together, the meanings of both imply that the other rapper writes watered-down lines as a result of his haste. This play on "made" and "maid" is a kind of **pun**—a play on like-sounding words often used to humorous effect—and is often referred to as a **punch line** in rap.

In the next chapter, we will consider flow in more detail, but a few aspects of Rakim's delivery and its relationship to the poetic devices deserve mention here. Bradley notes that "Rap follows a dual rhythmic relationship whereby the MC is liberated to pursue innovations of syncopation and stress that would sound chaotic without the regularity of the musical rhythm."[2] First, techniques like rhyming and alliteration often create a rhythm of their own that may coincide or conflict with the musical rhythm. Figure 2.1 interprets the third and fourth lines in musical meter. The numbers indicate where the musical beats fall: the underlined syllables are alliteration, and the italicized syllables are assonance. In the first line, the first two beats coincide with the "m" sound; beats 3 and 4 highlight the "a" sound. Both poetic techniques produce

Music	*mixed*	*mellow*	*Main*—	tains	to	*Make**	Melo—
dies	For *M*—	Cs	Moti—	vates	the	Br*ea*ks*	
1	&	2	&	3	&	4	&

Figure 2.1 Rakim, "Follow the Leader"

syncopation by creating the effect of an accent on weak parts of the beat. In the second line, beats 1 and 2 highlight the internal rhyme between "-dies" (beat 1) and "-Cs" (beat 2). Rakim starts two syllables marked with asterisks near the end of each line slightly before the beat, so that the vowel sounds end up on the beat.

Most of the poetic devices described above have to do with the sounds of the words: they are basically effects (some refer to these devices as "figures"). There is another class of poetic devices that affect the meanings of words (sometimes called "tropes"). Perhaps the two most common ways to invite comparisons in poetry are simile and metaphor. A **simile** is an implied comparison that uses the word "like" or "as" to draw the comparison; a **metaphor** is a direct comparison between two otherwise dissimilar objects. "Picture like a photo" is an example of a simile, as are "Stiff as if you're posin' " and "Planets are small as balls of clay" later in the first verse. "Follow the Leader" is full of colorful metaphors: "My magnum is a microphone murdering MCs;" "Dance, cuts rip your pants/Eric B on the blades bleedin' to death, call the ambulance," and "The stage is a cage, the mike is the third rail." Bradley suggests that similes are much more common than metaphors in rap because they are less ambiguous. "Similes shine the spotlight on their subject more directly than metaphors," he writes: "they announce their artifice from the beginning, leaving little room for confusion."[3] Many of the metaphors in "Follow the Leader" evoke violent images, but it's important to note that Rakim is not talking about physical violence; the violence is a metaphor for musical and lyrical skills. It's easy to miss this if you're not listening closely, and such casual listening can ultimately lead to a dismissal of the music based on assumptions about its content.

Some artists employ extended metaphors through multiple songs, or even through an entire album. The Wu-Tang Clan is exemplary in this regard, having created an entire fantastic, metaphorical world to inhabit that is rooted in Shaolin kung fu and the teachings of the Five-Percent Nation (see Chapter 8). The members of the group, many of whom have enjoyed solo careers as well, hail mostly from Staten Island, which they refer to as Shaolin. Kung fu and chess are both used as metaphors for lyrical skills, strategy, and discipline.

Hashtag rap, a style popularized by Kanye West, Big Sean, and Drake, came to popularity around 2010. The hash symbol (#) used on Twitter and other social-media platforms offers a way to categorize topics: including the hash symbol immediately before a word (i.e., #kanyewest) allows users to quickly search Twitter for other people who are talking about that topic. Hashtags have evolved into a way of tweeting asides, letting the audience know how you feel about a particular topic; for instance, "I just won the lottery #lucky." Kanye West coined the term (and claimed to have invented the style) on Funkmaster Flex's radio show in 2010: "Look at say the hashtag rap—that's what we call it when you take the 'like' or 'as' out of the metaphor. 'Flex, sweater red, #firetruck' "[4] The pause that typically precedes the "hashtag" word ("firetruck," in this example) could be interpreted as the space left by removing the "like" or "as." As with hashtags on social media, rap hashtags can also alert the listener to a rapper's "unstated" feelings.

While Kanye claims to have invented hashtag rap, examples of it appear well before the 2010 interview referenced above. Cam'ron's 2004 song "Girls" includes the line "And hope is hopeless, disappear in the air/#hocuspocus." Kanye's single "Barry Bonds" includes the line "And here's another hit/#Barry Bonds," a line that functions as a pun on the word "hit." Big Sean and Drake are best known for popularizing the style, with lines like Sean's "I live the life I deserve/#Blessed." Drake's verse on "Forever" includes the lines "Swimming in the money come and find me #Nemo/If I was at the club you know I balled (bald) #chemo." Tech N9ne raps "We in the opposite of blue suede shoes/#Elvis" on "Erbody But Me."

The history of rap can be viewed in terms of increasing complexity in both figures ("sound effects" like rhyme and alliteration) and tropes (metaphors and other comparisons). Early rap relies predominantly on end rhymes with clear line breaks. As rap evolved, internal rhymes, slant rhymes, and multisyllabic rhymes became more commonplace. Similes and metaphors evolved into increasingly clever and obscure punch lines, devices like personification gradually came into use, and hashtag rap represents a new way of suggesting comparisons.

SUBJECTIVITY

If rap music is first and foremost about telling stories, two questions naturally arise: who is telling these stories, and how are they told?[5] The answer to the first question deals with **subjectivity**. The answer to the second question, which will be addressed in the next section, deals with **narrative**.

The answer to the first question might seem obvious: the rapper is telling their story. The question quickly becomes problematic when we consider how many rappers have renamed themselves or—even more significantly—how many rappers employ several different personae in their performances. When we listen to Eminem, are we actually hearing Marshall Mathers? Or are we hearing him speak through the personality of Eminem, or Slim Shady? When we listen to Nicki Minaj, do we hear Onika Miraj (her birth name), Roman Zolanski, or Harajuku Barbie? Kool Keith of the Ultramagnetic MCs, who claims to be the inventor of the hip-hop persona, raps under 53 different names. In the case of these alter egos, is it possible to say that the stories they tell are true? Nelson George writes: "Black male pride is profoundly manifested in the renaming of oneself. No matter how much we love our parents, African-American males throughout the twentieth century have been notably uncomfortable with the Christian-based names they were given."[6] The renaming tradition has roots in groups like the Nation of Islam, in which members replaced their "slave" name—their last name—with an "X" (hence, Malcolm X, Clarence 13X, etc.). And in hip hop, the renaming is not solely a male strategy: most female rappers also rhyme under different names.

In broader terms, several archetypal characters have emerged over the course of rap's history, many of which have their roots in other elements of black culture. William Jelani Cobb suggests that the gangster evolved from the badman figure and the pimp from the trickster.[7] Figures like the gangster, pimp, and hustler pervade rap music; they are so pervasive, in fact, that they have given rise to sub-genres that bear their names. Tricia Rose writes about mainstream rap's "unholy trinity" of the gangsta, the pimp, and the ho.[8] Ice-T, Snoop Dogg, and Suga Free are examples of the pimp persona; Ice Cube and 50 Cent are among the representatives of the gangsta category; and Kool G Rap and Jay-Z are hustlers. While female rappers could in many cases be subsumed under these categories, Cheryl Keyes outlines four distinctly female personae found among rappers in the "golden age" of hip hop: the queen mother, the fly girl, the sista with attitude, and the lesbian.[9] The reliance on these stock characters can be traced to the homogenization of content that occurred as rap music became increasingly commercialized (see Chapter 6).

One of the things that critics found most troubling about the rise of gangsta rap on the West Coast in the late 1980s was the fact that many of these violent tales were told in the first person. As William Jelani Cobb writes, "By relaying [the rapper's] tale in the first person, the story itself carried greater realism, blazed a more indelible image in the mind of the listener and added to the cocktail of half-facts, overheard truths, and tabloid gospel that composed the artist's own sprawling legend."[10] At the very least, the first-person narrative created the illusion that the stories were indeed true, and, even if they were not true, they were at least believable. Even so, Cobb argues, "all autobiographies contain a quotient of fiction if only because memory is imperfect and in saying 'I' the MC is speaking for the invisible masses of his own hood."[11] In general, pronouns ("I," "you," "we") and many adverbs ("here," "now," "this") appear to convey factual information but are heavily dependent on context for their meaning. When Slick Rick starts "Children's Story" with the line "Once upon a time not long ago," we must consider whether "once upon a time" refers to 1989 (the year the song was released), the moment in which we are listening to the song, or some other point in time entirely. And just how long ago is "not long ago?" Such language choices simultaneously reinforce and challenge the rapper's credibility.

Not only can rappers inhabit different identities, but they can tell stories from different points of view or from different vantage points in time. Eminem raps as an obsessed fan in "Stan"; Nas raps from the point of view of a gun in "I Gave You Power"; and MC Lyte raps as a voice from the afterlife in her song "Cappuccino." Rappers who don't name their personae can nonetheless employ perspective shifts in their writing. In some cases, the perspective shifts happen within a single song. J. Cole's song "Lost Ones" provides a clear example of how these perspective shifts can structure a song.

LISTENING GUIDE 2.1

Artist: J. Cole
Song: "Lost Ones"
Album: *Cheers*
Record label: Shady/Interscope
Year released: 2003
DJ or Producer: Fredwreck and Eminem
Samples used: "Born of a Gentle South," Bo Hansson; "Big Poppa," The Notorious B.I.G.

Detroit rapper Obie Trice's "Follow My Life" begins with a graphic depiction of his birth. In the first verse, he recounts his childhood and his father's abandonment. We get a sense of the close relationship he had with his mother, as well as the kind of discipline she imposed. The single mother/absent father trope is common to a lot of rap songs, and we will explore its origins in Chapter 12.

The second verse chronicles Trice's time as a drug dealer, culminating with his being pulled over by the police. There is no third verse for the song, which may serve a dramatic role: we don't know what happened as a result of the traffic stop. We could guess that he either escaped or was arrested and that this song—and his rap career generally—is evidence of redemption. The next song on the album, "We All Die One Day," might provide some clues as to the aftermath: the hook includes the lines "It ain't considered a crime unless they catch you/We all die one day."

TIME	FORMAL UNIT	NEAL, "TIME-SHIFT"	COBB, "MALCOLM X FORMULA"	
0:00	Intro (4 bars)			
0:14	Verse 1 (20 bars)	Childhood	Birth	"11/14/77 . . ."
0:20			Dissolution of family	"Mom ain't breast feed . . ."
0:53			Experience of poverty	"Niggas on the corner gettin' money . . ."
1:13	Chorus (8 bars)			"Follow my life . . ."
1:37	Lead-in to verse 2 (4 bars)	Adulthood	Beginning of life as a hustler	(spoken dialogue; musical texture thins out)
1:49	Verse 2 (14 bars)			"Summer '94 . . ."
2:31				

Like the J. Cole song above, Trice's song demonstrates how form and content interact. While both songs rely on a conventional verse-chorus structure, each new verse heralds a change in content: a time shift in Trice's song, and a persona shift in Cole's.

If we ask who is telling the story, we can also ask who is *listening* to the story. Again, the answer might seem obvious at first: we are listening to the songs, and we are the audience to whom the lyrics are addressed. Individual listeners interpret a song in their own way, relating it to what they know about the artist, rap music in general, other media, and so on (this kind of listening will be taken up in more detail below, in the section on intertextuality). But every song also constructs a hypothetical idealized **listening subject** as well. Consider "Lost Ones": in the first verse, the speaker is addressing the woman; in the second verse, the woman is addressing the man. As the speaker's perspective shifts in this song, so does the listener's. We can learn a lot about each hypothetical listening subject by studying the speaker's verses carefully. For instance, Cole alerts us to the presence of someone else when he stops mid-sentence and says, "Hold up now—let me finish" (0:46). The line indicates that someone is trying to interrupt him. We get a sense of some of the conversations that the couple may have had previously—in a time before the conversation in the song starts—as we listen to the second verse. The third verse seems like a more direct address from the narrator to us as listeners, but the lyrics seem to be addressed to a male audience ("What about your seed?"; 3:46). Alternatively, we can imagine ourselves as eavesdroppers on the conversation between the couple, perhaps as we stand next to the narrator of the third verse, observing the scene from afar.

Cole's third studio album, *2014 Forest Hills Drive*, was noteworthy because it lacked **features**: the success (or potential failure) of the album rested on Cole's shoulders alone. This might suggest that we're only getting J. Cole's perspective through the entire album, but as we have seen, it's possible for a rapper to speak through different personae. The album achieved notoriety for going platinum and winning a number of awards in spite of the lack of features, leading many to speculate about future albums: would they, too, be feature-free? Cole's fourth studio album, *4 Your Eyez Only*, was released in December 2016, roughly two years after *2014 Forest Hills Drive*, and once again lacks features. One of the producers on the album, Elite, confirms a theory that fans put forth about the album: "There are moments where it parallels him and he speaks from his own perspective. [. . .] But the album is largely from a perspective that is not J. Cole."[12] Cole's independent, introspective nature lends itself to a deep exploration of the possibilities of storytelling.

When an artist is invited to perform a verse on another rapper's track, the guest verse is typically called a **feature**. Features are typically used to boost the career of one of the artists. In the case of up-and-coming artists, landing a feature could serve as a career stepping-stone—this was the case with Nicki Minaj on Kanye's "Monster," which we will examine in the next chapter. Having a well-known artist do a guest verse on a track works the same way, but could ultimately backfire if the guest artist's verse outshines the original artist's.

NARRATIVE

If subjectivity deals with who is telling stories (and who is listening to them), then **narrative** considers the ways in which these stories are told. A number of scholars have attempted to categorize these narrative strategies, and, despite their superficial differences, four basic narrative archetypes emerge: **reality**, **(auto)biography**, **diss**, and **party**.[13] Furthermore, a rapper can take a **chronological** or **lyric** approach to any of these four. In a chronological approach, a story unfolds in time; in the lyric approach, the rapper eschews chronology in favor of painting a picture. As with any categories—especially at this level of generalization—some overlap is natural; we will see some cases of this below.

Reality rap includes all the gritty tales of street life. The main objective of this style is to convince the listener that the events depicted actually happened. Gangsta rap and social commentary or "message" rap—which may initially appear to be opposites—both fall under this heading. The chronological narrative of many of these songs can be traced back to the genre's African roots. Many feature some obstacle that must be overcome, such as poverty, a rival artist or gang, the record industry, or some other institution. The protagonist may or may not be successful in their quest to overcome this obstacle—the quest might be comic (as in Lil Dicky's "$ave Dat Money") or tragic (as in Immortal Technique's "Dance with the Devil"). Grandmaster Flash & The Furious Five's "The Message" and Talib Kweli's "Get By" are examples of lyrical reality rap; Ice-T's "Midnight," Tupac's "Brenda's Got a Baby," and Ice Cube's "It Was a Good Day" are examples of chronological reality rap.

(Auto)biography relates the story of an individual or group: the subject of the song does not have to be the rapper himself or herself. Arguably, this narrative structure could be understood as a type of reality rap. Cobb traces the origin of the autobiographical in rap music to the autobiography of Malcolm X, distilling his life story into what he calls "the Malcolm X formula": "birth, the dissolution of his family, the experience of poverty and beginning of his life as a hustler, his incarceration, and his eventual redemption."[14] Quite a few rap autobiographies adhere to this formula, including Common's "I Used to Love H.E.R." (see Chapter 5), UGK's "One Day," and Obie Trice's "Follow My Life" (see below). While this archetype tends toward chronological narrative, boast raps are a common lyrical manifestation of this type. In lyrical instances, a rapper may boast about verbal or sexual prowess, toughness, wealth, or success in the industry. "Juicy" by The Notorious B.I.G., "Nuthin' But a G Thang" by Dr. Dre (feat. Snoop Doggy Dogg; see Chapter 11), and Kanye West's "Stronger" take this approach. In "Forest Whitaker," Brother Ali takes pride in his weight, blindness, and albino features by putting them front and center in the song.

Diss raps are the foundation of battle rapping. In a diss rap, the rapper hurls insults at an opponent. In a sense, it represents the opposite of the boastful lyric autobiography (one could argue, perhaps, that it is a kind of lyrical biography, where boasting is lyrical *auto*biography). In this style, wordplay is typically more important than the beat: the lyrics critique the target(s) in an effort to damage their reputation. It is not uncommon, though, for the dissing artist to rap over a track created by the target artist. "Roxanne's Revenge" by Roxanne Shanté, "South Bronx" by Boogie Down Productions, "Takedown" by Jay-Z (and Nas' response, "Ether"), and Hopsin's "Ill Mind of Hopsin 8" are all examples of this type.

Party raps tend to have lighter subject matter and are typically lyrical as opposed to narrative. These are songs that are meant for dancing, not contemplation: the beat is often more important than the words. The lyrics might be about sex, drugs, partying, or dancing. There are some songs that exist solely for the joy of wordplay or parody: songs by the Fat Boys, 2 Live Crew, and artists like Busdriver are more about the skill of rhyming than they are about communicating a specific message. Examples of party raps are The Sugar Hill Gang's "Rapper's Delight," "Summertime" by DJ Jazzy Jeff & The Fresh Prince, Soulja Boy's "Crank That (Soulja Boy)," and Asher Roth's "I Love College."

Iceberg Slim

Iceberg Slim, born Robert Beck in Chicago, Illinois, worked as a pimp before turning to writing after a short time in jail. Slim's first book, *Pimp* (1967), is an autobiographical chronicle of his life beginning in childhood and centering on his twenty-five years working as a pimp on the south side of Chicago: "Dawn was breaking as the big Hog scooted through the streets. My five whores were chattering like drunk magpies. [. . .] The inside of my nose was raw. It happens when you're a pig for snorting cocaine."[15] The colorful, gritty tales of street life that filled his nine books—fiction and nonfiction— ushered in the blaxploitation genre in film and inspired many rappers. Ice-T and Ice Cube both chose to name themselves "Ice" as an homage to Slim; Snoop Dogg and 50 Cent, among many others, portray the pimp lifestyle. In the introduction to *Doom Fox*, published after Slim's death, Ice-T praises him for showing the "the positive *and* negative sides of the game," an approach Ice-T and other gangsta rappers took to heart in their lyrics. "A real street hustler—whether he's out there selling drugs, pimping, or robbing banks—would never tell a child to do [as he did]."[16]

One theme of this book is the impact that technology, commercialization, and other external factors have had on the musical elements of rap, and rap's narrative structures are not immune to the influence of these factors. Greg Dimitriadis is one of the few authors who examines the impact of commercialization on musical form. Writing in 1996, he observed that:

> The decentralized face-to-face social dynamic which marked early hip hop has thus given way to a different dynamic, one mediated by way of commodity forms such as vinyl, video, and CD. These configurations have separated hip hop's focal discourse (i.e., "rap") from its early contexts of communal production, encouraging closed narrative forms over flexible wordplay and promoting individualized listening over community dance.[17]

Dimitriadis argues that recording has shifted the aesthetic of rap from a non-Western performance-based approach to a more Western—perhaps even "classical"—goal-directed narrative format, one that could be easily and endlessly reproduced. As rap has become more and more mainstream, it has been subjected to increasing pressure from market forces. These forces have changed not only the stories of rap, but also the ways in which those stories are told. It is important, then, to take into account the interplay among musical form, narrative, and subjectivity.

In the early days of rap, musical form had little impact on the overall structure of the lyrics. MCs would improvise over the beats the DJ was playing in order to move the crowd, and most of their material was improvised. Put another way, the MC was subservient to the DJ. Until about 1979, there really was no such thing as a rap "song": raps consisted of stock phrases ("Say ho!"; "Throw your hands in the air/And wave 'em like you just don't care!") that were assembled on the spot by MCs in response to their interactions with the crowd (improvisation in early rap is taken up in more detail in Chapter 5). Many of the first commercial rap releases—the first songs—were simply one long verse, like "Rapper's Delight." While that approach has largely fallen out of favor, artists occasionally still use it, like Tupac in "Brenda's Got a Baby" or Jay Electronica in "Exhibit C."

The most common song form was detailed at the beginning of the previous chapter: three 16-bar verses with a hook. At first glance, it might appear that musical forms like this would prove restrictive as artists try to manipulate their stories to fit into these standard song forms. As it happens, many artists used these forms to their advantage. The predictability of such forms encouraged artists to play with listeners' expectations. In "Midnight," Ice-T ends each verse with a cliffhanger, which serves to advance his story about being ambushed while hanging out in the parking lot of a convenience store. At the end of verse 1, he rhymes, "And they hadn't yet begun to fight/E hit the gas: it was one past midnight." The time stamp causes the listener to reconcile the fact that all the action in the first verse happened in a single minute. In lieu of a hook, the song features a variety of samples, sound effects, and spoken dialogue, all of which forestall the continuation of the drama in the second verse.

Some songs take an **epistolary** approach: each verse is a letter written to someone, as is the case with Eminem's "Stan," in which the first three verses are taken from a letter written to Eminem by an obsessed fan. The final verse consists of a letter written by the rapper to his fan, apologizing for not responding to the letters.

Music theorist Jocelyn Neal developed an analytical lens that she calls the "time-shift paradigm," in which the first verse typically describes birth or perhaps childhood; the second verse discusses middle age or the present; and the last verse suggests old age or the afterlife. The hook, rather than being dramatically static (as is often thought) serves to "fast-forward" to the next stage of life, and its meaning often shifts, given the context of the verses.[18] Although she developed the paradigm with country music in mind, it applies to many rap songs as well: the songs mentioned above in conjunction with Cobb's Malcolm X formula display the time-shift paradigm as well. Obie Trice's "Follow My Life" illustrates how the two storytelling techniques combine.

LISTENING GUIDE 2.2

Artist: Obie Trice
Song: "Follow My Life"
Album: *Cole World: The Sideline Story*
Record label: Dreamville/Roc Nation/Columbia
Year released: 2011
DJ or Producer: J. Cole
Samples used: "Theme from the Planets," Dexter Wansel

J. Cole provides three different perspectives, one in each 16-bar verse of the song. He uses basically the same tone of voice for each verse: it is mainly his language choices—changes in pronouns, for instance—that alert us to a shift in perspective. In the first verse (0:24), he presents the man's side of the conversation. It's not clear that this is Cole himself speaking: it's most likely a generic male perspective, with Cole speaking on behalf of the "invisible masses." This perspective is uncharacteristically sensitive, too, given the value placed on male promiscuity and "hardness" in rap. The first instance of the hook overlaps with the second verse, which starts with "She said . . ." (1:33) In this verse, Cole relates the woman's perspective. The tone of his voice changes somewhat, from the man's pleading to the woman's frustration. The third verse (2:57) presents the viewpoint of an omniscient narrator, someone observing the conversation. This verse functions in a similar fashion to the chorus in Greek drama, commenting on what the characters cannot perceive while informing the audience of what is actually happening. The "chorus" function is represented musically by the addition of multitracked vocal "echoes" in this verse. In this way it differs from the first two verses, in which the speaker is addressing the other partner, not the audience.

The hook of this song repeats three times, once after each verse. In each instance, the lyrics are practically identical, with one small change of pronoun. Cole uses the word "girl" in the first hook (1:11), suggesting that the man is addressing the woman. The line "And I ain't too proud to tell you that I cry sometimes about it" offers a rare display of male emotional vulnerability. In the second hook (2:35), Cole replaces "girl" with "boy," a subtle indication that the perspective has shifted. That the two hooks share lyrics reveal that, beneath the anger, fear, and confusion that the two characters display in their respective verses, both share an underlying sadness. The final occurrence of the hook (3:58) abandons the nouns, simply repeating "I ain't too proud to tell you that I cry sometimes about it."

INTERTEXTUALITY

When we listen to a song and try to discover its meaning, we often ask questions like "What feelings is this artist trying to evoke?" or "What was going on at this point in the artist's life, and how might it be reflected in this song?" In some cases, these questions have easy answers: if you can't tell by just listening, a quick web search will reveal that Ice Cube's "No Vaseline" was a result of his falling-out with the members of N.W.A., or that Kanye West's "Through the Wire" was written and performed while Kanye had his jaw wired shut as the result of injuries sustained in a traffic accident. Questions like this fall prey to something called the **intentional fallacy**; that is, we believe that there is some true meaning in a work of art and that we can decipher that meaning if we know the author's intentions when he or she created the work. Even in today's information-rich society, where volumes of information are readily available to us on mobile internet devices, it can be impossible to know an artist's true intention. Furthermore, it's possible that the author's intention changed over the course of production—songwriting can take weeks, months, or years—and since rap music is a collaborative effort (even on tracks with a single artist, producers, engineers, and others are always involved at some stage), we cannot possibly know the intentions of everyone involved, nor should we assume that everyone's intentions are crucial to understanding the song. Perhaps the engineer's intention was simply to finish the job so that he could return home in time for dinner.

This kind of listening also discounts the important contributions that each individual listener brings to the listening experience by privileging the artist's intentions as "true" and "correct." All listeners draw on a wide variety of reference points when they listen. And many (if not most) of our listening experiences occur without any kind of extensive background about the artist and his or her life circumstances. Imagine turning on the radio in the middle of an unfamiliar song. Your brain immediately starts making associations between the new stimulus and all of your prior listening experiences: "his voice sounds like Jay-Z, but earlier Jay-Z"; "I think the sample is from a James Brown song"; "This is another song about police brutality, like N.W.A.'s." The process of creating this web of associations is called **intertextuality**. Intertextuality suggests that texts (songs, lyrics, sounds) have no inherent meaning; instead, they develop meaning through their relationships with other texts. In contrast to the kind of listening described in the first paragraph, in which we seek a kind of "true" meaning, intertextuality opens the door for each listener to have the song mean something unique as a result of the individual associations. The multiplicity of meanings available for a song does not mean that one is somehow less true or correct than another, and they are certainly not less true than a listening that claims to evoke the artist's intent. Intertextuality suggests that each individual has a listening that is true for them. Furthermore, this perspective allows meanings to change over time, as old associations may be severed or reinforced, and new ones created.

Rap music (and hip-hop culture generally) is fundamentally intertextual as a result of its heavy reliance on borrowed material. Intertextuality is not synonymous with borrowing, however: *any* comparison you make while listening to a song creates (or destroys) a strand of the web, even if it results in a contrast ("this is definitely *not* a Jay-Z song"). Sampling is perhaps the most obvious manifestation of borrowing, and one of the most frequently asked questions about rap music gets at the distinction: do you have to know the source of a sample to understand the meaning of a song? In most cases, samples are chosen purely on the basis of their sound and not with the intention of making a thematic or topical connection between two songs. Returning to the radio example above, does it matter that you don't recognize the sample from "Apache" in the song? An intertextual hearing would say no. Maybe the sample has been slowed down or sped up or sliced so thin as to make it unrecognizable. In that event, even if the producer intended the sample to convey some kind of meaning ("this song is nostalgic for old-school hip hop"), that meaning could be lost if the sample is unrecognizable in the finished product.

Because the process of making these intertextual webs is a personal one, creating an intertextual listening guide for a song is challenging. Here, we will consider how such a web might be created with reference to two main songs, both titled "99 Problems"—one by Jay-Z and one by Ice-T. Given that Jay-Z's version is likely the more familiar of the two, we will start with that version. Starting with Jay-Z's version also highlights the fact that intertextuality is independent of chronology.

Jay-Z's "99 Problems" appeared on his 2003 release *The Black Album*. It's "almost a deliberate provocation to simpleminded listeners," he writes in *Decoded*. He calls the hook "a joke, bait for lazy critics."[19] In Jay-Z's song, each verse addresses a different problem and constructs a different context for the word "bitch." The first verse is directed at critics and ends with the second half of the hook, "I got 99 problems and a bitch ain't one." The second verse details a confrontation with a police officer who racially profiles Jay-Z: the lyrics "Son, do you know why I'm stoppin' you for? [. . .] You was doin' 55 in a 54" highlight the injustice (and perhaps even absurdity) of the stop. The verse ends with the police officer requesting a K-9 unit to search the car—the police dog in this case is the "bitch" in question. Jay-Z indicates that the verse ends ambiguously: the listener is left to guess how the situation ends. The third verse has Jay-Z ending up in the correctional system again, all because of the actions of another person who's "Tryin to play the boy [Jay-Z] like I'm saccharine." Like the second verse, the third verse also points out racial disparities in the system: "Half a mil' for bail 'cause I'm African."

The third verse starts with the line "Now once upon a time not too long ago," which for many listeners probably calls to mind any number of fairy tales, fables, or children's stories. In fact, the song "Children's Story" by Slick Rick is perhaps the most famous rap song to open with these lines. To some extent, the lines imply that what's about to follow is fiction but may have roots in truth; at the very least, the situation being described happened in the past. The associations we make between this "stock" opening line and the lyrics with which Jay-Z follows it help us to create meaning for the song. Not only does Jay-Z refer to Slick Rick with the opening of the third verse, but the first *four* lines of the verse are taken from a UGK song, "Touched." It's certainly possible to listen to Jay-Z's song, to enjoy it, to interpret it, without knowing any of these points of reference—the third verse makes sense and tells a clear story on its own terms; however, uncovering connections like this change our understanding and appreciation of the music.

The two versions of "99 Problems" have two immediate points of comparison: their titles and their hooks. Beyond that, they have very little in common: the subject matter and tone of each is quite different, and the musical tracks in the background don't sound alike at all. Ice-T's song is precisely the easy target for critics that Jay-Z alluded to: it's a list of all the different women that Ice-T and Brother Marquis (from 2 Live Crew) have at their disposal. One of the reasons the hook makes such good bait is because it invites comparison to a variety of songs *like* it (Jay-Z's own "Girls, Girls, Girls," or Ludacris' song "Area Codes," for instance). Jay-Z's song could thus almost be heard as a critique of Ice-T's, dismissing its frivolity by suggesting that many people are facing *real* problems. "List" songs like this have a long history. In the pop world, songs like R.E.M.'s "It's the End of the World as We Know It" and Billy Joel's "We Didn't Start the Fire" are of this type; in fact, an aria from Mozart's opera *Don Giovanni*

(1787), "Madamina, il Catalogo e Questo," is often called "the catalog aria," as Don Giovanni's assistant runs down a long list of his lord's amorous conquests.

In a 2014 interview with *Rolling Stone*, Ice-T was asked whether he liked Jay-Z's version of "99 Problems": "Yeah, I loved it. And Jay, instead of talking about bitches, he talked about a dog searching his car—which was a bitch—which was kind of clever. But it's kind of like, when you hear the real version, then you understand the hook. It makes sense."[20] In the interview, Ice-T implies that knowing his version of the song is crucial to an understanding of Jay-Z's song: an intertextual perspective would say that this is not so. The year before, Ice-T had announced that his hardcore band, Body Count, was back in the studio recording a fifth album. The album, *Manslaughter*, includes a mash-up of the two versions: Ice-T's lyrics with the beat from Jay-Z's version (here played by a live band). Listening to Body Count's version may generally call to mind other rap-rock hybrids like Run-D.M.C. (which also bears Rick Rubin's stamp), Public Enemy with Anthrax, Linkin Park, or Rage against the Machine.

Intertextuality also implies a comparison with other elements of culture that might not be immediately recognizable as texts. We compare the songs we hear to conventions of the genre in general: arguably, this is how we identify a rap song as opposed to, say, a country song or a jazz song (Chapter 6 takes up this point in more detail with a discussion of generic codes). We listen to it with reference to magazine articles, blog posts, and books like this one. We compare it to the prevailing cultural, political, and economic conditions of the time (hence the focus on the conditions in the South Bronx in Chapter 5). We could contend, for example, that Ice-T's "99 Problems" is a symptom of a prevailing culture of misogyny and patriarchy, reflecting the values held by that segment of society and playing into the stereotype of black men as promiscuous. If we understand Jay-Z's song as a critique of Ice-T's, then we might say it is a symptom of the broader systemic oppression faced by men in the black community.

Is it possible to listen to one version of "99 Problems" without knowing the other version, or anything about Slick Rick, fairy tales, or Mozart? Of course. Does recognizing all the points of reference in the song make listening to it more enjoyable? Not necessarily. Is it important to know that *The Black Album* was supposed to be Jay-Z's last album before retirement, or that Ice-T's album *Home Invasion* was his first after he was dismissed from Warner Brothers? Perhaps. The larger point is that, when we listen to music, we are constantly making comparisons to other things that we know in order to establish what a song means to us.

TRANSLATING RAP

Rap's poeticism pushes the boundaries of the English language in many ways, and it could be argued that, over the course of its history, it has *shaped* the language: phrases like "what up, G" and "bling bling" are now part of the American vernacular. Rappers transform language and, as they do so, imbue it with power—*nommo* (see Chapter 5). As rap spread around the country and around the world, it intersected with different languages and different cultures, shaping them as much as it was shaped by them. Rappers had to find ways to master and transform their own languages.

Writing with respect to Japanese rap, Ian Condry points out the tension between globalization, in which rap overall becomes more homogenous due to the multitude of influences (and mass-media dissemination), and localization, where the genre adapts to fit the needs of a local community.[21] This linguistic expansion further increased the available poetic devices available to artists. Consider the hook to Snow Tha Product's track "Vaquero": "I fell in love with a vaquero, Botas y sombreros/And I'mma cross him over I'mma pay for his pollero/And we goin' get married and he goin' get papers/But I'mma hunt him down if he tell me 'see you later.'" Snow mixes English and Spanish with ease in the hook. She rhymes "vaquero" and "sombreros" in the first line, and the first two lines end with slant rhyme in Spanish ("sombreros" and "pollero"). Lines 3 and 4 end with a slant rhyme in English.

From their earliest efforts, Japanese artists had to figure out how to reconcile the American hip-hop aesthetic with elements of Japanese culture. American rap records first appeared in Japan in the early 1980s; however, the movie *Wild Style*, which premiered in Japan in 1983, was the impetus for hip-hop culture—break dancing, initially—to take root there. As hip hop grew in popularity through the late 1980s, prominent rap acts such as Afrika Bambaataa, Run-D.M.C., and De La Soul played shows in Japan. Pioneering Japanese rappers faced a dilemma: should they rap in English or Japanese? The choice has both cultural and poetic repercussions.

Japanese rappers had to decide whether to write their raps in Japanese and risk alienating those who did not speak the language, or to rap in English, in which they were not as fluent.[22] As with many Japanese forays into global pop culture, they had to combat a general national stereotype of being inauthentic.[23] Even though English is the "original" language of rap, rappers from another country who try to rap in English could be seen as little more than cheap imitations. Many early Japanese rappers started rapping in English, believing that Japanese was ill-suited for composing raps; however, they soon returned to their Japanese roots, believing that they could express themselves more authentically in their native tongue. Furthermore, the subject matter of rap in Japan differs markedly from the subject matter of American rap. There is less income inequality in Japan, for instance; 99% of Japan's residents are ethnically Japanese (which suggests that racism is not an issue); and the country has generally low crime and gun-ownership rates.[24] Most Japanese rap is thus **party** rap.

Cultural considerations aside, rapping in Japanese presents a unique set of linguistic challenges. Rap in English relies on rhyming and stress accents, two linguistic elements that have no equivalent in Japanese. Rhyme and stress accent are how we define many English poetic forms: for example, an Elizabethan sonnet comprises fourteen lines of iambic pentameter—the stress-accent pattern—and has a rhyme scheme of *abab cdcd efef gg*. Instead of accent and rhyme, Japanese poems tend to rely on the number of syllables—more specifically, *moras* (an even smaller linguistic unit)—like the well-known 5-7-5 pattern of haiku. Each *mora* is spoken with the same duration but different pitch; changing the pitch accent changes the word's meaning, resulting in language full of homonyms. The nature of the Japanese language results in early experiments in rap that sound a lot like old-school American rap: a "sung" style with end rhymes that help articulate clear line breaks (as a result of the pitch accents).[25]

Scha Dara Parr's "Game Boys" provides a very early example of Japanese rap. The trio formed in 1988 and released its debut album in 1990. In 1994, their single "Kon'ya wa Bugī Bakku" ("Boogie Back Tonight") became the first million-selling Japanese rap song, and they made inroads into the United States via an appearance on De La Soul's track "Long Island Wildin'." The song "Game Boys"—also released in 1994—highlights the challenges faced by those trying to rap in Japanese: this track was recorded before the group really tried to rhyme in their songs.[26] Figure 2.2 includes a transliteration and translation of part of the first verse of "Game Boys." Every line in the first verse ends with the long "o" sound, which produces (or perhaps necessitates) very clear line breaks. The third line features internal rhyme,

Transliterated Japanese (verse 1)	English translation (verse 1)
Kyō wa doyōbi da dai shūgō	Today's Saturday and it's a big gathering
Famikon senshi ga min'na atsumō	The Famicom soldiers are all getting together
shirōto kurouto sorouto mō	When amateurs and experts gather then
masashiku sono ba wa soku senjō	Surely the place where they are will immediately
onōno jiman no waza o hirō	become a battlefield
aitsu ni makeji to min'na kisou	Each of them will show the techniques that they're
nikui ze zurui ze anchikushō	proud of
shirazushirazu to shinken shō	Everyone competes, thinking "I'm not gonna be
bu maketara kuyashisa ga tsukimatō	outdone by him"
makeru gurai nara shi nite⁻ yo⁻	I hate him, he's so cunning, that bastard
katawara ni oita igonjō	Unconsciously it turns into a real battle
makete tamaru ka boku do konjō	If I lose then frustration is dangled before me
tomadou koto naku nomerikomou	I'd rather die than lose, though
aikotoba "gēmu" de ikitōgō	I set my will nearby
yofuke ni gēmu wa saikōchō	Like I'd lose, I've got some serious guts
ashita wa nichiyōbi shinpai o muyō	Let's get completely absorbed without getting lost
janpu!	Hitting it off with the password of "game"
	Games are the climax late at night
	Tomorrow's Sunday; I'm worried, it's futile,
	Jump!

Figure 2.2 Transliteration and translation of Scha Dara Parr's "Game Boys" (verse 1)

comprising three three-syllable words (*shirōto, kurouto, sorouto*) each set to the same rhythm. The rhythmic similarities in this line and throughout the song are a result of the lack of stress accents and equal-length *moras*. In general, the first syllable of the text occurs on the first beat of the bar, and the last syllable of text in the line occurs on the last beat, with a long-short-short rhythm (*shi-ro-to, ku-rou-to, so-rou-to*) predominating.

As rap evolved in Japan, both artists and listeners went in search of more sophisticated lyrical techniques. Noriko Manabe outlines two strategies that Japanese rappers employ to create rhythm and rhymes: changing the syntax and borrowing from other languages. In Japanese, sentences must end with auxiliary verbs, and there is a limited number of these, which results in trivial end rhymes. K Dub Shine was among the first to experiment with Japanese syntax: he realized that rap in English relied on pairing important words and that he could do something similar in Japanese by focusing on key words and ignoring syntax and, in some cases, grammatically correct suffixes.[27] Japanese also borrows readily from other languages, including Chinese and English, and rappers began mining these languages for more rhymes. Manabe gives a few lines of "Slow Learner" by Rhymester to illustrate these borrowings in action: the lines appear in Figure 2.3.

The song quotes Bill Withers' hit "Ain't No Sunshine," mixing English and Japanese freely. Mummy-D (the rapper on this verse) rhymes the English "I know" with *sainou*, a word borrowed from Chinese but spoken with Japanese pronunciation.[28]

Different languages pose different challenges to the sonic elements of rap—things like rhyming, meter, and alliteration—to say nothing of the depth of meaning that figurative language like metaphor and personification can convey. Despite the emphasis on sound, there are those in the hip-hop community working to make rap music accessible to the deaf. Sharaya J, a protégé of Missy Elliott's, got her start as a dancer before transitioning to rap. She

Transliterated Japanese (verse 1)	English translation (verse 1)
Ain't no sunshine/Daga hi wa mada noboru	Ain't no sunshine, but the sun's still rising
I know, I know, *I know, I know, I know*	I know, I know, I know, I know,
Hito mo urayamu *sainou, sainou, sainou*	The talent that others envy

Figure 2.3 Excerpt from "Slow Learner" by Rhymester

incorporates American Sign Language (ASL) into many of her performances: in many cases, it seems organic to her choreography. In the video for "Shut It Down," she signs the refrain using the signs for "Shut (the door)" and then points down. The figurative meaning of the verbal lyrics is thus somewhat at odds with the literal meaning of what she is signing. Furthermore, ASL has its own grammar, distinct from English. In the verse, Sharaya J signs along with what she is rapping, but she forces the signs into English grammar for a more direct correlation between sight and sound, a strategy similar to that of Japanese rappers.

A provision of the 1990 Americans with Disabilities Act requires concert venues to provide an interpreter for the Deaf community when requested. Translating lyrics into ASL can be challenging and requires more than just conventional hand signs to convey meaning. Many common words and expressions have their own unique signs, and other words can be spelled out using letters of the alphabet. Any sign in ASL relies on five parameters—hand shape, palm orientation, location, movement, and facial expression—and a change in any one of these alters the meaning of the sign. Those who translate rap lyrics tend not to translate the material literally (that is, word-for-word); rather, they attempt to convey the general meaning of the lyrics. Facial expressions also take on an important role.

In the cases described above, we can see the reciprocal relationship between rap and language: language influences rap, and rap in turn influences language. This reciprocal relationship is examined further in the next chapter.

 OUTRO

Names you should know:

- Rakim
- J. Cole
- Iceberg Slim
- Obie Trice
- Jay-Z
- Ice-T
- Scha Dara Paar
- Rhymester
- Sharaya J

Terms you should know:

- Rhyme (end, internal, slant, multisyllabic, transformative)
- Alliteration, consonance
- Pun/punch line
- Syncopation
- Simile, metaphor, personification
- Hashtag rap
- Narrative (reality, (auto)biography, diss, party)
- Chronological
- Lyrical
- Subjectivity

- Feature
- Listening subject
- Epistolary

- Intentional fallacy
- Intertextuality

Questions for discussion/writing prompts:

1. Choose a song that you like and analyze it in terms of poetic devices, notions of subjectivity, and narrative.

2. How important is it that we know the circumstances of a song's creation? How important is it that we know the source of the samples (either musical or lyrical, in the case of rappers quoting other rappers)?

3. In 1999, Cypress Hill released a greatest-hits album, *Los Grandes Éxitos en Español*, which included their top hits translated into Spanish. Listen to one of the songs in the original English and then the same song in Spanish. How does translating the song affect the poetry? The rhythm?

Additional listening:

Poetic devices:

- "My Melody," Rakim
- "Mural," Lupe Fiasco
- "Uncommon Valor," R. A. The Rugged Man
- "True Mastery," Sa-Roc

Unusual approaches to rhyme:

- "Alphabet Aerobics" and "Chemical Calisthenics," Blackalicious
- "ABC/Guilty," Rapsody
- "Mathematics," Mos Def
- "Area Codes," Ludacris
- "Switch My Styles," Styles P

Subjectivity:

- "I Gave You Power," Nas
- "Lovesong," Jean Grae
- "Cappuccino," MC Lyte
- Kool Keith/Dr. Octagon, *Dr. Octagonecologyst*

Narrative:

- "Rewind," Nas
- "Before the Summer Broke (All Grown Up Version)," Jean Grae
- "Things Done Changed," The Notorious B.I.G.

Intertextuality:

- "Blood on the Leaves," Nina Simone; "Blood on the Leaves" and "New Slaves," Kanye West; "New Nat Turners," Jasiri X
- "C.R.E.A.M.," Wu-Tang Clan; "Paper Trail$," Joey Bada$$

NOTES

1 Adam Bradley, *Book of Rhymes: The Poetics of Hip Hop* (New York: Basic Civitas Books, 2009), 66.

2 Bradley 10.

3 Bradley 81. A simile is technically a kind of metaphor, one that uses "like" or "as" to highlight the comparison.

4 Amirah Mercer, "5 Things You Didn't Know about Hashtag Rap" *Mic* (June 3, 2013): https://mic.com/articles/45285/5-things-you-didn-t-know-about-hashtag-rap#.M06XFO2IF.

5 This is the focus of William Jelani Cobb, *To the Break of Dawn: A Freestyle on the Hip Hop Aesthetic* (New York: New York University Press, 2007), particularly chapter 4.

6 Nelson George, *Hip Hop America* (New York: Viking, 1998), 51.

7 Cobb 35. See also Eithne Quinn, *Nuthin' but a 'G' Thang: The Culture and Commerce of Gangsta Rap* (New York: Columbia University Press, 2005).

8 Tricia Rose, *The Hip Hop Wars* (New York: BasicCivitas, 2008).

9 Cheryl Keyes, *Rap Music and Street Consciousness* (Urbana: University of Illinois Press, 2002), chapter 7.

10 Cobb 112.

11 Cobb 112–3. See also Imani Perry, *Prophets of the Hood* (Durham, NC: Duke University Press, 2004), 38–9.

12 Edwin Ortiz, " 'The Album Is Largely from a Perspective That Isn't J. Cole's': Producer Elite on *4 Your Eyez Only*" *Complex* (December 10, 2016): www.complex.com/music/2016/12/elite-interview-on-j-cole-4-your-eyez-only.

13 These four types were distilled from work by Cobb 2007; Adam Krims, *Rap Music and the Poetics of Identity* (Cambridge: Cambridge University Press, 2000); Alexs Pate, *In the Heart of the Beat: The Poetry of Rap* (Lanham, MD: Scarecrow Press, 2010); and Perry 2004.

14 Cobb 130.

15 Iceberg Slim, *Pimp: The Story of My Life* (Los Angeles: Holloway House, 1969), 11.

16 Ice-T, Introduction to *Doom Fox*, by Iceberg Slim (New York: Grove Press, 1998), vi–vii.

17 Greg Dimitriadis, "Hip-Hop: From Live Performance to Mediated Narrative" *Popular Music* 15 no. 2 (May 1996): 179–95. Reprinted in *That's the Joint! The Hip Hop Studies Reader*. Ed. Murray Forman and Mark Anthony Neal (New York: Routledge, 2004), 421.

18 Jocelyn Neal, "Narrative Paradigms, Musical Signifiers, and Form as Function in Country Music" *Music Theory Spectrum* 29 no. 1 (Spring 2007): 41–72.

19 Jay-Z and dream hampton, *Decoded* (New York: Virgin Books, 2011), 55–6.

20 Kory Grow, "Ice-T Explains Why He Remade '99 Problems' and Brought Back Body Count" *Rolling Stone* (June 12, 2014): www.rollingstone.com/music/news/ice-t-explains-why-he-remade-99-problems-and-brought-back-body-count-20140612.

21 Ian Condry, *Hip-Hop Japan: Rap and the Paths of Cultural Globalization* (Durham, NC: Duke University Press, 2006).

22 Noriko Manabe, "Representing Japan: 'National' Style among Japanese Hip-Hop DJs" *Popular Music* 32 no. 1 (2013): 36. Manabe indicates that English is a required subject for Japanese students beginning in the seventh grade.

23 Manabe, "Representing," 35–6; Condry 12; Marcyliena Morgan, *The Real Hip Hop: Battling for Knowledge, Power, and Respect in the L.A. Underground* (Durham, NC: Duke University Press, 2009), 63.

24 Noriko Manabe, "Globalization and Japanese Creativity: Adaptation of Japanese Language to Rap" *Ethnomusicology* 50/1 (2006): 4.

25 This paragraph summarizes many of Manabe's observations about the language as presented in "Globalization."

26 Manabe, "Globalization," 8.

27 Manabe, "Globalization," 8.

28 Italics are in the original; translations are from Manabe, "Globalization," 11.

TIME LINE

2010   DJ Khaled releases "All I Do Is Win."

2010   Nicki Minaj features on Kanye West's "Monster" from his album *My Beautiful Dark Twisted Fantasy*.

IN THIS CHAPTER, YOU WILL LEARN ABOUT

- Listening to rappers' voices
- Techniques for describing a rapper's flow
- How language choices influence a rapper's voice

CHAPTER 3

Listening to Voice

OVERVIEW

In this chapter, we will survey different ways of talking about an MC's voice. Much as producers have their own sonic signature, each MC has a distinct voice. That voice is constituted not only by the MC's biology—male or female, high-pitched or low-pitched, nasal or chest voice—but also by the kinds of language choices they make. We can talk about the biological component of flow using the same parameters that we used in our discussion of sonic signatures. Language choices are a powerful marker of race and class identity. The biological and social, taken together, result in a rapper's flow (which we may think of as synonymous with voice at this point). This chapter culminates in an analysis of Nicki Minaj's verse on Kanye West's song "Monster," which is widely regarded as not only her best verse, but also one of the best verses of the 2010s.

INTRO

We can talk about the sound of the voice in many ways. We can contrast the deep, booming voices of Rakim and Chuck D with the nasal voices of Eazy-E and Slick Rick. We can talk about Ice-T's shouted delivery of the lyrics on "Midnight" and compare it to the more hushed tones of Jay-Z's "Minority Report," or we can talk about the way Kanye's voice becomes louder and more agitated over the course of "New Slaves." The tone of a rapper's voice can convey a variety of emotional states. The percussive quality of Cypress Hill frontman B-Real's voice is quite different from the singing style used by Bone Thugs-N-Harmony. In some cases, rappers inflect their voices differently within the same song: The Notorious B.I.G. raps both characters in "Gimmie the Loot." In many cases, we're not hearing a rapper's "natural" voice: their voice has been trained, or it could have been subjected to any number of technological processes. A voice with an accent can also connote location, as well as a sense of in- or out-group membership. KRS-One employs a Jamaican accent in "The Bridge Is Over"; many rappers from the southern states reveal their origins through a characteristic drawl.

We can use the same methodology here that we used to discuss sonic signatures in Chapter 1 and talk about voices in terms of pitch, intensity, duration, and sound color.[1] These terms provide a set of parameters for talking about elements of the voice that are independent from language choices. For the most part, a change in one of these parameters signals emphasis on a word or syllable. It is also worth mentioning that changes in one parameter are often accompanied by changes in another: the voice gets louder and higher-pitched, for instance. These parameters are also subject to technological manipulation as well, a subject that will be taken up later in this chapter.

Even though most rappers do not sing in the traditional sense, we can talk about the *pitch* of their voices in relative terms. Some rappers have higher-pitched voices (Eazy-E), and some have lower-pitched voices (like Rakim and Tyler the Creator). Women typically have higher-pitched voices than men. More specifically, it might not make sense to talk about whether a particular syllable is supposed to sound like C or C#, and it might not even make sense to talk about whether a rapper is in tune or out of tune. When we speak, our voices tend to descend in pitch over the course of a declarative statement, and they tend to rise in pitch toward the end of a question. Some rappers have a rather wide, expressive pitch range; others are narrower.

There are instances where rappers do sing, and it makes sense to talk about pitch in a more rigorous way; even here, though, there is a continuum, from the joyfully out-of-tune singing of Biz Markie, to the harmonies of Bone Thugs to more recent artists like Fetty Wap and Anderson. Paak. While singing in hooks is common—often, a different artist is hired just to sing the hook—singing in verses (especially by the *rapper*) is much less common. When a rapper does sing, it attracts special attention from the listener: why has the artist chosen to sing rather than rap? Similarly, if an artist is singing and that singing is badly out of tune, we might wonder why, given the available methods to fix it, they left it out of tune.

Autotune is a technology that originally referred to a particular software program (AutoTune, published by Antares) but has come to be a metonym for any real-time pitch-correction software. The pitch correction can be done subtly or very audibly, as it is in T-Pain's productions. Either way, many people consider pitch correction to be a form of cheating and use it to further their arguments about the inferiority of much contemporary pop music (rap included). The very audible use of autotune in music by T-Pain and others suggests not that they're trying to hide their poor singing, but that they're trying to call attention to the artificiality of the voice. The use of autotune peaked in the mid-2000s, at which point there was even an "I am T-Pain" smartphone app that allowed anyone to mimic the popular artist's signature sound. Jay-Z was not pleased with autotune's dominance of the airwaves and included "D.O.A." ("Death to Autotune") on his 2009 album *Blueprint 3*. Autotune features prominently in a lot of contemporary rap by artists like Future and Young Thug.

Intensity is the relative loudness or softness of the voice: it's the difference between shouting and whispering. A rapper's intensity can vary from song to song and even over the course of a single song.

Duration accounts for several parameters here. We can use "duration" to talk in general about a rapper's rhythmic choices. We can also use it to talk about the amount of separation or smoothness between syllables (staccato vs. legato, in musical terms).

Sound color is once again the trickiest to define. We might talk about the Beastie Boys' exaggerated New York accents, Chuck D's booming voice, Young Thug's mumbling, or Busta Rhymes' percussive style. A rapper's accent also influences our perception of sound color. Some artists even have signature **ad-libs**—grunts, moans, yelps, or other noises that are easily identifiable. Among the most well-known are Flavor Flav's "Yeah boy!"; Kanye's gravelly "heh"; Rick Ross' grunt; Lil B's "Swag," and Drake's "Yeah."

Voices can be altered naturally or through technological means like autotune. In *Something from Nothing: The Art of Rap*, MC Lyte tells Ice-T that she worked with Lucien George Sr. (who was the father of three members of Full Force) to develop a stronger voice: "[My voice] was teeny, tiny—no weight to it," she recalls.[2] "He would say 'get strong!' and 'come from here' [she points to her diaphragm].'" B-Real of Cypress Hill tells Ice-T: "It took a couple of years to get that [his unique delivery]. When we started, I was rapping in this voice that I talk in, and Muggs didn't like it and Sen was like 'I don't know.' [. . .] They said, 'if you don't do something about that voice, we're just gonna have you write rhymes for Sen Dog."[3] Kanye West's song "Through the Wire" was recorded after he was in an automobile accident. His injuries required his jaw to be wired shut in order to heal correctly. He recorded the track with his jaw wired shut, resulting in the unusual sound of his voice on the song.

Beat boxing is the skill of using the voice to imitate the sounds of drums, other percussion instruments, and turntable techniques. "Beat box" was a generic term that referred to early drum machines. In light of the poverty experienced by many early hip-hop artists, the story goes that beat boxing developed as a way to supply beats for rappers who could not afford turntables or a drum machine. In hip hop, the style was pioneered in the early 1980s by Doug E. Fresh, Sha-Rock, and The Fat Boys' Human Beat Box. Beat boxing, like turntablism, has split off from mainstream hip hop and become an art form in itself, with artists like Beardyman, Rahzel (formerly of The Roots), Eklips, Bellatrix, and Tom Thum among the most well-known and respected practitioners.

While there are many ways rappers can naturally change their voice, there are more ways that technology can alter its sound. Even the simple act of performing into a microphone and amplifying the voice changes it, denaturalizes it. Producers can add delay and reverb, both of which create a sense of space. The main difference between delay and reverb is the amount of time it takes for the reflection of the original sound to hit your ear: with reverb, the original sound is still present, as if you were making the sound in a small room; with delay, the original sound has dissipated, as if you were making the sound in a canyon.

DJ Khaled's **posse cut** "All I Do Is Win" provides an opportunity to compare the vocal qualities of four very different artists: T-Pain, Ludacris, Rick Ross, and Snoop Dogg. DJ Khaled is known for his ability to bring together top-shelf artists on collaborative projects—he's more of a behind-the-scenes figure—but he does the production work on this track, and we do hear his voice in short phrases throughout.

A **posse cut** is a song that features several artists, often from different labels, with each getting a verse. Songs by early rap groups are de facto posse cuts—the form certainly hearkens back to the cipher—they featured members of a particular crew or label. As groups became less prominent and solo artists came to dominate the airwaves, the posse cut became more of an "all-star" competition or reunion opportunity, generally in the spirit of friendly competition.

LISTENING GUIDE 3.1

Artist: DJ Khaled (feat. T-Pain, Ludacris, Rick Ross, and Snoop Dogg)
Song: "All I Do Is Win"
Album: *Victory*
Record label: E1
Year released: 2010
DJ or Producer: DJ Khaled
Samples used: (none)

The song starts with DJ Khaled enthusiastically shouting out his tagline: "DJ Khaled—we the best!" The hook, sung by T-Pain, follows (0:05). His delivery is the most like singing out of the group, which is not surprising considering hooks are often sung, and the *pitch* varies accordingly: his melody could be written in traditional musical notation or played on an instrument with relative ease. T-Pain is best known for pioneering the use—some might say overuse—of pitch-correction software (see the "Autotune" text box earlier in this chapter). Toward the end of the video, in fact, you can see him holding a mobile phone with the "I Am T-Pain" app, which made a rudimentary pitch-correction program available to the masses. T-Pain is a fine singer without the software, but the program adds a unique *sound color* (or *timbre*) to his voice. Rather than there being smooth glides from syllable to syllable as happens naturally when we sing or talk, the software makes it sound as though there are many little discrete steps as T-Pain moves from one pitch to another. This is most evident when he makes large, quick leaps, as he does from "go" to "up," and where he scoops up repeatedly into the word "win, win, win, and if you're goin' in . . ."—the highest pitches of the hook—toward the end.

Ludacris raps the first verse (0:30). His delivery is more speech-like than T-Pain's, but he does have a rather wide *pitch* range. Most of his lines start off with very short, fast notes and end with slightly longer, slower notes that drag behind the beat. His voice has a distinct growl, which you can hear in his "ow" and "aah" sounds, as in ". . . won't stop *now*" and ". . . sayin' Luda's *back*." His Southern roots (he grew up in Atlanta) come through in his inflections and word choices. In particular, the "ur" sound that appears in the words "verses," "servin'," and "versions" is drawn out in a characteristic Southern accent. Ludacris calls himself "the South's champion" and refers to collard greens, a soul-food staple. Leading into the hook, around 1:08, his words "all I" are electronically repeated as a stutter.

After a repetition of the hook (1:10), Rick Ross delivers the second verse (1:36). Ross' delivery stands in strong contrast to Ludacris': Ross' pitch range is narrower, his flow is generally slower and less rhythmically complex, and he is frequently behind the beat. On just about every other beat, the text in his verse is highlighted with an echo.

The hook appears again (2:13) and is followed by Snoop Dogg's verse (2:40). Despite his well-known status as a West Coast rapper, Snoop's delivery, which is often referred to as a "drawl," evokes the influence of the American South on black culture. His voice is the lowest-pitched of all the artists on the track and sounds more laid-back than the first two rappers: he works fewer syllables into each beat. This drawl is most noticeable at the ends of the first four lines. The rhyming words rely on the "oh" sound ("stove," "sold," "overload," and "old"): the pitch of his voice climbs to the "o" in each word and drops off dramatically after that.

One particularly interesting feature of this song is how the voices are normalized in terms of pitch. While it is very subtle, each voice has been tuned to have a "focal" pitch of D throughout the verse. That is not to say that each rapper speaks his syllables only on a single pitch; rather, it might be thought of in terms of an "average" pitch—taken together, the pitches intoned by the rappers center around D. This ultimately results in a fairly pleasing, consonant sound overall (which is important given the very pitch-focused nature of the synth tracks in the background) in contrast to the sublimely dissonant layering that we heard in Public Enemy's "Bring the Noise" (Chapter 1). While both tracks are very densely layered, studio wizardry in DJ Khaled's song results in a more harmonious sound overall.

FLOW AND RUPTURE

Tricia Rose contends that **flow**—and its "opposite," **rupture**—are, along with layering, the three fundamental components of the hip-hop aesthetic.[4] Looping the break beat creates flow, while the break itself and scratching techniques create ruptures. In graffiti, we can imagine long, uninterrupted bursts from a spray can, or the unbroken line of a magic marker. Full subway car graffiti pieces flowed through New York City's neighborhoods in the 1970s. In break dancing, we can think of the fluid motions of the dancers as they pop and spin, while a freeze is a rupture. Rupture might also happen as one dancer leaves the floor and another one enters. Transitions from footwork to floor work to spin could also be understood as ruptures (although one could make a similarly strong case that the transitions flow from one to the other, particularly in the case of skilled dancers).

In hip hop, flow most commonly refers to the synthesis of musical rhythm and lyrics. Felicia Miyakawa defines flow as "the musical application of the MC's skills to a poetic line," with individual styles determined by "phrasing, rhyme scheme, rhythmic play, timbre [sound color], and accents."[5] Kyle Adams defines flow as "all of the ways in which a rapper uses rhythm and articulation in his/her lyrical delivery."[6] Rappers' language choices can influence the musical decisions they make. Similarly, their rhythmic choices can shed new light on the lyrics they have composed.

Journalists often use colorful adjectives to describe an individual rapper's flow; however, we are going to develop a more generalized system for talking about flow, one that highlights the interplay between text and music in specific ways. Adam Krims developed a useful classification scheme for discussing the sound of a rapper's flow. Krims contrasts the **sung** style common to much early rap with **effusive** styles found in rap after about 1994.[7] Felicia Miyakawa argues that Krims' categories delineate old-school and new-school approaches to flow, respectively.[8] The effusive styles can be further divided into **speech-effusive** and **percussion-effusive**, with percussion-effusive being on the opposite end of the continuum from sung style. In short, the sung style sounds like singing: it's characterized by a relatively clear sense of pitch and rhythm. This style tends to feature end rhyme and very little internal rhyme, which often emphasizes clear line breaks. Rhythmically, the sung style is not particularly complex.

The effusive styles downplay the role of pitch and more closely resemble natural speech. This style was pioneered by MCs like Rakim and Nas in the late 1980s and early 1990s. The effusive style is so named because of the tendency of one line to spill into the next, an important point of contrast to the clear breaks of the sung style. Effusive style tends to be more complicated than the sung style: it features internal rhymes as well as end rhymes, and it features more sophisticated rhythms that not only divide but subdivide the beat. Put another way, there tend to be more notes or syllables packed into each beat in this style than in the sung style. The rhythmic divisions could be **syncopated**—that is, they emphasize not the beats themselves, but the notes "in the cracks," between the beats.

Most rap after about 1990 uses the speech-effusive style, although there are a few artists who tend to favor the percussion-effusive style. The percussion-effusive style treats the voice more like a percussion instrument, featuring sharp attacks. B-Real of Cypress Hill is perhaps the most well-known practitioner of this style.

The examples below contrast a passage in the sung style—the opening lines of Eazy-E's "Boyz-n-the Hood" (Figure 3.1)—with an example of speech-effusive style from The Notorious B.I.G.'s "Things Done Changed" (Figure 3.2). In Figure 3.1, the line breaks are very clear, and each line features an overall descent in pitch. The ends of lines 1 and 2 rhyme, and the ends of lines 3 and 4 rhyme; the only internal rhyme appears in the second line—"jockin'" and "clockin'"—and this is highlighted by the placement of each word on a strong beat and roughly the same pitch level. Most of the important words occur on the beat, and, for the most part, the beginnings of multisyllabic words also fall on strong beats. Beats are mostly divided into groups of two or three. In Figure 3.2, we hear a pair of long lyrical lines, each sprawling over two measures (1-2-3-4, 2-2-3-4). Lines 1 and 3 start after the first beat, and lines 2 and 4 start before the first beat: this is a clear example of what Krims means when he talks about "effusive" (students of poetry might

highest pitch	Cruis-	in'	down	the												
					street		in									
								my		Six-						
lowest pitch													four				
Beat count:	1	e	&	a	2	e	&	a	3	e	&	a	4	e	&	a

highest pitch																
	Jock-	**in'**	**the**						**Clock-**	**in'**	**the**					
lowest pitch					freaks								**dough**				
Beat count:	1	e	&	a	2	e	&	a	3	e	&	a	4	e	&	a

highest pitch	Went		to	the													
					park		to									
								get	the		**scoop**					
lowest pitch															Knuck-	le-
Beat count:	1	e	&	a	2	e	&	a	3	e	&	a	4	e	&	a

highest pitch	heads		out													
					there		cold									
									shoot-	**in'**	**some**					
lowest pitch													**hoops**				
Beat count:	1	e	&	a	2	e	&	a	3	e	&	a	4	e	&	a

Figure 3.1 Eazy-E, "Boyz-n-the Hood"

	1	e	&	a	2	e	&	a	3	e	&	a	4	e	&	a
		Shit,		it's	hard		be-	in'	**young**		from	the	**slums**		eat-	in'
	five-	cent			**gums**	not	know-	in'	**where**	your	**meal's**		com-		in'	from
			And	now	the	shit's	get-	tin'	**cra-**	zi-	er	and	ma-	jor		Kids
	young-	er	than	me	they	got		the	**Sky-**		**brand**		pag-		ers	
Beat	1	e	&	a	2	e	&	a	3	e	&	a	4	e	&	a

Figure 3.2 The Notorious B.I.G., "Things Done Changed"

call it "enjambment"). Biggie groups the lines into pairs using internal rhyme (in boldface) and a gradual decline in the pitch of his voice. The internal rhyme also serves to blur the line endings.

Cadence is another concept we can use when talking about flows. Cadence can be understood as how quickly the MC is rapping; maybe how many words per minute (or second or whatever). Cadence is not necessarily dependent upon tempo: a rapper could conceivably achieve a high syllabic density in a song with a slow tempo, and vice versa. Musicologist Alyssa Woods notes that slow cadences are not in any way inferior to faster cadences; rather, they can evoke different meanings (laid-back versus agitated, for instance).[9]

Adams further refines the qualities that define flow into two broad categories: metrical techniques and articulation techniques.

Metrical techniques

1. The placement of rhyming syllables
2. The placement of accented syllables
3. The degree of correspondence between syntactic units and measures
4. The number of syllables per beat

Articulative techniques

1. The amount of legato [smoothness or connection] or staccato [clipped, separated] used
2. The degree of articulation of the consonants
3. The extent to which the onset of any syllable is earlier or later than the beat[10]

Although we have already addressed many of Adams' criteria—and many are illustrated in the examples above—a few deserve further explanation. Adams' third metrical technique suggests that lyrical lines and bars may not correspond directly. In Figure 3.1, each syntactic unit corresponds to a bar; in Figure 3.2, there is one syntactic unit per two bars. Adams' fourth metrical technique corresponds roughly to my definition of cadence, the number of syllables per beat. The second articulative technique deals with accent: how forcefully the rapper projects the consonant sounds. The more forcefully the rapper projects these sounds, the more percussion-effusive the flow is. It can be difficult to hear whether the rapper is ahead of or behind the beat, but these aspects of flow can evoke meaning as well: rapping behind the beat might sound laid-back, whereas rapping ahead of the beat might suggest aggression or anxiety.

Rupture is any interruption in flow. Tricia Rose describes two kinds of rupture with respect to rap music: when scratching interrupts the flow, or when one musical passage is interrupted by another.[11] Miyakawa infers a third type of rupture from Rose's work, which happens when an MC changes up the flow.[12] Given the date of Rose's work—it was one of the first scholarly books on rap music—we might update her first type of rupture to include any instance of an instrument dropping out a texture in sample-based or newly composed beats.

LISTENING GUIDE 3.2

Artist: Blackalicious
Song: "Chemical Calisthenics"
Album: *Blazing Arrow*
Record label: MCA
Year released: 2002
DJ or Producer: DJ Cut Chemist
Samples used: "Strawberry Snocone, Part I," Seven from Eleven; "Improvisations by Jim Keltner," Jim Keltner; "Energy," Earth, Wind, and Fire; "Improvisations by Ron Tutt," Ron Tutt; "Organized Konfusion," Organized Konfusion

1. This song is a short masterclass in flow and rupture. There are a quite a few obvious points of rupture in the song, and they are given in the list below. As you listen, take note as to what happens in each, using the three types of rupture presented above.

- Rupture 1: 0:11 seconds
- Rupture 2: 0:34
- Rupture 3: 0:49
- Rupture 4: 1:46
- Rupture 5: 2:49
2. Find two other instances of rupture in this song and describe them.
3. Describe Gift of Gab's flow in this song. How does he negotiate the ruptures?

Technical aspects aside, a rapper with a good flow "moves easily and powerfully through complex lyrics."[13] Marcyliena Morgan suggests that flow is a kind of achievement: "When artists reach the level of flow, they often appear domineering and conceited and the audience is admiring and challenging."[14] Morgan claims that this achievement must be ratified by the listening audience, and that it is ultimately a source of pleasure for both performers and listeners.

LANGUAGE CHOICES

The sound of a rapper's voice adds another layer of meaning for us to discuss when we listen to music, but that sound is also influenced by the language choices that they make. As we've seen in the chapter on poetry, many of the poetic techniques surveyed—alliteration and rhyme, for example—involve manipulating the *sounds* of words. Adams goes so far as to propose a mode of listening that encourages attention to the *sound* of the words rather than their meanings: we should "treat the syllables of text simply as consonant/vowel combinations that occupy specific metrical locations."[15] Although such an approach might appear extreme at first glance, this is often the kind of listening we do the first time we hear a song, or when we are admiring a rapper's verbal dexterity. Words are invested with layers of meaning, including not just dictionary definitions and figurative meanings, but also connotations of race, class, and place. Language thus becomes a tool for reinforcing power structures and for challenging those structures already in place.

Among the most often heard criticisms of the genre during its infancy was that rappers do not use proper English in their lyrics. Such a claim carries with it political, class, and racial baggage: it offers a prime example of how a culture can invest words with meaning beyond their dictionary definitions. **African-American Vernacular English (AAVE)**, the dialect heard in many rap songs, is often construed in terms of deviation from "standard" English, thus signifying poverty, lower class, and lack of education.[16] This border is what Jennifer Lynn Stoever refers to as the "sonic color line," to be discussed in more detail in Chapter 12.[17] Russell Potter, Marcyliena Morgan, and others contend that the use of AAVE constitutes a form of resistance to the dominant (white, upper-middle-class) culture. Morgan argues that this resistance takes two forms: innovation in AAVE and repurposing of "proper" English (which she refers to as General English—GE—and is sometimes called Received Standard English, RSE). The transformation of a prefix like "dis-," which appears at the beginning of words like "disrespect," "disdain," and "discredit," into an autonomous word, "diss," is one example of such transformation. Snoop Dogg's trademark "-izzle" (as in "fo' shizzle," which means "for sure") is another example of this kind of innovation. Taking words like "fly" and "ill" and establishing new meanings for them is an example of the second strategy. "Fly" is no longer a verb, but an adjective; "ill" no longer means "unwell," but means "good." "Trap" has several GE meanings: it can mean a device to capture animals, or it can denote lying in wait to surprise others. In the southeastern United States during the late 1990s, "trap" referred to houses where drug deals were made. The word brought with it connotations of a lifestyle that was difficult to escape. As the 2000s dawned, "trap" referred to music that was about drug dealing and even came to signify a particular musical style as well: Metro Boomin, whose sonic signature we surveyed in Chapter 1, makes mostly trap beats.

Big L's song "Ebonics" (AAVE is sometimes referred to colloquially as "Ebonics") "breaks that slang shit down," demonstrating many of the language revisions that Morgan outlines. In the second line of the first verse, Big L combines three words with similar imagery, "high," "lifted," and "fly," but the GE meanings of the words differ from the definitions that Big L gives. The song was released in 1998—it was the last single he released before his death—and some of the language seems a bit outdated ("'Hit me on the hip' means 'page me'"). Some is region-specific: "730" in the second verse refers to Article 730 in the New York State Criminal Procedure Law, which deals with determining whether a defendant is fit for trial.

Efforts to capture this play with language in print have resulted in Ice Cube's album *AmeriKKKa's Most Wanted*, Ludacris' album *Word of Mouf*; Nelly's song "Hot in Herre," and Tech N9ne's "Erbody But Me." Rappers have also used creative approaches to spelling in their names, as in Tech N9ne, Ma$e, Too $hort, ?uestlove, and 2Pac. On the other hand, committing these kinds of linguistic variations to print has the potential to obscure levels of meaning, as in the case of homophones, where choosing one spelling might hide the meaning implied by the sound of the word: such is the case with Rakim's "Minute-Maid" line, referenced in the previous chapter, and Mos Def's line in "Dollar Day": "Don't get it twisted man, I dig U2 [the rock group?]/But if you ain't about the ghetto, well then fuck you too [U2?]" Rappers are even responsible for inventing words to suit their needs: "illmatic" (which now refers to Nas' debut album but was coined in 1991 by Cormega), "looptid" (in the "Humpty Dance": "I shoot an arrow like Cupid/I use a word that don't mean nothing, like looptid"), and "wanksta" (courtesy of 50 Cent).[18]

The N-word

The N-word is perhaps the most contentious word in hip hop. While some argue that the word is so hurtful it should be eliminated from the vocabulary, others contend that reclaiming the word allows them to divest it of its hurtful power. Some draw a distinction between ending the word with "-er" versus ending it with "-a," the former being derogatory and the latter being a term of endearment. Tupac insisted that N.I.G.G.A. stood for "Never Ignorant, Getting Goals Accomplished." In practice, though, it can be difficult to distinguish between the two. Robin D. G. Kelley writes that the word as it is commonly used in hip hop is "not merely *another* word for black"; instead, its meaning embraces issues of class and oppression typically associated with inner-city spaces.[19]

Debates have centered on who is allowed to use the word and exactly to whom the word refers. In a 1993 article for the *New York Times*, Michael Marriott quotes Bob Guccione Jr., then editor and publisher of *Spin* magazine, who saw the word as drawing a line between black and white: "In a sense, it empowers the black community in the white mainstream. [. . .] They can use a very powerful word like a passkey, and whites dare not, or should not use it."[20] This line has posed some interesting problems: can white fans say N.W.A.'s full name or talk about Jay-Z and Kanye's hit single "Niggas in Paris" without fear of criticism?

Potter suggests that languages are not monolithic, but multiplicities—that we engage in dialectic shifts on a regular basis. We talk one way when we are having dinner with our parents or meeting with a professor, and we talk another way when we get together with friends or take care of children. His claim is even more apparent in the case of artists who are bilingual in the more traditional sense of the word. We saw in the previous chapter Snow Tha Product mixing Spanish and English; Rhymester blending Japanese, Chinese, and English; and Sharaya J fusing American Sign Language with English. Poetic concerns aside, in each case the language choices made by these artists constitute a form of resistance, and they include some listeners while excluding others.

Loren Kajikawa suggests that rappers can project race based on their language choices. In his analysis of Eminem's "My Name Is," Kajikawa calls attention to the ways that the rapper signals his whiteness through the words he chooses. Whiteness, argues Kajikawa, is a dynamic construct, one that shifts with respect to the construction of blackness in mainstream hip hop. He suggests that the song's hook, "Hi! My name is. . .," "is about as 'square' and 'standard' a way as one could introduce oneself," noting that the placement of the word "Hi" on the downbeat "seems coated in forced sincerity."[21] Ultimately, Kajikawa notes, Eminem operates in a black sphere because he is rapping, and he is a very good rapper, at that. The likelihood of his enjoying the success that he did on the heels of either parody or skills alone is small.

The language choices in Macklemore's song "White Privilege" reveal a lot about his intended audience. Macklemore talks about "cultural appropriation," "gentrification," and stealing "their 40 acres"; he mentions Jimi Hendrix and Eric Clapton. Such language assumes a particular level of education and self-awareness among his listeners, who he acknowledges are primarily white. He also mentions the Central District, Beacon Hill, and the South End, which refer to neighborhoods in Seattle that were at one time predominantly composed of minorities but are rapidly becoming gentrified. Mentioning these neighborhoods implies a listener base that is familiar with Seattle's culture and geography. Macklemore's seriousness (in contrast to Eminem's parody) positions him as an outsider to hip-hop culture, despite the fact that he is an active participant in it.

A generation of Atlanta-based rappers who rose to fame in the mid-2010s, including Future, Young Thug, Rich Homie Quan, and Desiigner (who is from Brooklyn but sounds like these Atlanta rappers), have been characterized as "mumble rappers." Their lyrics tend to be less about poetic skill and more about spontaneous emotional expression. Heavy autotune and other effects further cloud the text. Shea Serrano describes Young Thug as "maybe the first post-text rapper": "He yelps and mumbles and takes words and strips them of all their meaning until they're just sounds and then splashes them on the floor."[22] These artists' language choices represent a fresh approach to the importance of the sound of lyrics—in this case, perhaps even at the expense of content.

Morgan argues that inclusivity of marginalized people is a hallmark of the hip-hop ethos and that comprehension of rap's evolving uses of language is a requirement for community membership.[23] The new ways of using language are not one-directional: the audience also participates in meaning-making. Conversely, those who cannot play rap's language games are excluded from the dialogue. The website Genius.com (formerly Rap Genius) provides one possible strategy for negotiating these group boundaries. Song lyrics (and other texts) are regularly added to the website, and users can sign in and annotate them, providing a way in for those who might be unfamiliar with the language.

LISTENING GUIDE 3.3

Nicki Minaj's Verse on "Monster"

Artist: Kanye West (feat. Jay-Z, Rick Ross, Nicki Minaj, and Bon Iver)
Song: "Monster"
Album: *My Beautiful Dark Twisted Fantasy*
Record label: Def Jam/Roc-A-Fella
Year released: 2010
DJ or Producer: Kanye West
Samples used: (none)

Nicki Minaj's verse on Kanye West's "Monster" is widely considered to be one of her best verses; *SPIN* magazine called it the "best verse of the 2010s"; Rick Ross—who also appears on the track—said her verse "proves she's one of the greatest"; and Kanye himself called it "the greatest of all time." An in-depth analysis of her verse will illustrate and synthesize many of the concepts outlined earlier in this chapter. The verse comprises a dialogue between two of Minaj's alter egos: Roman Zolanski (male) and Harajuku Barbie (female), beginning about 3:35 into the track.

The verse starts with Zolanski reciting lines 1–4 in a percussion-effusive near-monotone that almost bears a Jamaican accent. The first six lines feature *plosive* consonants: hard "g," "b," "t," and "k" sounds ("gangsta," "bad bitch," "Tonka," "Wonka," "king," and "conquer"). Minaj uses transformative rhyme to create the end rhymes and some internal rhyme. The first word of each of the first four lines begins on beat 1 of the measure (each line below corresponds to one bar). Line 2 includes the word "bitch," an example of a "reclaimed" term: "bitch" here is used as a term of empowerment. Minaj's voice is double-tracked at the end of the fourth line (the lyrics are italicized in the table below), resulting in a chorus effect. The first four lines, which appear in Figure 3.3, are accompanied by only a drum track.

In line 5, Minaj switches to a sung-style flow, and each line now begins before beat 1. These lyrics feature long "a" and "e" sounds, along with the nasal "m" and "n" sounds. The long "a" and "e" sounds are replaced with "ah" sounds beginning in line 7 ("monster," "Milan," "roster"). Kanye adds cymbal hits on beats 2 and 4 beginning in line 5, perhaps to compensate for the shift from percussion-effusive to sung style. The cymbals drop out after four lines as the percussion-effusive flow returns, and Minaj's voice takes on a slight warble in lines 9–12. In line 11, the words "all up" are repeated, resulting in a sound that resembles turntable scratching. Figure 3.4 includes lines 5 through 12.

For lines 13–14, Minaj switches personae to Harajuku Barbie: in the video, we see a pink-haired Nicki dressed in a white wedding gown, tied to a chair, addressing the camera directly, which visually reflects the shift. The end of line 12 overlaps with the beginning of line 13, reinforcing the sense that there are indeed two *different* voices at play. Barbie's voice is generally higher and less monotonous than Zolanski's, and the pitch varies more widely from high to low. Sibilant sounds ("s") with long

Line:																
1	Pull	up	in	a	mon-		ster	au-	to-	mo-	bile,	gang-		sta		
2	With	a	bad		bitch	that	came		from	Sri	Lank-		a			
3	Yeah	I'm	in	that	Ton-	ka	color	of	Wil-	ly	Wonk-		a			
4	*You*	*could*	*be*	*the*	*king*	*but*	*watch*	*the*	*queen*		*con-*	*quer/O-*	K,			
	1	e	&	a	2	e	&	a	3	e	&	a	4	e	&	a

Figure 3.3 Lines 1–4 of Nicki Minaj's verse on "Monster"

vowels dominate, and the articulation is less pronounced in these lines. These lines, which appear in Figure 3.5, are directed primarily at Lil' Kim, a rapper who has long held a grudge against Minaj.

Lines 16–20, which appear in Figure 3.6, are a return to Roman's persona—the switch actually takes place partway through line 15. Plosives and the long "i" sound feature prominently in the lines that follow. Tony Matterhorn is a Jamaican reggae artist, and "Dutty Wine" is the title of one of his songs. Including his name and the name of his song reinforces the Jamaican sensibilities that Minaj is trying to evoke in her Zolanski lines. The pitch of her voice drops significantly, and the tone becomes raspier, as she says "sign it" and "minded" at the ends of lines 19 and 20, highlighting the rhyme.

Lines 21–27 (Figure 3.7) are mostly in the Barbie persona, but Zolanski's voice emerges at the end of line 23, suggesting that maybe the two are in fact the same person. In line 26, Minaj alters the pronunciation of "me" ("may") to rhyme with "ye" ("yay"). Line 27 features two plays on words: "ménage," implying a ménage a trois, is a homophone with Nicki's last name, and Friday is a reference not only to the day of the week, but also to Minaj's debut album *Pink Friday*, which was released on the same day as Kanye West's *My Beautiful Dark Twisted Fantasy*. The words in boldface are accentuated by a synthesizer hit.

Minaj's voice is technologically altered in lines 28–30, as the words "pink," "think," "Now," and "for" are rapidly panned back and forth between the left and right channels. The video includes

Line: 5	first		things		first		I'll		eat		your		brains			Then
6	I'm	a	start		rock-	ing	gold		teeth		and		fangs			Cause
7	that's		what	a	moth-	er	fuck-	ing	mon-		ster		do	Hair-		
8	dres-	ser	from	Mi-	lan		that's	the	mon-		ster		'do	Mon-		
9	ster	Gius-	sep-	pe	heel		that's	the	mon-		ster		shoe	Young		
10	Mon-	ey	is	the	ros-	ter	and	a	mon-		ster		crew	And	I'm	
11	all	up	all	up	all	up	in	the	bank	with	the	fun-	ny	face		
12		And	if	I'm	fake,		I	ain't	no-	tice	cause	my	mon-	ey	ain't	*So*
	1	e	&	a	2	e	&	a	3	e	&	a	4	e	&	a

Figure 3.4 Lines 5–12 of Nicki Minaj's verse on "Monster"

Line: 13	let	me	get	this	straight,		wait,		I'm		the	roo-	kie?		But	my
14	fea-	tures	and	my	shows		ten		times		your	pay?			Fif-	ty
15	K		for	a	verse,		no		al-		bum	out?			Yeah,	my
	1	e	&	a	2	e	&	a	3	e	&	a	4	e	&	a

Figure 3.5 Lines 13–15 of Nicki Minaj's verse on "Monster"

Line: 16	mon-	ey's	so		tall		that	my	Bar-	biez	got-	to	climb		it	
17	Hot-	ter	than	a	Mid-	dle	East-	ern	Cli-		mate	vio-		lent		
18	Ton-	y	Mat-	ter-	horn		dut-	ty	wine	it,		wy-		lin'		
19	Nic-	ki	on	them	tit-	ties	when	I	sign		it			That's	how	these
20	nig-	gas	so		one-		track-		mind-		ed		But	real-	ly	
	1	e	&	a	2	e	&	a	3	e	&	a	4	e	&	a

Figure 3.6 Lines 16–20 of Nicki Minaj's verse on "Monster"

Line:																
21	real-	ly	I		don't	give	an	F		U		C		K			For-
22	get		Bar-		bie,		Fuck	Nic-	ki	cause	she's		fake				She
23	on	a	die-	t	but	her	pock-	et's	eat-	ing	cheese-		cake				And
24	I'll		say		bride		of	Chuck-	y	is	child's		play				Just
25	killed	a-	noth-	er	car-	eer,		it's		a	mild		day				Be-
26	sides		'Ye,		they	can't		stand		be-	sides		me				I
27	think	me,	you,	and	Am		should	mén-	age		Fri-		day/P-	p-	p-	p-	
	1	e	&	a	2	e	&	a	3	e	&	a	4	e	&	a	

Figure 3.7 Lines 21–27 of Nicki Minaj's verse on "Monster"

Line:																
28	Pink		wig,		thick	ass,		give	'em	whip-		lash				I
29	think		big,		get	cash,		make	'em	blink		fast				Now
30	look	at	what	you	just	saw,		this	is	what	you	live	for			
31	AAAHHH!					I'm	a	moth-	er-	fuck-	ing	mon-	ster!			
	1	e	&	a	2	e	&	a	3	e	&	a	4	e	&	a

Figure 3.8 Lines 28–31 of Nicki Minaj's verse on "Monster"

special effects at this point that visually echo the "scratching." Techniques like this foreground the artificiality of the voice. Lines 28–29 are closer to a sung-style (old school) flow, as they feature clear end rhymes and an overall descent in pitch. These lines appear in Figure 3.8.

Minaj's verse demonstrates a masterful use of all the techniques we have covered in this chapter. By evoking two different personae, we have the opportunity to compare and contrast techniques that a single rapper can use in a verse. Within each persona, there is considerable variation in voice, language choices, and approaches to flow. These aspects taken together are what makes this verse stand out among those of Minaj's peers.

OUTRO

Names you should know:

- DJ Khaled
- Eazy-E
- The Notorious B.I.G.
- Blackalicious
- Nicki Minaj

Terms you should know:

- Autotune
- Ad-lib
- Beat boxing
- Posse cut
- Flow (sung style, speech-effusive, percussion-effusive)
- Syncopation
- Cadence
- Rupture
- African-American Vernacular English (AAVE)

Questions for discussion/writing prompts:

1. Listen to the official remix for "All I Do Is Win," which (in addition to T-Pain and Rick Ross) features DJ Khaled, Diddy, Busta Rhymes, Nicki Minaj, Fat Joe, Jadakiss, and Swizz Beatz. Compare and contrast the flow of the rappers on this track. Alternatively, choose another posse cut and discuss the voices of the rappers on that track.

2. Find a verse by a rapper that you like and rewrite it in the voice of another rapper. Consider elements of flow, rupture, and language choices.

3. Listen to one of the songs mentioned in this chapter (or provided below) and find a word that you don't know the meaning of. Look it up in a variety of sources (Oxford English Dictionary, Urban Dictionary, or Genius.com, for example). Do any of these definitions make sense in the context of the song? What meaning(s) does the context of the song imply?

Additional listening:

Voice/posse cuts:

- "The Symphony," Marley Marl (feat. Masta Ace, Craig G, Kool G Rap, and Big Daddy Kane)
- "Scenario," A Tribe Called Quest (feat. Leaders of the New School)
- "Ain't No Fun," Snoop Doggy Dogg (feat. Nate Dogg, Kurupt, and Warren G)

Flow and rupture:

- "Crossroads," Bone Thugs-N-Harmony
- "Trap Queen," Fetty Wap
- "Insane in the Membrane," Cypress Hill
- "Break Ya Neck," Busta Rhymes

Beat boxing:

- "The Show," Doug E. Fresh and Slick Rick
- "Human Beat Box," The Fat Boys

Language choices:

- "Country Grammar," Nelly
- "Versace," Migos

NOTES

1 This approach has its roots in Alyssa Woods's dissertation, "Rap Vocality and the Construction of Identity" (Ph.D. Diss. University of Michigan, 2009).
2 Paul Toogood and Ice-T, *Something from Nothing: The Art of Rap* (Universal City, CA: Vivendi Entertainment, 2012). In the documentary, she repeatedly says "George Lucien."
3 Toogood.
4 Tricia Rose, *Black Noise: Rap Music and Black Culture in Contemporary America* (Hanover, NH: Wesleyan University Press, 1994), 38.
5 Felicia Miyakawa, *Five Percenter Rap: God Hop's Music, Message, and Black Muslim Mission* (Bloomington: Indiana University Press, 2005), 73.

6 Kyle Adams, "On the Metrical Techniques of Flow in Rap Music" *Music Theory Online* 13 no. 3 (2009): www.mtosmt.org/issues/mto09.15.5/toc.15.5.html, para. 1.

7 Adam Krims, *Rap Music and the Poetics of Identity* (Cambridge: Cambridge University Press, 2000), chapter 2.

8 Miyakawa 75. See also Woods 16.

9 Woods uses the term "tempo"; I prefer "cadence," for the reasons mentioned.

10 Adams paras. 8–9.

11 Rose, *Black Noise*, 39.

12 Miyakawa 81.

13 Rose, *Black Noise*, 39.

14 Marcyliena Morgan, *The Real Hip Hop: Battling for Knowledge, Power, and Respect in the L.A. Underground* (Durham, NC: Duke University Press, 2009), 82.

15 Kyle Adams, "Aspects of the Music/Text Relationship in Rap" *Music Theory Online* 14 no. 2 (2008): www.mtosmt.org/issues/mto.08.14.2/toc.14.2.html, para. 12.

16 Russell A. Potter, *Spectacular Vernaculars: Hip-Hop and the Politics of Postmodernism* (Albany: State University of New York Press, 1995), 58–9.

17 Jennifer Lynn Stoever, *The Sonic Color Line: Race and the Cultural Politics of Listening* (New York: New York University Press, 2016).

18 Ernest Baker, "The 15 Best Made-Up Words in Rap History" *Complex* (April 10, 2013): www.complex.com/music/2013/04/the-15-best-made-up-words-in-rap-history.

19 Robin D. G. Kelley, "Kickin' Reality, Kickin' Ballistics: Gangsta Rap in Postindustrial Los Angeles," in *Droppin' Science: Critical Essays on Rap Music and Hip Hop Culture*. Ed. William Eric Perkins (Philadelphia: Temple University Press, 1996), 137.

20 Michel Marriott, "Rap's Embrace of 'Nigger' Fires Bitter Debate" *New York Times* (January 24, 1993). Reprinted in *The Hip Hop Reader*. Ed. Tim Strode and Tim Wood (New York: Pearson Longman, 2008), 96.

21 Loren Kajikawa, *Sounding Race in Rap Songs* (Berkeley: University of California Press, 2015), 127.

22 Shea Serrano, *The Rap Yearbook: The Most Important Rap Song From Every Year Since 1979, Discussed, Debated, and Deconstructed* (New York: Abrams Image, 2015), 224.

23 Morgan 48.

IN THIS CHAPTER, YOU WILL LEARN ABOUT

- Influences on MCing
- Influences on DJing

CHAPTER 4

Listening to Influence

OVERVIEW

In the introduction to his book *The Dead Emcee Scrolls*, poet Saul Williams asserts "There is no music more powerful than hip-hop. [. . .] When the beat drops, people nod their heads 'yes,' in the same way that they would in conversation with a loved one, a parent, professor, or minister."[1] But what is the source of rap's power? Rap music consists of the rhythmic delivery of text over a looped beat. These two primary elements—MCing and DJing—arose from long traditions of figurative language and dance music that happened to coalesce in a unique way in the South Bronx during the 1970s. In African culture, the spoken word has power to influence the future. This power is called ***nommo***, and it originates as far back as the 1200s with a class of historian/musicians known as griots. The practices of the griots came to America via the slave trade and have undergone some transformations but nonetheless continued to advance the power of the word. Music enhances these powers by engaging not just the mind but the body as well. In this chapter, we will consider some of the linguistic and musical precursors of rap.

GRIOTS

Griots are storytellers who served as historians, advisors, teachers, and musicians to the ruling class in West Africa. Griots occupied a unique position in society because they functioned as mediators between the nobility and the people. They had the permission of the community to speak freely—to give good news and bad—and receiving this news, or listening to the stories of the griot, had the power to impact what happened later that day, that week, or that year. Griots' power lay in their ability to retell history in such a way that it was relevant to those listening at the time. The words of the griot possessed a power, called *nommo*, which could influence a listener's future course of action.[2]

The first professional griots date back to the thirteenth century, during the rule of Sundiata, a prince who founded the Mali Empire. The story of Sundiata, which has since been committed to print, was transmitted orally from generation to generation over hundreds of years by griots. To facilitate memorizing these long tales, the text was often set to music and accompanied by some sort of string instrument, like a guitar. These traditions were brought to America by the transatlantic slave trade from the 1600s to the1800s. The traditions were adapted by the slaves and their ancestors: traces of the practices can be found in black storytelling traditions like toasting and Signifyin(g) (to be discussed below). The griot was brought into American public consciousness by Alex Haley's 1976 novel *Roots*, which was made into a highly rated television miniseries the next year. Haley documented his quest to unearth his family's heritage, pursuing the trail all the way back to Gambia, where he met with a griot who made the final connections to his African heritage for him. Griots still exist today, although many of them have talent agents, use electronic instruments, and have otherwise "modernized" their image and skills to more closely resemble contemporary popular musicians.

The griots' long musical narrative poems are obvious precursors to MCing, the lyrical component of rap music. The ability to manipulate history resonates with rap music's tendency toward historical consciousness and self-critique, which are considered in the next chapter. Songs like MC Shan's "The Bridge" and Boogie Down Productions' "South Bronx" chronicle the early history of hip hop; Ice-T's "Gangsta Rap" does the same for West Coast rap. Many songs that refer to "back in the day," or begin with "once upon a time" or "here's a little story," also suggest a kind of historical frame.

SIGNIFYIN(G) AND THE DOZENS

Signifyin(g) (note the capitalization and "g" in parentheses) is, according to African-American-studies scholar Henry Louis Gates Jr., "a pervasive mode of language use" within the black community.[3] Signifyin(g) involves saying something about someone nearby using indirection or misdirection such that the person cannot respond. To do so, Signifyin(g) relies on the flexibility of language and the multiplicity of available meanings. Signifyin(g) encompasses a number of black oral traditions including toasting and the dozens. A **toast** is a long poem, reminiscent of the griot's tales, told in rhyming couplets (pairs of lines). It is typically full of profanity, humor, and boasting and is handed down through oral tradition. These toasts were usually presented informally—on street corners, in barbershops, and in bars. The subject of the poem is often a "trickster" figure, such as the monkey, or Stagger Lee (sometimes written as "Stagolee" or "Stack-O-Lee"), who uses his command of language to outsmart his foes.[4]

The "Signifyn' Monkey" poem is a well-known example of a toast and also offers a clear illustration of several forms of Signifyin(g). The poem features three characters: a monkey, a lion, and an elephant. The plot alone is a template for Signifyin(g): the monkey, who is tired of being pummeled by the lion, uses the power of his words to trick the lion into confronting an elephant, who then unknowingly does the monkey's bidding and beats up the lion. The tale is told in rhyming couplets and is often embellished with profanity.

LISTENING GUIDE 4.1

Artist: Rudy Ray Moore
Song: "Signifying Monkey"
Album: *The Second Rudy Ray Moore Album*
Record label: Comedians Inc.
Year released: 1970

Rudy Ray Moore's version of the "Signifying Monkey" is accompanied by drums throughout, and it sounds as though it was recorded in front of an audience: both are apparent from the outset of the recording. At 0:37, Moore begins with a standard opening for the poem: "Way down in the jungle deep/The badass lion stepped on the signifying monkey's feet." The poem unfolds mostly as a series of rhyming pairs of lines. Around 1:13, the monkey realizes that, while he can't beat the lion physically, he can outsmart him.

In an effort to enrage the lion, the monkey resorts to **the dozens** (1:49). The dozens is best known as a game of trading "Yo mama" jokes. Typically, participants stand in a circle (a cipher) and trade insults until someone cries or a fight breaks out. Here, the monkey implies that the elephant has said all kinds of lewd things about various members of his family.

While there is considerable variation in the details of each retelling, Gates observes that there are certain stock phrases that appear more or less intact in nearly every retelling of the poem: "full of gage" (3:12); "like a .44" (3:19) and "more dead than alive" (4:18). He uses these to make the point that there is no fixed text for the poem; rather, it exists as a "play of differences," a "repetition with revision."[5] In this way, the "Signifyin' Monkey" offers insight into how oral tradition works. While there is considerable variation in the details from storyteller to storyteller, the basic plot of the story and several "stock" phrases tend to stay unaltered. This is not unique to Signifyin(g), or to black aesthetics, but is rather a common thread among all types of improvisation, as we will see in the next chapter. Repetition with revision is a key element of black aesthetics: consider the common practice in jazz of different artists playing their own version of a "standard" like "Somewhere over the Rainbow" or "Summertime."

After the lion returns from his encounter with the elephant and confronts the monkey, the over-zealous monkey falls from the tree and risks being pummeled by the lion yet again (5:35). He tries once more—this time unsuccessfully—to use his wiles to escape the lion by appealing to the lion's sense of honor. The ending of the poem also tends toward the formulaic, as Gates notes.[6] This version ends with a repetition of the text "and signifying career."

Rudy Ray Moore

Rudy Ray Moore (1927–2008) was an actor, musician, and comedian known to many as the "god-father of rap." Moore started his career as a rock-and-roll singer and recorded a few singles, but he quickly turned to comedy. He recorded several moderately successful comedy albums in the late 1950s and early 1960s, but his career hit a turning point in 1970 when, as a clerk in a record store, he used to pay a regular visitor to recite toasts about Dolemite. Moore recorded the toasts and began incorporating his own versions into his routines. His later comedy albums, with titles like *Eat Out More Often* (1970), *The Streaker*, and *The Cockpit* drew on this toasting tradition, spinning excessively profane tales of badman/trickster figures like Shine, the Signifying Monkey, the Human Tornado, and Dolemite. Record-store owners typically kept the albums behind the counter in plain brown wrappers, to be sold only to those who asked.

In 1974, Moore marshaled his savings and produced a film version of *Dolemite*. The movie has become a cult classic and is an important film in the blaxploitation genre. Several other characters from Moore's stand-up acts transitioned into feature films, including *The Human Tornado* (1976) and *Petey Wheatstraw, The Devil's Son-in-Law* (1977). The *Disco Godfather* (1978) features Moore as a good guy, a former cop investigating an angel-dust ring; it was a flop, and Moore retreated to stand-up gigs.

Luther Campbell of 2 Live Crew told the *Miami Herald* that he patterned himself after Moore, and Snoop Dogg acknowledged Moore's influence in the liner notes to the 2006 re-release of the soundtrack to *Dolemite*: "Without Rudy Ray Moore, there would be no Snoop Dogg, and that's for real." In addition to collaborations with Snoop Dogg, Moore has appeared on albums with Busta Rhymes, Big Daddy Kane, and Eazy-E.

Comedians like Moms Mabley, Redd Foxx, Richard Pryor, and Dick Gregory also carried on the tradition of Signifyin(g) in their routines. Their raunchy comedy resurfaced in the work of Slick Rick, 2 Live Crew, and others. The insulting nature of the dozens manifests itself in contemporary rap in several ways, most noticeably in rap **beefs** or diss tracks. In the early days of hip-hop culture, Afrika Bambaataa saw the potential for rap music (and break dancing) to be a nonviolent means of settling disputes among the otherwise violent rival gangs in the Bronx: the power of the word sublimated the need for violence. As rap music matured, however, lyrical beefs would too frequently turn into violent confrontations between rappers and/or their crews. This violence peaked in the 1990s with the famous East Coast–West Coast (Bad Boy/Death Row) beef, which led to the deaths of two of the greatest voices in rap music: Tupac Shakur and The Notorious B.I.G.

Joseph Schloss suggests that sampling is a form of Signifyin(g), in that the process involves using someone else's music to tell your story.[7] In this case, the repetition with revision comes from the new context in which the sample is presented, as well as the way it is modified (sped up or slowed down, for instance) from its original version. Furthermore, the process of looping serves to recontextualize the sample: the end of it becomes juxtaposed against the beginning in a way that likely was not intended by the original artist(s). Repeating the same few measures of music over and over again forces the listener to hear them in new ways: Schloss writes: "As the end of the phrase approaches, the listener begins to anticipate its beginning. In the best beats, in fact, a virtual call-and-response develops in which a break actually answers *itself*." He goes on to argue that even when music not of African origin is sampled, the process of sampling "Africanizes" it.[8] Signifyin(g) thus provides a way to think about not only the power of the word, but also the power of the beat.

THE JAMAICAN CONNECTION

Jeff Chang argues that the birth of reggae in Jamaica served as a kind of blueprint for the birth of hip hop in the South Bronx some ten years later. After Jamaica gained independence from the United Kingdom in 1962, the island nation quickly fell into turmoil. "Seeing politics exhausted," Chang writes, artists like Bob Marley "channeled their energies into culture, and let it flow around the world."[9] Jamaica's newfound freedom precipitated the globalization of its culture, and Marley and his band The Wailers would come to be the face of Jamaican music (and revolutionary politics) for years to come. The liberation also resulted in a large exodus of Jamaicans and other West Indians, with many settling in the South Bronx. The families of rap's "founding fathers"—DJ Kool Herc (born Clive Campbell in Jamaica), who discovered the break beat; Grandmaster Flash (born Joseph Saddler in Barbados), who pioneered turntable technologies and techniques; and Afrika Bambaataa (born in New York to West Indian immigrants)—were among those who seized the opportunity to leave. There were three components of Jamaican musical culture that influenced early hip-hop culture: the sound system, reggae and dub, and toasting.

Jamaica's mobile DJ culture is often credited as a major influence on hip hop in the South Bronx. The mobile DJs were so called because they would transport their sound systems from place to place, often setting up in parks or other community gathering spaces, as opposed to club DJs, who worked at a fixed location. Chang writes, "The sound systems democratized pleasure and leisure by making dance entertainment available to the downtown sufferers and strivers."[10] These sound systems were typically homemade affairs, consisting of a single turntable, amplifiers, and dozens of speakers. Selectors—as the DJs were called—would manipulate the sounds of the records they were playing by adjusting the treble and bass controls and by fading some instruments and frequencies out, only to bring them back dramatically later.

Selectors would often challenge one another to see who had the most powerful system, with the audience deciding the winner.

The selectors typically played a blend of American rhythm and blues—artists like Chuck Berry and Fats Domino—and Jamaican styles like ska and reggae. Reggae (and ska) emerged in the Trench Town neighborhood of Kingston, Jamaica's capital city. Trench Town is the de facto music capital of Jamaica: reggae legends Bob Marley and Peter Tosh were born there, as was Kool Herc. Reggae is a hybrid of African and European musics and often features themes of social protest, black power, and pride. Boasts and insults are also prominent features, which undoubtedly came from the same African lineage as the Signifyin(g) practices detailed above.[11] Musically speaking, the African and Rastafarian rhythms ("riddims") are pushed front and center by the drums and bass.

When record producers were finished recording a track, they would often create several different versions of the track: one as-is (typically the A-side of the record) and another with no vocals—just instrumentals (the B-side). Remixes were, on occasion, also packaged along with the original, and cover versions in which artists would supply their own individual takes on a song were abundant. This notion of **versioning** is central to much Jamaican musical culture, and many aspects of African-American music as well. It resonates with Gates' idea that repetition with revision is a key component of African and African-American aesthetics and of Signifyin(g).

Dub, another Jamaican musical style that would influence rap, came about as an accident. In the late 1960s, recording engineer King Tubby was experimenting with fading the vocal and melodic tracks in and out on a reggae record he was working on. This left only the drum and bass—the "riddim." In performance, the selector could cut in vocals and melody instruments, manipulate the drum and bass levels, chant over the record, or let the crowd sing the lyrics. The "riddim" alone often appeared on the B-side of the single and was sometimes called a "dub plate." This strategy not only saved the labels money, but also gave the DJs a clean track to speak over. Dub led to a new style of performing in which the mobile DJs would speak in rhyme over the dub versions. This became known as **toasting** or **talk over** (note that this toasting is distinct from the toasting described in the previous section, although its origins are undoubtedly similar). U Roy, a DJ for King Tubby's system, was the first major talk-over star: he started releasing talk-over records in 1970.[12] Others followed suit, telling "badman" tales, boasting, and taunting over dub records. In many regards, then, dub is a clear predecessor to rap.

Mark Katz suggests that the importance of the Jamaican connection to hip hop's birth may be overstated. Kool Herc was only 12 when he and his family left Jamaica and came to America: it was unlikely he could have absorbed much of Jamaica's DJ culture at such a young age. He actually began his DJ career in the South Bronx playing reggae records at parties, but they did not generate the excitement that funk records did, so he quickly abandoned them. Furthermore, mobile DJ crews had been active in the New York City area for years prior to their appearance in the South Bronx.[13] Murray Forman suggests that the mobility of these New York DJs was a significant contributor to the dissemination of hip hop: while some DJs established certain clubs as hip-hop outposts, the mobile DJs brought hip hop to the people in their neighborhoods.[14]

Nonetheless, Jamaican influences continued to figure prominently in hip hop. Music theorist Adam Krims describes a wave of "Jamaicanness" that pervaded hip hop in the mid-1980s. Rappers like KRS-One and Smif-N-Wessun occasionally adopted a *patois*-style delivery in songs like "The Bridge Is Over" and "Sound Bwoy Bureill," respectively. Artists who wear their hair in dreadlocks often do so as a nod to Jamaican culture.[15] Central to Krims' observation is that hip hop's practitioners feel that it's important (or, it was important *at that time*) to emphasize this particular aspect of hip hop's origin story. (As a genre, rap music has always very aware and critical of its past, and this historical consciousness will be taken up in more detail in the next chapter.) More recently, in 2012, rapper Snoop Dogg announced that following a visit to Jamaica, he had been rechristened as Snoop Lion by a Rastafarian priest. He released a reggae and dancehall–inspired album and a documentary chronicling his journey and transformation, both titled *Reincarnated* (he has since returned to his original identity).

THE BLACK ARTS MOVEMENT AND THE LAST POETS

In the wake of Malcolm X's death in 1965, the prominent author LeRoi Jones wrote a letter urging black artists to carry on Malcolm's work. He moved from downtown Manhattan to Harlem, a historically black neighborhood, where he changed his name to Amiri Baraka and founded the Black Arts Repertory Theatre/School. Baraka coined the term "Black Art," and his poem of the same name serves as a manifesto for the movement. In the poem, Jones calls for "'poems that kill.'/Assassin poems, Poems that shoot/guns. Poems that wrestle cops into alleys/and take their weapons leaving them dead."[16] An essay by James T. Stewart titled "The Development of the Black Revolutionary Artist" encourages black artists to leave behind white artistic models and frame their aesthetics in terms of what is natural to their culture.[17] This seems to run contrary to Gates' implication that the predominantly white, male, European construct of the written word is an essential part of the frame, even though it ultimately becomes a vessel for a revisioning of oral tradition.[18] Music, Stewart argues, is particularly important in this regard because it "happens to be the purest expression of the black man in America."[19]

The movement was also inspired by Stokely Carmichael's call for Black Power. At the time, Carmichael was head of the Student Nonviolent Coordinating Committee (SNCC) and a close ally of Martin Luther King Jr. He gradually became disillusioned with nonviolence as a means of achieving the community's goals and would eventually change his name to Kwame Ture and become head of the **Black Panther Party for Self-Defense** (see Chapter 10). Many authors, poets, playwrights, visual artists, and musicians answered Jones' call, including Larry Neal, Gwendolyn Brooks, Audre Lorde, and Nikki Giovanni, to name but a few. Their works featured bold pro-black themes, and many were self-published.

Another group that emerged a few years later—in 1968—was The Last Poets. The group came into being at a park in Harlem during a celebration of Malcolm X's birthday. Its seven original members tackled issues like poverty and racism, which were pervasive in the black community at the time. Their strong social and political messaging encouraged listeners to act and led to their involvement with groups such as SNCC and the Black Panther Party. In performance, their poetry recitations were often accompanied by music: sometimes just bongos, and, later, a kind of free jazz. To that end, their performances situate them in the legacy of the griots. They recorded several albums, most notably their 1970 debut, *The Last Poets*. Infighting over writing and licensing credits ultimately created rifts among the members, but two of the original members, Umar Bin Hassan and Abiodun Oyewole, continued to perform as The Last Poets into the early 2000s.

LISTENING GUIDE 4.2

Artist: The Last Poets (feat. Umar Bin Hassan)
Song: "When the Revolution Comes"
Album: *The Last Poets*
Record label: Sunspots
Year released: 1970

"When the Revolution Comes" appears on The Last Poets' eponymous debut album. The poem uses the **refrain** (a short, repeated phrase of text) "When the revolution comes" as its backbone. The track features Umar Bin Hassan accompanied by the other members periodically engaging in call and response, doubling his words on the refrain, or chanting "revolution" in the background. A simple drum accompaniment—short-short-long, short-short (or high-high-low, high-high)—supports the text throughout most of the track.

Thematically, the track features themes of black power and white appropriation and critiques the complacency of the black community in the face of these issues. At about the 1:16 mark, the line "Guns and rifles will be taking the place of poems and essays" sounds like Baraka's call for "poems that kill." The intersection of Lenox and 125th Street is in Harlem, a historically black neighborhood in New York City, near where the Apollo Theater and other landmarks of black culture are located. The intersection also provides the title for Gil Scott-Heron's first album (see below). The Apollo Theater was operated by Frank Schiffman and Leo Brecher from 1935 until the late 1970s; Bin Hassan calls out the former at the 1:50 mark in the poem. Around the 2:10 mark, the drums stop, and the group repeats the chant "Party and bullshit" (later taken as a sample for a Notorious B.I.G. song with the same name), which fades just before the chilling final line.

In 1973, one of the Poets, Jalal Mansur Nuriddin (under the name "Lightnin' Rod"), teamed up with the funk band Kool & The Gang to record *Hustlers Convention*. Despite not selling very well and enduring a host of legal troubles, the album represents one of the most direct early influences on rap. The album consists of an extended toast detailing the escapades of two street hustlers, Sport and Spoon. Their first-person tales of life in the ghetto paved the way for gangsta rap. These tales were spread by word-of-mouth, and hip-hop pioneers like Fab 5 Freddy, Chuck D (of Public Enemy), Ice-T, and Nas knew the album by heart. Many of these same artists also sampled tracks from it on their own albums. Despite its importance to early hip hop, the album remains somewhat unknown among younger artists: "Because a lot of rappers happen to come from after that time, the media and powers-that-be have deemed these original storytellers as not being relevant," says Chuck D. He continues, noting that origins are important, as they help to shape the future.[20]

Although close in spirit to the group, Gil Scott-Heron was not a member of The Last Poets. While he was a student at Lincoln University in Pennsylvania, however, he attended a Last Poets performance at the school. Oyewole recalls Scott-Heron approaching him after the performance and asking about starting a group like the Poets. In contrast to the urgent, confrontational nature of the Poets' work, Scott-Heron relied more on subtlety and wit to convey his messages of social injustice. His debut album, *Small Talk at 125th and Lenox*, was recorded live at a club in New York City and includes many of his most famous pieces, such as "The Revolution Will Not Be Televised" and "Whitey on the Moon." His work became increasingly musical, thanks to working with producers like Nile Rodgers (of Chic; see below) and some of his albums even crept onto on *Billboard*'s R&B charts. Scott-Heron remained active into the 1990s, releasing a track that criticized the gangsta rap that he had influenced, called "Message to the Messengers" (1994).

The work of the Black Arts movement, The Last Poets, and others informed hip hop in several ways. First, Jones' call for an uncompromisingly black art opened the door for many writers and musicians whose works would directly influence members of the hip-hop community. Second, the recitation of poetry to musical accompaniment bears more than passing resemblance to early rap music. Rap's debt to these artists can be heard in their widespread sampling: A Tribe Called Quest samples Umar Bin Hassan's poem "Time Is Running Out" on their song "Excursions," Dr. Dre's *Chronic* opens with a sample from "The Shalimar," and Kanye West takes an extensive sample of Gil Scott-Heron's "Comment no. 1" for "Who Will Survive in America?" The importance and power of spoken word persists through vehicles like Russell Simmons' *Def Poetry Jam*, artists like Saul Williams and Sarah Jones, and the practice of a cappella raps.

FUNK

As a musical style, funk is a synthesis of the vocal stylings of soul, the driving beat of rock, and the improvisational nature of jazz. It emerged in the mid-1960s, a time of both progress and tragedy in the fight for civil rights. While segregation and other racist policies were being dismantled by Martin Luther King Jr. and his allies, and Muhammad Ali was voicing his opposition to the Vietnam War, the assassination of Malcolm X left a void in leadership in the black community. The Black Arts movement represents one effort to fill this void, as mentioned above, while radio host and author Rickey Vincent argues that the mantle of leadership fell on the shoulders of James Brown and Sly & The Family Stone, vanguards of the so-called First Funk Dynasty.[21] Songs like Brown's "Say It Loud (I'm Black and I'm Proud)" and Sly & The Family Stone's "We Are Family" came from the same culture that spawned the Black Panther Party, according to Vincent.[22]

Many critics honor James Brown's "Papa's Got a Brand New Bag, part I," which was released in the summer of 1965, as the first real funk song, although traces of the style can be found in earlier Brown hits as well. Funk has several defining musical characteristics. The first, and perhaps most distinctive, is the drumming pattern. In a typical funk beat, the emphasis falls on the first beat of the measure, the downbeat. This contrasts with early rock styles, in which the "backbeat" (that is, beats 2 and 4) was emphasized. This shift in feel creates a strong sense of forward momentum, which is carried along by the way the drummer, and other musicians fill in the space before the next downbeat.

To help propel the music forward, even the non-percussion instruments (that is, guitar, bass, horns, and even the voice) tend to be used percussively: the guitar is often relegated to a rhythmic role (as opposed to the guitar solos that characterized heavy metal and progressive rock at the time), sometimes playing only a single chord throughout a song; the slap-bass sound characterizes a good deal of funk (that is, hitting the strings with the thumb and pulling them with the fingers so that they "snap" against the fingerboard); and horn sections punctuate phrases with one or two clipped notes. Funk's vocal style came from gospel music and the church: lyrics are shouted, sometimes in call-and-response style, or chanted (often by the entire group together). Many of the bands were very large and had a tribal or familial feel to them, and, as funk evolved in the 1970s, grew more racially and gender diverse. Sly & The Family Stone, for example, was unique in that the band included both men and women of different races.

Funk shares some musical and aesthetic attributes with rap music. Funk is very repetitive, for instance, often repeating a single one- or two-bar idea for an entire song. This phrase is often harmonically static (that is, consisting of only one or two chords) but rhythmically very active. The emphasis on percussion—that is, not just using drums, but treating *anything* as a percussion instrument—finds its offspring in sample-based rap as well as the percussion-effusive style of rapping (as discussed in the previous chapter).

LISTENING GUIDE 4.3

Artist: James Brown
Song: "Funky Drummer"
Album: *In the Jungle Groove*
Record label: Polydor
Year released: 1986

James Brown's "Funky Drummer" is quite possibly the most sampled song in rap, hence its inclusion here. Originally issued in 1970 on two sides of a 45 single, the extended version on the compilation album *In the Jungle Groove* is the version we will consider here. The song consists mostly of a repeated groove that is four beats long. Brown's lyrics seem very much off the cuff and consist of short exclamations, many of which are instructions to the band. The harmony rarely changes, sustaining one single chord throughout.

The key to this track (and funk drumming in general) is to listen to the smallest subdivisions of the beat, which in this song appear consistently in the hi-hat (a small pair of cymbals that are open and closed via a pedal, but can also be played with sticks). The hi-hat keeps a constant pulse throughout that divides each beat into four equal parts. This constant subdivision is characteristic of funk drumming. The bass drum marks beat 1, as does the three-note horn figure. The snare drum highlights beats 2 and 4 (the "backbeat"). After saxophone and keyboard solos, the song seems to begin again (3:13) as the introductory riff reappears. Around 4:36, Brown warns the band that he's going to call for a drum solo, and he asks the drummer—18-year-old Clyde Stubblefield—not to change what he's doing, perhaps for fear of losing the groove. After Brown counts "1-2-3-4," (5:32), the break starts (5:34); it lasts for eight bars. Starting in bar five, Brown begins repeating "Ain't it funky?" before counting the band back in with a double-time "1-2-3-4." Around 6:29, Brown says, "The name of this tune is 'The Funky Drummer,'" almost as if he's naming it on the fly.

The sample shows up in tracks such as Public Enemy's "Bring the Noise" (see Chapter 1), Eric B & Rakim's "Lyrics of Fury," Dr. Dre's "Let Me Ride," Nicki Minaj's "Save Me," and hundreds of other tracks. Listen to some of these songs and consider how the sample's identity changes in the different contexts.

As DJs in the 1970s raided their parents' record collections, they found many funk recordings. These recordings were popular with hip-hop DJs for a few reasons. First, they represented a move away from disco, which was reigning at the time largely because it had been co-opted by white America. Second, they were often thought to embody strong notions about what it means to be black (e.g., James Brown's "Say It Loud (I'm Black and I'm Proud)"). Finally—and most importantly—they *sounded good* and were easy to dance to. Many classic breaks come from the funk era, including James Brown's "Give It Up or Turnit A Loose" and "The Funky President." If James Brown's music was the foundation for hip hop on the East Coast, George Clinton and Parliament-Funkadelic laid the groundwork for West Coast rap. MC Hammer, one of the most commercially successful rap artists of the early 1990s, sampled Parliament in his first big hit, "Turn This Mutha Out," and "U Can't Touch This" features a sample from Rick James' "Superfreak." Dr. Dre's G-Funk production style, which is heard most clearly on his 1992 album *The Chronic* (see Chapter 11), relies heavily on the sounds of Clinton and his bandmates.

While the popularity (and, some would argue, the quality) of funk waned into the late 1970s and early 1980s, the rise in popularity of hip hop over the next two decades led to a renewed interest in the genre, as hip-hop DJs, producers, and fans started chasing down the sounds that comprised their favorite tracks. Disco was largely to blame for funk's waning popularity, but even disco owes funk a debt of gratitude.

DISCO

Disco and hip hop have a contentious relationship. On one hand, it is easy to see the rise of hip hop as a reaction to disco, which had gotten its start among the marginalized communities (i.e., black, Latinx, and queer) in the city but was eventually co-opted by white culture. On the other hand, hip hop owes many of its early technological foundations to disco. Among the things that made disco unique was its emphasis on studio production: unlike most musical genres of the 1960s and '70s, live performance was not an important part of disco culture. Artists and producers created lavish studio recordings, which were then played by DJs in clubs. In contrast to the mobile DJs described above, these DJs made their living in the clubs. The DJ rose to prominence around this time for two reasons: first, few bands agreed to play in clubs whose clientele consisted largely of these marginalized groups; second, hiring a DJ for the night was a lot less expensive than hiring a band.

Disco is fundamentally dance music, and imagining disco culture often brings to mind images of cocaine-filled parties at places like Studio 54 lasting into the small hours of the morning. The need for continuous music to support this scene resulted in extended club mixes of songs, which were often issued on 12-inch records (as opposed to the smaller 7-inch 45-rpm singles). A 12-inch record could hold anywhere from 15 to 22 minutes (depending on the speed) as opposed to the roughly four minutes of the 7-inch. Disco DJs used a setup with two turntables linked by a crossfader to avoid any breaks in the music (which would have, of course, led to breaks in the dancing). The crossfader allowed the DJ to transition smoothly between records, fading one out while gradually bringing up the volume on the other. Both the 12-inch single and the two-turntable setup became important in the early days of hip hop.

Disco was reaching the height of its popularity in the mid-1970s, just as rap music was getting its start. The popularity of disco came about as a result of its appropriation by white culture, which was made most visible with the release of the movie *Saturday Night Fever* (1977) starring John Travolta. The soundtrack to the movie reinvigorated the career of the Bee Gees, an Australian group who had had some minor successes in the disco world. The film and the soundtrack set many sales records at the time and provided an early success story of using a film to cross-promote an album (and vice versa). Disco became a fixture on radio and television across the country, spreading it far beyond the urban context in which it had developed. Records such as *Sesame Street Fever* (1978) and *Mickey Mouse Disco* (1979) show how disco came to permeate every aspect of mainstream American culture.

By the end of the 1970s, however, disco faced a rapid decline in popularity. Much of the backlash against disco was racist and homophobic, disguised as criticism of the music and exemplified by the opposition's rallying cry of "disco sucks." Rap would later face similar criticisms: rappers don't play instruments, for instance, and they just steal other people's music. Such criticisms are dismissive of the genre's roots in music in black and Latinx cultures, where such aesthetics are common, and reinforce negative stereotypes of people of color as unskilled and criminal.

Throughout the rise and fall of disco in mainstream American culture, there remained a strong subculture that sought to keep the music among the communities that had started it. DJs like Lovebug Starski, Eddie Cheeba, and DJ Hollywood spun disco records in clubs around New York City and were among the first to recite rhymes over the records they played. Sylvia Robinson heard Lovebug Starski rapping over disco records at Harlem World, which prompted her and her son, Joey, to start scouting for rappers to sign to their failing record label. Their search ultimately gave rise to Sugar Hill Records and what many consider to be the first rap *song*, "Rapper's Delight" (more on this in Chapter 6). Many of Sugar Hill's releases have a noticeable disco influence: "Rapper's Delight" features the beat from Chic's 1979 disco hit "Good Times," and several other early rap singles use it, or one closely derivative of it (Spoonie Gee's "Monster Jam," for instance).

LISTENING GUIDE 4.4

Artist: Chic
Song: "Good Times"
Album: *Risqué*
Record label: Friday
Year released: 1979

TIME	MUSICAL CHARACTERISTICS	LYRICS	DESCRIPTION
0:00	Bass line that mostly alternates between two notes, E (low) and A (higher) Bass drum on beats 1 and 3; snare drum on beats 2 and 4 Funk guitar	None	Introduction
0:18	The texture thickens with the addition of piano and synthesized strings. "Disco claps" appear on beats 2 and 4. Throughout the song, the lyrics are sung by a group.	"Good times . . ."	Chorus
0:53	The texture thins out as instruments are removed and the bass line is simplified.	"Happy days are here again . . ."	Verse 1
1:27	The texture thickens with the addition of piano and synthesized strings. The bass line is embellished. "Disco claps" appear on beats 2 and 4.	"Good times . . ."	Chorus
2:03	The texture thins out as instruments are removed and the bass line is simplified.	"A rumor has it . . ."	Verse 2. The lyrics are different, but the music is the same as in verse 1.
2:37	The texture thickens with the addition of piano and synthesized strings. The bass line is embellished. "Disco claps" appear on beats 2 and 4.	"Good times . . ."	Chorus
3:11	The texture remains thick here, like the chorus.	None	Outro. The instruments continue playing the repeated figure as the music fades out.

The disco hit "Good Times" enjoyed a six-week run at number 1 on *Billboard*'s R&B charts and later landed at the top of the pop chart. It became the foundation of "Rapper's Delight" (1979) and influenced Queen's hit "Another One Bites the Dust" (1980). Members of Chic eventually sued Sugar Hill for copyright infringement, but only after the rap song had become a hit.

Musically, the song relies on two alternating chords. The bass line is the clearest place to hear the change: it alternates between a low note (the open E string) and a higher note (the open A string). Because it uses only two chords, it can be difficult to differentiate musically between the verse and chorus in this song. Although the chords do not change from verse to chorus, the texture does change. The bass line is embellished—it sounds more complicated—and other instruments are added, creating a fuller texture. One of the most notable additions to the texture of the chorus are the ubiquitous "disco claps," which appear on the second and fourth beats of each measure.

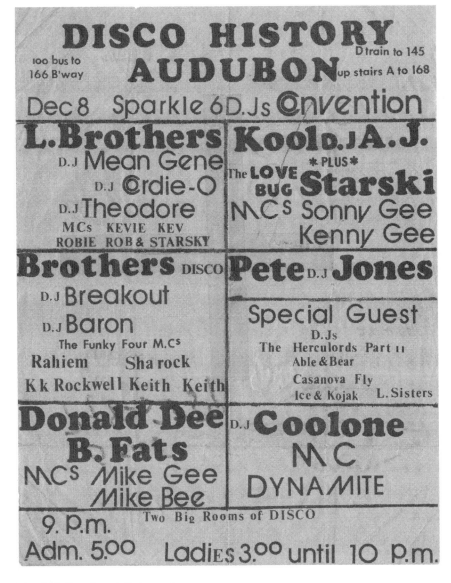

Figures 4.1 and **4.2** Flyers for early hip-hop parties
Source: Images courtesy of the Cornell University Library Hip Hop Collection

Figures 4.1 and **4.2** (Continued)

As a result of the close ties between disco and rap, the recording industry initially made little distinction between rap and disco records. Many early rap records—particularly those on the Sugar Hill label—use popular disco tracks underneath the rap. As musicologist Loren Kajikawa observes, the disco handclaps and crowd noises appeared on many rap records, and many artists promoted themselves and their music as disco.[23] The Fat Boys originally called themselves the Disco 3; DJs included "disco" in their names (like DJ Disco Wiz); and promotional materials regularly referred to the parties as disco parties.

Disco fashion was common in the rap scene, as was a fascination with the zodiac (see Busy Bee's rap in Chapter 5, for instance). Robert Ford Jr., a writer for *Billboard*, penned some of the first widely read articles on the phenomenon that would become rap music and makes explicit the connection with disco: "The requests [for obscure R&B records] come from young black disco DJs from the Bronx who are buying the records just to play the 30 seconds or so of rhythm breaks that each disk contains."[24] The title of another Ford article, "Jive Talking N.Y. DJs Rapping Away in Black Discos," also makes the relationship clear. The article relates that "many black disco promoters now use the rapping DJs to attract young fans to one-shot promotions."[25] As rap started to gain popularity and become more commercial, it forged its own identity, distinct from disco. The beats, subject matter, fashion, and other aspects began to crystallize into what we now know as hip hop.

OUTRO

Names you should know:

- The Last Poets
- James Brown
- Rudy Ray Moore
- Gil Scott-Heron

- Amiri Baraka
- James Brown
- Chic

Terms you should know:

- Griot
- Nommo
- Signifyin(g)
- The dozens
- Toasting (note: two different meanings)/ talk over

- Versioning
- The Black Arts movement
- Refrain
- Funk
- Disco

Questions for discussion/writing prompts:

1. What are some musical precursors to rap? What are some linguistic precursors to rap? How did each contribute to the development of rap?

2. How is the power of the word or the power of the beat manifest in each of these precursors?

3. Are there similarities across the different sources of early hip hop? For instance, what, if anything, do funk and disco have in common?

4. To what extent are any of these elements (still) present in contemporary rap music?

Additional listening/viewing:

- *Dolemite!* Rudy Ray Moore
- *Small Talk at 125th and Lenox*, Gil Scott-Heron

- *The Last Poets*, The Last Poets
- *Hustlers Convention*, Lightnin' Rod and Kool & The Gang
- "Papa's Got a Brand New Bag," "Give It Up or Turnit A Loose," "Funky Drummer," James Brown
- "Tear the Roof off This Sucker," "Atomic Dog," Parliament

NOTES

1 Saul Williams, *The Dead Emcee Scrolls: The Lost Teachings of Hip-Hop and Connected Writings* (New York: MTV Books/Pocket Books, 2006), xi.
2 Thomas A. Hale, "Griot," In *The Oxford Encyclopedia of African Thought*. Ed. F. Abiola Irele and Biodun Jeyifo (New York: Oxford University Press, 2011).
3 Henry Louis Gates Jr., *The Signifying Monkey: A Theory of African-American Literary Criticism* (Oxford: Oxford University Press, 1988), 80.
4 Eithne Quinn and Imani Perry trace the legacies of these trickster figures in contemporary rap music: see Quinn's *Nuthin' but a "G" Thang: The Culture and Commerce of Gangsta Rap* (New York: Columbia University Press, 2005), chapters 5 and 6; and Perry, *Prophets of the Hood* (Durham, NC: Duke University Press, 2005), chapter 4.
5 Gates 60–1.
6 Gates 55.
7 Joseph Schloss, *Making Beats: The Art of Sample-Based Hip Hop* (Hanover, NH: Wesleyan University Press, 2004), 138.
8 Schloss 138.
9 Jeff Chang, *Can't Stop, Won't Stop: A History of the Hip-Hop Generation* (New York: St. Martin's, 2005), 23.
10 Chang 29.
11 Dick Hebdige, *Cut 'n' Mix: Culture, Identity, and Caribbean Music* (London, New York: Methuen, 1987), 43.
12 Hebdige 84.
13 Mark Katz, *Groove Music: The Art and Culture of the Hip Hop DJ* (New York: Oxford University Press, 2012), 25–7.
14 Murray Forman, *The 'Hood Comes First: Race, Space, and Place in Rap and Hip-Hop* (Middletown, CT: Wesleyan University Press, 2002), 73.
15 Adam Krims, *Rap Music and the Poetics of Identity* (Cambridge: Cambridge University Press, 2000), 152–4.
16 Amiri Baraka, "Black Art," in *Black Fire: An Anthology of Afro-American Writing*. Ed. Amiri Baraka and Larry Neal (New York: Morrow, 1968), 302.
17 James T. Stewart, "The Development of the Black Revolutionary Artist," in *Black Fire: An Anthology of Afro-American Writing*. Ed. Amiri Baraka and Larry Neal (New York: Morrow, 1968), 3–11.
18 Gates ch. 4.
19 Stewart 3.
20 Graeme Thomson, "Hustlers Convention: Rap's Great Lost Album" *Guardian* (January 30, 2014): www.theguardian.com/music/2014/jan/30/hustlers-convention-rap-lost-great-album-hip-hop.
21 In an effort to prevent funk's history from being "whitewashed," rap producer Ashem "The Funky Man" Neru-Mesit laid out three funk dynasties: The First Funk Dynasty (1965–1972) included James Brown and Sly & The Family Stone. The United Funk Dynasty (1972–1976) came about as blaxploitation genres were peaking and the TV show *Soul Train* was popular. This era tended to feature multiracial/ethnic groups that included both men and women. George Clinton and Parliament-Funkadelic heralded the Golden Age of Dance Music, which spanned roughly 1976–1980. See Rickey Vincent, *Funk: The Music, The People, and the Rhythm of the One* (New York: St. Martin's, 1996), 10–11.
22 Vincent 52.
23 Loren Kajikawa, *Sounding Race in Rap Songs* (Berkeley: University of California Press, 2015), 42–3.
24 Robert Ford Jr., "B-Beats Bombarding Bronx: Mobile DJ Starts Something with Oldie R&B Disks" *Billboard* (July 1, 1978). Reprinted in *The Pop, Rock, and Soul Reader*. Ed. David Brackett (New York: Oxford University Press, 2005), 390.
25 Robert Ford Jr., "Jive Talking N.Y. DJs Rapping Away in Black Discos" *Billboard* (May 5, 1979). Reprinted in *The Pop, Rock, and Soul Reader*. Ed. David Brackett (New York: Oxford University Press, 2005), 391.

1954	New York City starts taking possession of buildings in the South Bronx to make way for Robert Moses' Cross Bronx Expressway.
1973	At a party in the South Bronx, DJ Kool Herc uncovers the power of the break.
1977	A citywide blackout plunges New York into darkness for twenty-four hours.
1979	The radio show *Mr. Magic's Rap Attack* premieres on WHBI in Newark, New Jersey.
1981	"The Adventures of Grandmaster Flash on the Wheels of Steel" is released.
	—The Funky Four + 1 becomes the first rap group to perform on *Saturday Night Live*.
	—Chief Rocker Busy Bee battles Kool Moe Dee on Christmas Eve.
1982	Afrika Bambaataa, the Rock Steady Crew, and others play concerts in London and throughout France.
1984	U.T.F.O. Releases "Roxanne Roxanne," sparking a response from Roxanne Shanté, which ultimately leads to dozens of response records in the "Roxanne Wars."
1994	Common releases *Resurrection*.
2014	A radio station in Houston, KROI, becomes the first in the nation to broadcast a "classic hip-hop" format.

IN THIS CHAPTER, YOU WILL LEARN ABOUT

- The social, political, and economic crisis from which hip hop emerged
- Pioneers of DJing and MCing
- The role of improvisation in early hip hop
- Hip-hop culture's historical self-awareness

CHAPTER 5

Listening to History

OVERVIEW

Hip-hop culture originated in the South Bronx in the 1970s amid social and political turmoil in New York City. Each of the so-called Founding Fathers of rap—DJ Kool Herc, Grandmaster Flash, and Afrika Bambaataa—contributed something significant to the style. Early hip hop emerged from the fusion of African-American and Caribbean styles, but contributions by Puerto Ricans and women—largely overlooked in many histories of hip hop—played an important role. Hip hop was first and foremost party music, and it was the responsibility of the DJs and their MCs to keep the party going. Rap existed only as live performance in its early days and was primarily improvised: it would be almost five years until the first rap record was released. Since its beginnings, rap has been a very self-aware genre, recording, revising, and repeating its histories.

SOCIAL, POLITICAL, AND ECONOMIC CONDITIONS

New York City was facing tough times in the 1970s. Mayor Abe Beame inherited a mess when he took office in 1974: the city was $1.5 billion in debt. Beame had to put a freeze on hiring city employees and was ultimately forced to lay off nearly 38,000 city employees, including sanitation workers, teachers, police officers, and firefighters. Despite these efforts, the city was still on the verge of bankruptcy in 1975, and Beame petitioned the federal government for help. The president's response was summed up on the front page of the *Daily News* in characteristic New York bluntness: FORD TO CITY: DROP DEAD. Fixing the city's problems was of paramount importance, because the country's bicentennial celebrations were just around the corner, and the city was due to host the 1976 Democratic Convention. To that end, the mayor cracked down on the adult-entertainment industry that had taken over much of Times Square, and other illicit activity, finding any reason to put thousands of New Yorkers behind bars.

Economically speaking, the Bronx was perhaps the hardest hit of New York City's boroughs. Thousands of manufacturing jobs dried up, leaving many unemployed. Unemployment rates hovered around 60% and were as high as 80% for teenagers. The median annual income of a Bronx resident was about $2,500. As it became increasingly difficult to keep apartment buildings filled with residents, landlords realized that they could make more money simply by burning down their buildings and collecting insurance money. Between 1973 and 1977, nearly 30,000 fires were set in the Bronx: on one day in 1975, forty fires were set during a three-hour period.[1] Some fires were set by families who knew that they would be given relocation assistance: "We'd go to a fire and the furniture would be [moved] out on the street and the building would be burning," says Santo Puglisi, a firefighter in Brooklyn.[2] Due to the layoffs, it was virtually impossible for the short-staffed fire departments to keep up. After the fire, vandals—sometimes hired by the landlords—would return to steal plumbing and wiring in order to sell it as scrap. This devastated the Bronx landscape and left many without homes; namely, those who could not afford to move to other, more expensive parts of the city or the suburbs.

Robert Moses was a visionary city planner who was active in New York City in the mid-twentieth century. Moses is responsible for creating thousands of acres of parks, hundreds of playgrounds, and public swimming pools (he was an avid swimmer in his youth and was on the swim team as an undergraduate at Yale). Many iconic locations in New York City—Lincoln Center, the United Nations, and many of the massive suspension bridges that connect the city to the outer boroughs and New Jersey— are the direct result of Moses' work. Moses believed that the hardworking (mostly upper-class and white) residents of Manhattan deserved opportunities to get out of the city and enjoy nature, to spend time at a nearby beach or park. To facilitate this, he claimed thousands of acres of land by using eminent domain laws, proceeding to build highways and bridges to allow those with automobiles (only the wealthiest—again, typically white—residents) to get away.

Not only did Moses want to give the well-to-do access to these amenities, he wanted to keep "undesirables" away. In his biography of Moses, titled *The Power Broker*, Robert Caro contends that many of Moses' planning decisions were clouded by his racist tendencies. Overpasses were built just too low for buses to pass through (assuming that only the poor and people of color took buses); swimming pools along Manhattan's border with Harlem hired only white lifeguards and kept the water temperature a few degrees colder—Moses believed that the black community couldn't tolerate the colder water.[3] In 1948, construction began on what would become Moses' most infamous project: the Cross Bronx Expressway.

The Cross Bronx Expressway (CBE) was planned to be a stretch of highway only seven miles long, one mile of which was to cut right through the middle of one of the poorest neighborhoods in the country. Ultimately the CBE crossed 113 streets, other expressways (some of which were also in-progress Moses projects), subways and elevated train lines, sewers, and power lines. The plan also required the Bronx River to be rerouted, something that one of the project engineers claimed was the least of their problems.[4] In the path of the highway were 54 buildings that contained about 1,500 apartments housing nearly 5,000 people. Neighborhood residents opposed to the plan organized and hired a team of engineers who proposed an alternate route that would impact only nineteen families in six buildings—it would have extended the road by a quarter mile—but Moses wouldn't hear of it.

As conditions in the Bronx worsened, and as the CBE construction became imminent, many of the middle-class (mostly white) residents moved to places like Long Island and New Jersey. High-rise apartment buildings were constructed along the edges of the proposed highway in order to accommodate the displaced residents. The city offered a small sum of money for relocation assistance. On January 1, 1954, the city took possession of 150 buildings, and two weeks later it started shutting off heat and water in an effort to force people to vacate. Buildings were torn down floor by floor, ultimately forcing everyone living within to find a new place to live. Not long after construction finally got underway, the project stalled until 1957. Residents had to live in close quarters amid a half-demolished wasteland, and many familiar community gathering places—churches, schools, barbershops, nightclubs—were gone. When construction finally resumed, residents were surrounded by the constant sound of earthmovers and blasting.

The crisis in the Bronx reached a tipping point on July 13, 1977. A particularly hot, humid day placed unusually large demands on the city's power grid. When a lightning strike incapacitated one of the transformers outside of the city, the entire metropolis was plunged into darkness for twenty-four hours. DJ Disco Wiz and Grandmaster Caz were hosting a party in the park on the evening of the blackout. They tapped into a streetlight for power to run their sound system, and, as a result, the streetlight blew out—a typical occurrence:

Caz: While he [Wiz] did his thing, I'm just waitin'. He turns off, it's my turn. I throw on one record over here, boom, the crowd is goin' nuts, 'cause they know I'm gonna get into my thing. [. . .] I bring in the record "Love, loove, looooovve . . ." It just slows to a stop.
Wiz: The light blew out—
Caz: Went off. The whole set went off.
Wiz: Two lights blew out.
Caz: —and then the streetlights started goin' out one at a time, all the way up the block, like "poof, poof, poof, poof, poof." We looked at each other. I go "Oh shit," 'cause we're plugged into one of the streetlights, and I thought we blew out the whole street! The whole neighborhood went dark.
Wiz: And you know what it was? It was the blackout of '77.[5]

Pandemonium ensued. Nearly 1,000 fires were set, and looting was rampant. Police arrested more than 3,000 people: when the backseats of the police cars were full, suspects were stuffed in the trunks, and precincts quickly ran out of room to house prisoners. Looters stole anything they could get their hands on, but diapers and canned food were among the most frequently taken items—a reflection of the "reality of lack" (to borrow a phrase from KRS-One) that pervaded neighborhoods like the South Bronx. Willis Barnes, who was among those arrested for looting that night, explains: "You steal a color TV and I have a van loaded with Pampers, and I bet I can sell all those Pampers before you sell that TV. In the ghetto, people ain't got no money for color TVs, but they got a lot of babies and they got to have Pampers."[6] Most importantly for our purposes, the chaos allowed many aspiring DJs to acquire turntables and sound systems, luxuries that most of them never would have been able to afford. Disco Wiz remembers: "It's funny, 'cause I have a theory. [. . .] Before that blackout, you had about maybe five legitimate crews of DJs. After the blackout, you had a DJ on every block. . . . That blackout made a big spark in the hip-hop revolution." Grandmaster Caz agrees: "Everybody was a DJ. Everybody stole turntables and stuff. Every electronic store imaginable got hit for stuff. Every record store. Everything. That sprung a whole new set of DJs."[7] Were it not for the opportunities afforded by the blackout, rap music may have evolved very differently.

While the story of hip hop's origins is often cast as a response to the terrible conditions in the South Bronx—or, more forcefully, that the conditions in the South Bronx were *responsible* for hip hop's birth—Joseph Schloss contends that the legend is a bit of a misnomer. Being a DJ required a considerable amount of money to purchase not only equipment but also records (many DJs' collections easily number in the thousands). Another myth that is often perpetuated is that there were no school music programs—"regular" instruments were not available—and that is why kids turned to hip hop. Legendary producer Prince Paul refutes that notion, claiming that "everybody went to a school that had a band. You could take an instrument if you wanted to. [. . .] But, man, you playing the clarinet isn't gonna be like, BAM! KA! Ba-BOOM-BOOM KAH! Everybody in the party [saying] 'Oooohhhhh!'"[8] Simply put, correlation does not equal causation: the oppressive conditions in the South Bronx did not create hip hop, nor did hip hop emerge as a response to those conditions. These are, however, the conditions in which these artists came of age, and many facets of their lives are reflected in the music.

FOUNDING FATHERS

Block parties offered an opportunity for the residents of these neighborhoods to get together and forget about their troubles, if only for a night. DJs would roll out enormous speaker systems, a pair of turntables, and their record collections and inspire the crowd to dance all night long. There are three DJs central to any early history of hip hop: Kool Herc, Grandmaster Flash, and Afrika Bambaataa. These three are often referred to as hip hop's Founding Fathers. All three were DJs active in the South Bronx in the late 1970s, and each contributed something unique to rap's musical style.

Kool Herc

Kool Herc was born Clive Campbell in Jamaica, where he grew up around the nightlife music scene. In 1967, he and his family moved to the South Bronx and ended up right in the path of Moses' expressway. He became a graffiti artist in high school: his tag "Clive is Cool" meshed with his nickname, "Hercules" (he was very tall and strong), and he ultimately became known as Kool Herc. Herc and his sister held a party on August 11, 1973, to raise money to buy back-to-school clothes. During this party, Herc had a revelation that would change the course of popular music. "I was smoking cigarettes and I was waiting for the records to finish. And I noticed people was waiting for certain parts of the record," he recalls. That part was the **break**: the spot on the record where most of the instruments would drop out, leaving only the percussion to carry the groove. Rather than play the entire song, Herc would cue up and play only the break, and then he would switch over to the other turntable, which had a different break ready to go. Herc called this technique the "merry-go-round." "And once they heard that," he said: "that was it, wasn't no turning back. They always wanted to hear breaks after breaks after breaks after breaks."[9] Among Herc's favorite breaks were "Apache" by the Incredible Bongo Band and "Give It Up or Turnit A Loose" by James Brown. Herc began calling those who danced to these selections "break boys," or "b-boys" for short.

Grandmaster Flash

If Kool Herc discovered the unbridled power of the beat, Grandmaster Flash figured out how to harness its power. Born Joseph Saddler in Barbados in 1958, Flash moved to the South Bronx as a child. Flash admired what Kool Herc was doing—isolating break beats by using two turntables—but he felt that Herc's technique was sloppy: the beat would sometimes be interrupted while Herc cued the next record, and his performances were occasionally punctuated by dead air, which dissipated the energy of the party. Flash made several significant contributions to the art of DJing. He studied electrical engineering at a trade school and put his skills to work developing a device that allowed him to hear one record in the headphones while the other went out through the speakers. This innovation resulted in much neater cuts from record to record as a result of more exact cueing.

LISTENING GUIDE 5.1

Artist: Grandmaster Flash
Song: "The Adventures of Grandmaster Flash on the Wheels of Steel"
Album: (single)

Record label: Sugar Hill
Year released: 1981
DJ or Producer: Grandmaster Flash (DJ)/Sylvia Robinson & Joey Robinson Jr. (producers)
Samples used: "Good Times," Chic; "Rapture," Blondie; "Another One Bites the Dust," Queen; various early rap tracks from Grandmaster Flash & The Furious Five, The Sugar Hill Gang, and Spoonie Gee

TIME	MUSICAL CHARACTERISTICS	LYRICS	DESCRIPTION
0:00	Sample from Spoonie Gee's "Monster Jam"	"You say one for the . . ."	
0:10	Sample from Blondie's "Rapture"	"Fab 5 Freddy . . ."	
0:25	Sample from Chic's "Good Times" Scratching	"Good times"	Sample also refers to "Rapper's Delight" by The Sugar Hill Gang
0:34	Sample from Incredible Bongo Band, "Apache" Scratching		
0:51	Sample from Queen, "Another One Bites the Dust"		Musically, this sample is quite similar to "Good Times."
1:04	Scratches in rhythm to "Another One Bites the Dust"		
1:17	"Good Times"		
1:35	Sample from "Freedom" by Grandmaster Flash & The Furious Five	"Grandmaster cut faster!"	
2:14	Sample from "The Birthday Party" by Grandmaster Flash & The Furious Five		"Good times" cut in
3:33	Sample from The Hellers, "Life Story"	"Why don't you tell me a story . . ."	
4:07	Sample from The Sugar Hill Gang, "8th Wonder"		
5:20	Sample from *Flash Gordon* (1980 film)		

"The Adventures of Grandmaster Flash on the Wheels of Steel" is one of the earliest commercially recorded examples of what DJing must have sounded like in the Bronx during hip hop's early years. It also serves as an example of hip hop's postmodern aesthetics. The song consists of samples of disco, rock, new wave, and early rap, as well as dialogue from a movie. The composition is Flash's assemblage of these disparate elements.[10]

Russell Potter suggests that this record is important because it challenges the prevailing inauthentic sound of hip hop that had been circulating mainly as a result of Sugar Hill's other records: hits like "Rapper's Delight" (to be discussed in the next chapter) didn't reflect the kind of music that was being made in the South Bronx and surrounding areas during the 1970s. Sugar Hill Records presented a cleaned-up, disco-influenced version of rap that was supported by studio musicians, not DJs. Potter writes, "Finding a way to put hip-hop's indigenous modes of production onto the very vinyl that it founded itself on cutting into pieces was no small task, but if anyone could do it, it was Grandmaster Flash."[11]

Furthermore, "Adventures" provides an early example of hip hop's historical consciousness. By choosing the samples that he did, Flash tells a story of the early days of hip hop. His choice of "Good Times" is an obvious reference to "Rapper's Delight," the song that put Sugar Hill Records (and rap music) on the map. Blondie's song "Rapture" references Fab 5 Freddy, an important figure in the early days of hip hop. While Blondie was a new-wave group, they quickly adopted the speech-like delivery of rap music, as you can hear in excerpts that Flash chose (we will look at "Rapture" in more detail in the next chapter). The fact that Flash chose rap records by his peers to sample also supports this idea that this recording is a kind of historical document ("Why don't you tell me a story?" the little girl asks around 3:33 into the track). Potter contends:

> The impact of "Adventures" was immediate and sent everyone in the business back to the drawing boards. What Sylvia Robinson and her peers had never understood, Flash had realized and put into practice: hip-hop was not able to *record* itself until it could sample its own previously recorded selves, until the audience for *records* knew as well as the club crowds the precise *situatedness* of each of its outbursts.[12]

Afrika Bambaataa: Master of Records

Bambaataa was a DJ well known for his eclectic music tastes. If Herc discovered the breakbeat, and Flash honed the technique, Bambaataa opened up the repertoire of musical styles that could be played. The "Master of Records" (as he is sometimes called) took great pride in getting people to dance to music they ordinarily would not consider listening to. While Herc and Flash played funk, rock, and disco, Bambaataa played everything from oldies to calypso to reggae: "I even played commercials that I taped off the television shows, from *Andy Griffith* to the *Pink Panther*, and people looked at me like I was crazy."[13] His eclectic tastes aroused the curiosity of many partygoers, thus he also took great pride in concealing his sources, doing things like soaking records to remove the labels or buying decoy records while he was out **digging in the crates**.

Bambaataa was also keen to incorporate new technology like synthesizers and drum machines into his music. This often resulted in a sound that was much more futuristic than that of his contemporaries; in fact, many people credit Bambaataa with laying the foundation for many genres of electronic dance music, like techno and house. His 1982 hit "Planet Rock," which we will look at more closely in Chapter 10, uses the Roland TR-808 drum machine, along with the Fairlight Computer Musical Instrument, an early digital sampling synthesizer.

"Digging in the crates" ("digging" for short) is slang for "looking for records." Plastic milk crates were the ideal size for storing 12-inch records: they can hold roughly 75–100 discs. DJs and producers go to great length to find not only rare or unique recordings, but also recordings that are part of the hip-hop canon. Beyond record stores, committed DJs will canvass yard sales, thrift shops, and old dance clubs. In his book *Making Beats*, Joseph Schloss recounts the story of one producer who, while on vacation, went door to door asking complete strangers whether they had records they'd be willing to part with.

Schloss discusses four additional outcomes of digging: a connection to hip-hop tradition, paying dues, education, and socialization. Digging formed a cornerstone of early hip-hop culture, and modern producers seek to preserve this connection with the past. DJs and producers might advertise that the beats on an album were taken from the original vinyl, implying that they did the work required to locate the rare tracks themselves. Education means not only learning about classic hip-hop sample sources, but also learning about different genres of music, like jazz, bluegrass, and classical. Finally, for many producers, digging allows them to forge bonds with other producers, both locally and abroad, as they pursue a shared passion.

Digging has diminished in popularity somewhat as a result of the rise of digital synthesizers and samplers, the disappearance of record stores, and the rise in online shopping. Schloss also relates the sentiment of some producers that "all of the good stuff has been used."[14]

IMPROVISATION

Improvisation was the foundation of early hip hop. When we think of improvisation, we tend to think of things that are unique, novel, and ephemeral, but studies of improvisation across many different modalities have shown that improvisation involves the intersection of two systems: a lexicon (that is, a dictionary, of sorts) and a grammar (a set of rules for organizing material). When we speak, we choose words that we (and others) already know the meanings of, and we arrange them in ways that are familiar to members of our speech communities: for instance, English speakers typically put the subject of a sentence before the verb; German speakers place the verb at the end of a sentence. When jazz musicians improvise, they are not "inventing" notes, chords, or scales: they are relying on formulas that they have rehearsed over and over again, and they fit those formulas into the structure of a preexisting song—the "changes"—in real time. Improvisation in hip hop is no different: artists take a series of "moves" that they've mastered and arrange them in real time into preexisting structures.

Many aspects of the DJ's art are improvisatory. Records and turntables are the preexisting material in this case, and finding new ways to play those records—mixing, punch phrasing, cutting, and so on—is where improvisation takes place. Furthermore, many of the early DJ setups were improvised. Herc started with guitar amps, and he would use the "channel" switch on the amp to switch back and forth between records. Tony Tone, a "hook-up man" (that is, he was responsible for setting up the equipment) for DJ Baron and DJ Breakout, describes building a set of speakers out of fifty-five-gallon drums: "The speakers faced down so you could get a bass reflex, and it would shoot out—you could hear it for at least ten blocks."[15] Grandmaster Flash would take various electronic components—amplifiers, transistors, wiring—from broken-down cars and find ways to incorporate them into his system. Even plugging these systems into streetlights was a form of improvisation.

So far, we've focused only on the role of DJs in the early days of hip hop. Early MCing sounded very different from what we hear in contemporary rap, and this was mostly a result of improvisation and interaction with the crowd during a live DJ performance. MCs would call for the dancers to "wave their hands like they just don't care" or "say ho." There was very little in the way of clear structure or plot in these early rhymes; rather, they were typically pieced together in performance from bits that the MC had memorized. As MCs began taking on increasingly important roles, and their routines became more complex, they too began to battle. The 1981 battle between Chief Rocker Busy Bee and Kool Moe Dee was one of the earliest and highest-profile MC battles, and, according to many, it fundamentally changed the way MCs rhyme. An exploration of both sides of the battle reveals a lot about how improvisation works in rap.

LISTENING GUIDE 5.2

Artist: Chief Rocker Busy Bee (aka Busy Bee Starski)
Song: "Battle with Kool Moe Dee"
Album:——
Record label:——
Year released: 1981
DJ or Producer: Kool DJ AJ

TIME	MUSICAL CHARACTERISTICS	LYRICS	DESCRIPTION
0:40	In rhythm	"Is _____ in the house?"	Busy Bee starts by asking the audience where they're from.
1:00	Spoken naturally; call and response	"Say ho! Ho!"	Bee gets the crowd to clap their hands.
1:12	In rhythm	"Is it Burger King?"	Bee polls the audience as to their favorite fast-food restaurants.
1:38			
1:57	In rhythm	"Is it Cancer?"	Bee polls the audience as to their zodiac signs.
2:34	4 x couplets in common measure (8+6; *ab, ab*)	"Now for those of you . . ."	This bit is clearly pre-rehearsed and not improvised.
3:00	Sung	"Spurs that jingle, jangle, jingle . . ."	Bee uses a familiar "ditty."
3:12	Call and response	"Somebody say sex!"	
3:50	Call and response	"Say [19]82. . ."	Bee time-stamps the performance (not surprising in the live context).
4:32		"Ba diddy bop"	Busy Bee's signature bit, a throwback to doo-wop (you can hear the crowd scream)
4:40	6 x rhyming couplets (8+8; *aa, bb*)	"Right now y'all . . ."	

Chief Rocker Busy Bee Starski was a well-known celebrity club rapper, and his recordings provide an example of what rap sounded like in its earliest days. Starski was affiliated with Bambaataa's Zulu Nation for a time and was considered a champion battle rapper in his day. In rap's early days, the winner of a rap battle was the one who could rock the party the hardest: these were not battles as we think of them today, where one rapper insults the other one. Starski was best known for his live performances and released very few records. He faced off with Kool Moe Dee at Harlem World on Christmas Eve, 1981, in a battle that would set the stage for the years of beef to come. A bootleg recording of the performance quickly became one of the most circulated tapes of the time. Busy Bee's appearance in the movie *Wild Style* includes several performances.

Busy Bee rocked the crowd by using a variety of call and response techniques like asking them to clap, "polling" them, and directing them to repeat things that he said. Call and response is a fundamental element of many African art forms: it's viewed as a more "democratic" mode of performance—there's little to no separation (or distinction) between performer and audience. Busy Bee's performances consisted of a variety of pre-rehearsed bits that were strung together in different ways

Is	Man—	HAT—	tan	in	the	House?	
Is	it	BUR—	ger	King?			
Is	It	CAN—	cer?				
4	&	1	&	2	&	3	&

Figure 5.1 Busy Bee's "poll" formula

in response to his interactions with the audience. Some were staples of the hip-hop vernacular: "say ho!" "somebody scream!" and so on. His performance lacks any kind of story or narrative that we've come to expect in much contemporary rap music: his sole motivation is to move the crowd.

In contrast to many popular songs, Busy Bee's performance lacks a clear form: there's nothing like a verse or catchy hook for listeners to hang on to. This lack of clear structure is indicative of the improvised nature of the set. But his material isn't entirely made up on the spot: the rhyming couplets, for instance, come off as too polished. The "polls"—asking about where people are from, restaurants, and zodiac signs—rely on a preexisting rhythmic formula that is common to all of them: the formula appears in Figure 5.1.

Such an approach frees up mental processing time: Busy Bee can rely on these preexisting formulas and fill in the blanks on the fly. Providing support for this hypothesis is a seeming mistake by Busy Bee: in the restaurant poll, he says "Burger King" twice—once at the beginning and once at the end. Listening to other recordings of Busy Bee performing, we hear that many of these same structures reappear. They may be in different orders: he might start with a different zodiac sign, for instance, or put the restaurant bit toward the end of his performance rather than the beginning, like it is here.

LISTENING GUIDE 5.3

Artist: Kool Moe Dee
Song: "Battle with Busy Bee"
Album:——
Record label:——
Year released: 1981
DJ or Producer: DJ Easy Lee

TIME	MUSICAL CHARACTERISTICS	LYRICS	DESCRIPTION
6:38	Natural speech; no music	"1–2, 1–2"; "In the place to be . . ."	Moe Dee is passing time while the DJ gets set up.
7:13			
7:32	Music starts		
8:34		"Party after party, the same old shit . . ."	Criticizes Busy Bee's reuse of material
8:54		"I'll take the title right here on the spot/How can I take a title you ain't got?/You're not number one, you're not even the best/And you can't win no real MC contest"	Transition from attack on Bee to Moe Dee The implication is that Moe Dee is a *real* MC and Busy Bee isn't.

TIME	MUSICAL CHARACTERISTICS	LYRICS	DESCRIPTION
9:35		"Now you popcorn peanut toy MCs/Never ever ever heard no rhymes like these/Cause my intent from the time I sent/Is to say those rhymes that I invent"	Moe Dee proclaims his originality.
10:30		"That ba-diddy-bop . . . ain't no thing"	Takes aim at Busy Bee's signature bit
10:35	Rapid-fire staccato sixteenth-note delivery		Alternates four-bar verses with LA Sunshine. This is clearly intended as a display of Moe Dee's *virtuosity*. The rhythm is highlighted by the alliteration and internal rhyme, which results in a machine-gun-like sound.

Kool Moe Dee was a member of The Treacherous Three, a group that also included Special K, LA Sunshine, and DJ Easy Lee (whose names are mentioned on the track). Moe Dee was known as someone who took time to write his rhymes down, carefully planning what he was going to say, and trying to craft lyrics with a message.

While it, too, is mostly improvised, Moe Dee's style differs markedly from Busy Bee's. His rap is basically one long, relentless verse, delivered in rhyming couplets. Whereas Busy Bee's rhymes were addressed to the crowd, Moe Dee's rhymes directly attacked Busy Bee. This represents a fundamental shift in how MCs operated: it was no longer about the crowd; instead, it was about the rapper. Nonetheless, Moe Dee relies on preexisting structures, too; namely, the rhyming couplet. In the spoken introduction, we hear another improvisatory tactic: listen for how many times Moe Dee says "1–2, 1–2" and "In the place to be" (which, incidentally, rhymes with "Kool Moe Dee," "Treacherous Three," and "Busy Bee Starski"). Both of these recurring fragments are used to fill time: it would be awkward (and not particularly braggadocious) if he just stood on stage waiting for the DJ to get set up and said nothing. Instead, he fills what could have been dead air with these stock phrases.

In the first part of his attack, Moe Dee salutes Busy Bee for his ability to move the crowd but then begins to criticize his lack of originality ("If you was money man/You'd be counterfeit"). He accuses him of reusing material ("Record after record, rhyme after rhyme/Always wanna know your zodiac sign"), biting (stealing) his name from Love Bug Starski (another prominent early MC), and buying rhymes from Spoonie Gee.

In the second part of the attack, Moe Dee claims his superiority chiefly through claiming his originality. The coup de grace occurs near the end with the rapid-fire delivery of his lines, full of internal rhyme and alliteration, a clear display of Moe Dee's verbal skills.

In one of the earliest essays on break dancing, Sally Banes describes the style of dancing in terms that resonate with the approach taken here. Break dancing is a way to "flaunt a unique personal style within a conventional format."[16] Dancers stand in a circle (similar to the cipher of early rap freestyle battles) and each takes a turn dancing in the center, which lasts from ten to thirty seconds. Dancers have a sort of grammar (Banes refers to it as a "script") for organizing a series of "stock expressions" (the lexicon). Banes outlines the script as "entry-footwork-spin-freeze-exit." She writes:

> The entry, the footwork, and the exit were like the stock expressions and nonsense syllables that sandwich narrative content in a rap. They provided a rhythmic frame for the freeze, an improvised pose or movement, which broke the beat. [. . .] And besides their aesthetic function, these segments were a way for the dancer to "tread water" between strokes, to free the mind for strategizing while the body went through familiar, uninventive paces.[17]

Banes suggests that preexisting (i.e., planned, rehearsed) material—stock expressions—are combined in novel ways in real time according to a sort of grammar or script. These preexisting movements can be used to buy time while the dancer formulates his or her next move, much like Kool Moe Dee's use of "1–2, 1–2."

Banes also enumerates on the cross-cultural art forms that combine to form break dancing: black dance, ballroom dance (the Charleston and Lindy Hop), the Brazilian martial art *capoeira*, kung-fu movies, French pantomime, and cartoons.[18] The improvisatory nature of hip hop is evident from the diverse cultural forms (both "high" and "low," Eastern and Western) it draws on and the ways in which it combines and repurposes the elements of each culture into something new. Jorge Pabon writes that "half" of the dance forms associated with hip hop developed in New York (i.e., up-rocking and b-boy/b-girling) while the other half originated on the West Coast (i.e., popping and locking). These forms combined under the general heading of break dancing.[19] Schloss contends that break dancing actually got its start in Brooklyn, years before Kool Herc's famous party.[20] Such claims undermine the prevailing origin story that hip hop was in fact born in the South Bronx.

OTHER CONTRIBUTIONS

Most histories of hip hop (including this one, so far) outline the African and Caribbean influences on the genre that were then expanded upon by the "Founding Fathers." Such a retelling marginalizes the roles of two other significant groups: the Latinx community (in particular, Puerto Ricans) and women. As early as the 1990s, scholars were lamenting the erasure of the contributions of women and Latinxs to hip hop.[21] Many of these scholars cite the increasing commercialization of rap music as the reason for this erasure; this phenomenon is covered in more detail in the next chapter. Furthermore, as artists like Public Enemy, KRS-One, and the Native Tongues collective began to address more Afrocentric themes, rap became increasingly identified as *black* music, and those who did not conform to that image were pushed out. The Latinx community's role in b-boying and graffiti has been reasonably well documented; however, their contributions to the musical aspects of hip hop are relatively underexplored. Even during the peak of their fame, the visibility of Latinxs in rap was low: Charlie Chase, the DJ for the Cold Crush Brothers, acknowledges that many people didn't recognize that he was Puerto Rican because he was behind the group DJing—out of sight—and he gained his reputation through tapes of his that circulated.[22] Many other well-known hip-hop groups had Latinx members whose identities were masked by either their individual stage names or their membership in a rap group: in addition to Chase, Prince Whipper Whip, Ruby Dee, and Prince Markie Dee of the Fat Boys were all Latinx.

Chase was a part of hip hop from the beginning: "When I started doing rap, there were no Hispanics doing it. If there were, I didn't know about it."[23] He came of age in the South Bronx and Brooklyn, admiring the skills of Grandmaster Flash. Chase, who was a bass player in several Puerto Rican music groups, came from a musical family and had a deep knowledge of the island's musical heritage. During his DJ sets, he would sneak in bits of salsa records or Tito Puente songs. Despite his high profile as a member of the Cold Crush Brothers, rapping in Spanish seemed like an insurmountable task at the time. "I always stressed the point that I was Hispanic doing rap music," he told Juan Flores: "but I couldn't do it in Spanish, you understand? But that was my way of opening the doors for everybody else to do what they're doing now."[24] The first bilingual rap release was 1981's "Disco Dream" by Mean Machine. While the song doesn't feature any extended rhyming in Spanish—the Spanish lyrics were mostly short catchphrases—it opened the door for other bilingual rappers to expand on it. The group was signed to Sugar Hill Records but was dropped by the Robinsons after they made some disparaging remarks about the label on a radio show.

The Rock Steady Crew

The Rock Steady Crew is probably the most well-known of the early break dance crews. The group was founded by Jo Jo and Jimmy D, and later members included Mr. Freeze (one of the first "official" white b-boys), Frosty Freeze, and Richard "Crazy Legs" Colon, who became (and remains) the leader and figurehead of the crew. They were at one time also members of the Zulu Nation, and in 1982 they toured Europe with Bambaataa and other hip-hop artists. The crew went on to appear in many early hip hop–related films, like *Wild Style, Style Wars, Beat Street,* and *Breakin'*. Their appearance in the 1983 movie *Flashdance* introduced b-boying to a much wider audience—it was, in fact, Crazy Legs dressed as Jennifer Beals' character who performed the final dance scene. The group still exists today and has become a franchise name for b-boy crews around the world.

William Jelani Cobb notes that Kool Herc is the undisputed father of hip hop but contends that the "mother of hip hop" post remains vacant.[25] While she was not a rapper, one could certainly nominate Sugar Hill's Sylvia Robinson for the position. Today, female artists constitute a small minority in mainstream rap, but MCs like Lisa Lee, Sha-Rock (the "plus 1" of the Funky Four + 1), the Sequence, and graffiti artists like Sandra "Lady Pink" Fabara were important contributors to the early days of hip hop. Not everyone agrees: Nelson George writes, "I would argue that if none of these female artists had ever made a record, hip hop's development would have been no different."[26] Such a claim suggests that the contributions of female MCs were negligible; however, those contributions were innovative in that they had to stake a claim in a territory that was (and is even more so now) male-dominated. With respect to their male counterparts, Cobb writes that artists like Kool Moe Dee and Melle Mel had to invent the genre as they went—there were no precedents for what they were doing—and the same could be said for the female artists that George names.[27]

The Sequence, widely regarded as the first all-female rap group, signed to Sugar Hill Records. The trio released a few records, including 1979's "Funk You Up"—which was the second release by Sugar Hill Records—and "Monster Jam" with labelmate Spoonie Gee. In addition to being the first female rap crew, the Sequence has the distinction of being the first well-known rap group from the South: the trio hailed from South Carolina. They caught the ear of Sylvia Robinson when The Sugar Hill Gang played a show in Columbia, South Carolina (their hometown) and auditioned for her backstage. Another Sugar Hill act, The Funky Four + 1, featured Sha-Rock, the only other female MC on the label's roster. In 1981, the group became the first rap act to perform on *Saturday Night Live* (the episode was hosted by Blondie's Deborah Harry). Sha-Rock also appeared on the news program *20/20* and in the 1984 film *Beat Street*. These appearances helped establish the image of a female MC.

The most notorious of these early MCs was Roxanne Shanté, who achieved notoriety by taking on U.T.F.O. In 1984, U.T.F.O. and Full Force released a song titled "Roxanne, Roxanne," in which a woman rejects attempts by each member of the group to seduce her: each of the three group members pleads his case in his own verse. The group was scheduled to perform a concert for WBLS, but when the group canceled, Shanté teamed up with popular hip-hop radio host Mr. Magic and his Juice Crew to release a song that took aim at the group. "Roxanne's Revenge," which was recorded by the 14-year-old in one take, originally featured Shanté rapping over U.T.F.O.'s beats, a highly confrontational move. After facing legal action, Shanté's DJ Marley Marl created a new instrumental track for the song's commercial release. The song is the first real response record in rap history, paving the way for the Bridge Wars (see Chapter 10) and many other beefs to follow. Shanté pulls no punches in her response, which calls out U.T.F.O. members by name and directly addresses many of the lines in their song: "I said I met these three guys and you know that's true/Let me tell you and explain them all to you."

Shanté first refuses to dignify Kangol by using his name. She dismisses the Educated Rapper's elementary name rhymes, uncovering it as little more than a ploy to seduce. Finally, she accuses Doctor Ice of trying to impress with his "pig Latin"—all the medical specialties he lists—which is even more effective because of a double meaning of the word "pig." U.T.F.O. fired back, bringing on an artist who came to be known as The Real Roxanne. Ultimately, dozens of response records followed.

Mr. Magic

Mr. Magic hosted one of the first rap radio shows, *Mr. Magic's Rap Attack*, which launched in 1979 on WHBI in Newark, New Jersey. WHBI was a public-access station: Magic sold advertisements so that he could afford to buy airtime. He would play tapes of live hip-hop shows—some recorded just earlier that night at clubs down the street from the radio station—and have guests from New York's hip-hop scene. In 1983, he moved to WBLS, a commercial station in New York City. Along with his engineer Marley Marl, he built a stable of rappers that called themselves the Juice Crew. Among its members were Big Daddy Kane, MC Shan, Kool G Rap, Roxanne Shanté, and Biz Markie.

Magic's show paved the way for stations like KDAY, the first all hip-hop station in Los Angeles, and for programs like the *Stretch and Bobbito Show* and Jay Smooth's *Underground Railroad*. His influence appears in rap lyrics by a host of artists, including Nas, Tupac, Biggie, and Jay-Z. His ongoing rivalry with DJ Red Alert, who had a show on New York's KISS-FM, led to the so-called Bridge Wars that catapulted Boogie Down Productions to fame.

NOSTALGIA

Even though rap music and hip-hop culture in general is quite young, its forty-year history has already produced its share of nostalgia: any verse that includes the phrase "back in the day" longs for a time when things were somehow better. Nostalgia implies that there is some problem in the present that didn't exist in the past: the word "nostalgia" essentially means a longing for the return home. Literary theorist Svetlana Boym argues that nostalgia is in fact a yearning for a different *time*, not necessarily a different place (more precisely, she argues that it's a yearning for time that is constructed as space). She suggests that nostalgia is the mirror image of progress: "The fantasies of the past [are] determined by the needs of the present, and have a direct impact on the realities of the future," she writes.[28] In music, this can take one of two forms: a reengagement with music, artists, and cultures of the past, or an attempt to rebuild, evoke, or reconnect with the past using contemporary materials.[29]

Hip hop's first noticeable nostalgic turn came with the rise of the underground (the rise of the underground is discussed more fully in the next chapter). The radical changes that commercialization brought to the genre were met with stark criticism from those who saw it as their duty to protect and preserve rap's past. Common's "I Used to Love H.E.R." is one such song that seems to long for the past in light of the changes the genre was undergoing.

LISTENING GUIDE 5.4

Artist: Common
Song: "I Used to Love H.E.R."
Album: *Resurrection*
Record label: Relativity
Year released: 1994
DJ or Producer: No I.D.
Samples used: "The Changing World," George Benson; "I'm Gonna Do You," Jungle Brothers; "Still Talkin'," Eazy-E; "Fly, Fly, the Route, Shoot," If

The title, "I Used to Love H.E.R.," sets a nostalgic tone for the song, with Common looking back to better days. Many people believe that "H.E.R." stands for "hearing every rhyme," but in an interview on *Yo! MTV Raps*, Common says it stands for "Hip hop in its Essence is Real." In this case, Common implies that there is something inauthentic about contemporary rap, and that authenticity—the "real"—can only be found at hip hop's origins. This personification of hip hop as a woman is not unique—Nas does this as well in "Hip Hop Is Dead," as does DJ Khaled in "Hip Hop," for example—but it does open the song up for a more careful interpretation. Traditional notions of the feminine suggest that hip hop is delicate, emotional, nurturing, and so on. Personifying hip hop as a woman, though, stands in stark contrast to the objectification of women commonly found in rap music around this time. Common plays into this a bit, as the love interest in the song becomes increasingly sexualized, promiscuous, and money-hungry.

The song leads with a hook that calls to mind the early days of hip hop with its "Yes, yes y'all/To the beat y'all. . .," phrases that were pioneered by some of rap's first MCs. In discussing the origins of the track, Common recalls: "I grew up on Gang Starr and Pete Rock, stuff like that. That's what was on their choruses, so that's what we did."[30] In so doing, the hook longs for a past when hip hop was pure and about rocking the party, not making money. Mickey Hess observes that the past Common (and others who pen similar songs) longs for is roughly the six-year period between 1973 (the "invention" of rap) and 1979 (when rap's first singles hit the airwaves). During that period, Common would have been a toddler (he was born in 1972) and thus could not have any recollection of the culture, nor have participated in it.[31] Hess invokes Renato Rosaldo's idea of "imperialist nostalgia," a state in which one mourns that which they helped destroy.

Imperialist nostalgia implies that Common is to some degree complicit in the destruction of the art form that he mourns. His complicity is evident in part via the form of the song. Common includes three 16-bar verses with a hook—a stock commercial formula—to critique the changes that rap went through as it became increasingly commercial. Furthermore, these three verses exemplify the "time-shift" paradigm outlined in Chapter 2: each verse suggests a different stage of life—both Common's and hip hop's. Hess writes that artists engaging in this kind of critique typically fall back on their live performance skills as a way of reconnecting with hip hop's origins (when it was only live performance). Common's use of "Yes, yes, y'all" and similar phrases call to mind the live, improvised performances of early rappers like Busy Bee.[32]

While the album did not sell well initially—it barely made it onto the *Billboard* charts—it was praised by critics. The success of this song helped bring Common to mainstream attention, in part because Ice Cube interpreted it as an attack on West Coast rap (Common is from Chicago). The song sparked a beef between the two: Ice Cube counterattacked with a verse on Mack 10's song "Westside Slaughterhouse" that boldly stated that hip hop started on the West Coast. In response, many East Coast rappers came to Common's defense, escalating the growing feud between East Coast and West Coast styles. Common responded with "The Bitch in Yoo," which is regarded as one of the most brutal diss tracks in rap history. Ultimately the two reconciled, with help from Louis Farrakhan, who was the leader of the Nation of Islam at that time.

Popular music is full of stories about artists who died too young, presumably before they could reach their full potential. Hip hop has more than its fair share of artists in this category: Scott La Rock (of Boogie Down Productions), Tupac Shakur, The Notorious B.I.G., and producer J Dilla are among the names that come to mind. As music theorist Justin Williams notes, these artists become symbols in their passing, marking changes of generation and style. They achieve "symbolic immortality," as their fame lives on through their music. Sales of an artist's music tend to spike at the time of their passing, and many artists continue to "live on" through posthumous releases. In one sense, the artists have been silenced; in another sense, they continue to speak to audiences through constructed spaces of mourning. The film *Tupac: Resurrection* presents a particularly uncanny example of this. The movie, which appeared in 2006 (ten years after Shakur was murdered) is an autobiography that was pieced together from interviews that he did. The effect is one of Tupac narrating his life from beyond the grave—even the title suggests a return from the dead, with strong Christian undertones (imagery in the film—particularly at the beginning—reinforces these undertones).[33] The 2012 Coachella festival took Tupac's resurrection a step further: a lifelike hologram of Shakur performed on stage with Snoop Dogg and Dr. Dre.[34] Holograms of Eazy-E and Ol' Dirty Bastard (who are also deceased) have since appeared in concert.

Fans long for the rappers they grew up with, whose careers may have gone into hibernation, to release new material. Implicit in this desire is a hope that the new material will be contemporary and relevant and that it might have a positive influence on the current scene. Unfortunately, neither of these desires typically materializes, but that doesn't prevent fans from hoping. A 2014 article in the *New Yorker* sought to get to the bottom of a mystery making the rounds on the internet: an unknown rapper who went by the name Your Old Droog had been posting tracks to the music sharing site SoundCloud. His anachronistic style led many to speculate that Your Old Droog was a pen name for Nas: "droog" in Russian means "friend," both rappers end their phrases with the same "raspy sigh," and Droog made references to obscure elements of 1970s culture, just as a 40-year-old "with a nostalgia problem" would.[35] Later in the article, the author, Jay Caspian Kang, observes that "nearly every MC in New York these days, from Joey Bada$$ to Action Bronson, sounds like a nineties rapper" and that Droog's case was "hopeful wish fulfillment for hip-hop fans in their thirties, many of whom cite Nas' [1994] début album, *Illmatic*, as the purest possible distillation of hip-hop's potential." Action Bronson's style has been compared to Wu-Tang Clan's Ghostface Killah, and the comparisons have led to the two of them exchanging strong words. Kang's point—that fans are eager and willing to believe that their 1990s idols are still active *as they were in the 1990s*—is evidence of a longing for what they perceive as better times.

In 2015, Dr. Dre released his long-awaited third studio album, *Compton*. The album appeared sixteen years after the release of *2001* and featured the now-50-year-old Dre orchestrating rhymes by a who's who of rap, including Eminem, Snoop Dogg, and Kendrick Lamar. Lamar, a Compton native, was riding the success of his 2012 major-label debut, *Good Kid, M.A.A.D. City*, and the alliance with Dre connected those who were nostalgic for gangsta rap's past with those shaping its future. Dre's album was set to coincide with the release of the film *Straight Outta Compton*, which told the story of N.W.A. The movie, which starred Ice Cube's son, was both a critical and a box-office success, and Dre and Cube's involvement lent the film a stamp of authenticity. The soundtrack—which is distinct from Dre's *Compton*—featured remastered classic N.W.A. tracks as well as solo efforts released after the group split up.

At the Coachella music festival in 2016, Ice Cube brought out the remaining members of N.W.A.—minus Dr. Dre—along with Lamar and Eazy-E's son to perform with him, capitalizing on the popularity of the movie and reinforcing Lamar's link with the group. The movie and subsequent "reunion" exemplify the two strands of nostalgia mentioned above. On one hand, fans look back longingly on the music that N.W.A. created nearly thirty years ago and could hear it again in the context of both the film and the Coachella performance. That Dre and Eazy-E could not (or, in Dre's case, perhaps, would not) be there highlights the present reality. On the other hand, Lamar represents a new incarnation of the same spirit that brought N.W.A. into being. If nostalgia means "longing for the return home," the present state of N.W.A. shows that, even if a return home is possible, that home is forever changed. Lamar represents progress: he quenches the longing of fans for a time when hip hop that dealt with social issues could be commercially viable and musically satisfying at the same time.

These various strands of nostalgia coalesced in the rise of the "classic hip hop" radio format. In October 2014, Houston radio station KROI-FM 92.1 became Boom 92, the country's first classic hip-hop station. The all-news station had once attempted an all-Beyoncé format as a stunt and was surprised by the results. This new format was an effort by the ailing radio industry to bring back listeners who had flocked to satellite ("Backspin" is Sirius XM's old-school hip-hop channel) and streaming radio. Within a few months, ratings at the station had tripled, as listeners enjoyed tracks by Biggie, Missy Elliott, and other stars of the 1980s and '90s. Other stations followed in Philadelphia, Dallas, and Atlanta and met with similar success—Atlanta eventually ended up with three such stations. The format attracted the prime 35- to 49-year-old demographic that advertisers covet: it's "the hip hop you grew up with," Boom 92 proclaims. In a *New York Times* article about the new format, Tom Silverman, founder of Tommy Boy Records, says "Hip hop has now entered the realm of credible nostalgia."[36]

Tom Silverman

In 1981, Tom Silverman founded Tommy Boy Records in New York City. During the 1970s, Silverman had been writing and circulating a newsletter for DJs called *Dance Music Report* and had established connections with many artists in the area. When he first encountered Afrika Bambaataa in the early 1980s, he invited him to record a demo, and, on the heels of its success, Silverman signed other artists from the Bronx. The label went on to sign groundbreaking artists like De La Soul, House of Pain, and Queen Latifah. Silverman also helped launch the New Music Seminar, an industry gathering that ran from 1980 to 1995 and was relaunched in 2009. The Seminar's "Battle for World Supremacy" was inspired by Silverman's frequent visits to the T-Connection, a club where Bambaataa used to DJ. These battles were among the first formal DJ competitions: they were held from 1981 to 1994 and spawned many imitators, most notably the DMC World Championships, which launched in 1985.

OUTRO

Names you should know:

- Chief Rocker Busy Bee
- Kool Moe Dee
- Robert Moses
- DJ Kool Herc

- Grandmaster Flash
- Afrika Bambaataa
- The Rock Steady Crew
- Tom Silverman

Terms you should know:

- The four pillars of hip hop

- Digging in the crates

Questions for discussion/writing prompts:

1. Describe the social, economic, and political conditions that gave rise to hip-hop culture in the 1970s.

2. Describe the similarities and differences between Busy Bee's and Moe Dee's styles. What elements are improvised? What elements seem to be pre-planned? Are there elements of either style that persist into hip hop today?

3. In an interview with Kevin T. Robinson, Grandmaster Flash discussed his innovations in terms of turntable technique and equipment modification and described his realization as "figure[ing] out how to control time." In what ways does Flash "control time" in "Adventures on the Wheels of Steel?"

4. Lil Yachty claimed in an interview that he cannot even name five songs by Tupac Shakur or The Notorious B.I.G., and he generally expresses disregard for hip hop's history. How important is it for new artists to understand the history of the genre? Why do you think such an understanding is or is not important?

Additional listening/viewing:

Founding Fathers:

- Ahearn, Charlie. *Wild Style*. New York, NY: Wild Style Productions, Ltd.; Burbank, CA: Rhino Entertainment Co., 1983.
- Silver, Tony. *Style Wars*. New York: Public Art Films, 1983.
- Recordings of *Mr. Magic's Rap Attack* offer a different kind of window into early hip hop. Audio files of the shows can be downloaded from blogs like old-school-hiphop-tapes.blogspot.com.

Improvisation:

- Fitzgerald, Kevin. *Freestyle: The Art of Rhyme*. New York: Palm Pictures, 2000.
- *Pioneers of Hip-Hop, vol. 1: Busy Bee*, Busy Bee

Nostalgia:

- "Meteor Hammer," Ghostface Killah (feat. Action Bronson)
- "Nutty Bars," Your Old Droog
- *Straight Outta Compton* soundtrack (2015)

NOTES

1 Jeff Chang, *Can't Stop, Won't Stop: A History of the Hip-Hop Generation* (New York: St. Martin's, 2005), 15.
2 Jonathan Mahler, *The Bronx is Burning: 1977, Baseball, Politics, and the Battle for the Soul of a City* (New York: Picador, 2005), 210.
3 Robert A. Caro, *The Power Broker: Robert Moses and the Fall of New York* (New York: Knopf, 1974), 513–14.
4 Caro 841.
5 Jim Fricke, *Yes Yes Y'all: The Experience Music Project Oral History of Hip-Hop's First Decade.* Ed. Charlie Ahearn and Experience Music Project (Cambridge, MA: Da Capo Press, 2002), 131.
6 Robert Curvin and Bruce Porter, *Blackout Looting: New York City, July 13, 1977* (New York: Gardener Press, 1979), 9.
7 Fricke 133.
8 Joseph Schloss, *Making Beats: The Art of Sample-Based Hip Hop* (Hanover, NH: Wesleyan University Press, 2004), 28–9.
9 Chang 79.
10 Mark Katz offers a similar listening guide in his Figure 3.4: see *Groove Music: The Art and Culture of the Hip Hop DJ* (New York: Oxford University Press, 2012), 80.
11 Russell A. Potter, *Spectacular Vernaculars: Hip-Hop and the Politics of Postmodernism* (Albany: State University of New York Press, 1995), 47.
12 Potter 47.
13 Fricke 49.
14 Schloss ch. 4.
15 Katz 49.
16 Sally Banes, "Breaking," in *Fresh: Hip Hop Don't Stop.* Ed. Nelson George, Sally Banes, Susan Flinker, and Patty Romanowski (New York: Sarah Lazin, 1985). Reprinted in *That's the Joint! The Hip-Hop Studies Reader.* Ed. Murray Forman and Mark Anthony Neal (New York: Routledge, 2004), 14.
17 Banes 15.
18 Banes 18.
19 Jorge Pabon, "Physical Graffiti: The History of Hip-Hop Dance," in *Total Chaos: The Art and Aesthetics of Hip-Hop.* Ed. Jeff Chang (New York: Basic Civitas Books, 2006), 18.
20 Joseph Schloss, *Foundation: B-boys, B-girls, and Hip-Hop Culture in New York* (New York: Oxford University Press, 2009).
21 See the first three essays in *Droppin' Science: Critical Essays on Rap Music and Hip Hop Culture.* Ed. William Eric Perkins (Philadelphia: Temple University Press, 1996).
22 Juan Flores, "Puerto Rocks: New York Ricans Stake Their Claim," in *Droppin' Science: Critical Essays on Rap Music and Hip Hop Culture.* Ed. William Eric Perkins (Philadelphia: Temple University Press, 1996), 89.
23 Flores 88.
24 Flores 90–1.
25 William Jelani Cobb, *To the Break of Dawn: A Freestyle on the Hip Hop Aesthetic* (New York: New York University Press, 2007), 39.
26 Nelson George, *Hip Hop America* (New York: Viking, 1998), 184.
27 Cobb 47.
28 Svetlana Boym, "Nostalgia and Its Discontents" *Hedgehog Review* (Summer 2007), 8.
29 These two forms are distillations of Boym's (ibid.) restorative and reflective nostalgia.
30 Insanul Ahmed, Andrew Barber, and Keenan Higgins, "The Making of Common's *Resurrection*" *Complex* (October 29, 2011): www.complex.com/music/2011/10/the-making-of-commons-resurrection.
31 Mickey Hess, *Is Hip Hop Dead? The Past, Present, and Future of America's Most Wanted Music* (Westport, CT: Praeger, 2007), 33.
32 Hess 33.
33 Lauren Lazin, dir. *Tupac Resurrection* (Atlanta: Amaru Entertainment, 2003).

34 Justin A. Williams, *Rhymin' and Stealin': Musical Borrowing in Hip Hop* (Ann Arbor: University of Michigan Press, 2013). Chapter 4 is titled "The Martyr Industry" and looks at the ways artists are "immortalized" after death.

35 Jay Caspian Kang, "Nas Is Not Your Old Droog" *New Yorker* (August 25, 2014): www.newyorker.com/culture/culture-desk/nas-your-old-droog.

36 Ben Sisario, "Classic Hip Hop is Spreading on the Radio Dial" *New York Times* (December 15, 2014): www.nytimes.com/2014/12/16/business/media/classic-hip-hop-is-spreading-on-the-radio-dial.html.

TIME LINE

1979	"King Tim III (Personality Jock)" by The Fatback Band and "Rapper's Delight" by The Sugar Hill Gang are the first commercially available rap recordings.
1980	Kurtis Blow becomes the first rapper to sign with a major record label (Mercury).
1981	Blondie's "Rapture" becomes the first song that features rapping to hit no. 1 on the *Billboard* Hot 100.
1983	Herbie Hancock releases "Rockit," which introduces hip-hop DJing to a wider audience, courtesy of Grandmixer D.ST's scratching on the track.
1984	Russell Simmons and Rick Rubin launch Def Jam Records.
	—Run-D.M.C. release their eponymous debut album.
	—The movies *Breakin'* and *Beat Street* bring hip hop to the big screen.
1985	LL Cool J releases his debut, *Radio*.
1986	Run-D.M.C.'s *Raising Hell* becomes the first rap album to go platinum.
	—The Beastie Boys debut with *Licensed to Ill*.
1988	*Yo! MTV Raps* premieres.
1989	The Good Life Café in Crenshaw, California, starts hosting hip-hop open-mic nights.
1991	*Billboard* magazine, which publishes record-sales data, adopts SoundScan in order to tabulate more accurate sales data.
	—Public Enemy and Anthrax collaborate on "Bring the Noise."
1995	Four friends launch Rhymesayers Records in Minneapolis, Minnesota.
1996	Congress passes a Telecommunications Act that deregulates media properties.

IN THIS CHAPTER, YOU WILL LEARN ABOUT

- How rap became mainstream
- The rise of the hip-hop underground
- How rap music crosses over into other musical styles

CHAPTER 6

Listening to Commercialization

OVERVIEW

Commercialization and commodification often go hand in hand. **Commodification** is the process by which an idea (or something otherwise not traditionally commercial) is transformed into something that can be bought or sold; **commercialization** is how an object is bought and sold. The first rap singles appeared in 1979 and were markedly different from the kind of music that was being played in the South Bronx. Labels like Sugar Hill, Def Jam, and Tommy Boy were among the first to focus solely on rap music, and helped the music reach audiences outside of New York City during the 1980s. Several important changes in the music industry in the 1990s catapulted rap to the top of the *Billboard* charts and forced major labels to take notice. As hip-hop culture became mainstream and popular, it mingled with other genres of music, leading some to believe that it lost its power. Those artists and fans sought refuge in the underground, where they preserve hip hop's history and push its artistic limits.

HIP HOP'S FIRST DEATH

It didn't take long before rap music caught the ear of the record companies, and the first commercial rap records appeared in 1979. Once the new genre became a commodity, its form and content started to change. Jeff Chang refers to rap's appearance on wax as "hip hop's first death"; S. Craig Watkins says that 1979 was "both the beginning and the end of the hip-hop movement."[1] It is important to emphasize that early rap was predominately a live experience: there were no real commercially available recordings of rap until 1979, and the rap music that did circulate consisted largely of cassette-tape recordings of live shows. Record labels had approached artists like Grandmaster Flash, but they turned down offers, unsure of how an improvised set that typically lasted hours would translate into recorded media.

Many histories of hip hop contend that The Sugar Hill Gang's "Rapper's Delight" is the first rap song released on record. In fact, it was the *second* rap record to be released: "Personality Jock" by King Tim III & The Fatback Band was released about a month before. The song appeared as a **"B-side"** to a bigger hit and consequently did not receive the kind of promotion that it needed to cement its place in history. Nevertheless, "Rapper's Delight" was an unlikely vehicle for introducing rap to the outside world. First, none of the members of The Sugar Hill Gang was really a part of the South Bronx scene, and they weren't otherwise rappers. Second, the instrumentals behind them were played by live musicians, not a DJ. Finally, many of the rhymes were not original to the group members: Sylvia wrote some, and some of Big Bank Hank's rhymes were stolen from his friend Grandmaster Caz. Grandmaster Flash heard the song and remembers thinking, "'Well, damn, I heard these rhymes by [Grandmaster] Caz.' But this guy who was a bouncer at the club is saying these rhymes on the record. These other two guys, I didn't have a clue who they were." Grandmaster Caz said: "At the time, hip hop was limited to a small group of people. Whatever you did, everybody knew what it was and who was doing it," implying that The Sugar Hill Gang were outsiders.[2]

"Rapper's Delight" was eventually a huge success for the Robinsons, but its success came only after considerable risk. Rap was a new genre, not heard by too many people outside of the Bronx (and "Rapper's Delight" was clearly unlike anything coming from the Bronx), so its popularity was quite serendipitous. Robinson decided to release the song as a 12-inch single—much like a disco club mix—which was about four times more expensive than the standard 7-inch single. A 12-inch held about fifteen minutes' worth of music, in comparison to the roughly four minutes on a 7-inch. Robinson then had to get the song on the radio. After much prodding, the song debuted on two radio stations, WESL-AM in St. Louis and WBLS-FM in New York City. After the record finally aired in St. Louis, Robinson received an order from a local distributor for 30,000 copies of the record. Michael Ellis, an executive at New York's WKTU-FM, said that the station received "between 100 and 150 calls each day [requesting the record], which is ten times as many calls as we have received on any other record."[3] Joey Robinson recalls a radio DJ telling listeners to "Stop calling, we're not going to play the record any more. We're going to play it at 7 o'clock, we're going to play it at 10 o'clock, we're going to play it at 12 o'clock."[4] Watkins argues that rap's unlikely emergence on the scene would probably be the last time that "an unknown, untested, and unproven style of music" could break into the mainstream as it did, given the subsequent consolidation of record labels and media outlets.[5] These first rap records were followed quickly by the first rap record by a female artist, Lady B's "To The Beat Y'All" and Steve Gordon & The Kosher Five's "Take My Rap, Please," which was the first white rap act as well as the first rap parody.

Sugar Hill Records

Sugar Hill Records was the first record label devoted solely to rap music. Founded in 1979 by Sylvia Robinson and her eldest son Joey Jr., the Englewood, New Jersey–based label was a last-ditch effort to save the family business. Since the 1950s, Robinson had had several minor successes as a performer and producer, but business was sliding off. One night, Sylvia heard Lovebug Starski rapping at Harlem World (later, the site of the Busy Bee/Kool Moe Dee battle) in New York City and, believing that this new style could save the business, enlisted her son to help her find some rappers. They found Big Bank Hank working at a pizza shop and rapping along to a tape of a Cold Crush Brothers show. Hank recalls: "Picture this: I'm full of pizza dough, and I'm like, 'Okay, they want me to come outside and audition in the car?'"[6] Hank was their first signee, and Wonder Mike and Master Gee soon followed. The label would eventually sign Grandmaster Flash & The Furious Five, Spoonie Gee, The Sequence, The Treacherous Three, and The Funky Four + 1.

The Sugar Hill sound is strongly influenced by disco, and lyrics for the most part are variations on the party-rocking lines of "Rapper's Delight" (which uses and reuses many phrases that were by that time commonplace in hip hop). A majority of the label's releases feature a live house band—one of the last house bands in the record industry—playing the music (that is, no DJ or sampling). It's worth noting, however, that the band sought to *imitate* the kind of looping and cutting that early hip-hop DJs practiced.[7]

LISTENING GUIDE 6.1

Artist: The Sugar Hill Gang
Song: "Rapper's Delight"
Album: (single)
Record label: Sugar Hill
Year released: 1979
DJ or Producer: Sylvia Robinson
Samples used: "Good Times," Chic (the rhythm tracks were not sampled, but played by Sugar Hill's house band)

TIME	MUSICAL CHARACTERISTICS	LYRICS	DESCRIPTION
0:00	Instrumental intro (8 measures)		Hi-hat, bongos, cowbell, piano and bass play an opening riff.
0:17			Bass plays "Good Times" riff, accompanied by disco claps on beats 2 and 4.
0:34	Verse 1 (20 measures)	"I said a hip, hop . . ."	Wonder Mike
1:18	Verse 2 (30 measures)	"Check it out, I'm the C-A-S-A . . ."	Big Bank Hank. Many of these rhymes were stolen from Grandmaster Caz.
2:23	Verse 3 (50 measures); the new verse starts halfway through the "sample"	"Well it's on and on . . ."	Master Gee
4:07	Verse 4 (14 measures)	"I said a hip, hop . . ."	Wonder Mike. Starts similarly to his opening lines in verse 1
4:37	Break (8 measures)		Like the introduction
4:56	Verse 5 (16 measures)	"A hip, hop . . ."	Wonder Mike
5:29	Verse 6 (60 measures)	"Well I'm Imp the Dimp . . ."	Big Bank Hank
7:33	Verse 7 (48 measures)	"It was seven o'clock . . ."	Master Gee
9:05	Verse 8 (48 measures)	"I say a can of beer . . ."	Wonder Mike
10:47	Verse 9 (46 measures); the new verse starts halfway through the "sample"	"I go to the halls and . . ."	Big Bank Hank
12:18	Verse 10 (42 measures)	"Well like Johnny Carson . . ."	Master Gee. During this verse, the song dissolves and fades out.

"Rapper's Delight" is unusual in many ways. The listening guide above breaks it down into verses according to who's rhyming, but an argument could be made that it's really two *very* long verses, interrupted only by the break in the middle. There's no real catchy hook or anything that would make this radio-friendly, especially given its extraordinary length.

While the verse lengths are indicated in measures above, another way to listen to the song involves listening for the phrase length, which in this case is four measures. When the bass line starts over again, four measures have passed. The texture of the music changes every two phrases. For two statements, it's just bass, piano, and percussion. For the next two, a funk/disco guitar and keyboard are added. This pattern continues throughout the song, adding a bit of variety to the backdrop.

The lyrics are very lighthearted, but they paved the way for much rap music to come. The rappers brag about partying, their possessions, and their sexual prowess. Many of the phrases were in common use by MCs in the South Bronx by this time: "hip hop," "and you don't stop," and "'til the break of dawn," for example. Most of the lyrics are in **common measure**, a poetic device that features alternating lines of eight and six syllables with rhymes at the end of the six-syllable lines:

Now what you hear is not a test (eight syllables)
I'm rappin' to the beat (six syllables)
And me, the groove, and my crew (eight syllables)
Are gonna try and move your feet (six syllables)

Perhaps the most important thing about "Rapper's Delight" is that it shifted the focus from the DJ (where it had been in the Bronx scene) to the MC, a change that ultimately transformed the entire genre.

While the status of "first rap record" may be up for debate, it's well-known that Kurtis Blow was the first rapper to sign with a major label. After getting his start with the DJs Grandmaster Flash and Joseph Simmons—then known as "Son of Kurtis Blow" and later as Reverend Run—he was signed to Mercury Records in 1980, thanks in large part to his savvy manager, the young Russell Simmons (Joseph's brother). Blow made a name for himself with the independent release "Christmas Rappin'" and followed up with the very successful single "The Breaks," which made it to number 5 on the R&B charts and became the first rap single certified gold (and only the second 12-inch gold single in history; the other was a Barbara Streisand/Donna Summer duet) by the Recording Industry Association of America (RIAA).

The RIAA

The Recording Industry Association of America (RIAA) certifies albums based on the number of units sold. The criteria vary for different formats (single, EP, LP, etc.), but generally speaking, "gold" certification means 500,000 units sold, "platinum" means one million sold, and "multi-platinum" means two million sold. The rare "diamond" certification is reserved for albums that sell more than ten million copies. At the time of this writing, OutKast, Eminem, MC Hammer, Tupac, and Biggie are the only rap artists to appear on the diamond certification list.

As popular music consumption moves more toward a streaming model, in which fewer and fewer people are paying for individual albums and/or songs, these numbers become harder to measure and, arguably, less meaningful. Rihanna's 2016 album *ANTI* was certified platinum within twenty-four hours despite selling very few copies: the album was first leaked and then officially made available for free on the streaming platform TIDAL (which was launched by Jay-Z in early 2015) to users who entered a download code. Close to 1.5 million copies were downloaded within the first twenty-four hours of the album's release, but very few of these were actually purchased by listeners: mobile-communications giant Sprint had bulk-purchased the album to enable the giveaway. In exchange, the company sponsored Rihanna's tour. In 2017, Kanye West's *Life of Pablo* became the first album to go platinum based on streams alone.

"The Breaks" is also important because it introduced hip hop to Europe. Producer J. B. Moore recalls: "When we finally got the deal at Mercury, it was because it was releasable in

England. The record was discovered by a newly arrived English A&R man in Los Angeles as a tape on his desk. [. . .] The record broke the Top 30 over there."[8] Journalist Nelson George offers further clarification, indicating that "his contract didn't come through the black department [at Mercury]." According to George, executives in charge of black music were actually skeptical about rap's potential for success.[9] Blow's full-length album, *Kurtis Blow*, was quite successful, breaking into the top 10 on the R&B charts (there were no rap charts at the time). Subsequent releases did not fare as well, although Run-D.M.C. covered his hit "Hard Times" and Nas recorded a version of "If I Ruled the World."

LISTENING GUIDE 6.2

Artist: Kurtis Blow
Song: "The Breaks"
Album: (single)
Record label: Mercury
Year released: 1980
DJ or Producer: J.B. Moore; Robert Ford Jr.
Samples used: (none)

TIME	MUSICAL CHARACTERISTICS	LYRICS	DESCRIPTION
0:00	Intro Clap accompaniment on beats 2 and 4	"Clap your hands, everybody . . ."	Listen for the "crowd" noise throughout: it functions almost like a laugh track on television.
0:09	Guitar starts (4 measures)		
0:17	Verse 1 (4 measures)	"Brakes on a bus . . ."	
0:25	Refrain (2 measures)	"These are the breaks . . ."	
0:29	Break (8 measures) Guitar drops out; bass line is featured		
0:47	Verse 2 (16 measures) + refrain + break (percussion feature)	"If your woman steps out with another man . . ."	Note the call and response (1 measure each)
1:42	Break continues (8 measures)	"Throw your hands up . . ."	Note the crowd interaction here.
2:00	Instrumental verse (8 measures)	"Break down!"	
2:17	Verse 3 (4 measures) + refrain + break (guitar feature)	"Breaks on a stage . . ."	
2:46	Break continues (8 measures)	"To the girl in brown . . ."	
3:04	Break continues: percussion solo for first 4 measures; rest of band joins for 12 measures	"Break down!"	
3:37	Verse 4 (4 measures) + refrain +	"Brakes on a plane . . ."	
3:52	Break (42 measures); keyboard solo		
5:20	Break continues (8 measures)	"Just do it . . ."	
5:36	Verse 5 (16 measures) + refrain + break (42 measures)	"Say last week you met the perfect guy . . ."	Call and response
	Fade out		

"The Breaks" represents an attempt to capture the live experience of rap music, thus the crowd noise throughout and the call-and-response sections. It's also noteworthy for the long break sections, which were intended for dancing. The shaded area above indicates that the smaller musical units—the verse, refrain, and break—combine to form larger, more significant units of structure.

Like many of the Sugar Hill recordings, the record uses a newly recorded background track played by a live band. The B-side of the record contains the instrumental tracks alone and is labeled the "do-it-yourself" version. The "do-it-yourself version" provided many aspiring rappers with the inspiration and material they needed to start honing their craft.

DEF JAM'S EARLY DAYS

The Sugar Hill Gang and Kurtis Blow may have paved the way for the first generation of rap recording artists; however, it was the fledgling label Def Jam that would solidify rap's place on the national stage. In 1984, Russell Simmons—Kurtis Blow's manager—went on to form Def Jam Records with Rick Rubin, a New York University student who was interested in this new genre of music. Def Jam's greatest accomplishment was helping rap cross over to a wider—mostly white—audience. Simmons and Rubin accomplished this in three main ways: by changing the sound of rap from the disco and funk of "Rapper's Delight" and "The Breaks" to a more hard-rock sound; by promoting the first all-white rap crew, The Beastie Boys; and by introducing the rap ballad through LL Cool J.

Russell Simmons

From his humble beginnings as Kurtis Blow's manager, Russell Simmons has emerged as one of hip hop's elder statesmen. Born in Queens, New York, Simmons partnered with Rick Rubin (see below) to start Def Jam Records. He also helmed Rush Management and at one time or another was responsible for the careers of artists as diverse as EPMD, DJ Jazzy Jeff & The Fresh Prince, Warren G, Slick Rick, and Wu-Tang's Method Man. Simmons had many interests outside of music as well: he was one of the founders of Phat Farm clothing; he coproduced a number of films, including Eddie Murphy's *Nutty Professor*; he launched HBO's *Def Comedy Jam* in 1991; and he became the driving force behind several philanthropic initiatives as well. More than just a manager, Simmons is, as Nelson George puts it, "an ambassador promoting hip hop culture to whoever wants to sample it" and a role model for the next generation of hip-hop entrepreneurs.[10]

While they never officially signed with Def Jam Records, Run-D.M.C. could be considered honorary members: they were managed by Russell Simmons, and many of their songs were produced by Rubin. The trio comprised Reverend Run (Joseph Simmons; Russell's brother), DMC (Darryl McDaniels), and their DJ Jam Master Jay (Jason Mizell). The group, which hailed from the middle-class neighborhood of Hollis, Queens, was responsible for many significant firsts in the rap world: they were the first group to appear on the cover of *Rolling Stone*, the first to land a high-profile endorsement deal (with Adidas), and the first artists to have a rap album certified platinum (1986's *Raising Hell*). Their tremendous success is a direct result of their crossover appeal. Run-D.M.C. frequently used rock samples (as opposed to funk) to build the backdrop for their raps, which drew the attention of white fans. The use of rock samples was not original to Run-D.M.C.: many classic break beats came from this repertoire (see Chapter 1). A glance at the titles of many of their hit songs reveals that they aligned themselves with the rock world: "King of Rock," "Can You Rock It Like This," and "Rock Box" (although it was not uncommon for MCs to talk about "rockin' the mic"). Their collaboration with rock veterans Aerosmith laid plain the merger of the two styles.

LISTENING GUIDE 6.3

Artist: Run-D.M.C. (feat. Aerosmith)
Song: "Walk This Way"
Album: *Raising Hell*
Record label: Profile
Year released: 1986
DJ or Producer: Jam Master Jay/Rick Rubin
Samples used: "Walk This Way," Aerosmith

Run-D.M.C.'s crossover single, "Walk This Way," features Aerosmith and helped Def Jam negotiate the divide between black and white audiences. At the time, Aerosmith—one of the most well-known rock-and-roll bands of the 1970s—was coming out of a rough patch: the band was on hiatus as its members were in and out of rehab for drugs and alcohol. By covering an Aerosmith classic, Run-D.M.C. helped relaunch Aerosmith's career, and Aerosmith's name recognition brought a new audience into contact with rap music. The video for "Walk This Way" illustrates the crossover strategy that Def Jam was aiming for. At the opening of the video, both groups are rehearsing in separate rooms: a wall divides the two and the cutaway fourth wall allows us to observe both groups at once. Aerosmith, on the left, is bathed in white light, while Run-D.M.C. is in the dark. Aerosmith's lead singer, Steven Tyler, becomes increasingly frustrated once he realizes that it's not his band performing their song, and he eventually breaks through the wall, just in time for the song's hook. The shot of him singing through the hole in the wall, bathed in the glow of white light, portrays him as the savior, bringing light to the dark world of hip hop.

The video transitions to what appears to be an Aerosmith concert: the live concert performance video was ubiquitous among heavy-metal acts around this time. The composition of the audience, visible in a few brief shots, seems to bear this out: it consists of mostly white teenagers. Run-D.M.C. appear on the scene (in their trademark Adidas sneakers with no laces) and join the band, at one point even teaching Tyler their dance moves. Near the very end of the video, a Run-D.M.C. sign descends, calling into question whose concert (and, more significantly, whose audience) we're actually seeing.

Rick Rubin

If Simmons was the business side of Def Jam, Rick Rubin was the musical mind behind the operation. Easily recognizable by his long beard, Rubin was a guitarist in a hardcore band who had a fondness for rap. Rubin brought his hard-rock sensibilities to bear on rap, encouraging artists to rely on standard song forms—a few verses with a hook instead of the sprawling, shapeless songs that characterized rap's old school—and to craft albums that were "full artistic statements."[11] During his tenure at Def Jam, Rubin also produced a thrash metal act, Slayer. He split with Def Jam in 1988 to form Def American, taking Slayer with him, and signing a number of other heavy-metal bands, the controversial comedian Andrew Dice Clay, Houston rappers Geto Boys, and Seattle's Sir Mix-A-Lot. Rubin continues to work as a producer, having branched out to work with acts as diverse as Johnny Cash, The Dixie Chicks, Metallica, The Red Hot Chili Peppers, and Adele.

The Beastie Boys were the first significant white rap crew and were, in effect, the mirror image of Run-D.M.C. Two of The Beastie Boys were members of a hardcore band before they evolved into a rap trio. MCA, Ad-Rock, and Mike D were three white kids from New York City whose rock-infused sound appealed to Rubin, who was also in a hardcore band at the time.

Rubin's roommate at New York University brought him their first single, an unusual track called "Cookie Puss" (named after a Carvel Ice Cream cake). The song features an unremarkable rap beat, but most of the "lyrics" consist of a prank call recording. The demo was indicative of the sense of humor that would pervade The Beastie Boys' debut album *Licensed to Ill* (1986; see Chapter 9 for a listening guide for "Paul Revere"). The album, a tongue-in-cheek send-up of the rock- and rap-star lifestyle, became the first rap album to top the *Billboard* album charts and was Def Jam's fastest-selling album to date. *Licensed to Ill* featured samples from hard-rock legends Led Zeppelin, Black Sabbath, and AC/DC. The Beastie Boys had a messy split with Def Jam in 1988. Their sophomore album, 1989's *Paul's Boutique* (on Capitol/EMI Records), is a landmark of sample-based hip hop.[12]

Ad-Rock brought a demo by a 17-year-old prodigy—James Todd Smith, better known as LL Cool J ("Ladies Love Cool James")—to the attention of Def Jam. LL had a wide range as an artist: he could battle with the best of them (and did, with Kool Moe Dee, Canibus, and Ice-T), spin gritty street tales, and be romantic, all within a single album. His 1985 debut, *Radio*, was Def Jam's first platinum album. *Bigger and Deffer* followed in 1987, and the pioneering rap ballad "I Need Love" became the first song to top *Billboard's* R&B charts. Love was not a common topic in rap music to this point: more often, artists bragged about their sexual escapades and avoided the emotional aspects.

LISTENING GUIDE 6.4

Artist: LL Cool J
Song: "I Need Love"
Album: *Bigger and Deffer*
Record label: Def Jam
Year released: 1987
DJ or Producer: LL Cool J, L.A. Posse
Samples used: "Zoraida's Heartbeat," Jayson Dyall

TIME	MUSICAL CHARACTERISTICS	LYRICS	DESCRIPTION
0:00	Solo keyboard melody (4 measures)		The Yamaha synthesizer plays long, single notes.
0:10	Verse 1: Vocals start; hi-hat added (4 measures)	"When I'm alone in my room . . ."	The thin musical texture—single synthesizer melody and hi-hat—signal tranquility and solitude. Note LL's hushed delivery of the text, in contrast to his usual aggressive style.
0:22	Verse 1 continues; keyboard plays chords under the original melody Fuller drum sound with snare, hand claps (16 measures)	"There I was . . ."	

TIME	MUSICAL CHARACTERISTICS	LYRICS	DESCRIPTION
1:05	Hook (8 measures) A different keyboard sound plays a descending figure to contrast with the new ascending figure in the original keyboard part	"I need love . . ."	
1:27	Verse 2: texture is the same as verse 1 (16 measures)	"Romance, sheer delight . . ."	
2:10	Hook (8 measures; musically, same as above)	"I need love . . ."	
2:32	Verse 3: texture is the same as first two verses (16 measures)	"I wanna kiss you . . ."	
3:15	Hook (8 measures; musically, same as above)	"I need love . . ."	
3:37	Verse 4: texture is the same as the first three verses (16 measures)	"See what I mean?"	
4:21	Hook (8 measures; musically, same as above)	"I need love . . ."	
4:43	Outro (8 measures) The musical texture thins out. The text here is spoken out of rhythm, not rapped.	"Girl, listen to me . . ."	This spoken text recalls the soul ballads of the 1970s by artists like Barry White and Isaac Hayes and paved the way for similar spoken (or rap) breaks on R&B tracks into the 1990s.
5:05	Outro continued (fade out) The texture is similar to that of the verses.		

LL's star eventually began to fall as a new wave of socially conscious artists began to emerge on the East Coast and as gangsta rap started to rise on the West Coast. As the major labels began to pursue rap artists more aggressively, Def Jam became part of PolyGram Records and is now part of Universal Music Group. With rap's white audience growing, the conditions were ripe for the next wave of commercialization, one that would have a lasting impact on the genre.

SOUNDSCAN AND THE RISE OF GANGSTA RAP

By the late 1980s, there was room on the airwaves for all kinds of rap: the political rhetoric of Public Enemy, the eccentric De La Soul, the family-friendly DJ Jazzy Jeff & The Fresh

Prince, and the empowering Queen Latifah. As the 1990s approached, hip hop's public image began to change. Hip hop's image in the media was predominately a safe, almost comedic one. At the top of the charts were artists like MC Hammer, Vanilla Ice, and DJ Jazzy Jeff & The Fresh Prince. Novelty acts like The Fat Boys covered songs that the previous generation grew up with, like "Wipeout," "Louie Louie," and "The Twist" (which featured Chubby Checker, the artist who popularized the original version of the song). MC Skat Kat was Paula Abdul's animated sidekick in her 1989 video for "Opposites Attract." The movie *Flashdance* (1983) was a box-office success that featured a break-dancing scene featuring the Rock Steady Crew. Inspired by that film's success, hip-hop films like *Breakin'* and *Beat Street*, both released in 1984, concocted fictitious stories around the lives of inner-city b-boys and b-girls.

Breakin' and *Beat Street*

Capitalizing on the success of the 1983 film *Flashdance*, Hollywood released two movies in the summer of 1984 that brought hip-hop culture to a wider audience: *Breakin'* (dir. Joel Silberg) and *Beat Street*. *Breakin'* tells the story of a young jazz dancer who becomes interested in break dancing and finds herself in the middle of a bitter rivalry between two hip-hop crews. The film features a young Ice-T in his acting debut. While *Breakin'* primarily features break dancing, *Beat Street* engages with all four elements of hip hop. Written by pioneering hip-hop journalist Steven Hager, the movie tells the stories of two brothers—a DJ and a b-boy—an aspiring MC, and a graffiti artist, as they chase their dreams in New York City. The movie features a who's who of early hip hop, including Afrika Bambaataa, Grandmaster Flash & The Furious Five, Kool Herc, The Rock Steady Crew, and The New York City Breakers. Even though Hollywood "cleaned up" hip-hop culture for both films, the films succeeded in exposing hip-hop culture to a broad audience.

Rap music came to television as well, in the form of *Yo! MTV Raps*, which premiered in 1988. Launched in 1981, MTV was one of the most heavily test-marketed television networks in history: their target audience was white suburban males between the ages of 12 and 34. In its early days, the network was criticized for showing videos by white artists almost exclusively—even Michael Jackson's videos were not in rotation until his record label threatened to pull all of their videos from the network. By 1988, the network could not ignore the popularity of hip hop among its target demographic, and *Yo! MTV Raps* premiered with a mix of videos, in-studio performances, and interviews. Similar shows on other networks followed suit. BET (Black Entertainment Television) had *106 and Park* as well as the late-night *BET Uncut*, which provided an outlet for increasingly graphic videos.

Hip-hop culture also began creeping into advertising. A McDonald's commercial featured Chicken McNuggets that rapped ("'cause we can't sing!'") and b-boyed ("We have this dance where we spin around/Get real dizzy then we all fall down") to a rock-inspired beat. The tone of the commercial recognizes the power of hip hop to influence young people while showing the older generation's disdain and dismissal of the culture in the guise of humor. Even the town of Bedrock—home to the Flintstones—could not escape the reach of rap. In a commercial for the cereal Fruity Pebbles, Barney Rubble, dressed like a member of Run-D.M.C., raps to trick Fred Flintstone out of his breakfast in 1989: "I'm the master rapper and I'm here to say/I love Fruity Pebbles in a major way." Both commercials reflect the image of Run-D.M.C., who helped bring rap music into the mainstream, as we saw earlier. Furthermore, the use of animation indicates that rap is now being used to market products to children. Rap's appearances in commercials like this began to dilute the socially conscious messages found in much of the music.

Rap's image underwent a change in the early 1990s, and several interdependent forces set this change in motion. The first was the rise of rap in locations outside of New York City (see Chapter 11). The second was an important shift in how record sales were tabulated. The third was a set of laws passed that altered the telecommunications landscape.

Billboard is a music-industry magazine that is best known for its sales charts. The charts tabulate sales of albums and singles across a variety of genres—there's a country chart, an R&B chart, a classical chart, and so on. *Billboard*'s "Hot 200" chart ranks the best-selling albums across all genres. Those in the industry carefully watch the charts to see what's popular, and they base many of their decisions on what the charts look like at any given time. Until about 1990, the rankings on the *Billboard* chart were calculated mostly by asking record-store owners what was selling well that week—more like an informal poll than a list based on "hard" data. Not surprisingly, the rankings were easily swayed: representatives from labels would frequently bribe those whom they talked to in order to get the answer that they wanted. To some extent, then, the *Billboard* charts reflected what the industry *wanted* to be selling. At the top of the charts in early 1991, for instance, were artists like Mariah Carey, Michael Bolton, Wilson Phillips, and Sting—artists who might be considered "adult contemporary." The only rap artists on the charts at that time were Vanilla Ice and MC Hammer, rappers whom many would consider more "pop" than "rap"; put another way, they were "safe" choices.

In 1989, *Billboard* held a meeting to discuss ways to improve sales tracking. The result of this meeting was SoundScan, a point-of-sale system that tallies each barcode scanned at the cash register. At the outset, this was a far more objective measure than the previous informal polling (although the industry soon figured out how to influence this system as well). Sound-Scan debuted in 1991, and when the initial tallies came in, the music industry was shaken up: the adult contemporary that had long dominated the charts was replaced by artists like Garth Brooks (country); Nirvana (grunge); Guns 'n' Roses and Metallica (heavy metal); and Ice Cube and Public Enemy (rap). These were all genres that had been grossly underrepresented in the previous charts. The new Hot 200 offered a more accurate picture of sales across *all* genres, not just pop. The industry had underestimated the sales figures for these other genres: they thought that rap had roughly a 6% share of the market, but once the figures came in, they saw that the figure was closer to 12%. While 12% still might not seem like a particularly large segment, recognizing that the market for rap was *twice* as big as they had thought motivated record companies to take action. Figure 6.1 shows the difference between the Top 10 albums across all genres for March 16 and November 16, 1991.

Not only did SoundScan yield more accurate sales data, but also it allowed the industry to track *where* certain records were selling. Most surprisingly, the data revealed that most rap music was being bought by suburban *white* youth (the target audience for most music sales), not the black youth to whom it was originally marketed. Moreover, the audience was very young, ranging from 11 to 13 years old. As radio programmer Glen Ford observed: "Early and pre-adolescents of both genders are sexual-socially underdeveloped—uncertain and afraid of the other gender. Tweens revel in honing their newfound skills in profanity; they love to curse. Males, especially, act out their anxieties about females through aggression and derision."[13] The arrival of gangsta rap at the top of the charts indicated that white America was interested in and willing to support this kind of music.

The new data also led to more intensive, localized marketing approaches, and the involvement of major record labels and media outlets allowed regional scenes to flourish as a result of the resources that those entities could mobilize: they could either sign up-and-coming local artists or buy small, independent labels outright. Music critic Nelson George wrote, "Rap's gone national and is in the process of going regional."[14] Rap's growing presence on

Pos.	Album	Artist	Pos.	Album	Artist
1	*Emotions*	Mariah Carey	1	*Ropin' the Wind*	Garth Brooks
2	*To the Extreme*	Vanilla Ice	2	*Death Certificate*	Ice Cube
3	*The Soul Cages*	Sting	3	*Too Legit to Quit*	MC Hammer
4	*Wilson Phillips*	Wilson Phillips	4	*Use Your Illusion II*	Guns 'n' Roses
5	*I'm Your Baby Tonight*	Whitney Houston	5	*Metallica*	Metallica
6	*Please Hammer, Don't Hurt 'Em*	MC Hammer	6	*Diamonds*	Prince and the N.P.G.
7	*Some People's Lives*	Bette Midler	7	*Use Your Illusion I*	Guns 'n' Roses
8	*Into the Light*	Gloria Estefan	8	*Emotions*	Mariah Carey
9	*Shake Your Money Maker*	The Black Crowes	9	*Nevermind*	Nirvana
10	*Gonna Make You Sweat*	C&C Music Factory	10	*Cooleyhighharmony*	Boyz II Men

Figure 6.1 Top 10 songs in the *Billboard* Hot 100 in March 16 vs. November 16, 1991

the national scene inspired artists in places other than New York and Los Angeles to begin writing and producing rap music that was inspired by their own unique situations. These new regional styles, in turn, were heard around the country and inspired the next generation of rap artists. Chapter 11 looks at the distinct characteristics of some of these regional styles.

The music industry was going through a period of rapid consolidation around this same time. Independent labels were thriving and, as a result, served as a kind of research and development laboratory for the major labels. SoundScan's data revealed that independent labels actually had a much larger share of the market than originally thought, and the major labels perceived this as a threat. When artists from an independent label began enjoying success, major labels would either rush to sign the artists (as happened with many of the grunge artists on Sub Pop around this time) or simply buy the independent label outright (as was the case with Def Jam's acquisition by Sony, then Polygram). By 2005, five companies controlled the vast majority of mainstream media outlets in the United States; at the time of this writing, that number has shrunk to three: Warner, Universal Music, and Sony. Universal Music, currently the largest of the three, is home to Capitol Records, Def Jam, Interscope Geffen A&M, Virgin, and Republic Records. Capitol Records oversees Priority Records, the label that launched N.W.A. in the late 1990s. Interscope is home to Aftermath Entertainment (founded by Dr. Dre), Shady Records (Eminem's label), and G-Unit Records. Republic Records is home to Cash Money, Lil Wayne's label. As Tricia Rose points out, rap beefs seem a little more tame and a lot more like a marketing ploy when you realize that the artists involved are employed by the same company.[15] These companies own more than just record labels: many of them are affiliated with television and online outlets (Warner has entered a partnership with the free music-streaming site SoundCloud; Universal owns video-streaming service VEVO; they hold stakes in audio-streaming apps like Spotify and Rdio and the music-recognition app Shazam). Universal's parent company, Vivendi, has a stake in NBC Universal, which is owned by cable-television and internet giant Comcast. Another media giant, Viacom, owns MTV, VH1, CMT, and BET and their subsidiaries (at one point, it owned CBS and its affiliates as well).

The Telecommunications Act of 1996 led to a further narrowing of what kind of music made its way to the airwaves. "The goal of this new law," according to the FCC, "is to let anyone enter any communications business—to let any communications business compete in any market against any other."[16] In effect, prior to the passage of this act, there was a limit to how many media outlets a given entity could own: a company could own only forty radio stations nationwide, for instance, and only two in any given market. The Act lifted this restriction entirely so that there was no limit to the number of media outlets a corporation could own. Advertising giant Clear Channel was a major beneficiary of this act: the company quickly went on to acquire nearly 1,300 radio stations in all formats—sports, news, pop, rap—across the country, allowing them to reach nearly a third of the US population. The company changed its name to iHeartMedia in 2014, to reflect its entry into the digital age, and launched the iHeart-Radio app, which allowed it to standardize streaming content among all of its stations.

There were several consequences to this massive consolidation: homogenization of content, a shift from the local to the national, and pressure on remaining small media outlets to conform. Nas' song "Hip Hop Is Dead" from the album of the same name (2006) bemoans the fact that "Everybody sound the same/Commercialize the game." Rose observes: "In the early 1990s, [. . .], programmers played popular songs an average of 40 times per week. By the end of the decade that number had jumped to 140 plays per week."[17] The end result of all these changes was that mainstream rap music became a commodity: a way to sell a very specific image of blackness to an audience of largely young, white, male consumers. The diversity and variety that had characterized rap to this point started to fade as gangsta rap ruled the airwaves. These forces also led to a shift away from hip-hop crews toward solo artists, who were easier to manage and promote.

THE UNDERGROUND

The commercial turn that rap took in the 1990s separated it from the communities that had created it and turned it into a commodity, something meant to be bought and sold. While this chapter in rap's history is often framed in terms of what the genre lost, commercialization also helped rap in some ways. Certainly an argument could be made that the music's newfound visibility was a net positive: rap music was now heard all over America via mainstream outlets. SoundScan's ability to measure not just what was being sold, but also *where* it was being sold, facilitated this growth. This flourishing of regional sounds and their subsequent appearance on the national stage led musicologist Adam Krims to suggest that the perception of homogenization as a consequence of commercialization is inaccurate.[18]

In response to the commercialization of hip hop, the early 1990s also saw the emergence of the hip-hop **underground**, in which artists sought to preserve the essence of hip hop by advancing it as an art form in the face of its increasing commercialization. "Underground" has several different connotations when talking about rap music. To some, it simply means noncommercial (that is, rapping for art's sake, not for financial gain) or independent (that is, without the resources of a major label, or signed to an independent label); to others, it is synonymous with socially conscious or message rap. Both ways of thinking share the common idea of freedom of expression: artists can make whatever kind of music about whatever subject they want without pressure from music industry insiders to sell records. It is important to note, though, that even those who rap for art's sake are subject to market forces, and it is also possible to be a mainstream rapper with socially conscious material.

James Peterson builds an elegant case for understanding the underground as a place where roots (and routes) are found. Imani Perry suggests that one interpretation of "keepin' it real" emerges in light of rap's commercialization: underground artists "keep it real" by staying true to the roots of hip hop.[19] This attitude is essentially nostalgic, with artists attempting to regain what they perceive was lost (and remains missing) from the commercialized form of the music. Underground artists Signify on mainstream rap, Peterson argues, performing the kind of critique from within that has always been a characteristic of rap. The perpetuation and evolution of Signifyin(g) is a valued attribute of underground rap. The very nature of the underground makes it difficult to generalize; thus we will examine two prominent groups that have been fixtures in the hip-hop community for almost two decades: the hip-hop collective Project Blowed and the record label Rhymesayers Entertainment.

"Rapper" vs. "MC"

Just as there is disagreement over the distinction between "rap" and "hip hop," fans of the music often make distinctions between MCs and rappers. William Jelani Cobb writes: "Every MC raps, but not every rapper is an MC. [. . .] The difference between a rapper and an MC is the difference between smooth jazz and John Coltrane, the difference between studio and unplugged."[20] According to Cobb (and many others), rappers are in the business for the fame and money; the MC is in it for love of the art. Cobb suggests that Nelly, P Diddy, and Master P are rappers, while Nas, KRS-One, and Lauryn Hill are MCs. The dividing line can be understood in terms of mainstream versus underground, or possibly old school versus new school. There are, however, artists that straddle the divide, earning mainstream commercial success while staying true to the art form: LL Cool J, Tupac, Biggie, Jay-Z, and Eminem are among them. Acknowledging the difference, Jay-Z raps in "Moment of Clarity": "If skills sold, truth be told/I'd probably be lyrically Talib Kweli/Truthfully I wanna rhyme like Common Sense/But I did [sold] five mil[lion], I ain't rhymed like Common since."

Project Blowed

In December 1989, the Good Life Café, a health-food store the Crenshaw neighborhood of Los Angeles, began hosting open-mic nights. One of the owners' sons, R.K. Blaze, was an aspiring rapper who asked his mother whether he and his friends could use the space after hours as a workshop to hone their skills. The workshop went by the name Underground Radio (in part because the local hip-hop radio station had recently gone off the air). Among the earliest participants were Aceyalone, Mikah 9, P.E.A.C.E., and Self-Jupiter, who would become known collectively as the Freestyle Fellowship.

In keeping with the values espoused by the health-food store, Blaze's mother B. Hall had one rule—no swearing. "The no-cussing policy wasn't about us being uptight church people," she said: "it was about wanting the atmosphere of a serious arts workshop. Most of the crowd respected the rule, some said it made rapping more challenging."[21] Freestyling was another important aspect of the Good Life scene: even those who wrote rhymes were expected to adapt them on the fly. All the artists involved sought to push the boundaries of what was possible in rap, delivering rapid-fire barrages of rhymes about esoteric topics over beats from a wide variety of genres. If a rapper got up on stage and couldn't move the crowd, he or she was met with chants of "Please pass the mic!" The Good Life scene provides a clear example of rap's self-critical apparatus at work. The prohibition on cursing, the emphasis on improvisation, and the role of the crowd are all ways in which those involved pushed against mainstream rap music. These aesthetics not only sought to recapture hip hop's "good old days," but also served to advance the genre.

The Good Life shows ended in 1997, but Project Blowed, a coalition of rappers who got their start at Good Life, began hosting an open-mic night on Thursday at KAOS studios. In addition to the members of the Freestyle Fellowship, the group included Abstract Rude (who would later sign with Rhymesayers), Busdriver, Ellay Khule (aka Rifleman), the members of Jurassic 5, Medusa, and many others. Some established rappers, such as Common, Fat Joe (who broke the rules and swore), Kurupt, and Ice Cube, also came through the open-mic night either to listen or to test their skills.

LISTENING GUIDE 6.5

Artist: Busdriver
Song: "Imaginary Places"
Album: *Temporary Forever*
Year released: 2002
DJ or Producer: Paris
Samples used: Johann Sebastian Bach's Badinerie from the third orchestral suite; Niccolo Paganini's caprice no. 5 for solo violin

TIME	FORM	LYRICS	NOTES
0:00	Intro (1 bar)		Repeated flute figure (L-s-s, L-s-s x4) Bass drum on beats 1, 2, 3 & 4 & The flute figure is "sampled" from Bach (although played live on this recording).
0:03	Verse 1 (4 bars)	"I'm just here to hold your hand . . ."	Busdriver's rapping largely matches the rhythm and pitch contour of the flute. The bass note marks the first beat of each measure.
0:15	(v. 1 continues; 2 bars)	"Cause I'm accused of lewd conduct . . ."	The flute figure changes, gradually ascending; the pitch of Busdriver's voice mimics it, getting higher and more excited.
0:22	Verse 2 (4 bars)	"I'm just here to hold your hand . . ."	
0:34	v. 2 continues (2 bars)	"I play dead songs on the silk screen. . .	Same as at 0:15
0:40	Verse 3 (4 bars)	"I'm just here to hold your hand . . ."	
0:52	v. 3 continues (2 bars)	"Twenty-four-hour surveillance . . ."	Same as at 0:15, but Busdriver's voice starts at a higher pitch.
0:58	Verse 4	"I'm just here to hold your hand . . ."	
1:11	v. 4 continues (2 bars)	"My name is Mr. Busdriver . . ."	Same as 0:15
1:16	Bridge		All the instruments in the previous verse drop out, and a few guitar chords take the inertia out of the music.

TIME	FORM	LYRICS	NOTES
1:21	Bridge cont'd (12 bars)	"Kids . . . if you want to piss off . . ."	Clarinet, drums and bass create a more relaxed feel; guitar chords. Busdriver can be heard humming along, somewhat out of time, in the background. The tempo here is only about 10 bpm slower than the previous one; the absence of the quick notes in the flute and the presence of the long notes in the clarinet create the illusion that it's much slower.
2:02	DJ solo (8 bars)		The texture again changes and the flute returns, this time sampling the Paganini. The DJ scratches in time with the rapid (but steady) rhythm of the flute and even tries to match its pitch. Busdriver can be heard in the background humming along with the flute. This functions like the guitar solo in heavy metal songs.
2:26	Like intro (0:00 above) Bach flute part returns	"Gotta do my shout-outs now . . ."	
2:29	Verse 5 (4 bars)	"I'm just here to hold your hand . . ."	"Shout-outs" are a common trope in rap, dating back to early rap radio shows during which DJs would call out names of listeners and artists.
2:41	Outro		The tempo is now twice as slow and gradually gets slower; this creates the illusion of the texture thinning.

This song samples two well-known pieces of classical music, one by Bach and one by the famous violinist Niccolo Paganini. The choice of classical music is significant because of what it connotes. Classical music is typically regarded as the music of old, rich, white people: it suggests a listener who occupies a certain social status—think of how often classical music appears in advertisements for luxury items. Using classical music in this song might suggest that Busdriver's performance deserves to be considered high art, that it conveys a particular status to the listener. Conversely, we could make an argument that Busdriver is trying to bring classical music to a new audience. More broadly, perhaps Busdriver is encouraging listeners to question any kind of distinction between "high art" (classical, European, wealthy) and "low art" (popular, non-white, working-class).[22]

Lyrically, the song could be understood as a tongue-in-cheek critique of organized religion—specifically Christianity—and the kinds of promises it makes. Lyrics aside, this song is all about **virtuosity**; that is, demonstrating a very high level of skill. Busdriver achieves a remarkable feat in this song: he is able to keep up with the rapid flute melody, rapping in virtually the same rhythm at the same fast tempo, and even matching (to some extent) the pitch inflection of the flute. In the song's break, DJ Paris scratches in rhythm with the Paganini excerpt while Busdriver hums along. It's uncommon for rappers to synchronize their lyrics so closely with the beat as Busdriver does, which suggests that he chose to do so to make a point.

Backpack rap is often synonymous with underground rap, in which the focus is on lyrical craft. Backpack rappers tend to avoid topics that are common in mainstream commercial rap, such as money and expensive cars; in fact, many say that the "backpack" is a component of the style because these rappers lack the material wealth of their mainstream counterparts and must rely on walking and public transportation to get from place to place. Also, backpacks are used for carrying books; thus "backpack" may symbolize the intelligence of rappers in this style. The term is associated with artists like Kanye West, Joey Bada$$, Hopsin, and other mostly college-educated rappers.

Rhymesayers

On its website, Minneapolis-based label Rhymesayers draws a parallel between the struggle that birthed hip hop in the 1970s and the challenges that aspiring rap artists faced in light of the major-label takeover of rap in the 1990s. The label grew out of the Headshots crew, with producer Anthony "Ant" Davis, rappers Sean "Slug" Daley and Musab Saad, and CEO Brent "Siddiq" Sayers joining forces to launch the label in 1995. Both Slug and Siddiq worked at record stores in the Twin Cities, which not only helped them become known in the local music scene but also afforded them a behind-the-scenes look at the record industry. Their experiences led them to open Fifth Element, a record store in Minneapolis dedicated to Rhymesayers and other local artists. The store was staffed by artists and hosted open-mic nights.

Because they lacked the support of radio and television, Rhymesayers artists had to build their fan base through grueling tour schedules. "We were definitely some of the first to independently build a following out of touring," said Slug. "We built those followings hand-to-hand by hitting small cities and going back to them twice a year."[23]

LISTENING GUIDE 6.6

Artist: Eyedea and Abilities
Song: "Now"
Album: *E&A*
Year released: 2004
DJ or Producer: Abilities
Samples used: OutKast, "B.O.B."; Dead Prez, "It's Bigger Than Hip Hop (Remix)"

This song is widely credited as one of the best songs released on the Rhymesayers label. Both MC Eyedea and DJ Abilities honed their craft in battle: Eyedea won the "triple crown" of MC freestyle contests—Scribble Jam (1999), Blaze Battle, and the Rock Steady Battle (both 2000)—and Abilities holds three DMC titles. Tragically, Eyedea died of a drug overdose in 2010 at the age of 28.

Questions:

1. In what ways does this song Signify on mainstream rap?
2. In a *Complex* magazine article, Slug praised this particular song, claiming: "That's what they did best, matching old school values with new school vision."[24] How does this song exemplify "old school values?" What might the duo's "new school vision" include?
3. Around the 2:00 mark, Abilities starts scratching a sample from Dead Prez's song "It's Bigger Than Hip Hop"—"Sick of the same old thing. . . ." Why do you think he may have chosen this particular sample? Does his scratching affect our interpretation of it?
4. Compare and contrast this song with Busdriver's "Imaginary Places."

CROSSING OVER

The crossover success of Run-D.M.C. and The Beastie Boys was not the first example of rap commingling with other genres, nor would it be the last. Properly speaking, the term "crossover" was first used to talk about songs that started life on one of *Billboard*'s "genre" charts (R&B, country, gospel, etc.) but eventually crossed over to the Hot 100 chart, which ranks the most popular singles across all genres. Musicologist David Brackett suggests that a chart like the Hot 100 "centers" music by defining a mainstream, while the genre charts marginalize styles by keeping them outside of that mainstream; thus, a move from one of the genre charts to the Hot 100 signals a broader acceptance of that style. This also points to the shifting identities of both "mainstream" and "popular" as categories.[25] Colloquially, the term "crossover" describes music that blends elements of two or more otherwise distinct genres. Justin Williams' work on borrowing provides a useful framework for talking about how music from one or more genres is borrowed into another genre.

In Chapter 2 of his book, Williams examines the influence of jazz on hip-hop culture from 1989 to 1993 in the context of a renewed interest in jazz in popular culture generally. In order to examine the ways in which jazz manifests itself in rap songs, Williams lays out a set of jazz **codes**; that is, sonic and visual elements that are understood as unique identifiers of a particular style or genre. Among the jazz codes Williams discusses are acoustic (upright) bass lines, saxophone, muted trumpet, and jazz guitar sounds.[26] These codes extend to the visual realm too: the video for Digable Planets' 1992 single "The Rebirth of Slick (Cool Like Dat)" is shot in black and white in what appears to be a speakeasy. The artists are backed by a jazz combo and dressed as we might expect jazz performers in the 1940s to have dressed. In some sense, these codes are akin to the idea of "sonic signatures" (presented in Chapter 1) in that they are considered by most to be the defining characteristics of the genre—they essentialize it. As with sonic signatures, though, the identity of these codes is often not apparent until they appear as borrowings.

Earlier in his book, Williams outlines six borrowing strategies that hip-hop artists use. While Williams intends these strategies to illuminate how rap pulls in materials from other styles, or how newer rap music draws on (or refers to) older rap, the strategies prove equally valuable for exploring how hip-hop culture is borrowed into other genres. Figure 6.2 lays out these six strategies, provides examples, and offers ways in which they manifest in both sonic and visual texts.

	Definition/Examples	Found In
A. Image	Break dancing, graffiti, turntables, live battles, fashion, urban space	Music videos, cover art, CD booklets, live performance
B. Sampling and borrowing	Using "classic" break beats (e.g., "Apache," "The Big Beat"); scratching and other vinyl sounds	Musical Signifyin(g) in hip-hop beats
C. Peer references	Referencing rappers, historically important DJs, break-dancing crews	Lyrical content
D. Verbal quotation	Allosonic and autosonic quotations from hip-hop films and recordings	Lyrical content
E. Stylistic allusion	Imitating earlier styles of rap music, or the flow of a particular artist without direct quotation Using older technological equipment (such as the Roland TR-808 drum machine)	Either (or both) beat or flow
F. Nostalgia	Often based on art vs. commerce "Back in the day" as pure, peaceful, fun, more creative, uncorrupted	Lyrical content, though nostalgia can be a sentiment demonstrated by all types of borrowing

Figure 6.2 Justin Williams' borrowing strategies

An **allosonic** quotation incorporates previous material by rerecording it or performing it live, like in jazz performance of a standard. An **autosonic** reference quotes previous material by means of digital or analog sampling. The examples below elaborate on how these borrowings occur.

In the early 1980s, Fab 5 Freddy was making connections between hip-hop artists in the outer boroughs and movers and shakers in the downtown arts scene (these meetings are lightly fictionalized in *Wild Style*), which included new-wave acts like Blondie. Blondie's 1981 song "Rapture" was one of the first crossover songs to achieve widespread airplay: it was the first song that featured rap to reach number 1 on the *Billboard* Hot 100, and a case could be made that it was the first rap video that MTV ever aired. Deborah Harry, the lead singer, sings the first half of the song and raps most of the second half over a funk beat played by the band. The rhythmically spoken text over the funk beat (combined with the almost obsessive repetition in the rap) could both be considered **stylistic allusion**. In her rap, Harry mentions both Fab 5 Freddy and Grandmaster Flash, a case of **peer reference**. Freddy and graffiti artist Lee Quinones have cameos in the video, and Flash was supposed to appear but didn't show and was replaced with graffiti artist Jean-Michel Basquiat. The images of DJs and graffiti in an outdoor, urban environment connected the uptown aesthetic of hip hop with the downtown aesthetic of new wave. These borrowed elements, taken together, comprise a set of codes—albeit an incomplete one (there's no b-boying)—for early hip-hop culture.

What "Rapture" did for MCing, Herbie Hancock's 1983 song "Rockit" did for DJing. Hancock, a well-known jazz-fusion keyboard player, enlisted Grandmixer D.ST to scratch throughout the song. The surreal video played regularly on MTV, and Hancock, D.ST, and the rest of the band performed the song live at the Grammy Awards in 1984 (the song won a Grammy that year for Best R&B Instrumental Performance). "Rockit" marked the mainstream debut of the turntable *as an instrument*, and having Hancock's name on the project legitimized its use (as Katz notes, the progressive nature of the collaboration was beneficial for Hancock as well). The song consists largely of a sequenced drum track, programmed on the Oberheim DMX, a repeated keyboard figure played by Hancock, and D.ST's scratching. Hancock's use of turntables in the song comprises several of the borrowing strategies above: the image of the turntable appearing on stage with the jazz group reinforces its status as an instrument, not merely a playback device. Grandmixer D.ST's performance can also be understood as sampling or stylistic allusion.

Heavy metal also made fast friends with rap: both genres appealed to essentially the same demographic, so this should not be surprising. While much heavy-metal activity was centered in Los Angeles and the Bay Area, Anthrax was one of the few heavy-metal bands that called New York City home. The members of Anthrax admired rap music and released an original parody rap, "I'm the Man," in 1987. Later, they would go on to collaborate with Public Enemy on a version of "Bring the Noise" (see Chapter 1). Chuck D was initially skeptical of the idea but realized that such a project would highlight the similarities of the two genres. The collaboration basically consists of Anthrax playing an "instrumental" version of the Bomb Squad's production on the song; members of Anthrax also rap on the track. The performance as a whole could be considered an allosonic quotation of Public Enemy's song by Anthrax: while it doesn't digitally sample the song, the band makes an effort to recreate the sound and energy of the original. Their strategy suggests, perhaps, that sampling itself is not a code, but the resultant sound—the "hip-hop sublime"—is. Since both genres are typically criticized as "noisy," the crossover seems almost natural. The song appeared on albums by both bands—Public Enemy's *Apocalypse '91: The Enemy Strikes Black* and Anthrax's *Attack of the Killer B's* (both from 1991)—and the two groups ended up touring together. The collaboration paved the way for new styles of music like nu-metal and rapcore. These bands—bands like Korn, Limp Bizkit, and Rage against the Machine—have roots in the instrumental styles of heavy metal and grunge, but the vocal delivery tends toward rap, and, in some cases, the music incorporates turntablism and sampling. Ice-T's hardcore band, Body Count, sparked a national controversy in 1992 with the song "Cop Killer" (see Chapter 12).

In the 2000s, rap-country hybrids started to appear. St. Louis rapper Nelly teamed up with country artist Tim McGraw to record the single "Over and Over" in 2004; it appeared on Nelly's fourth album, *Suit*. Other country-rap collaborations include "Cruise" by Florida Georgia Line featuring Nelly (see below), "Save a Horse (Ride a Cowboy)" by Big and Rich, and the poorly conceived "Accidental Racist" by Brad Paisley featuring LL Cool J. All three songs reflect how homogenized popular music has become not just within a genre, but *across* genres too. Many of the themes that people associate with commercial rap music have close parallels in mainstream country music: misogyny, materialism (cars in rap music; pickup trucks in country music), violence, and substance abuse (drugs in rap music; beer in country music).[27] Both genres are closely tied to a particular location: country is associated with rural America—the South in particular—and rap is associated with urban America, especially the coasts. Sales figures reflect a slightly different reality: most country music is bought in urban areas, places like New York and Los Angeles (which is maybe not surprising, given their status as population centers), while most rap music is bought by white suburbanites.

LISTENING GUIDE 6.7

Artist: Florida Georgia Line (feat. Nelly)
Song: "Cruise (Remix)"
Album: *This Is How We Roll*
Record label: Big Loud Mountain/Republic Nashville
Year released: 2013
DJ or Producer: Joey Moi; Jason Nevins

The original version of this song is often held up as an archetype of "bro-country," a hybrid style that blends country music with elements of rock and rap. It became the best-selling digital country single in 2014, and the remix peaked at number 4 on the Hot 100 chart in late 2013.

Listen to the song, watch the video, and answer the questions below.

1. What *lyrical* elements or themes are borrowed from rap?
2. What *musical* codes are borrowed from rap?
3. What *visual* codes are borrowed from rap?
4. What themes in this song are shared by both rap and country?

While hip-hop producers have included a variety of classical music in their productions (see, for instance, Nas's "I Can" and Puff Daddy's "I'll Be Missing You"), the classical-music world has been reluctant to assimilate rap music into its sphere. This is in large part due to classical music's reliance on music of the past: people attend concerts to hear music from hundreds of years ago, and they tend to shun contemporary works. Many of the conventions of classical music are at odds with conventions of rap music: the reliance on sheet music, live instruments and performance (as opposed to recordings), concert etiquette, and the like. In 2014, the Seattle Symphony accompanied local rap legend Sir Mix-A-Lot in a performance of his hit "Baby Got Back." Before the song starts, Mix-A-Lot warns the audience that "what I want to do now is something you really should not do," signaling his awareness that he's about to violate some of classical music's conventions. He invites "some of the ladies" in the audience to join him on stage. Breaking the "fourth wall" like this—inviting audience members to the stage—is virtually unheard of in classical concerts. While the performers and audience members are clearly enjoying themselves, the classical music-world at large was outraged, largely as a result of the clashing of codes.

Examining borrowing strategies in these crossover works helps illuminate what many listeners consider to be the stylistic markers of rap. Furthermore, the changes in *what* is borrowed highlight shifts in the public perception of what constitutes rap. Turntables were replaced by sampling and electronics; images of graffiti were replaced by luxury cars and objectified women.

OUTRO

Names you should know:

- The Sugar Hill Gang/Sugar Hill Records
- Lady B
- Kurtis Blow
- Def Jam
- Run-D.M.C.
- Russell Simmons

- Rick Rubin
- The Beastie Boys
- LL Cool J

- Project Blowed
- Rhymesayers

Terms you should know:

- Commercialization
- Commodification
- Common measure
- B-side
- SoundScan

- Underground
- Backpack rap
- Virtuosity
- Codes
- Autosonic vs. allosonic quotations

Questions for discussion/writing prompts:

1. Listen to a recording of "Personality Jock" by King Tim III & The Fatback Band. How is it similar to or different from "Rapper's Delight?" Why, do you think, did it not achieve the same popularity?

2. A number of songs criticize the commercial turn that rap took (see below for some examples). Choose one of these songs, and examine the music and lyrics in terms of the material in this chapter.

3. Find a record label and research it. When and where was it started? Who are some artists that are (or were) on the label? Is it an independent label or a subsidiary of a larger label?

Additional listening/viewing:

Sugar Hill:

- "Monster Jam," Spoonie Gee meets The Sequence
- "That's the Joint," Funky Four + 1
- "Showdown," The Furious Five meets The Sugar Hill Gang

Def Jam:

- Schultz, Michael. *Krush Groove*. Burbank, CA: Warner Home Video, 1985.
- *Raising Hell*, Run-D.M.C.
- *Licensed to Ill*, Beastie Boys
- "I Can't Live without My Radio," "Rock the Bells," "Mama Said Knock You Out," and "Around the Way Girl," LL Cool J

Pop rap:

- *Please Hammer Don't Hurt 'Em*, MC Hammer
- "Ice Ice Baby," Vanilla Ice
- "Wild Thing," Tone Lōc
- "Parent's Just Don't Understand," DJ Jazzy Jeff & The Fresh Prince

Songs critical of pop rap:

- "Check the Rhime," A Tribe Called Quest
- "The Rape Over," Mos Def
- "It's Bigger Than Hip Hop," Dead Prez
- "Hip Hop Is Dead," Nas

NOTES

1 S. Craig Watkins, *Hip Hop Matters: Politics, Pop Culture, and the Struggle for the Soul of a Movement* (Boston: Beacon Press, 2005), 10.
2 Jim Fricke, *Yes Yes Y'all: The Experience Music Project Oral History of Hip-Hop's First Decade*. Ed. Charlie Ahearn and Experience Music Project (Cambridge, MA: Da Capo Press, 2002), 188–9.
3 Watkins 17.
4 Fricke 185.
5 Watkins 17.
6 Fricke 182.
7 Loren Kajikawa, *Sounding Race in Rap Songs* (Berkeley: University of California Press, 2015).
8 Fricke 193.
9 Nelson George, *Hip Hop America* (New York: Viking, 1998), 59.
10 George 83–5.
11 George 66.
12 See Amanda Sewell, "*Paul's Boutique* and *Fear of a Black Planet*: Digital Sampling and Musical Style in Hip Hop" *Journal of the Society for American Music* 8 no. 1 (February 2014): 28–48.
13 Cited in Tricia Rose, *The Hip Hop Wars* (New York: BasicCivitas, 2008), 16.
14 George 131.
15 Rose, *Hip Hop*, 18.
16 Federal Communications Commission, "Telecommunications Act of 1996," 2013. www.fcc.gov/general/telecommunications-act-1996.
17 Rose, *Hip Hop*, 87.
18 Adam Krims, *Music and Urban Geography* (New York: Routledge, 2007), 98–9.
19 James Peterson, *Hip Hop Underground and African-American Culture* (London: Palgrave Macmillan, 2014), 34; Imani Perry, *Prophets of the Hood* (Durham, NC: Duke University Press, 2005), chapter 7.
20 William Jelani Cobb, *To the Break of Dawn: A Freestyle on the Hip Hop Aesthetic* (New York: New York University Press, 2007), 8.
21 Brendan Mullen, "Down for the Good Life" *LA Weekly* (June 21, 2000): www.laweekly.com/music/down-for-the-good-life-2132192.
22 Williams makes similar arguments about the relationship between jazz and rap in his chapter 2: see Justin Williams, *Rhymin' and Stealin': Musical Borrowing in Hip-Hop* (Ann Arbor: University of Michigan Press, 2013).
23 Andres Tardio, "Rhymesayers: An Oral History of the Indie Rap Empire" *MTV News* (December 4, 2015): www.mtv.com/news/2616582/rhymesayers-20th-anniversary-oral-history-atmosphere.
24 Chaz Kangas, "Slug Talks Complex's 25 Best Rhymesayers Songs" *Complex* (May 2, 2011): www.complex.com/music/2011/05/best-rhymesayers-songs/sunshine.
25 David Brackett, "What a Difference a Name Makes: Two Instances of African-American Music," in *The Cultural Study of Music*. Ed. Martin Clayton, Trevor Herbert, and Richard Middleton (New York: Routledge, 2003), 241.
26 Williams 54.
27 It could be argued that this perceived difference between the two genres goes back to the early marketing of hillbilly and race records in the 1940s. The lyrical content and musical structure of both styles often had more in common than not: the musician's race was typically the only dividing line.

TIME LINE

1989 Queen Latifah releases her debut album, *All Hail the Queen*.

1991 Salt-N-Pepa release *Blacks' Magic*.

2000 50 Cent is shot nine times outside of his grandmother's house in Queens.

2012 Frank Ocean reveals that he had a romantic relationship with a man.

—Macklemore and Ryan Lewis release "Same Love" in support of marriage equality in their home state of Washington.

2014 Le1f performs "Wut" on *The Late Show with David Letterman*.

IN THIS CHAPTER, YOU WILL LEARN ABOUT

- Mainstream rap's commodification of gender and sexuality
- The dialogic relationship between masculine and feminine
- Hip hop's relation to queer culture

CHAPTER 7

Listening to Gender and Sexuality

OVERVIEW

In addition to what we might call the "purely musical" aspects of rap, particular facets of the culture have also been commodified. Among these, black gender stereotypes are perhaps the most prominent. In this book, we will understand gender as a set of practices—a performance—governed by cultural norms. As such, it is typically distinguished from sex, which is biologically determined. Prior to the 1990s, hip hop had space for diverse representations of masculine and feminine. As the major labels gained more and more control over rap music, gender in hip hop became more narrowly defined, with **heteronormativity** and **hypermasculinity** becoming the point of reference for any other expressions of gender. "Heteronormative" means that male and female are the only two genders and that heterosexuality is the normalized way to express sexuality. "Hypermasculinity" is an exaggerated display of qualities typically considered masculine: strength, aggression, and violence, for instance.

As we saw in Chapter 5, women played an important role in the early days of hip hop. They rapped about many of the same topics as their male counterparts, but through a woman's perspective. Tricia Rose writes that beyond these shared concerns, female rappers also have to address sexual politics in a way that men do not.[1] To fully understand how gender plays out in hip hop, we need to consider that gender in hip hop is both **dialogic** and **intersectional**. That is, gender performance emerges as interactions take place both within and across gender roles. Intersectionality acknowledges that individuals can be subjected to multiple forms of oppression, such as racism and sexism.

MANY MEN

Masculinity in rap music has changed considerably from the early days of gangsta rap to the present. Gangsta rap's first-person tales of robbery, drug-dealing, killing, and sex also showcase the environment that gave birth to the street economy: the 'hood or the ghetto.[2] Songs like Ice-T's "6 in The Mornin'" and "Addicted to Danger," N.W.A.'s "Dope Man," and Cypress Hill's "Locotes" highlight the dangers of living in south-central Los Angeles. "6 in The Mornin'" showcases all the players in the street economy: outlaw, gambler, gangster, and pimp; "Midnight" describes in vivid detail an unprovoked attack on Ice-T and his crew; and "Addicted to Danger" chronicles a drug deal gone bad as the result of a double-cross. "Dope Man" illustrates the dangers present on all sides of the drug trade. "Locotes" ends abruptly with the death of the protagonist. These cautionary tales did not glamorize the streets; rather, they were an effort to raise awareness of the conditions that many who live in low-income areas face. Behind the violence, these songs present men as vulnerable victims of circumstance, acting in their own defense. These themes were quickly and easily twisted into narratives of aggression, fearlessness, and domination once gangsta rap went mainstream in the 1990s.

The commodification of rap music that took place in the 1990s coincided with the ascendency of both gangsta rap (Ice-T and N.W.A.) and black nationalist rap (Public Enemy, X-Clan), which resulted in a mainstreamed image of black masculinity characterized by strength, aggression, violence, and misogyny.[3] **Hypermasculinity** is the exaggerated performance of these behaviors—typically understood as male—that we see in much mainstream rap music, and it is often described as an effort to reclaim masculinity, to dismiss the vulnerability. bell hooks argues that black men are subject to the "feminizing gaze" of white patriarchy, an observation that illuminates the intersection of race and gender. Given the ways in which men, most typically those of lower socioeconomic status, have been deprived of their ability to provide—lack of available employment, education, or money, perhaps as the result of incarceration—they often fall back on their instinct to protect.

Images of black hypermasculinity have a long history—dating from slavery, to the 1910s (when it was believed cocaine not only made black men murderous and expert marksmen, but also made them impervious to bullets), to later professional sports. They persist into the present, where the gangsta, pimp, and hustler stereotypes prevail in mainstream rap music, and songs like 50 Cent's "Many Men"—in which he recounts being shot nine times and surviving—echo claims made nearly a century ago.

LISTENING GUIDE 7.1

Artist: 50 Cent
Song: "Many Men (Wish Death)"
Album: *Get Rich or Die Tryin'*
Record label: Shady/Aftermath/Interscope
Year released: 2003
DJ or Producer: Darrell "Digga" Branch, Eminem, and Luis Resto
Samples used: "Out of the Picture," Tavares

The song starts with a short skit that recreates the scene of 50 Cent's 2000 shooting. The skit positions the song as a true story, a claim that is reinforced by other details in the lyrics: 50 was an amateur boxer and compares himself to Muhammad Ali in the first verse (although Ali comparisons are not uncommon in rap), and he also recounts his days as a drug dealer, a profession he entered when he was barely a teenager. The authenticity of this narrative makes the masculine stereotypes easier to accept as true.

The hook, which follows the skit (0:18), outlines the two themes of the song: potential and resilience. 50 Cent is well known for crafting catchy hooks, and it is important to note that he *sings* this hook. Rapping is coded as masculine, particularly in contrast to the R&B sound that dominated the charts in the 1980s as rap grew in popularity. Lord Jamar of Brand Nubian said that it was a way to "sing without singing" and "write poetry without being a poet, like a soft poet." Sister Souljah praised rap for "bringing back strong male voices."[4] 50 believes that he survived the shooting incident because he still has work to do: "I'm tryin' to be what I'm destined to be" (0:24). The metaphor of the diamond in the rough (0:59) supports this theme as well. At the end of the third verse, 50 rhymes, "Now it's clear that I'm here for a real reason/'Cause he got hit like I got hit, but he ain't fuckin' breathin'." 50 survived an attack that would have killed an "ordinary" (or perhaps a "lesser") man, and his survival marks him as special.[5]

The resilience theme emerges from the intersection of victimization ("Niggas tryin' to take my life away") and hypermasculinity, a "the-best-defense-is-a-good-offense" strategy. Because vulnerability is associated with weakness, 50 has to overcompensate through his aggressiveness. The first verse is full of hypermasculine posturing: he feminizes his foes by calling them "pussies" (0:54) and touts his skill with knives (1:14; "ox" is slang for knife) and guns. In the second verse, he draws comparisons between himself and other strong male figures: the mobster Paulie from the movie *Goodfellas* (2:16) and Malcolm X (2:20; "By any means" refers to a famous line in a speech of Malcolm's).

In a profile for *Rolling Stone*, Touré wrote that after the shooting 50 Cent began working out almost obsessively, sculpting the muscular body that has appeared on many album and magazine covers. 50 Cent is often seen posing shirtless, revealing his physique and tattooed body, or in a bulletproof vest, all of which reinforce the hypermasculine "cool pose." Nonetheless, the attack left permanent damage, most noticeably to his mouth:

> There was now a large, squarish hole through the left side of his lower jaw and a piece of bullet left in his tongue. He'd lost a bottom tooth and a U-shaped chunk of his gums, but his lazy tongue and the hole in his jaw gave him a slur like no one in hip-hop. "There's a different sound now when I talk, 'cause of the air around the tooth," 50 says. "Gettin' shot just totally fixed my instrument."[6]

The changes to his speech are an audible reminder of 50 Cent's ordeal, one that pervades his output since 2000.

Despite the deep-seated misogyny that characterizes much rap music, many rappers have very strong relationships with their mothers. This is not surprising, given the matriarchal nature of the African-American family, a theme that we will explore in more depth in Chapter 12. What is surprising is the willingness of rappers to express these kinds of emotions publicly in a genre of music that rejects displays of male sensitivity, associating them with women and weakness. bell hooks argues that black masculinity is rooted in the body and the cultural meanings inscribed in it by the "imperialist white-supremacist capitalist patriarchy" (her way of articulating hegemony). The body is strong, charged with physical labor, hypersexualized, and violent. The emphasis on the body comes at the expense of the mind and spirit: men in general are taught to repress their emotions. This "cool pose"—looking physically tough and downplaying any emotions that might be perceived as weak—has been widely discussed in studies of black masculinity: it's often presented as a mechanism to compensate for the power that has been denied black men by society. It is precisely this cool pose that has become commodified as an integral component of rap music.[7] Drake, in particular, has faced criticism on this front. A self-proclaimed "nice guy" who has made a career rapping about the emotional component of relationships, he has been called "a fuckin' piece of shit" by DMX and "a straight pussy" by Lil' Kim; Chris Brown encouraged him to come out of the closet.[8] Challenging Drake's sexuality represents an effort to feminize him, a topic that we will explore in more detail below.

Many rappers have penned songs to their mothers: Jay-Z's affection for his mother comes through in "December 4th" (see Chapter 2); OutKast's "Ms. Jackson" pays homage to mothers-in-law; Kanye's "Hey Mama" expresses his devotion to his mother (whose unexpected death in 2007 affected him deeply), and J. Cole's "Apparently" asks his mother for forgiveness. Tupac's "Dear Mama" is perhaps the most well-known love letter in this realm, and it embodies both sides of what hooks talks about in terms of black masculinity. Released while Tupac was in prison, the song garnered numerous accolades: not only was it a platinum-seller and *Billboard*-chart topper, it earned Tupac a Grammy nomination and later became only the fourth rap record to be added to the Library of Congress' National Recording Registry ("Rapper's Delight," "The Message," and Public Enemy's "Fight the Power" were the first three).

LISTENING GUIDE 7.2

Artist: Tupac Shakur
Song: "Dear Mama"
Album: *Me against the World*
Record label: Amaru/Interscope/Jive
Year released: 1995
DJ or Producer: Tony Pizarro
Samples used: "In All My Wildest Dreams," Joe Sample; "Sadie," The Spinners

Set against a down-tempo R&B beat, Tupac's song takes the form of a letter to his mother—it is an example of an epistolary song (see Chapter 2). The lyrics demonstrate an unconditional love that flows both ways: despite their flaws and the hardships that both of them encountered, their love for one another remained constant. Tupac's mother, Afeni Shakur, was deeply involved with the Black Panther Party for Self-Defense, and while her activism and radical politics certainly influenced her son's worldview, they also made the family's life challenging: she was pregnant with Tupac when she was incarcerated as a member of the "Panther 21" (more on this in Chapter 10). Tupac recounts her struggles with crack cocaine: "And even as a crack fiend, Mama/You always was a black queen, Mama," he rhymes in the first verse (0:57). The reference to "black queen" resonates with the "queen mother" figure (who we will encounter later), a nurturing caregiver. To some extent, Tupac's mother (and many others in similar situations) is fulfilling both the stereotypically masculine roles of provider, protector, and disciplinarian and the stereotypically feminine role of caregiver.

Tupac also acknowledges his own tribulations and admires his mother for always being there for him, working long hours, coming home and cooking for the family, and making "miracles for Thanksgiving." Just as Tupac's mother negotiated masculine and feminine roles, we could argue that Tupac is exploring two different roles in this song as well. He talks about his run-ins with the law and his (brief) career selling drugs as a way to earn money—common black male stereotypes—but he also relates that he and his half-sister shared tears (0:28), that he was "huggin' on my mama from a jail cell" (0:42) and that he is generally grateful for her sacrifices. Such a display of feelings and emotions contrasts with what society says it means to "be a man."

Eminem is an important exception here: his strong negative feelings toward his mother are the subject of songs like "Cleaning Out My Closet." This could be interpreted as another way that Eminem articulates his difference from black culture—through the harsh, vocal rejection of his mother. She even sued him for defamation at one point, asking for $10 million in damages (she was awarded $1,600). In stark contrast to these feelings, Eminem's love for his daughter Hailie is apparent in tracks like "Hailie's Song," and she even lent her voice to "My Dad's Gone Crazy." Being a devoted father also diverges from the black masculinities found in mainstream rap. Many rappers are quick to dismiss their "baby mamas" or to encourage abortions after unprotected intercourse: the so-called "Plan B" pill figures prominently in recent songs like Lil Uzi Vert's "Safe House" and Migos' "Plan B." Both scenarios absolve the man of any responsibility and shift that responsibility onto the woman.

SISTAS WITH ATTITUDE

Prior to about 1994, rap allowed for more diverse representations of women. In conversation with musicologist Cheryl Keyes, MC Lyte describes three distinct eras of female MCs: "Sha-Rock, Sequence [discussed in Chapter 5], that to me is the first crew. Then you've got a second crew, which is Salt-N-Pepa, Roxanne Shanté, The Real Roxanne, me, Latifah, [Monie] Love, and Yo-Yo. Then after that you got Da Brat, Foxy Brown, Lil' Kim, Heather B."[9] Keyes proposes four strategies of empowerment that female rappers use to gain entry into the overwhelmingly male arena: the **Queen Mother**, **Fly Girl**, **Sista with Attitude**, and **Lesbian**.[10] The first three of these strategies have strong ties to historical stereotypes of black women, the Mammy, Jezebel, and Sapphire. As rappers reclaim and revise these stereotypes, they work to diminish their negative power. This can create a fine line between empowerment—liberation from the stereotypes—and reinforcement of them.

Around the time that MC Lyte's third crew rose to popularity—roughly 1994—the number of female rap artists declined sharply. From 2003 (Lil' Kim's *La Bella Mafia*) to 2010 (Nicki Minaj's *Pink Friday*), no albums by female MCs were certified platinum. Awards shows dropped categories specific to female artists, and the number of women signed to major labels dropped from forty in the 1990s to three in 2010.[11] The disappearance of female MCs was accompanied by a shift in representation as women in rap began to lose agency and came to be defined solely in terms of heteronormative hypermasculinity as subjects of the male gaze. Put more simply, women no longer had much say in how they were represented in rap. Increasingly, women were forced to perform in masculine roles in order to get a "way in" to mainstream rap. Keyes' categories need to take into account the ways in which they emerge from dialogue with masculinities (which could also be essentialized into the gangsta, pimp, and hustler figures presented in Chapter 2).

Sistas with attitude use defiance as their empowerment strategy: they can be frank, arrogant, and aggressive—qualities typically associated with men. The category emerges from the Sapphire stereotype, which casts black women as loud and angry. Many who adopt this approach have reclaimed the words "bitch" (and "ho"), "using it to entertain or provide cathartic release," while others take issue with any use of the term.[12] As anthropologist Jason Haugen observes, it can be difficult to tell when an artist is using the term as one of solidarity or domination because some artists switch quickly between meanings.[13] As a term of domination, the word is also divisive: Tricia Rose devotes a chapter of *The Hip Hop Wars* to dismantling the oft-repeated defense that using the word "bitch" is acceptable because "There are bitches and hos." Given the sexualized—in some cases, borderline pornographic—nature of the lyrics and images associated with these rappers, many would say such a claim is easy to substantiate. Rose argues that for a male rapper to say "'I am not referring to all black women when I use these terms' (which suggests that *some* women are 'bitches and hos') is sexist name-calling that normalizes sexism for all women, especially black women."[14] Efforts to reclaim the word keep it and its many contested meanings in circulation.

Keyes lists quite a few female MCs who are members of well-known (largely male) hip-hop crews, like Roxanne Shanté (The Juice Crew), Eve (DMX's Ruff Riders), and Lil' Kim (Junior M.A.F.I.A. and Bad Boy Records). These crews function as sponsors on some level, with the female members behaving like "just one of the guys." Some of the artists also use the word "nigga" fraternally to refer to themselves and members of their crew. In addition to the baggage already attached to this word, its use by female MCs is noteworthy because it is often gendered masculine when used as a term of solidarity. Imani Perry writes that many early female hip-hop artists were able to make inroads into the genre by "occupying styles of presentation and archetypal roles coded as male."[15] Citing the prominence of the "bad-man" archetype throughout black culture, Perry refers to these artists as "female badmen." She describes badmen as being perceived both as a hero and as a threat, existing outside the law, and basing much of their identity on the ability to exert control over the female body: hip hop's hustler, pimp, and playa archetypes all stem from the badman image.[16] Taking the position of "female badman" thus affords opportunities to critique the overwhelmingly mas-culine nature of the genre.[17] Adopting lyrical themes of violence enables these women to spar with their male peers, choose "violence over victimization" by asserting control over their own bodies (or, perhaps, control over male bodies), express anger (which is typically coded male), and present instability (which is often repressed in the role of nurturing caregiver).[18]

LISTENING GUIDE 7.3

Artist: Lil' Kim (feat. The Notorious B.I.G.)
Song: "Queen Bitch"
Album: *Hard Core*
Record label: Undeas/Big Beat/Atlantic
Year released: 1996
DJ or Producer: Carlos "6 July" Broady, Nashiem Myrick
Samples used: "Hey, That's No Way to Say Goodbye," Roberta Flack

Lil' Kim's tone of voice is deep, authoritative, and direct, all qualities associated with masculinity. The aggressive posture that she takes is not new: female MCs have engaged in battle raps from the begin-ning (recall the "Roxanne Wars" from Chapter 5). She often refers to herself as "Queen Bitch," and this song outlines the reasons she claims that title. In this case, she uses the word in the sense of dom-inance and power, which is clarified with the addition of "Queen." In the first verse, she connects the word "bitch" with a number of assertive adjectives: "Queen bitch, supreme bitch/Kill a nigga for my nigga by any means bitch/Murder-scene bitch/Clean bitch, disease-free bitch." These lines highlight her dominating personality, her willingness to commit violence ("by any means" is likely a reference to a line from a Malcolm X speech, in which he said the black community would secure their rights "by any means necessary"), and her control over her body. Throughout the song, she refers to her male friends as "niggas," reinforcing her membership in the men's club. Kim invokes fellow Brooklyn rapper Notorious B.I.G.'s name early in the song, and he contributes a few lines in the second verse. She also shouts out their crew, Junior M.A.F.I.A., in the first verse. Given that this song appeared on Kim's debut album, it is not surprising that Biggie appears as a "sponsor," providing his seal of approval.

She adopts what might be considered a very masculine "pimp" stance in terms of her sexuality. The line "Got buffoons eatin' my pussy while I watch cartoons" implies that men—whom she values only for their ability to give her sexual gratification—are giving her pleasure but she pays them no mind. In the second verse, she relates her ability to give men erections and refers to male-stripper act The Chippendales (who could also be interpreted as bodies in the service of female pleasure). Furthermore, she does not rely on men to provide for her: she buys or takes by force what she wants. She shops for designer goods, makes her own money, and will "stick [up] your moms for her stocks and bonds."

Haugen proposes that we disengage the content and presentation strategies from gender: rather than labeling these "masculine" traits, we should think of them as elements of a gangsta aesthetic shared by men and women.[19] Decoupling these lyrical themes from gender associations could pave the way for breaking down the strong gender binary in hip hop.

"bitch" and "ho" are used in rap to refer not only to women, but to men as well. In an interview with *Playboy* magazine, Ludacris asks: "How can you say I'm degrading women, when I call myself a ho? I'm degrading myself! Look at me. I'm rich and successful and degrading the hell out of myself. [. . .] Rappers may degrade women, but we degrade men, too, so that pretty much cancels itself out."[20] Using the word in this context adds another layer to the problem. Not only does it emasculate the man to whom it refers, but it reinforces the stereotype of women as weak or untrustworthy. Rose claims that arguments like Ludacris' do not hold up, because the only way the word can work as an insult is if it is already attached negatively to women.[21] The emasculation of black men throughout history makes the use of these terms even more damaging. This emasculation has led to repeated attempts to reclaim masculinity, and rap music represents yet another effort to that end.

Considering a pair of related songs—one by Sir Mix-A-Lot and one by Nicki Minaj— reveals some of the ways in which gender is constructed dialogically.

LISTENING GUIDE 7.4

Artist: Sir Mix-A-Lot
Song: "Baby Got Back"
Album: *Mack Daddy*
Record label: Def American
Year released: 1991
DJ or Producer: Rick Rubin, Sir Mix-A-Lot
Samples used: "Technicolor," Channel One

Artist: Nicki Minaj
Song: "Anaconda"
Album: *The Pinkprint*
Record label: Young Money/Cash Money/Republic Records
Year released: 2014
DJ or Producer: Polow da Don, Da Internz
Samples used: "Baby Got Back," Sir Mix-A-Lot

Sir Mix-A-Lot's "Baby Got Back" opens with a woman saying: "Oh my God, Becky! Look at her butt. It is so big. She looks like one of those rap guys' girlfriends." The woman has a thick "valley girl" accent, which sonically identifies her as white. The way the line is delivered implies a conversation with another white friend, and a black woman perhaps just out of earshot, an image that the music video confirms. This opening highlights differing perspectives of female beauty and is followed by Mix-A-Lot proclaiming, "I like big butts and I cannot lie." The video features women's backsides prominently, ultimately casting them as objects of male desire.[22]

Nearly twenty years later, Nicki Minaj's "Anaconda" takes the beat from Mix-A-Lot's song and samples two lines as well: the opening "Oh my gosh . . ." and "My anaconda don't want none unless you got buns, hon[ey]."[23] In the song, Minaj boasts about her power over men, referring to them as "boy toys" and talking about the expensive things they buy in exchange for sex. The men waiting in line for her are effectively disposable, and the repetition of the hook ("By the way, what'd he say/He can tell I ain't missin' no meals . . .") implies that her encounters with each of them are interchangeable. The video features women of diverse of body types and critiques Hollywood's ideal image of female beauty ("Fuck them skinny bitches") but, like Mix-A-Lot's song and video, could ultimately be read as women's complicity in the projection of such images, as rendered through the male gaze.

When Minaj's video failed to receive a nomination for Video of the Year at the 2016 MTV Video Music Awards, Minaj took to Twitter and accused the industry of bias toward one specific body type (or, against diverse body types), namely a thin, white image of femininity, embodied that year by Taylor Swift, who was nominated for her video "Bad Blood." Swift assumed Minaj was referring to her, and the two exchanged tweets over the next few days. An article in the *Guardian* notes that in the course of the conversation, Minaj had been cast as "the angry black woman," the Sapphire. The article asserts that even the photos chosen by news outlets to report on the coverage reinforced the stereotype. What many failed to see was the intersectionality at work in this argument: Minaj was calling attention to racism in the music industry, which Swift and many others misinterpreted as sexism.[24]

The relationship between Mix-A-Lot's and Minaj's songs is dialogic: Mix-A-Lot's beat and lyrics figure prominently in Minaj's track, and both celebrate voluptuous women, but from different points of view. Ultimately, both songs and videos toe the same line between cultural critique and objectification.

As rap became more and more mainstream, masculinity moved to the forefront and women were relegated to serving as little more than "props" in videos: they did not speak (or rap) and were simply there to boost the male ego. Imani Perry writes that rappers use women not only to create an "imaginative patriarchy," but also as an "expression of wealth and sexual power in the face of racialized economic powerlessness."[25] Many argue that if the women voluntarily participate in the video shoots—whether they are compensated or not—then there is no harm done. Tricia Rose writes that, whereas men can earn money as gangstas, pimps, and hustlers, sex is the only "street economy" readily available to women.[26] Psychologist Carolyn West writes that this exploitation typically follows one of six "scripts": Diva, Gold Digger, Freak, Gangster Bitch, Baby Mama, and Earth Mother. In each case, the woman is defined by sexual transactions. The Diva trades sex for wealth and social standing; the Gold Digger trades sex for basic needs like groceries and rent; the Freak is interested in only her own sexual pleasure; the Gangster Bitch brags about her sexual conquests; the Baby Mama uses her child as leverage against the father; and the Earth Mother "exudes a more subtle sexuality," resembling Keyes' Queen Mother category. Carolyn West contends that the incessant reproduction of these scripts causes lasting harm to young girls who try to emulate what they see.[27]

Videos like the one for Nelly's "Tip Drill" are emblematic of this trend. The song, which includes the lines "It must be your ass because it ain't your face," and "It ain't no fun unless we all get some," is accompanied by a music video that features Nelly and his crew showering dozens of scantily clad women with money, gazing at them, and touching them. The most notorious scene appears near the end of the video: having run out of money to throw around, Nelly swipes his credit card down a woman's backside. This scene was the subject of a good deal of public debate, and it ultimately came back to haunt him. Nelly had a sister who suffered from leukemia (she passed away in 2005) and he started a foundation that tested prospective bone-marrow donors (not just for his sister). In 2004, when Nelly wanted to bring his bone-marrow drive to Spelman College in Atlanta, the women of Spelman told Nelly's representatives that they would host the drive if Nelly agreed to talk about the representation of women in his music. Nelly refused; the women of Spelman—believing both issues to be important—organized their own bone-marrow drive. William Jelani Cobb summarized the situation for Byron Hurt: "It's like saying 'just shut up and give me your bone marrow.'"[28]

Despite the rampant misogyny, women continue to listen to and support rap music. Many writers, like Michelle Wallace, have described their relationship with hip hop as an abusive one. In "Confessions of a Hip Hop Critic," journalist dream hampton described the disconnect she felt in having to defend misogynist rap artists from critics.[29] As Mark Anthony Neal and others have observed, black women will often jump to defend black men from criticism even when the actions of those men are hurtful to them, because they believe that the good of black culture as a whole is more important than their own individual welfare.[30] Rose contends that in many cases, those who criticize hip hop's sexism often cast it as an attack on the black men who propagate such images, rather than addressing the sexism and objectification at the core of the debate.[31]

FLY GIRLS AND QUEEN MOTHERS

The **Fly Girl** is characterized by her fashion sensibility and eroticism, which Keyes suggests has roots in the so-called blaxploitation films of the 1970s (*Dolemite*, *Shaft*, *Superfly*, and *Foxy Brown*, for instance). Fly Girls typically wear clothes that accentuate their figures; Keyes argues that foregrounding sexuality in this way is a political act, because it "calls attention to aspects of black women's bodies that are considered undesirable by mainstream standards of American beauty."[32] It does, however, run the risk of reducing women to sex objects: to paraphrase Rose, there is a fine line between explicit and exploitative.[33] A double standard also applies to women who flaunt their sexuality in hip hop: promiscuous women are often denigrated as hos, while a man with multiple sexual partners is praised as a pimp or playa. The Fly Girl grows out of the Jezebel, which stereotypes black women as promiscuous and always desiring sex. According to West, this stereotype has historically been used to justify acts of sexual aggression and violence toward black women.[34]

The Fly Girl's display of sexuality is tied to a strong sense of individuality; the two manifest in themes of *responsible* sex. TLC, for instance, often adorned their clothes with condoms: one member of the group, Left Eye, emphasized her nickname by wearing a condom over her left eye. Songs like TLC's "Waterfalls" (1994) and Salt-N-Pepa's "Let's Talk about Sex" (see below) deal with these themes musically; the latter was even turned into a public-service announcement that addressed facts and rumors about AIDS, a disease that had a profound impact on the black community. The ability to deny men sex remains one of the strongest forms of power that women have over men, and it runs as a theme through rap songs as early as "Roxanne's Revenge" (see Chapter 5). Tricia Rose points to the line "Never trust a big butt and a smile" from Bell Biv DeVoe's hit "Poison" as emblematic of the kind of power that women wield over men.[35]

LISTENING GUIDE 7.5

Artist: Salt-N-Pepa
Song: "Let's Talk about Sex"
Album: *Blacks' Magic*
Record label: FFRR Music
Year released: 1991
DJ or Producer: Hurby Luv Bug
Samples used: "I'll Take You There," The Staples Singers

Salt-N-Pepa's "Let's Talk about Sex" exemplifies Tricia Rose's claim that "explicit is not always exploitative."[36] Salt-N-Pepa talk frankly about the perils and pleasures of sex—"how it is and how it could be"—from a woman's point of view. Throughout the song and the video, they acknowledge the contradictions that female artists face: the song even begins with a hesitation: "I don't think we should talk about this [. . .] People might misunderstand . . ." The theme of censorship pervades both the song and the video, subtly framing the explicit/exploitative distinction as a function of gender: an exploitative song by a male artist has a better chance of making it on the radio (or television) than an explicit song by a female artist. The second verse deals with the emotional aspects of sex, describing a woman who uses sex to get what she wants from men, but, despite the gifts, feels unfulfilled. The third verse encourages condom use by making the point that birth-control pills cannot prevent sexually transmitted infections. Both scenarios are quite explicit, albeit in a very different way from the typical lyrics of male artists.

The video includes a wide variety of representations of both men and women. Salt-N-Pepa appear first in form-fitting black dresses, and later in baggy New Jack–style outfits. In a few scenes, they "cross-dress" as construction workers, catcalling at the men who walk by. Men in the video appear as background dancers (a role usually reserved for women). Images of children hint at one of the many "good things and the bad things that could be."

Salt-N-Pepa is one of the few groups with a female DJ, Spinderella. Female MCs are rare, but female DJs and producers are even more scarce. Both Rose and Mark Katz highlight this imbalance, noting that, in general, women are not encouraged to pursue technology and that the informal environment in which these skills are passed on and developed is often male-dominated, making it difficult for women to gain entry and acceptance.[37] The physical strength required to move turntable rigs and dozens of crates of records is also cited as a barrier to female engagement in DJing, at least in the early years of hip hop: Katz observes that, if the physical aspects were really limiting, then the shift to digital (CDs and mp3s) has opened more space for female DJs. He writes that female DJs are subject to the same biases that their MC counterparts face: "when they're not invisible, they're too visible"—either they are not taken seriously, or they are judged solely on their looks.[38]

Despite the independent streak, it has been (and remains) challenging for female MCs to enter mainstream hip hop in any capacity. Too often—likely as a result of deep-seated stereotypes—female MCs are accused of sleeping their way to success (or are encouraged to do so behind the scenes). Nicki Minaj confronts her critics with their assumptions about her success in the opening lines of her song "Only": "I never fucked [Lil] Wayne, I never fucked Drake/All my life, fuck's sake." (As founder of Young Money Records, Lil Wayne was responsible for signing Minaj and is credited with launching her career.) Furthermore, female rappers are more likely to be accused of having male ghostwriters (that is, having a man write the lyrics that they perform). Many of Salt-N-Pepa's early hits—including "Let's Talk about Sex"—were written by their producer, Hurby Luv Bug.

The **Queen Mother** figure is descended from the Mammy stereotype. The Mammy often assumes the role of caretaker, most often for the children of the white parents that employ her, and often at the expense of caring for her own children. In her role as mother figure, the Mammy is asexual. She is often portrayed as full-figured, and her appearance is downplayed through her conservative dress and the bandana that typically adorns her head, hiding her hair. West writes that the Mammy's appearance reinforces white notions of beauty, mainly through opposition; that is, the Mammy image comprises everything that white men have been socialized *not* to find beautiful.[39]

In hip hop, Queen Mother figures tend to embody an Afrocentric aesthetic, which is conveyed not only by the topics they rap about but also in the way they dress: their clothing often reflects images of African royalty. The embrace of Afrocentrism is one of the strategies that rappers use to upend the Mammy stereotype: here, the object of care is history and roots. Many of these rappers were associated with the Zulu Nation and the Native Tongues collective (see below), and some had ties to the Five-Percent Nation (see Chapter 8). Queen Mothers are seen as nurturing leaders: their songs feature themes of female and community empowerment, and they command respect from their listeners by virtue of their maturity and intelligence.

Native Tongues

The Native Tongues collective, which came together in the late 1980s, continued the spirit of Afrika Bambaataa's Zulu Nation. Comprising De La Soul, A Tribe Called Quest, and Jungle Brothers (which included an MC named Afrika Baby Bam), the group later expanded to include Queen Latifah, Monie Love, Black Sheep, Black Star (Mos Def and Talib Kweli), Common, and Leaders of the New School. Their aesthetic is most clear on De La Soul's *3 Feet High and Rising* (1989), ATCQ's *People's Instinctive Travels and the Paths of Rhythm* (1990), and Jungle Brothers' *Straight Out the Jungle* (1988). The Jungle Brothers' album was released a few months before N.W.A.'s similarly titled *Straight Outta Compton*, but the musical stylings could not be more different. Inspired in part by New York City's vibrant jazz scene, much of the Native Tongues' music is characterized by eclectic sampling with an emphasis on jazz sounds. Lyrically, the music covered a wide variety of topics ranging from the bohemian to the socially conscious, all with strong roots in Afrocentrism.

LISTENING GUIDE 7.6

Artist: Queen Latifah (feat. Monie Love)
Song: "Ladies First"
Album: *All Hail the Queen*
Record label: Tommy Boy
Year released: 1989
DJ or Producer: DJ Mark the 45 King
Samples used: "Listen to the Music," King Errisson; "Daisy Lady," 7th Wonder

Queen Latifah is a clear example of Keyes' Queen Mother, as demonstrated by the lyrics and video for her song "Ladies First." The video begins with images of historically significant black women: Harriet Tubman, Madame C. J. Walker, Sojourner Truth, Angela Davis, and Winnie Mandela. These images situate Latifah as part of a long tradition of politically active black women. Both Latifah and Monie Love, a British rapper who is featured on the song, boast about their lyrical skills while reminding listeners that "A woman can bear you, break you, take you" (0:22).

The video includes women of different body types and skin tones, highlighting diversity and critiquing social constructions of beauty. At times, two "fly girls" flank the artists, dancing, while Latifah and Love present themselves as powerful through their Afrocentric dress, posture, and lyrical abilities. Latifah in particular assumes a leadership role—the queen—as she moves what look like large chess pieces across a map of South Africa. Images of that country's apartheid struggle—a system of enforced racial segregation that stretched from about 1948 until Nelson Mandela's election in 1994—permeate the video. As Robin Roberts contends, Latifah's song and video highlight the intersection of racism and sexism through the use of apartheid imagery. Roberts notes the power of music video to combine multiple texts—in this case, feminist lyrics and images of racism—to create a more complex message.[40] That Latifah is addressing not only sexism but also racism is emblematic of the community caregiver role ascribed to Queen Mothers.

Often, when hip hop is personified, rappers portray it as a Queen Mother figure: it is nurturing and loving, and it cares about the community. In "Hip Hop Is Dead," Nas refers to hip hop as "his first wifey"; Common constructs hip hop as a woman throughout "I Used to Love H.E.R." (see Chapter 5). In many of these songs, the once-caring Queen Mother devolves into the stereotype of the "ho" as rap becomes increasingly commercialized. Rap has thus lost its caring nature, becoming an object of male desire and pleasure, no longer deserving of respect.

SAME LOVE?

One damaging consequence of the heteronormative hypermasculinity that dominates mainstream hip hop is the homophobia that emerges from it. Homophobia has a long history in hip hop, stretching back to songs like "Rapper's Delight" ("I said he's a fairy, I do suppose/ Flying through the air in pantyhose") and "The Message" ("Spend the next two years as an undercover fag"). Cheney links rap's homophobia to the male-dominated world of black nationalist groups like the Nation of Islam and the Five-Percent Nation, who suggested that a woman's primary role was procreation for the advancement of the race. This heteronormativity is, of course, not unique to black culture: it can be traced back to the patriarchal Christian beliefs upon which the United States was founded.[41] As Perry notes, when female artists refuse to behave as sex objects, or when they behave in ways traditionally coded masculine, they face charges of lesbianism.[42] Just as "bitch" and "ho" are problematic, particularly when they refer to a man, so are homosexual slurs like "fag" and "homo." The same problem arises: when used as an insult, the word implies that queer people are somehow weak and inferior to heterosexuals. "No homo" became a popular refrain in hip-hop culture as a way of distancing oneself from any claim that might be perceived as a sign of homosexual desire. Lil Wayne's hit "Lollipop" begins with the phrase, serving as a disclaimer for the rest of the song.

Tim'm, a member of the pioneering queer HomoHop crew Deep Dickollective, suggests that, while the pioneering work of contemporary queer artists is important, the culture needs "a reexamination of how we've imagined hip-hop in ways that have de-emphasized and discounted Queer presence." He observes that most questions about homosexuality in rap are addressed to MCs, not to DJs, graffiti artists, or others. Furthermore, pioneering graffiti artists Jean-Michel Basquiat and Keith Haring were both gay, and hip hop's roots in disco link it very directly with queer culture.[43] Even today, mainstream hip hop has a strong undercurrent of homoeroticism that often goes unremarked. Images of shirtless male rappers covered in tattoos, oiled up and showing off their physiques, with their pants sagging low, are very erotic: as Tim'm tells Byron Hurt, "It's not only women looking at those images."[44]

The sagging pants come from prison culture, where they indicate which role someone plays in male-on-male sex. Nelson George notes that "the committing of homosexual acts behind bars is rarely commented on." He continues: "Because they often occur through rape or psychological coercion they are not viewed as acts of sexual orientation but as manifestations of control and domination, both reflections consistent with a 'gangsta mental' or gangster mentality. If sex is taken, from this viewpoint, it is not an act of love but power."[45] Songs like Ice Cube's "No Vaseline," a diss track aimed at his former N.W.A. bandmates and their manager, Jerry Heller, emphasizes both the power and pain dynamics of this kind of sex act: " 'Cause you're getting fucked out [of] your green/By a white man with no Vaseline." The metaphor of Heller—the white man—as a pimp persists through the song, which feminizes the members of N.W.A. Cheney writes that the song succeeds because there is no talk of male gratification, only the brutality of the act.[46] Descriptions of male-on-male prison sex appear in raps written by those who have served time, such as Mac Dre and Beanie Sigel.

> **HomoHop** was a style of hip hop that emerged in the Bay Area in the early 1990s, comprising a group of queer artists who openly challenged hip hop's homophobia. Rainbow Flava pioneered the style; Tori Fixx, Deep Dickollective, and God-des and She were among the other acts associated with it.

While images of lesbian eroticism (as constructed through a heteronormative male lens) are common in videos by male artists, those same artists are often quick to distance themselves from male homosexuality. 50 Cent said that he chose to avoid gay people because "he was uncomfortable with their thoughts," implying that gay men have different thoughts than straight men (or women). Claims such as this also imply that queer rappers would be inclined to rap only about "queer topics," which is not the case. Le1f is rather dismissive of a "gay rap" category: in an interview with Alex Frank for *Fader*, he said: "I am gay, and I'm proud to be called a gay rapper, but it's not gay rap. That's not a genre. My goal is always to make songs that a gay dude or a straight dude can listen to and just think, This dude has swag. I get guys the way straight rappers get girls."[47]

Keyes cites Queen Pen as a pioneer in the **Lesbian** rap category, noting that rap music in general tends toward homophobia and that the intersectionality of race and sexuality is relatively new ground to break. That Keyes can only name one rapper that fits this category is telling. Given the relative paucity of female rappers, those brave enough to identify as lesbian—a claim which could open them up to criticism on racial, gender, and sexuality fronts—remain comparatively rare. In an interview with the *New York Times*, Pen said: "I'm black. I'm a female rapper. I couldn't even go out of my way to pick up a new form of discrimination."[48] Pen is widely credited as being the first to bring up homosexuality in a rap song, her 1997 single "Girlfriend," and many commentators were not surprised that it was a woman, not a man, who addressed it first.

Some fifteen years later, in 2012, Macklemore and Ryan Lewis released "Same Love" in support of Referendum 74, an initiative that would legalize same-sex marriage in the state of Washington. Macklemore's sudden rise to fame has not been without its critics: his status as a rapper has been challenged on the basis of his skin color, the "popular appeal" of his songs, and his willingness to tackle subject matter that is often considered taboo in the realm of hip hop. He is acutely aware of these contradictions, as he has made clear in his music and in interviews. "Same Love" was championed by many for bringing the issue of same-sex marriage front and center and for beginning to dismantle the wall of hip hop's homophobia; however, criticism emerged on two fronts. Those who do not consider Macklemore to be part of the hip-hop community were quick to distance themselves from him because of his skin color and pop sound. Many in the queer community—particularly the growing community of queer rappers—were critical of Macklemore (who is straight) succeeding on the basis of his privilege (white-, cis-, and hetero-). Rather than use his platform to elevate queer voices in hip hop, Macklemore spoke *for* them. As intersectionality is a theme of this chapter, it is worth noting that race tends to trump sexuality, as it does with gender as well. Tim'm and Juba agree that the black gay community has little in common with—or interest in mingling with—the white gay community.[49]

Macklemore's song was released around the same time that Frank Ocean, in a letter posted on his website, publicly acknowledged that his first love was a man.[50] The post queered Ocean's sexuality, suggesting the possibility of other sexual preferences. While not a rapper per se, Ocean is well known in the hip-hop community: he was a member of the Odd Future collective, and he contributed hooks to a number of well-known songs, including two tracks on the Jay-Z/Kanye collaboration *Watch the Throne* (2011). The hip-hop community at large was supportive of his announcement, with artists like Jay-Z, fellow Odd Future member Tyler the Creator (who would later ignite debates about his own sexuality), and even mogul Russell Simmons expressing their admiration. Snoop Dogg (who was going by "Snoop Lion" at the time) was quick to qualify the announcement, noting in an interview with the *Guardian* that Ocean "ain't no rapper. He's a singer."[51] Mark Anthony Neal argues that former president Obama's very public performance of black masculinity, "thoughtful, adaptable, and even progressive (if we consider the stance on same-sex marriage) has given many male rap artists the cover to explore the nuances of their manhood." Following Obama's endorsement of gay marriage, many rappers—Jay-Z, T.I., Ice Cube, Snoop Lion, and Kendrick Lamar—voiced their support for the policy.[52]

In the last decade or so, another underground queer rap movement, this time centered in New York City, has begun to gain strength. Artists like Mykki Blanco, Zebra Katz, Le1f, Cakes Da Killa, and Azealia Banks all identify as queer, and their music and videos often reflect their identities. Le1f's song "Wut" dropped a few weeks after Ocean posted his letter, and it became a viral sensation. The timing led some widely read sites (*Bossip* and *World Star Hip-Hop*) and critics to suggest a connection between the events, as though Ocean had opened the floodgates: *World Star*'s headline read: "This Is What Happens When Rappers Start Admitting Their Gay? Hip-Hop Artist Le1f—Wut."

LISTENING GUIDE 7.7

Artist: Le1f
Song: "Wut"
Album: *Dark York*
Record label: Greedhead, Camp & Street
Year released: 2012
DJ or Producer: 5kinAndBone5
Samples used: (none)

Le1f's hit "Wut" is an infectious dance track that articulates aspects of queer culture chiefly through its beat, imagery, and language choices. The beat has a strong dance-club feel to it, with the prominent saxophone octaves (A-flat, and the A-flat an octave higher) and rapid "disco" handclaps. In the video, Le1f shakes his butt in a pair of tight purple short shorts and perches on an oiled-up shirtless man wearing a Pikachu mask. Wearing masks and dancing—some of which could be considered "vogueing"—can be traced back to New York City's queer ballroom scene, which originated in the 1960s. Members of the community, organized into "houses" (many of which were named after famous fashion designers), participated in competitions that included lip-synching, impersonating famous people, dressing in drag, and dancing.

In the lyrics, Le1f brags about how men—black and white, closeted or openly gay—lust after him. Boasting about his sexual prowess puts him in line with many mainstream rappers, who do the same, but from a heterosexual perspective. In a way, Le1f's claims ridicule those of his heteronormative counterparts: he really can have *anyone* he wants, and the partners he describes highlight the possibilities of a more fluid approach to gender and sexuality. He refers to "swishers" and says he's "light in his loafers," both of which are old (derogatory) euphemisms for being gay. Taking lines like this and putting them front and center is akin to a strategy described by Mickey Hess, *inversion*. Hess talks about inversion with respect to white rappers, who parody their whiteness in order to deflect criticism on that basis (inversion will be discussed in more detail in Chapter 9). Here, Le1f is putting his homosexuality on display, using archaic terms in hopes of depriving his critics of using such terms against him, or perhaps suggesting that such homophobic attitudes are out of date.

"Wut" achieved some notoriety because of the beat's resemblance to Macklemore's "Thrift Shop," a song which was released about a month after Le1f's. This similarity, coupled with the release of "Same Love" earlier that year, led Le1f to criticize Macklemore's apparent insensitivity. Following Macklemore's wins and performance at the 2013 MTV Video Music Awards, Le1f took to Twitter to express his outrage: "that time that straight white dude ripped off my song then made a video about gay interracial love and made a million dollars," followed by "do proceeds go to any gay people? The HRC [Human Rights Campaign, an LGBTQ advocacy organization]? Aids foundation? Or does this straight white man keep the money?" While Macklemore is certainly aware of his role in the white appropriation of black culture, he seems less concerned with the ways in which he has profited from queer issues: instead of raising up the voices of artists in that community—like Le1f—Macklemore has effectively silenced them by taking center stage.

Le1f was invited to perform on *The Late Show with David Letterman* in March 2014 (some two years after the single's release), marking the first time an out rapper appeared on a late-night network television program. The rapper tweeted his gratitude, grateful that Letterman invited him to perform "as a musician and not a spectacle."

Artists like Mykki Blanco and Angel Haze are pushing the gendered binaries of the genre even further. Blanco identified as trans for a few years in the early 2010s and began using female pronouns but decided against transitioning. Haze describes herself as agender and pansexual: "If you call me 'him' or 'her' it doesn't matter to me. I don't consider myself of any sex. I consider myself an experience."[53] In an interview with the *Guardian*, Blanco observes that straight rappers can rap about whatever they want and the media doesn't bat an eye, but virtually everything a queer rapper does is taken as a political act.[54] When she announced that she was HIV-positive in June 2015, the story was picked up by several mainstream media outlets that had otherwise paid her career little mind. "Never before had *Time Magazine* wrote about me," she tells Ann-Derrick Galliot, "but when I came out as HIV-positive, *Time* Magazine was like, 'Mykki Blanco, rapper announces. . . .'"[55] Her viral hit "Wavvy" oscillates between masculine and feminine performances, and a lavish ballroom scene serves as the centerpiece of the video. The lyrics confront some of the stereotypes that queer rappers have faced ("This fag can rap") and also seem to imply that some of his detractors in the rap community might be in the closet themselves: "I pimp slap you bitch niggas with my limp wrist, bro/What the fuck I gotta prove to a room full of dudes/Who ain't listening to my words cuz they staring at my shoes?"

Despite the progress that has been made, homosexuality is still taboo in mainstream rap. In early 2017, *Rolling Stone* interviewed Atlanta-based rap trio Migos, whose single "Bad and Boujee" was at the top of the charts. The group was praising the diversity of their hometown when the author, Jonah Weiner, asked their opinion on iLoveMakonnen's—a fellow Atlantan—recent announcement that he was gay:

"Damn, Makonnen!" Quavo bellows after an awkward interlude. I mention support I saw online for Makonnen's decision. "They supported him?" Quavo asks, raising an eyebrow. "That's because the world is fucked up," says Offset. "This world is not right," Takeoff says. "We ain't saying it's nothing wrong with the gays," says Quavo. But he suggests that Makonnen's sexuality undermines his credibility, given the fact that "he first came out talking about trapping and selling Molly, doing all that."

He frowns. "That's wack, bro."[56]

Migos would go on to say that the world is messed up *because* Makonnen was forced to conceal his identity, but that explanation appears to be little more than damage control. The belief that his sexuality somehow undermines his credibility goes to show that stereotypes have deep roots and die hard.

 OUTRO

Names you should know:

- 50 Cent
- Tupac Shakur
- Lil' Kim
- Sir Mix-A-Lot
- Salt-N-Pepa
- Queen Latifah
- Native Tongues

- Macklemore
- Frank Ocean
- Queen Pen
- Le1f
- Mykki Blanco
- Angel Haze

Terms you should know:

- Heteronormative
- Hypermasculinity
- Dialogic
- Intersectionality

- Queen Mother (Mammy)
- Fly Girl (Jezebel)
- Sista with Attitude (Sapphire)
- HomoHop

Questions for discussion/writing prompts:

1. As with any kind of categories, Keyes' categories are fluid: Missy Elliott, Lauryn Hill, and Nicki Minaj are among the artists that seem to cross Keyes' categories with relative ease. Listen to some songs by these artists, and talk about which categories they inhabit. Or, choose an artist that you're familiar with, and discuss which empowerment strategies she might use.

2. Many MCs object to being called "female MCs" or "gay MCs," yet these labels seem to persist, despite the hip-hop community's growing acceptance of female and queer artists. Are the terms useful or divisive? In what ways?

3. Consider songs in which a rapper speaks "on behalf of" an underrepresented group, such as Macklemore's "Same Love," J. Cole's "Lost Ones," and Lupe Fiasco's "He Say She Say." Do these songs further equal representation or hinder it?

4. Compare Rick Ross' "B.M.F. (Blowin' Money Fast)" with a remix by House of LaDosha, "B.M.F. (Black/Model/Famous)." How does each articulate aspects of gender and sexuality? In what ways is the House of LaDosha's song a critique of Rick Ross' track? Alternatively, compare and contrast Macklemore's "Same Love" with Angel Haze's track of the same name.

Additional listening/viewing:

Female MCs:

- DuVernay, Ava. *My Mic Sounds Nice*. Los Angeles: Forward Movement, 2010.
- Lauryn Hill
- Medusa
- Jean Grae
- Rapsody
- Saroc the MC
- K'Valentine

Male-female dialogue:

- "It's a Man's World," Ice Cube (feat. Yo-Yo)
- "Only" Nicki Minaj (feat. Drake and Lil Wayne)
- "Don't Fight the Feelin'," Too $hort (feat. Rappin' 4-Tay)

"Bitch":

- "Da Baddest Bitch," Trina
- "Me and my Bitch," Notorious B.I.G.
- "Ain't Nothin' but a Word to Me," Too $hort (feat. Ice Cube)
- "Bitch Bad," Lupe Fiasco
- "Cookie Cutter Bitches," Snow Tha Product

Queer hip hop:

- Hinton, Alex. *Pick Up the Mic*. Los Angeles: Rhino Films, 2006.
- "Wavvy," Mykki Blanco
- "I'ma Read," Zebra Katz
- "New Phone (Who Dis)," Cakes da Killa
- *Herstory*, Young M.A.

NOTES

1 Tricia Rose, *Black Noise: Rap Music and Black Culture in Contemporary America* (Hanover, NH: Wesleyan University Press, 1994), 146–7; Cheryl Keyes, *Rap Music and Street Consciousness* (Urbana: University of Illinois Press, 2002), 186.

2 See Charise L. Cheney, *Brothers Gonna Work It Out: Sexual Politics in the Golden Age of Rap Nationalism* (New York: New York University Press, 2005), 6, and Robin D. G. Kelley, "Kickin' Reality, Kickin' Ballistics: Gangsta Rap in Postindustrial Los Angeles," in *Droppin' Science: Critical Essays on Rap Music and Hip Hop Culture*. Ed. William Eric Perkins (Philadelphia: Temple University Press, 1996), 124.

3 This is the main argument of Cheney's book.

4 Cheney 64.

5 50 Cent believed that Darryl "Hommo" Baum was the one who shot him, although authorities investigated Irv Gotti and his Murder Inc. labelmates in connection with the shooting. Murder Inc. was also suspected in the shooting death of Run-D.M.C.'s Jam Master Jay, which may have been related to 50's shooting.

6 Touré, "50 Cent: The Life of a Hunted Man" *Rolling Stone* 919 (April 3, 2003).

7 bell hooks, *We Real Cool: Black Men and Masculinity* (New York: Routledge, 2004). See also Mark Anthony Neal, *New Black Man* (New York: Routledge, 2005), and Tricia Rose, *The Hip Hop Wars* (New York: BasicCivitas, 2008).

8 These criticisms of Drake are not solely on the basis of his lyrical output: his light skin, his Canadian heritage, and his early career as a child actor also undermine his authenticity. Furthermore, Drake himself makes efforts to separate himself from rap's mainstream that limit his effectiveness as a role model in the genre. See Kris Singh and Dale Tracy, "Assuming Niceness: Private and Public Relationships in Drake's *Nothing Was the Same*" *Popular Music* 34 no. 1 (January 2015): 94–112.

9 Keyes 188.

10 Keyes chapter 7.

11 Erik Nielson, "Where Did All the Female Rappers Go?" *NPR Code Switch* (March 4, 2014): www.npr.org/sections/codeswitch/2014/03/04/285718351/where-did-all-the-female-rappers-go.

12 Keyes 200.

13 Jason D. Haugen, "'Unladylike Divas': Language, Gender, and Female Gangsta Rappers" *Popular Music and Society* 26 no. 4 (2003): 434–5.

14 Rose, *Hip Hop Wars*, 173.

15 Imani Perry, *Prophets of the Hood* (Durham, NC: Duke University Press, 2005), 156.

16 Perry 128–9.

17 Perry 159.

18 Perry 162–5.

19 Haugen 430.

20 Quoted in Rose, *Hip Hop Wars*, 171.

21 Rose, *Hip Hop Wars*, 171.

22 See also Rose's discussion of this song in *Black Noise* (Hanover, NH: University Press of New England, 1994), 168–9.

23 In Mix-A-Lot's version, the text is "Oh my *God*"; Minaj changes it to "gosh."

24 See Nosheen Iqbal, "The Nicki Minaj Debate Is Bigger Than Taylor Swift's Ego" *Guardian* (July 22, 2015): www.theguardian.com/music/2015/jul/22/nicki-minaj-debate-bigger-than-taylor-swifts-ego and Todd VanDerWerff, "The Taylor Swift and Nicki Minaj Twitter Feud, Explained" *Vox* (July 22, 2015): www.vox.com/2015/7/21/9012179/taylor-swift-nicki-minaj-twitter.

25 Perry 127.

26 Rose, *Hip Hop Wars*, 174.

27 Carolyn West, "Still on the Auction Block," in *The Sexualization of Childhood*. Ed. Sharna Olfman (Westport, CT: Praeger), 89–102.

28 Byron Hurt, *Hip-Hop: Beyond Beats and Rhymes* (Northampton, MA: Media Education Foundation). See also Rose, *Hip Hop Wars*, 209–13, and S. Craig Watkins, *Hip Hop Matters: Politics, Pop Culture, and the Struggle for the Soul of a Movement* (Boston: Beacon Press, 2005), 216–19.

29 Hampton originally posted the letter to her Tumblr feed; it has since been removed. See Andrew Martin, "Dream Hampton Says She's Done with Hip Hop" *Complex* (August 16, 2012): www.complex.com/music/2012/08/dream-hampton-says-shes-done-with-hip-hop.

30 See, for instance, Neal 11.

31 Rose, *Hip Hop Wars*, 157.

32 Keyes 194–5.

33 Rose, *Hip Hop Wars*, 122–4.

34 Carolyn West, "Mammy, Jezebel, Sapphire, and Their Homegirls: Developing an 'Oppositional Gaze' toward the Images of Black Women," in *Lectures on the Psychology of Women*. 4th ed. Ed. Joan Chrisler, Carla Golden, and Patricia Rozee (New York: McGraw Hill, 2012), 294; see also hooks 53.

35 Rose, *Black Noise*, 172–3.

36 Rose, *Hip Hop Wars*.

37 Mark Katz, *Groove Music* (New York: Oxford University Press, 2012), 241–7 and Rose, *Black Noise*, 57.

38 Katz 241–7.

39 West, "Mammy, Jezebel, Sapphire," 289–91.

40 Robin Roberts, "'Ladies First': Queen Latifah's Afrocentric Music Video" *African American Review* 28 no. 2 (Summer 1994): 245–57.

41 Cheney 104.

42 Perry 157.

43 Juba Kalamka and Tim'm West, "It's All One," in *Total Chaos: The Art and Aesthetics of Hip-Hop*. Ed. Jeff Chang (New York: Basic Civitas Books, 2006), 199–200.

44 Hurt 2006.

45 George 44.

46 Cheney 114–15. The strong anti-Semitic content is worth mentioning too.

47 Alex Frank, "Gen F: Le1f" *Fader* 81 (July 23, 2012): www.thefader.com/2012/07/23/gen-f-le1f.

48 Laura Jamison, "A Feisty Female Rapper Breaks a Hip-Hop Taboo" *New York Times* (January 18, 1998).

49 Kalamka and West 201.

50 Frank Ocean, "Whoever You Are, Wherever You Are . . ." http://frankocean.tumblr.com/post/26473798723.

51 "Snoop Lion Meets the Guardian's Simon Hattenstone" *Guardian* (April 6, 2013): https://www.theguardian.com/music/2013/apr/06/snoop-dogg-lion-interview.

52 Rahiel Tesfamariam, "Has Obama Made Hip-Hop Rethink Masculinity?" *Washington Post* (May 25, 2012): www.washingtonpost.com/blogs/she-the-people/post/has-obama-made-hip-hop-rethink-masculinity/2012/05/25/gJQAmulhpU_blog.html. See also Travis Gosa and Erik Nielson, "Introduction," *The Hip Hop and Obama Reader*. Ed. Travis Gosa and Erik Nielson (New York: Oxford University Press, 2015), 17.

53 David Smyth, "Angel Haze, Interview: 'At Home, I'm Dead. But On Stage, I'm God'" *Evening Standard* (January 15, 2016): www.standard.co.uk/goingout/music/angel-haze-interview-at-home-i-m-dead-but-on-stage-i-m-god-a3157611.html.

54 Dorian Lynskey, "Mykki Blanco: 'I Didn't Want to Be a Rapper. I Wanted to Be Yoko Ono'" *Guardian* (September 15, 2016): www.theguardian.com/music/2016/sep/15/mykki-blanco-i-didnt-want-to-be-a-rapper-i-wanted-to-be-yoko-ono.

55 Ann-Derrick Galliot, "Mykki Blanco Explains the Meaning of Every Song on *Mykki*" *Fader* (September 13, 2016): www.thefader.com/2016/09/13/mykki-blanco-album-track-by-track-interview.

56 Jonah Weiner, "Migos' Wild World: One Night in the Studio with 'Bad and Boujee' Trio" *Rolling Stone* (February 8, 2017): www.rollingstone.com/music/features/bad-and-boujee-inside-atlanta-rap-trio-migos-wild-world-w465205.

TIME LINE

1964   Clarence 13X founds the Five-Percent Nation in Harlem.

1982   MC Sweet's *Gospel Beat: Jesus Christ*, considered by many to be the first Christian rap album, is released.

1990   Brand Nubian releases *One for All*.

1992   Spike Lee's movie *X*, an adaptation of *The Autobiography of Malcolm X*, premieres.

1993   Rev. Calvin Butts threatens to smash boxes of rap CDs with a steamroller during a protest of the music.

1995   The Million-Man March takes place in Washington, DC.

2002   T-Bone releases *Gospel Alpha Mega Funky Boogie Disco Music*.

—KJ-52 releases "Dear Slim."

2003   KJ-52 follows "Dear Slim" with a remix ("Dear Slim, Part II").

2004   Lecrae founds Reach Records in Dallas, Texas.

—Matisyahu releases his debut, *Shake Off the Dust . . . Arise*.

2014   Lecrae's album *Anomaly* becomes the first album to top both the Hot 200 and Gospel charts in the same week.

2016   Kanye West releases *The Life of Pablo*, calling it a "gospel album."

—Chance the Rapper releases *Coloring Book*.

IN THIS CHAPTER, YOU WILL LEARN ABOUT

- The Five-Percent Nation and rap music's relationship with Islam
- Anti-Semitism, rap, and Orthodox Judaism
- Early examples of and the recent mainstreaming of Christian rap

CHAPTER 8

Listening to Religion

OVERVIEW

Religion has always been an important element of rap music, and it manifests itself in three main ways: artists whose material openly reflects their religious orientation, artists who have left rap and converted to the religious life, and artists who hold strong religious beliefs that are not necessarily reflected in their music. Many historians of rap find early templates for the genre's vocal delivery in the cadences of black preachers. Artists like Kurtis Blow and Ma$e have left the music industry and gone on to become ordained ministers. While Christianity had an early and lasting influence on rap music, two groups with ties to Islam—the Nation of Islam (NOI) and a splinter group, the Five-Percent Nation—also had a profound effect on the culture in the late 1980s and early 1990s. More recently, hip hop with overtly Christian themes has moved out of the shadows and is becoming increasingly visible, as artists like Lecrae and Chance the Rapper have released albums with strong roots in the church.

THE FIVE-PERCENT NATION

One of the most important influences on early hip hop—and one of the most misunder-stood—is the Five-Percent Nation, which is also known as the Nation of Gods and Earths (NGE). The Five-Percent Nation was formed in Harlem in 1964 when Clarence 13X and his followers split from the **Nation of Islam** over theological differences. An article in the *New York Amsterdam News*, a black-owned newspaper, described the Five Percenters as "a hate group trained in the ways of Islam and karate."[1] The group takes their name from Lost Found Lesson Number 2—a series of questions that must be answered to gain admission into the Nation—which claims that 85% of the population are slaves to 10% of the population, who lie to the poor in order to maintain control over them. The remaining 5% are "Poor Righteous Teachers," who are responsible for leading the 85% out from the shadow of the 10%. Among the artists affiliated with the Five-Percent Nation are Aceyalone, Rakim, the Wu-Tang Clan, Brand Nubian, Nas, AZ, Busta Rhymes, and Black Thought (of the Roots). Other rappers have a loose affiliation or were members at one time, including Erykah Badu and Queen Latifah. The Five-Percent Nation and the NOI appealed to a growing segment of the black community who were becoming skeptical of mainstream religions, Christianity in particular.[2]

Sister Soulja called hip hop a "blessing because the [Poor] Righteous Teachers, Brand Nubian, and KRS-One have actually been the educational system for black kids, in place of the so-called educational system that is entirely financed by the American government."[3] It is the primary duty of the Five Percent to "civilize the uncivilized," and many Five

Percenter MCs refer to themselves as teachers and their listeners as students. In addition to sharing NOI and Five Percent lessons, Five Percenters lead by example and share personal narratives of conversion: musicologist Felicia Miyakawa talks about GZA's conversion as relayed in his "B.I.B.L.E. (Basic Instructions Before Leaving Earth)."[4] His story and others like it share a framework with the Malcolm X narrative (see Chapter 2). Here, imprisonment is a metaphor for lack of knowledge—being a prisoner of the 10%—and redemption comes from gaining the wisdom to become part of the Five Percent. Rakim sums it up in "Follow the Leader": "I'm here to break away the chains, take away the pains/Remake the brains."

LISTENING GUIDE 8.1

Artist: Brand Nubian
Song: "Wake Up (Reprise in the Sunshine)"
Album: *One for All*
Record label: Elektra
Year released: 1990
DJ or Producer: Brand Nubian
Samples used: "Everybody Loves the Sunshine," Roy Ayers Ubiquity

A close reading of "Wake Up (Reprise in the Sunshine)" by Brand Nubian provides an introduction to many of the beliefs of the Five Percenters. The lyrics begin with an illustration of the **Supreme Alphabet**, a method of interpreting texts, similar to interpreting acronyms or acrostics: "The attribute Hagi Helper to Another God/In need He Allah God Islam" (0:33) Here, "Hagi"—a Muslim who has traveled to Mecca—is broken down into its constituent letters, and words beginning with each letter are assembled into short phrases, unlocking alternate "meanings" for the word: "Helper to Another God In need" and "He Allah God Islam." In the Five Percent teachings, "Mecca" refers to Harlem. Members of the Nation believed that all black men are divine—that they are gods—in contrast to the NOI claim that W. Fard Muhammad alone was Allah. The idea that all black men are gods is echoed a few lines later: "This Asiatic black man is a dog spelled backwards" (0:45). The reference to "Asiatic" is not a reference to Asia as we think of it, but rather a reference to the Middle East, and northeastern parts of Africa, where many believe that humans first emerged.

The Supreme Alphabet occurs in other places in the song as well: in response to the question "Did we receive more gold?" (2:25) the answer is "God, Now Cipher"; "Now Cipher" is "no." The song ends with the line "Please Educate Allah's Children with Equality," which spells "peace." There is not a one-to-one correspondence between a letter in the Supreme Alphabet and a specific word; rather, the Alphabet should be thought of in terms of a method of uncovering meaning. Compare "P.E.A.C.E." above with the Wu-Tang Clan's song "C.R.E.A.M.," which stands for "Cash Rules Everything Around Me": both words contain A, E, and C, but their "translations" are different in each. The Supreme Alphabet is also used to reinforce the beliefs of the Nation: "Allah" can be rendered as "Arm, Leg, Leg, Arm, Head," offering support for the fact that God appears in human form.

The song continues: "The maker, the owner, the cream of the planet Earth/Father of civilization, God of the universe" (0:48). This line, together with the previous line, comprises Student Enrollment Lesson no. 1: "1. Who is the Original man? [Answer:] The original man is the Asiatic Black man; the Maker; the Owner; the Cream of the planet Earth—God of the Universe." The next lines touch on Student Enrollment Lessons 7 and 8:

7. How much of the useful land is used by the original man? 23 million square miles
8. How much of the useful land is used by the Colored man? 6 million

Here, "colored" refers to white people: Five Percenters believe that Yacub, the devil, selectively bred light-skinned people and that the lighter the skin, the closer to the devil a person is. The end of the first verse references these ideas as well.

All men are gods in the Nation; women are Earths. When Grand Puba raps "Preacher got my old Earth puttin' money in the pan" (1:03), he's referring to his female partner (who may or may not be his wife; children are moons or stars). The next few lines reflect the belief that the 10% teach the 85% to believe that God is a "spook in the sky," rather than walking among them. This sentiment is echoed near the end of the song, when Puba raps, "Lyin' who is God."

The lyrics of the bridge ("They put our Wisdom before us/That makes it Wisdom Knowledge . . ."; 1:54) relate the **Supreme Mathematics**, a numerological system of unlocking truths and correspondences in the universe. In the Supreme Mathematics, each number corresponds to a specific value:

1. Knowledge
2. Wisdom
3. Understanding
4. Culture or Freedom
5. Justice or Power
6. Equality
7. God
8. Build or Destroy
9. Born
0. Cipher

Here, the group is simply counting from one to zero using the values ascribed to the numerals. The Supreme Mathematics appears elsewhere in the song: near the end of the first verse, Grand Puba says, "I wrote this on a day of Wisdom Power" (1:34), which would be the 25th. The Supreme Mathematics is further evidence of the importance of numbers and numerology to the Nation: as we have seen, many of the Student Enrollment Lessons involve measurements of land area, distances, and populations. Prospective members also need to memorize a set of Solar Facts, comprising distances from the sun to each of the planets in the solar system: Earth, for instance, is 93 million miles from the sun.

The call-and-response section that follows (2:15) and some of the last verse draw from English Lesson C-1, another doctrine that the Five Percenters share with the NOI:

21. Did I hear you say that some of the seventeen million do not know that they are Muslims?
22. YES, SIR!
23. I hardly believe that unless they are blind, deaf, and dumb.
[. . .]
25. CAN THE DEVIL FOOL A MUSLIM?
26. NOT NOWADAYS,
27. Do you mean to say that the Devil fooled them three hundred seventy-nine years ago?
28. Yes, the T R A D E R made an interpretation that they receive G O L D for their labor—more than they were earning in their own country.
29. Then did they receive gold?
30. NO. The Trader disappeared and there was no one that could speak their language.

Not all raps by Five Percenters are as didactic as Brand Nubian's song; many are much more subtle. In "Follow the Leader," Rakim raps "God by nature, mind raised in Asia/Since you was tricked, I have to raise ya." The lines might go by without much notice, but knowing the Nation's beliefs about divinity, humanity's origins in Asia, and the "tricknology" of the 10% shed new light on these lines.

Beyond the Supreme Mathematics and the Supreme Alphabet, some common expressions in hip hop can be traced to the Five Percent Nation. While its origins date back to biblical times, the phrase "Word is Bond" was popularized by the Five Percenters. It comes from Lost Found Muslim Lesson no. 1:

> 11. Have you not learned that your word shall be Bond regardless of whom or what?
>
> Answer: Yes. My word is Bond and Bond is life, and I will give my life before my word shall fail.

Another phrase in hip-hop along these lines is "What['s] up, G?" where "G" is short for "God," not "gangsta," as is typically thought. Other elements of Five Percenters' beliefs manifest themselves in more recent hip hop, with some rappers echoing the idea of god among us. Ralph C. Watkins cites an interview with Ja Rule: "Who is God? Is Ja Rule God? Has he become God? Yes, and more to the point, God is us. We are God."[5] Some rappers even adopt theistic monikers, such as Kanye West calling himself Yeezus, or Jay-Z, J-Hova [Jehovah]. As Watkins suggests, the subtle spelling changes hint at the difference between mainstream and hip-hop ideas of deities. The Five Percent Nation's skepticism toward mainstream Christianity also lingers into more contemporary mainstream hip hop, a topic that we will examine in more detail later in this chapter.

Malcolm X's assassination in 1965 was a catalyzing moment in the struggle for civil rights. As the leader of the Nation of Islam, his fiery rhetoric had inspired millions to take a stand against racism in America. Juan M. Floyd-Thomas frames Malcolm X's rhetoric as a "jihad of words" and articulates this in terms of the twofold nature of jihad: "striving within the self" and "striving within the path of Allah."[6] We can conceive of the first as an effort to effect change in the self, and the latter as an effort to change the culture. As we saw in Chapter 5, arts movements like funk, the Black Arts movement, and The Last Poets can be understood as attempts to fill the void left by Malcolm X's death. The legacy of these groups continues in rap, particularly as the genre became more Afrocentric in the mid- to late 1980s. Floyd-Thomas suggests that these artists continue the "jihad of words" through their lyrics. Many groups, including Public Enemy, refer to Nation of Islam leaders like Louis Farrakhan: recall that "Bring the Noise" (see Chapter 1) starts with samples from a speech by Malcolm X, and the first verse includes the line "Farrakhan's a prophet that I think you ought to listen to." KRS-One and Boogie Down Productions Signified on a famous image of Malcolm X for the cover of their album *By All Means Necessary.*[7]

The 1992 release of Spike Lee's cinematic adaptation of *The Autobiography of Malcolm X* and the crass commercialization of the "X" symbol that accompanied it abruptly halted the flow of hip hop in this vein.[8] While the NOI was mostly quiet through the 1980s and 1990s, the so-called "Million-Man March" in October 1995—a "Day of Atonement" for black men—brought them back into the national spotlight. The March was widely criticized for reinforcing the patriarchal leadership inherent not only to Islam (generally) but also to other mainstream religions.

Hip Hop and Judaism

Jewish identity is complex: it comprises elements of ethnicity (Jewishness) and religion (Judaism). A number of prominent rap artists have been Jewish or have converted to Judaism, including The Beastie Boys, MC Serch, Drake, Shyne, Mac Miller, Remedy, and Asher Roth. Other members of the Jewish community have played important roles behind the scenes, like Rick Rubin and Lyor Cohen (both affiliated with Def Jam) and Jerry Heller (associated with Ruthless Records and N.W.A.).

The relationship between the black and jewish communities has been both cooperative and confrontational. The Jewish community played an important role in establishing the NAACP (National Association for the Advancement of Colored People). Prominent Jewish leaders lobbied Congress and mobilized their congregations during the Civil Rights movement in the 1960s. New Yorkers Michael Schwerner and Andrew Goodman traveled to the South to assist with a voter-registration drive and were murdered by the Ku Klux Klan—along with James Chaney, a young black man from Mississippi—during the summer of 1964. The rise of the Black Power movement in the late 1960s put a strain on these relations. In 1991, riots broke out in the Crown Heights neighborhood of Brooklyn after a motorcade transporting an esteemed rabbi struck and killed a young black child. A few years later, Khalid Abdul Muhammad, at the time a spokesman for the Nation of Islam, called Jews "bloodsuckers" in the course of a hate-filled tirade that also targeted whites and Christians. The speech ultimately resulted in his being condemned by both houses of Congress and dismissed from the Nation of Islam.

Shortly before the Crown Heights riots and Muhammad's speech, anti-Semitic attitudes nearly brought about the end of Public Enemy. In a 1988 issue of *Melody Maker* magazine, Public Enemy's Professor Griff remarked that "If the Palestinians took up arms, went into Israel and killed all the Jews, it'd be alright." Jeff Chang notes that PE frontman Chuck D still cites this as the beginning of the group's "meltdown."[9] Subsequent comments by Griff put forth increasingly offensive and indefensible claims: he refused to wear gold chains during an interview because of Jewish support for apartheid in South Africa ("Is it a coincidence that the Jews run the jewelry business, and it's named *jew-elry*?" he responded to David Mills, a reporter for the *Washington Times*). Even Chuck D at one point pushed back, saying "it's all right to even be derogatory to Blacks. Just don't be derogatory to most of the people in the business. Ninety percent of the business is operated by Jews, who started it." Griff was suspended, reinstated, and ultimately fired from the group as a result of his views.[10]

Griff's views and Chuck D's response highlight a tension between the black artists and the Jewish men who engage in the business side of the music industry. Jewish artists have historically been mediators of black culture: consider the work of Tin Pan Alley songwriters like Irving Berlin, or the Gershwins, who translated black music like jazz and ragtime into more acceptable European models, or the number of Jewish artists like Al Jolson who would perform in blackface. James Baldwin observes that the Jews were doing the "dirty work" of the Christians: they were the landlords and shopkeepers who were, in essence, the "face" of the white community in predominantly black neighborhoods. After considering the trauma inflicted on the black community (slavery and racism) and the Jewish community (the Holocaust and anti-Semitism), Baldwin goes so far as to say "The Jew, in America, is a white man."[11] Baldwin's remark signifies a change in the way that members of the Jewish community were being viewed in America.

Part of Baldwin's argument is that, while they were initially considered a separate race, Jews were ultimately able to assimilate into mainstream American culture in a way that African Americans were not. "Jewish" became a marker of ethnicity, religion, or both, but many Jews in America—in particular, those of Eastern European heritage—identified and were identified as white. The conflation of Jewishness and whiteness privileges the experiences of Ashkenazi Jews such that in America, Jewishness has become synonymous with the experiences of Eastern European Jews. This conflation in turn marginalizes the experiences of Sephardic (of Spanish and Portuguese descent), Mizrahi (of Middle Eastern heritage), and various African Jewish communities. While many Jewish people in the United States benefit from white privilege, they are nonetheless subjected to anti-Semitism originating from both the political left and the right: the left tend to view them as part of the "establishment," while the right still marginalize them as non-white. Abroad, Ashkenazi Jews may or may not be recognized as white.

Loren Kajikawa reveals that one of the first rap songs on record was a parody titled "Take My Rap, Please," by Steve Gordon and the Kosher Five. Released in 1979—roughly a month after "Rapper's Delight"—Kajikawa claims that the record boasts a number of firsts: it is the first rap record by a white artist, the first rap parody, and the first to bring up issues of race and ethnicity.[12] By juxtaposing Jewish cultural references with a disco track (recall that rap music at this time was closely associated with disco; see Chapter 4), Kajikawa observes that the song shows how "from its very beginning as a commercial genre, [rap] could make identity audible."[13] Indeed, many of the first Jewish rap artists were essentially novelty acts. 2 Live Jews, whose debut album was titled *As Kosher as They Wanna Be* (1990) and featured the single "Oy, It's So Humid" clearly parodied 2 Live Crew's work, and it functions in the same way as "Take My Rap, Please": by juxtaposing two apparently contradictory identities.

LISTENING GUIDE 8.2

Artist: 2 Live Jews
Song: "Oy, It's So Humid"
Album: *As Kosher as They Wanna Be*
Record label: Hot Productions
Year released: 1990

This parody track is clearly based on 2 Live Crew's "Me So Horny": it features a quick 808 beat, with an added klezmer fiddle line (klezmer music is an Ashkenazi Jewish folk music tradition, often featuring violin or clarinet melodies that evoke the voice). The musical background juxtaposes the two contrasting identities and mimics the Miami bass sound in particular (see Chapter 11); however, the subject of the song—humidity—is evocative of Miami's climate and, by extension, Florida's reputation as a retirement destination. This is a more subtle way in which the group negotiates black and Jewish identities, by juxtaposing Miami's reputation as a nightlife center and retirement destination.

The group consists of two white men, MC Moisha (Eric Lambert) and Easy Irving (Joe Stone), who are themselves Jewish and performing in character of stereotypical elderly Jewish men. Exaggerated accents signify their Jewishness (or at least rule out blackness), and their language choices also clearly mark them as Jewish. Throughout the song, the duo repeatedly drops references to Jewish culture, using Yiddish words like "schmucks," and referring to foods like bagels, blintzes, corned beef, and smoked salmon. The song highlights elements of what American society has come to identify as Jewish; however, these elements can all be traced to practices of the Ashkenazi Jews, who emigrated to the United States from Eastern Europe. Much like mainstream commercial hip hop, which commodifies a very specific kind of black masculinity, songs like this represent one of many Jewish identities, reinforcing these tropes while marginalizing other experiences of Jewishness and Judaism.

Seattle MC Nissim's career demonstrates that Jewish identity in the United States is far from monolithic. Nissim converted to Orthodox Judaism in 2011. Prior to his conversion, Nissim recorded as D. Black and was poised for success in the secular rap world: his father was a member of a pioneering Seattle hip-hop group, the Emerald Street Boys, and Black had collaborated with well-known producers Vitamin D and Jake One, among others. The black Orthodox community is quite small: some estimates put the size of the black Orthodox community in the United States between 20,000 and 150,000 people.[14] Despite the fact that they are more likely to identify as jewish first and black second, black Orthodox jews still have to grapple with racism not only from society at large, but also from the broader Orthodox community in which they claim membership.[15]

LISTENING GUIDE 8.3

Artist: Nissim (feat. Yisroel Laub)
Song: "A Million Years"
Album: *Lemala*
Record label: LittleBox
Year released: 2016
DJ or Producer: Yosef Brown

The video chronicles a pilgrimage made by Nissim as he carries the Torah scrolls (which contain the first five books of the Bible). Dressed in traditional Hasidic clothing (white shirt; dark pants, vest, coat, and hat) for much of the video, Nissim raps about finding and serving God; however, he never mentions God's name in the course of the song (which could be out of respect). The subject of the song could thus be open to interpretation; however, there are enough contextual clues—particularly in the video—to establish God as the being to whom the verses are directed.

"A Million Years" is a song about Nissim's personal beliefs: it serves not only to test the boundaries of Orthodox Judaism but also to connect contemporary Judaism with "the cool." Nissim's instrumental track would be at home under many mainstream commercial artists: there are, for instance, no quotations from or clear influence of Jewish music in it. The lyrical content—recited in English, not Hebrew—is almost generically spiritual and could easily be heard sympathetically by Christians, Muslims, and others.

Throughout the video, Nissim is subjected to the gaze of mostly white people—who may or may not be Jewish—which reinforces the notion that, despite his deep faith, he is *seen* as black. The clothing he wears as he carries the Torah (and the Torah itself) identify him as Jewish, most likely adding to the onlooker's curiosity.

Nissim has collaborated with Simon Benzaquen, a Seattle-area rabbi who is committed to preserving and transmitting Ladino, the dialect of Sephardic Jews. Benzaquen recognized the shared struggle of both the Jewish and black communities—exemplified by their song "Sores"—and the power of music to keep language alive. On the track, Nissim raps the verses, and the rabbi sings the hook in the tradition of a cantor.[16]

Drake is the most visible Jewish rap star today. His father was black and his mother, Jewish: they separated when Drake was five years old, and he was raised by his mother. While he does not typically put his religion front and center—and is occasionally evasive in his discussions of it—the video for his song "HYFR" shows the rapper getting the lavish bar mitzvah he dreamed of as a young man (he did have a modest bar mitzvah as a child). Judah Cohen suggests that the Jewish rap movement is part of a cultural project to make Judaism cool, and this strategy relies on pushing the boundaries of "a complacent Jewish tradition," reinforcing some aspects of Judaism while updating others in an effort to preserve the faith.[17] While Cohen is not directly addressing Drake or his music, many fans have found ways to reconnect with their Jewish identity as a result of their encounters with Drake's music.[18]

As discussed in the previous chapter, other rappers have feminized Drake because of his "nice guy" persona. While his demeanor, his Canadian heritage, and his background as a child star all contribute to this persona, his identification as Jewish could be a contributing factor. Cohen contends that hip hop's hypermasculinity appealed to Jewish men, who were frequently portrayed as weak, neurotic, and otherwise feminine—Woody Allen and Jerry Seinfeld are good examples—and that music provided a safe space to experiment with shifting relationships between gender and faith.[19] While Drake does not engage in the kind of hypermasculine posturing associated with many mainstream gangsta rappers, he is not one to back down from a beef, as evidenced by his quick and sharp responses to Meek Mill during their 2015 feud.

EARLY CHRISTIAN RAP: T-BONE AND KJ-52

It may seem like a paradox that mainstream Christianity would want to be associated with a genre of music that, on the surface, advocates just about everything Christians are opposed to; however, that might be precisely why hip hop was attractive to Christian musicians. The subjects of rap songs (and, in many cases, the artists themselves) inhabit a world of sin and immorality and need to be saved. Religious leaders like Rev. Calvin Butts, head of Harlem's Abyssinian Baptist Church, and Rev. Paul Scott have inveighed against rap's immorality, with Butts famously staging an event in 1993 during which he was going to crush boxes of rap CDs with a steamroller (he did not go through with it and ended up leaving the boxes in front of Sony headquarters).[20] Some within the Christian rap community see making music as their mission: Houston-based Nuwine strives to reach "those who don't know God [. . .] the sick, the rebellious, the angry, the hurting. [. . .] Why do the well people need a physician? It's the sick people that need a physician."[21]

Monica Miller argues that mainstream religion is one of many forces that claim hip hop is deviant: it is responsible for "moral panics," and, as such, the people who participate in hip-hop culture—both producers and consumers—need to be saved. Such an outlook, she suggests, reinforces the hegemonic nature of religion and diminishes any contributions that hip hop may have made to religion. Churches have made efforts to reach out to those in the hip-hop community and "save" them:

> These church-based projects (attempting to keep the institutional church relevant in a changing cultural economy) cloak their religious messages with a thugged-out Hip-Hop twist. This troubling approach has culminated in a hegemonic project that relies upon appropriating the stylistic elements (e.g., appropriating rap music by replacing the original language with Christian terms and theology, making churches more "Hip Hop friendly" by dressing in clothing that is traditionally worn in Hip-Hop culture, and using Hip-Hop slang and vernacular intentionally in order to capture the attention of their target audience) of Hip-Hop culture as tools of evangelization.[22]

The church's view of hip hop as deviant is rooted in many of the stereotypes of black life that are regularly perpetuated by the mainstream media in general and hip-hop culture in particular.[23] While it could be argued that this was the project of much early Christian rap, lately, rap has begun to engage more visibly with the church on its own terms, with artists like Lecrae and Chance the Rapper paving the way for a more organic hip-hop Christianity.

Christian rap emerged in the early 1980s: MC Sweet's *Gospel Beat: Jesus Christ* (1982) is widely considered the first Christian rap album. TobyMac and dc Talk were the only two artists to enjoy some mainstream success. Dc Talk's album *Jesus Freak* (1995)—a departure from their more rap-oriented albums—went double platinum and reached number 16 on the *Billboard* Hot 200 (best-selling albums across all genres). Christian rap artists have to negotiate the thorny intersection of religion and commerce, which is not always easy.[24] The typical

Christian rap album is produced on a budget that is roughly 10% of a commercially success-ful mainstream album. These low budgets most often manifest in the quality of the beats: most artists are unable to afford the high costs of sample licensing. Consequently, in the early days of Christian hip hop, many of the beats are newly composed and lack the quality of their mainstream counterparts. In a 1997 *Billboard* article, Mike Allen, known on the radio as DJ Majik, observed: "There's an interesting thing happening in the 'gospel rap' arena. This music is no longer just people yelling 'Jesus' over some weak beats. The music is becoming something people want to buy. Although we were appealing to the gospel consumer, people weren't buying the records because they just weren't any good."[25]

Christian rap relies on refashioning metaphors often found in secular rap. Mainstream rap's focus on conspicuous consumption is one of many metaphors that Christian hip hop turns on its head: rather than the pursuit of material wealth ("For the love of money is the root of all evil," 1 Timothy 6:10), Christian rappers use riches as a metaphor for salvation ("But my God shall supply all your need according to his riches in glory by Christ Jesus," Philippians 4:19).[26] In addition to "riches," underground economies like selling drugs are refashioned as evangelizing, spreading God's word. As mentioned earlier in the chapter, nar-ratives of conversion or redemption closely mirror the Malcolm X formula given in Chap-ter 2. Rather than a descent into hustling, the protagonists find themselves in a spiritual nadir, a state from which only God can rescue them. Neal notes a religious variant of the time-shift paradigm in which God assumes the role of father figure and the promise of an afterlife represents the future.[27]

One of the few early Christian rappers who successfully merged Christian content with admirable rap skill is T-Bone. T-Bone was raised in the Mission District of San Francisco. Both of his parents were preachers, yet his upbringing mirrors that of many other rappers. He grew up among the gangs, pimps, and hustlers of the area, and he related to the music of N.W.A. and other gangsta-rap artists, but he converted to Christianity after a good friend of his was killed in a drive-by shooting. His background and his lyrical skills provided him the street credibility to bridge the gap between Christian and mainstream styles. His artistry has been recognized with several Dove Awards (the Christian-music equivalent of the Grammys) and a Grammy nomination for his 2001 album *Last Street Preacha.*

LISTENING GUIDE 8.4

Artist: T-Bone
Song: "Blazin' Mics"
Album: *Gospel Alpha Mega Funky Boogie Disco Music*
Record label: Flicker
Year released: 2002
DJ or Producer: Chase
Samples used: (none)

This song showcases T-Bone's verbal dexterity as well as the ways in which many Christian rappers reimagine common tropes in mainstream hip hop. From the start, his verses are full of dense internal rhymes, alliteration, and other sonic devices. Consider the first seven lines:

I'm sweet like cinnamon when I'm spittin' this lyrical *venom*
Givin' the rappers the blues like *denim*

When I'm **killin'** '**em, fillin'** '**em** with the<u>s</u>e <u>s</u>yllable
<u>S</u>ynonym<u>s</u> of adren<u>a</u>line <u>s</u>pillin' off my <u>s</u>piritual tongue
Then numbin' 'em like peni<u>c</u>illin
Plu<u>s</u> I'm tryin' to reach the lo<u>s</u>t like **Gilligan,** God **willin'**
The <u>s</u>piritual **healin'** will <u>s</u>top the drug **dealin'** and **killin'**

Repetition of the "s" sound (underlined above) figures prominently throughout these opening lines. A few multisyllabic transformative internal rhymes are also packed into this opening, starting with "-innim-" (italicized above) and followed by "-illin-" (boldface). T-Bone pronounces some of the "-innim-" words to approximate rhyme with the "-illin-" words, resulting in a very uniform sound throughout the beginning of this verse.

Many rappers use the drug economy as a metaphor, and T-Bone is no exception. Unlike his peers, who use it as a metaphor for their music (or the music industry), T-Bone uses it as a metaphor for evangelizing. In the second verse, he alludes to selling crack ("the first to slang cane and baking soda") before his spiritual awakening. After finding God, he compares preaching to "slangin' holy rock on the curb" with his "eyes blurred from the Holy Ghost." In a similar vein, he aligns himself with Vito Corleone—the Godfather (from the Mario Puzo novel-turned-film)—referring to himself as "Bone Cor-

Figure 8.1 Album cover for *Gospel Alpha Mega Funky Boogie Disco Music*
Source: Photos courtesy of Rene Sotomayor

Figure 8.2 Album cover for *Bone-A-Fide*

leone" and invoking his name in the hook. T-Bone's use of Corleone's name could also be an oblique reference to God the Father, although it seems unlikely that he would equate himself with God in this direct fashion. The album cover for *Gospel Alpha Mega Funky Boogie Disco Music* mixes sacred and secular images as well. T-Bone appears dressed as a pimp, in a white suit, red shirt, and floor-length fur coat, and leaning on a walking stick. The overall image resembles a stained-glass window or icon.

The album cover for 2005's *Bone-A-Fide* features an image of T-Bone styled as the revolutionary Che Guevara, another image common to a lot of socially conscious rap. More recently T-Bone has referred to himself as "Boney Soprano," a reference to the main character Tony Soprano from the acclaimed HBO mob series *The Sopranos*.

On the basis of his skills, T-Bone caught the attention and respect of some well-known secular rappers, a few of whom he would go on to collaborate with. As his own music trended toward the more secular, he collaborated with KRS-One, E-40, Chino XL, and Mack 10.

KJ-52's (*It's Pronounced "Five-Two"* is the title of one of his albums) story is also not unique. His parents divorced when he was young, and he grew up in one of the poorer neighborhoods of Tampa, Florida. Since 2000, KJ-52 has released nearly a dozen albums, collaborated with many of the top names in Christian rap, and taken home his fair share of awards. Much of his success can be attributed to his resemblance to Eminem, a comparison that ultimately brought him into a (rather one-sided) dialogue with the self-proclaimed "rap god." In 2002, KJ-52 released "Dear Slim," an epistolary song that Signified on Eminem's hit "Stan." In short, "Stan" consists of a series of letters sent to Eminem by an obsessed fan named Stan. As time goes by and there is no response from Eminem, Stan becomes increasingly disturbed and starts engaging in the kind of violence that Eminem raps about. In the last verse, Eminem finally writes a kind letter back: he had been too busy to write, but putting off replying to Stan had had tragic consequences. "Dear Slim" takes a similar approach: KJ-52 writes letters to Eminem, drawing comparisons between their lives and praising Eminem's talent but encouraging him to turn from his sinful ways. The song made waves when MTV's *Total Request Live* aired the first verse, with the VJ framing the song as a diss to Eminem. A pastor gave a copy of the CD to Eminem backstage at the MTV Video Music Awards and encouraged him to listen to "Dear Slim"; whether Eminem listened to the song is unknown. In 2003, KJ-52 released a "remix" titled "Dear Slim, Part II," that follows up on the VMA exchange.

The "Dear Slim" saga provides a clear example of Miller's contention that Christian hip hop can reinforce the hegemony of the church as it labels participants in mainstream hip hop deviants. Throughout the song, KJ-52 compares himself to Eminem, even acknowledging that he is a longtime fan ("See I heard your first album; it was called *Infinite*"). In KJ-52's eyes, Eminem is deviant, having sold his soul for riches ("What good's all kinds of dough, plus all kinds of flow/To gain a world of fans but suffer the loss of soul?"), but is worthy of (and capable of) salvation, as KJ advises him. Unlike T-Bone's song, KJ-52 takes direct aim at a very specific target, the reigning rap god of the 2000s, and endeavors to bring him into the church by dressing his message in hip-hop fashion.

LECRAE'S *ANOMALY* AND CHANCE THE RAPPER'S "BLESSINGS"

The quest for an individual spirituality can be challenging, particularly for members of marginalized communities who may wonder how a just God could allow the kinds of injustices that they are regularly subjected to. Sociologist William J. Wilson found that fewer than 29% of inner-city residents claim any kind of affiliation with a formal religious organization.[28] We saw how the Five-Percent Nation used rap music to educate the masses about their beliefs and how the Christian community evangelized through rap. Many elements of the Five Percent doctrine have since become integral parts of hip-hop culture, demonstrating one way that music can spread the message. In the previous section, we looked at how Christianity tried to "save" hip-hop culture: in this section, we will examine how hip-hop culture is trying to reinvigorate Christianity.

To some extent, there has always been a religious element to rap. In addition to the Christian rappers discussed earlier in this chapter, there are rappers who profess faith as part of their personal life and may rap about spiritual topics. There are those artists like Kurtis Blow, Reverend Run, and Ma$e, who became preachers, and others who had very public conversions or religious awakenings. Loon, formerly of Bad Boy Records, converted to Islam and left rap; The Beastie Boys' MCA converted to Buddhism; and Snoop Dogg experimented with Rastafarianism—he changed his name to Snoop Lion after a visit to Jamaica in 2012, releasing a documentary and reggae album in early 2013. KRS-One's book *The Gospel of Hip Hop: First Instrument* (which Miller observes is even styled like a Bible, featuring an embossed leather cover and silk bookmark) proposes a hip-hop religion—one that would replace Christianity, Judaism, and Islam—positioning himself as the central, Jesus-like figure ("I AM HIP HOP.").[29]

In the 2010s, elements of Christianity began appearing with greater regularity in mainstream hip hop. This was the result of two trends: Christian rappers enjoying mainstream success, and mainstream rappers leveraging their profile to rap about Christian topics.

Lecrae's 2014 release *Anomaly* became the first album to top both *Billboard*'s Hot 200 and Gospel charts in the same week. Known by many as a Christian rapper, Lecrae describes himself as a "rapper who happens to be Christian": "I'm not ashamed of my faith, but I think it really does kind of capsize [*sic*] my art," he relates.[30] Lecrae's response mirrors those of women and queer rappers that we saw in the previous chapter. Critics say that Lecrae's Christian messages "sneak up on you," but the messages of unity, love, and justice are in many ways similar to those found in a good deal of socially conscious rap. In 2004, Lecrae founded Reach Records, which boasts a roster of Christian artists including Andy Mineo, Tedashii, and Trip Lee.

LISTENING GUIDE 8.5

Artist: Trip Lee (feat. Lecrae)
Song: "Manolo"
Album: *Rise*
Record label: Reach Records/Sony
Year released: 2014
DJ or Producer: Gawvi
Samples used: (none)

Trip Lee's "Manolo" fits the mold of just about any trap song from the mid-2010s. The beat features the deep bass and rapid hi-hat that characterizes trap, and, on the surface, the song is about a gun. The lyrics are delivered in the clipped, compound meter often heard in trap. On the surface, the song is about a gun—Lee even uses the slang "burner"—but a more careful reading reveals that the gun is a metaphor for truth it contains.

The title of the song, "Manolo," was the result of producer Gawvi's improvisations in the booth. In the context of hip hop, the word evokes several possible interpretations: it could refer to a luxury item, like Manolo Blahnik shoes (in the same spirit as Future's song "Maison Margiela"); it could refer to Tony Montana's sidekick, Manolo "Manny" Ribera, in the movie *Scarface* (a favorite gangster hero); or some exotic place: "It sounds like an Italian city or something," Lee told *HipHopDX*.[31] After looking up the word, the two were surprised to learn that in Spanish, it means "God with us" (it is related to "Emmanuel").

Unlike the more heavy-handed songs in the previous section, the Christian message of this song is buried deep underneath the metaphor. The only lyrical clues to uncovering the message are "flippin' the page," Lecrae's line "Got plenty ammo got old and new, they both testify, Lord" (a subtle reference to the Old and New Testaments), and a few veiled references to scripture. This song rejects the conversion narratives of T-Bone and KJ-52's songs in favor of a more personal reflection. This is not a case of (to paraphrase Miller) the church dressing itself up in hip-hop clothes; rather, songs like this demonstrate the potential for a new approach to theology that emerges organically from rap music, that treats it not as a disease, but as a cure. Lee asks listeners to give the music a chance: "I do try to have truth in my music, but I think people assume it's going to be something else and don't give it a chance. [. . .] If it's dope, keep listening to it. If not, then move on."[32]

While Lecrae may be bringing Christian rap into the mainstream, artists like Kanye West and Chance the Rapper are bringing mainstream rap more in line with its Christian counterpart. Kanye's music (and personality) has consistently engaged with religion, from his song "Jesus Walks" to the album *Yeezus*, which features a track called "I Am a God," spirituality is clearly an important, if challenging, topic for him. His 2016 album *The Life of Pablo* is, by his admission, a gospel album, the subject of which is the life of the apostle Paul. The first track, "Ultralight Beam," evokes Paul's conversion to Christianity. While traveling, Paul—who was at the time a nonbeliever and persecutor of Christians—was blinded by divine light. He remained blind for three days, after which his sight returned instantly, and, as a result of this experience, he converted to Christianity.

The song features all the trappings of a church service: organ, tambourine, soloists (The-Dream and Kelly Price) with a gospel choir, a sermon (delivered by Chance), and a blessing (courtesy of Kirk Franklin). It recalls mid-century gospel music by groups like The Dixie Hummingbirds, Five Blind Boys of Mississippi, and The Sensational Nightingales, which Kanye, Chance, and others may have heard in church in their youth. The beat is sparse, driven by the ebb and flow of the organ chords. Kanye's delivery in the hook is characterized by repetition and call and response with the choir, much as a preacher might lead the congregation. Chance's verse is the centerpiece of the song. In it, he proclaims the strength of his faith and his willingness to stand up for others. He conflates hip hop and religion—secular and sacred—in the lines "I made 'Sunday Candy'; I'm never going to hell/I met Kanye West; I'm never going to fail." The lines recall one of Kanye's lines from "Otis," which appeared on 2011's *Watch the Throne*: "I made 'Jesus Walks'; I'm never going to hell." Chance's homage also positions Kanye as a kind of religious figure—a teacher or shepherd, perhaps.

Many critics wrote that Chance's verse on "Ultralight Beam" represented his coming-of-age, a transition from the mischievous kid suspended from high school for marijuana (as he appears on his first mixtape, *10 Day*) to the clean, community leader who, in 2017, pledged $1 million to the Chicago public school system. A few months after *Pablo* was released, Chance debuted *Coloring Book*, another album that leaned toward gospel music.

LISTENING GUIDE 8.6

Artist: Chance the Rapper
Song: "Blessings"
Album: *Coloring Book*
Record label: (self-released)
Year released: 2016
DJ or Producer: The Social Experiment
Samples used: "Let the Praise Begin," Fred Hammond and Radical for Christ

While Trip Lee's song is a religious song cloaked in trap sounds, Chance's song is more like hip hop dressed as gospel music: *Spin* magazine says that the song "may be the most explicitly religious track of Chance's career."[33] Much of the song resonates closely with Chance's verse on "Ultralight Beam." The hook, which opens the song, implies that God has been good to Chance, since Chance has been faithful. The two main blessings that Chance is referring to are his new daughter and his success as an independent artist, both of which he touches on in the verses that follow.

Chance delivers his verses with his characteristic laid-back flow: he weaves in and out of the beat, approximating normal speech patterns on occasion. The laid-back flow could be an embodiment of the security that his faith brings him. In the first verse, he hints at his success as an independent artist: "I don't make songs for free, I make 'em for freedom" (0:42). As an independent artist, Chance does not have to play by industry rules, but he also risks being excluded from significant recognition in the industry. Despite the obstacles, he made history as the first unsigned artist to appear on *Saturday Night Live* and the first artist to land an album on the *Billboard* charts on streams alone, having never

actually sold an album. In addition, the American Academy of Recording Arts and Sciences, the organization that sponsors the Grammys, changed the eligibility criteria in order for his album to compete,
a decision that he foreshadowed in his "Ultralight Beam" verse.

Later in "Blessings'" first verse, in one densely packed line—"Jesus' black life ain't matter:
I know, I talked to his daddy" (0:55)—Chance critiques the standard image of Jesus as white, makes a
connection between the unjust death of Jesus and police killings of young people of color, and frames
those who acknowledge one but not the other as hypocrites. The line also leads into a mention of
Chance's responsibilities as a new father and how God will support him through this part of his life.
Verse 2 indicates that his daughter may have been an unexpected blessing but that she "became his
everything."

Chance incorporates a number of biblical references as well. In the first verse, he refers to Psalm
119 ("Order my steps . . ."; 1:02) and the Battle of Jericho (Joshua 9; 2:24), and more generally refers
to the imagery of the sword as God's word (as did Trip Lee) and the trumpet. The trumpet plays several
roles in the Bible: it was used to knock down the walls of Jericho, to gather communities, and to cue
apocalyptic events, among other things. It so happens that Nico, Chance's close friend and leader of
The Social Experiment, is a trumpet player—he went by the name Donnie Trumpet for some time—
and his playing can be heard throughout the track.

Hip hop's long-standing relationship with religion has clearly shifted over the years. The
relationship is symbiotic: rap is music of oppressed communities, and religion offers hope
and the possibility of salvation.

OUTRO

Names you should know:

- Five-Percent Nation (Nation of Gods and Earths)
- Nation of Islam
- Brand Nubian
- Matisyahu
- Nissim
- T-Bone
- KJ-52
- Lecrae
- Reach Records
- Chance the Rapper

Terms you should know:

- The Supreme Alphabet
- Supreme Mathematics

Questions for discussion/writing prompts:

1. Listen to Mos Def's song "Mathematics." Can you argue that this song represents
a critique of the Five-Percent Nation (specifically the Supreme Mathematics)? What
information would you give to support your hypothesis? (You might also listen to
Erykah Badu's "On and On," which is sampled in the Mos Def song.)

2. Choose a religion not covered in this chapter, and find rap music associated with it.
How does the music engage with the religious doctrine?

3. Compare "Manolo" to Tupac's "Me and My Girlfriend" or Nas' "I Gave You Power."
How does each artist use the gun?

Additional listening:

Five-Percent Nation:

- "Wu-Revolution," Wu-Tang Clan
- "B.I.B.L.E. (Basic Instructions Before Leaving Earth)," GZA
- "The 18th Letter," Rakim
- "On and On," Erykah Badu

Judaism:

- "King without a Crown," Matisyahu
- "Harmony," DeScribe
- *R.E.L.I.G.I.O.N.*, Black Hattitude
- "Never Again," Remedy

Christianity:

- "Jesus Walks," Kanye West
- *Anomaly*, Lecrae

NOTES

1 Felicia Miyakawa, *Five Percenter Rap: God Hop's Music, Message, and Black Muslim Mission* (Bloomington: Indiana University Press, 2005), 16.
2 Charise L. Cheney, *Brothers Gonna Work It Out: Sexual Politics in the Golden Age of Rap Nationalism* (New York: New York University Press, 2005). See chapter 5 in particular.
3 Ernest Allen Jr., "Making the Strong Survive: The Contours and Contradictions of Message Rap," in *Droppin' Science: Critical Essays on Rap Music and Hip Hop Culture*. Ed. William Eric Perkins. (Philadelphia: Temple University Press, 1996), 182.
4 Miyakawa 43.
5 Ralph C. Watkins, "Rap, Religion, and New Realities: The Emergence of a Religious Discourse in Rap Music," in *Noise and Spirit: The Religious and Spiritual Sensibilities of Rap Music*. Ed. Anthony B. Pinn (New York: New York University Press, 2003), 190.
6 Juan M. Floyd-Thomas, "A Jihad of Words: The Evolution of African American Islam and Contemporary Hip-Hop," in *Noise and Spirit: The Religious and Spiritual Sensibilities of Rap Music*. Ed. Anthony B. Pinn (New York: New York University Press, 2003), 50. While often (mis-)translated as "holy war," Floyd-Thomas notes that "jihad" actually means "struggle" or "striving."
7 Floyd-Thomas 52.
8 Floyd-Thomas 53.
9 Jeff Chang, *Can't Stop, Won't Stop: A History of the Hip-Hop Generation* (New York: St. Martin's, 2005), 283.
10 Chang 282–92.
11 James Baldwin, "An Open Letter to the Born Again" *Nation* (September 29, 1979): Reprinted online July 23, 2014. www.thenation.com/article/open-letter-born-again.
12 Loren Kajikawa, *Sounding Race in Rap Songs* (Berkeley: University of California Press, 2015), 20.
13 Kajikawa 20.
14 "The Black Orthodox: Double Consciousness and the Pursuit of God" *New York* (December 23, 2012): http://nymag.com/news/features/black-jews-2012-12.
15 Trymaine Lee interviewed nearly a dozen members of the community, and most identified as Jewish first and black second. See "Black and Jewish and Seeing No Contradiction" *New York Times* (August 27, 2010). See also Michael Martin, "Black Family Bears Unique Jewish Distinction" *Faith Matters (NPR)*: www.npr.org/templates/story/story.php?storyId=92230958.
16 Naomi Tomky, "Meet the Rapping Rabbi of Seattle" *Forward* (May 21, 2015): http://forward.com/culture/308586/meet-the-rapping-rabbi-of-washington-state.

17 Judah Cohen, "Hip Hop Judaica: The Politics of Representin' Heebster Heritage" *Popular Music* 28 no. 1 (January 2009): 2.

18 Michael Fraiman, "Jew from the 6ix: Dissecting Drake's Complicated Relationship with Judaism" *Canadian Jewish News* (March 16, 2017): www.cjnews.com/perspectives/jew-from-6ix-drakes-complicated-relationship-judaism.

19 Fraiman 3, 15.

20 Clifford J. Levy, "Harlem Protest of Rap Lyrics Draws Debate and Steamroller" *New York Times* (June 6, 1993).

21 Quoted in Pinn 16.

22 Monica R. Miller, *Religion and Hip Hop* (New York: Routledge, 2013), 27.

23 Tricia Rose lays out the conservative case against hip hop in the first five chapters of *The Hip Hop Wars* (New York: BasicCivitas, 2008).

24 See Christina Zanfagna's "Kingdom Business: Holy Hip Hop's Evangelical Hustle" *Journal of Popular Music Studies* 24 no. 2 (June 2012): 196–216.

25 Antracia Merrill, "The Other Side of Rap" *Billboard* 109 no. 31 (August 2, 1997): 47.

26 Biblical references to the King James Version.

27 Jocelyn Neal, "Narrative Paradigms, Musical Signifiers, and Form as Function in Country Music" *Music Theory Spectrum* 29 no. 1 (Spring 2007): 48.

28 Watkins 185.

29 Miller critiques *The Gospel* at length, along with similar writings by 50 Cent and RZA of the Wu-Tang Clan (*Religion and Hip Hop*, ch. 3).

30 Sasha Savitsky, "Lecrae: I Put Faith in Hip-Hop" *Fox News* (October 2, 2014): www.foxnews.com/entertainment/2014/10/02/lecrae-put-faith-in-hip-hop.html.

31 Victoria Hernandez, "Trip Lee Discusses 'Rise,' His Faith & T.I.'s Role In Promoting Fatherhood in Hip Hop" *HipHopDX* (October 23, 2014): http://hiphopdx.com/interviews/id.2611/title.trip-lee-discusses-rise-his-faith-t-i-s-role-in-promoting-fatherhood-in-hip-hop.

32 Hernandez.

33 Britt Julius, "Review: Chance the Rapper Turns Atheists into Believers on *Coloring Book*" *Spin* (May 18, 2016): www.spin.com/2016/05/review-chance-the-rapper-coloring-book.

TIME LINE

1986	The Beastie Boys release *Licensed to Ill*.
1988	The *Source* is first published.
1990	Vanilla Ice's "Ice Ice Baby" becomes the first rap song to hit number 1 on the *Billboard* Hot 100.
2003	The Himalayan Project releases *Wince at the Sun*.
2010	Omar Offendum releases *SyrianamericanA*.
2015	Lil Dicky releases "$ave Dat Money."

IN THIS CHAPTER, YOU WILL LEARN ABOUT

- How rap reflects shifting definitions of blackness
- How Muslims and South Asians in the United States use hip hop to engage with blackness
- The role of white rappers and audiences in the growth of hip hop

CHAPTER 9

Listening to Race and Ethnicity

OVERVIEW

Cultural ideas about "what it means to be black" or "what it means to be white" have evolved over time and differ from place to place. Since its origins, rap music has been identified as black music, and to engage with rap music at any level is to negotiate a relationship with blackness. Throughout its history, hip hop has "sounded" blackness in different ways, even as societal definitions of blackness have changed. After forty years, white rappers are still an anomaly, which suggests to some that rap continues to resist white appropriation (unlike rock and roll, disco, or jazz, for instance). On the other hand, the fact that the major media corporations are largely run by white men and that close to 70% of rap music is bought by white people would seem to suggest otherwise. While discussions about race in hip hop are often framed in terms of black and white, it is useful to explore how other communities of color have embraced rap music and navigated the issues of race and oppression that are central to the genre.

SOUNDING BLACKNESS

Imani Perry unequivocally claims that rap is black American music: "Even with its hybridity: the consistent contributions from nonblack artists, and the borrowings from cultural forms of other communities, it is nevertheless black American music." She cites four central characteristics of rap to support her point:

1) Its primary language is African American Vernacular English.
2) It has a political location in society distinctly ascribed to black people, music, and cultural forms.
3) It is derived from black American oral culture.
4) It is derived from black American musical traditions.[1]

William Jelani Cobb makes a similar claim: "Hip hop, we are told, has gone universal. And yet, my references to this as a black art form are intentional."[2] Both Perry's and Cobb's claims are quite bold: they could be read as dismissive of the contributions of Latinx artists (see Chapter 5) or suggesting that the influence of white media empires and audiences can be disregarded. Their claims, by extension, imply that Latinx rap artists (or Desi, or Muslim, as we will discuss later) have to engage with hip hop's blackness to some extent.

bell hooks takes a contrary position. Writing in opposition to a claim articulated by Todd Boyd—that contemporary hip hop is descended from a black nationalist impulse and therefore, somehow more authentically black—she writes:

> This is the stuff of pure fantasy, since not only is hip hop packaged for mainstream consumption, many of its primary themes—the embrace of capitalism, the support of patriarchal violence, the conservative approach to gender roles, the call to liberal individualism—all reflect the ruling values of imperialist white-supremacist capitalist patriarchy, albeit in black face.[3]

Even if we accept Boyd's claim, Cherise Cheney observes that many of the black nationalist organizations that preceded hip hop exhibited these values as well, so it should be no surprise that they are later reflected in hip-hop culture.[4] Just as rap's commodification of hypermasculinity has forced all other expressions of gender and sexuality to the margins of the genre, its commodification of blackness has forced other expressions of race and ethnicity to the margins. The commodification of gender and race—which are clearly intertwined in rap—has come about as the result of white involvement in the production and consumption of the music.

In their landmark study, Michael Omi and Howard Winant define race as "a concept which signifies and symbolizes social conflicts and interests by referring to different types of human bodies."[5] Ideas about race are not fixed: they vary from place to place and have changed throughout history. They can be reinforced, challenged, and transformed—a process Omi and Winant call "racial formation"—by the media, through political action, or via other avenues. They can be internalized by the groups that they oppress. But to say that race is strictly a social construct ignores the legacy of racism that people of color have faced—and continue to face—ranging from slavery to mass incarceration, and including personal attacks and microaggressions: this denial is at the core of the "I don't see color" or "I don't see race" claim. Furthermore, discussing race purely in terms of black and white marginalizes the experiences of Latinx, Native, Middle Eastern, and Asian Americans, all of whom have come to have a stake in hip-hop culture. Such a binary approach also fails to account for the relationships between these other minority communities, like the tension between the black and Korean communities detailed in Chapter 11.[6]

Taking Cobb's and Perry's positions as a point of departure, we can say that to be authentic in rap music requires establishing some believable connection with blackness.[7] Given the role the mainstream media plays in the dissemination of rap, it should come as no surprise that blackness in rap is often defined by the industry, which validates hooks' claim. It is possible for several different kinds of blackness present at any one moment. In his book *Sounding Race in Rap Songs*, Loren Kajikawa observes that N.W.A., Public Enemy, and A Tribe Called Quest were at the height of their popularity at roughly the same time, and all three were considered authentic despite the different images of blackness each projected.[8] To engage with rap music involves reinforcing, challenging, or transforming the dominant images of what it means to be black. Rap can thus "sound race" through its music and lyrics; that is, it is possible for non-black artists to be considered authentic in rap provided they can successfully negotiate the genre's prevailing representations of blackness.

Kajikawa builds a case that rap music *sounds* blackness and that the ways in which the music does this shift, in tandem with changing definitions of blackness. The social construction of blackness not only shaped hip hop, but also was shaped by hip hop. As mentioned in Chapter 4, early rap was viewed as a continuation of disco. Disco was associated with the black, Latinx, and queer communities, who went to clubs to dance. The backlash against disco reached a fever pitch with Steve Dahl's "Disco Demolition Night" at Comisky Park in

Chicago in 1979, the same year that "Rapper's Delight" was released. The anxiety surrounding disco was fueled largely by fears that music of queer subcultures was replacing rock: the Village People in many ways personified disco at the time, making numerous television and concert appearances and appearing on the cover of *Rolling Stone* that year.

Once the music was disengaged from the clubs, its identity as primarily black music began to coalesce. In the 1980s, blackness in hip hop was not monolithic. As we saw in Chapter 7, prior to around 1994, there was room for many kinds of gender representations, and the same could be said for blackness. Blackness in the 1980s was shaped by President Reagan's neoliberal policies, which led to rapid deindustrialization of many urban areas and large numbers of unemployed blacks and Latinxs, and the introduction of crack cocaine and its fallout, including an escalating War on Drugs that resulted in a steep rise in incarceration rates within the black community. Consequently, blackness became associated with poverty, crack, welfare, and criminality. Rap groups engaged with these prevailing images of blackness in different ways and, in doing so, constructed narratives of blackness that challenged the dominant media representations. The three groups that Kajikawa mentioned—Public Enemy, A Tribe Called Quest, and N.W.A.—illuminate a few of the many possible representations.

In "Bring the Noise," Chuck D raps, "Radio stations, I question their blackness/They call themselves black, but we'll see if they play this." The lines imply that Public Enemy and its music are even blacker than—or more authentic than—mainstream ideals of blackness; or, more precisely, that mainstream ideals of blackness are inauthentic and inaccurate. Kajikawa makes the point that, in the late 1980s, "Public Enemy sounded blacker to those convinced that real blackness (i.e., hip hop authenticity) personifies defiance, rebelliousness, and political engagement."[9] Public Enemy's revolutionary politics recalled groups like the Black Panther Party for Self-Defense (see Chapter 10) and reinforced stereotypes that conflated blackness and violence. Public Enemy played into these stereotypes with its imagery as well: many photos of the group members show them dressed in military garb, sometimes camouflage, or dress uniforms with berets (also reminiscent of the Panthers). Musically speaking, their beats—produced by the Bomb Squad—echoed the discord that they perceived in society.

A Tribe Called Quest and similar groups—many of their fellow Native Tongues members, for instance—connected with blackness through Afrocentric lyrics and an embrace of jazz, which was enjoying a resurgence during the 1980s.[10] Justin Williams quotes an interview with Gang Starr's Guru at the opening of his chapter: "The so-called jazz hip hop movement is about bringing jazz back to the streets. It got taken away, made into some elite, sophisticated music. [The jazz hip hop movement is] bringing jazz back where it belongs."[11] Guru's statement contains several important implications: First, that jazz came from the streets and *belongs* in the streets resonates with hip hop's growing identification as music from the streets. Second, that jazz's "sophistication" has made it somehow less authentic, and aligning it with hip-hop culture would restore its authenticity. As Williams argues in the course of his chapter, hip hop's assimilation of jazz elevated that particular style of rap into a kind of "elite, sophisticated music," whose association with smoky jazz clubs, the Black Arts movement, and "the cool" separated it from Public Enemy's radical politics and N.W.A.'s West Coast gangsta image.

Williams indicates that gangsta rap quickly became the yardstick against which other releases were measured. He cites an article in which the author praises Digable Planets for "taking the high road" paved by De La Soul and ATCQ, "all but ignor[ing] gangsta culture."[12] N.W.A., on the other hand, embraced the media narratives of young, black, male gangsters from the inner city, rhyming about the struggles they faced on a daily basis as a result of the conditions in which they lived. First-person narratives of drug dealing, pimping, criminal activity, and encounters with the police presented the members of N.W.A. as victims of circumstance, doing what they could to survive. This subject position is quite different from Public Enemy's radical politics or ATCQ's cool, bohemian sound.

The three groups represent three different ways in which blackness can be constructed, and it is important to note that all three groups were at the height of their popularity at the same time, roughly 1989–1991. As rap's popularity grew in the late 1980s, the increased focus on specifically black aesthetics crowded out many non-black artists, resulting in a more widespread perception of rap music as fundamentally black music. Moving into the 1990s, blackness in hip hop became increasingly monolithic and associated closely with hyper-masculinity. In contrast, Anthony Kwame Harrison observes that the hip-hop underground constitutes a space that is far more welcoming of people from different racial and ethnic groups and that the underground, in particular, is leading to new forms of racial formation that undermine the black/white binary so often invoked in conversations about hip hop.[13] This is another way in which the underground preserves the aesthetics of the old school and fights against the forces of commercialization.

"MUSLIM COOL" AND "HIP-HOP DESIS"

While the beliefs and practices of the Five Percenters deviate substantially from what the majority of Muslims believe and practice, for many listeners the Five-Percent Nation is the first and maybe only exposure to Islam that they encounter in rap music. For others, the Five-Percent Nation functions as an introduction to other sects of Islam: a number of rappers who began their careers as Five Percenters, including Ghostface Killah and Rae-kwon, both of the Wu-Tang Clan, have since converted to Sunni Islam. Other rappers, such as Mos Def, Lupe Fiasco, Brother Ali, Q-Tip, DJ Khaled, and Freeway, identify as Sunni Muslim; however, identifying as such does not necessarily mean that their music reflects their beliefs.

Hisham Aidi writes that more and more mosques have been appearing in the inner cities to compensate for the loss of government social services, supplementing the work that Christian churches have historically done.[14] As young people seek a way of organizing their lives, many turn to religion. While some are drawn to Christianity, more and more minority youth view it as the religion of the establishment and have started gravitating toward Islam—whether it be Sunni Islam, the Nation of Islam, or the Five-Percent Nation—as part of an oppositional identity.[15] As we saw in the previous chapter, some members of the black community gravitated toward the Nation of Islam or the Five-Percent Nation as a way of opposing mainstream Christianity. A similar process has been taking place among Muslims in America looking to connect with their black identity and heritage.

In her ethnography of Muslims in Chicago, Su'ad Abdul Khabeer argues that some Muslim-Americans use hip hop as a way to engage with blackness, an aspect of their identity that is often deemed secondary to their Muslim way of life. She writes:

> Early scholarship on Islam in the United States told a diaspora narrative in which Muslims emigrated from an "Islamic homeland" to the "West." The narrative centered on a bicultural clash between "American" and "Muslim" identities. [. . .] Moreover, it locates Blackness and critical race studies at the fringes of the study of U.S. American Islam.[16]

Khabeer suggests that conversations about Muslim-Americans tend to focus on religion and diaspora, not skin color. Engaging with hip hop allows Muslims in America to connect with blackness while challenging the orthodoxy of the faith. Hip hop thus helps inform what it means to be Muslim, and vice versa.[17]

Omar Offendum is a Syrian-American rapper whose uses his music to build community. "We've been taught to tell people what we're not—we are not terrorists, we are not extremists—but for me, a lot of it was telling people really what we are."[18] His music tends to explore his identity as an Arabic Muslim living in the United States—much like the early paradigm that Khabeer mentions. By participating in hip-hop culture, he establishes a connection between his Muslim Arabic roots, his American life, and blackness. In some songs, he raps in both Arabic and English, as in the hook to his song "Destiny": he says, "It's hard livin' in the West when I know the East got the best of me [. . .] Bilingual is what I'm blessed to be," and concludes the hook in Arabic. While the beats are clearly hip hop, the third verse features a melody played by what sounds like a mizmar, a double-reed instrument (like the oboe) that is common in Middle Eastern cultures. His track "Straight Street" illustrates another way in which he connects the two cultures.

LISTENING GUIDE 9.1

Artist: Omar Offendum
Song: "Straight Street"
Album: *SyrianamericanA*
Record label: Cosher, Ink
Year released: 2010
DJ or Producer: Oddisee
Samples used: (none)

"Straight Street" is about a street in Damascus, Syria, on which the apostle Paul is said to have walked. Near the eastern terminus of the road is Bab Sharqi, one of the seven Gates of Damascus. The street is rich with history, and Offendum's pride for its history and culture provided the impetus for this song. "'A Street Called Straight' [sic] really means a lot to me, because it was a song inspired by a real place . . . one of the most ancient urban places in the world. Given that hip hop is an urban culture, and more specifically a street culture, to be able to talk about one of the oldest, longest-lasting urban experiences in the world was very powerful for me."[19]

The conflicts in Syria in the 2010s have left Damascus transformed. Writing in the *New Yorker*, Rania Abouzeid observes the influx of people from elsewhere in the country who have fled to Damascus to escape the violence. She describes concrete barriers and blast walls, rationing of food and gasoline, and frequent power outages.[20] The conditions there mirror those described in many rap songs. "There's a lot of songs out there about life on the streets," he says at the beginning of the song, "But this one is about *the* street." Offendum casts the song as a journey down the street: each of the three verses begins with the distance he has traveled: "I took a stroll down the Street Called Straight/Met a medicine man about a third of the way/Predecessor to the pusherman." Offendum draws connections between the past and the present, between life in Damascus and life "in the streets" in the United States.

Miss Undastood is a New York City–based Muslim MC. She raps in a hijab (head scarf), which functions as a visible symbol of her Muslim faith, and her manner of dress seems at odds with how women are typically portrayed in mainstream hip hop: a post on her Facebook page says, "Let's be clear . . . Many of these Rap Females are not Prettier than Me . . . They just wear less." Her identity is shaped by her race, religion, and gender, and these factors all shape her music. The third verse of her song "Gone Too Far" begins with the lines

"Police fire first and think after/When will they realize that our lives matter?" She mentions the names of Mike Brown, Eric Garner, and Tamir Rice, three African-American men who were killed by police. By invoking rhetoric associated with the Black Lives Matter movement, Miss Undastood forges an alliance between the Muslim, black, and female communities to which she belongs: "We're all in this together, this is our fight," she rhymes.

As with the Muslim artists, the diaspora plays a central role in rap by many desi artists. The word "desi" refers to any South Asian—Indian, Pakistani, Sri Lankan, or Bangladeshi— living abroad. In her ethnography of "hip-hop desis," Nitasha Tamar Sharma relates that, in general, desis tend to sidestep issues of race. Racial formation in these communities is complex, hinging on the intersection of their dark skin color with their status as "model minorities." Both South and East Asians (i.e., Chinese, Japanese, Korean) have been accorded model minority status as a result of generally high levels of education and socioeconomic status, family integrity, and respect for authority figures. While this may seem complementary, there are two main problems with such a label. First, it functions as a measuring stick for other minority communities—the black community in particular—and often is used as leverage against them: if members of one minority group are able to achieve "the American dream," why is it so difficult for other minority groups? Second, it disregards the oppression that "model minority" communities *do* face as a result of their skin color or place of origin (consider, for instance, the Japanese internment in the United States during World War II).[21]

Participating in hip-hop culture allows desis to create racialized identities that foreground the effects of racism that they experience, making race visible and expressing "a political consciousness of inter minority solidarity."[22] To engage with hip hop is to engage with blackness, which produces an apparent conflict between the desi's "model minority" status and the disadvantaged status of the black community, disadvantages that in some cases are defined in opposition to the success of desis. Here, Sharma suggests that viewing race in terms of a binary opposition is limiting: "the artists embrace 'both/and' rather than 'either/or' distinctions."[23]

The Himalayan Project's song "Postcards from Paradise" is a nostalgic look at Vadodara, the city in India that rapper Chee Malabar once called home (he moved with his family to the United States when he was 12 years old).

LISTENING GUIDE 9.2

Artist: The Himalayan Project
Song: "Postcards from Paradise"
Album: *Wince at the Sun*
Record label: Red Bench Records
Year released: 2003
DJ or Producer: Rainman
Samples used: (none)

In painting a vivid picture of the city's resilience despite the damage done by colonialism, the lyrics make connections with the kind of urban life in the United States that rap typically portrays. The "postcards from paradise" highlight the discrepancies between the images of India that circulate in the United States—Malabar alludes to Gandhi and mentions Deepak Chopra, the "Taj Mahals, camels, and snake charmers." The latter serve as reminders of how Westerners have fetishized "the Orient" throughout history. The postcard images could also function as a metaphor for the model minority status, while the conditions that Malabar describes reflect the reality of how he is perceived as a result of his race.

The reality that Malabar presents in the song has much in common with the conditions described in many hip-hop songs that portray life in "the ghetto": disease, housing projects, drugs, and prostitution. He traces these problems to British colonialism (India was a British colony from 1858 to 1947), which "left more than English literature, cricket, whiskey, and tea." Malabar praises the resolve of his fellow Indians, likening the situation to "a rose grow[ing] through cracks of concrete," which is a reference to a well-known poem by Tupac Shakur.

Both Muslims and desis have come under increased scrutiny in the United States following the events of September 11, 2001, largely based on how they look. Offendum recalls that once 9/11 happened, he suddenly became "that Muslim rapper" or "that Arab rapper": "People were questioning my Americanness because I was against the war."[24] The visibility of rappers who are Muslim helps dispel the notion that all Muslims are Arab. Furthermore, the different sects of Islam that are represented in hip hop helps debunk the impression of a singular Islam, divisions that are made even more clear as a result of the conflict between Sunni Muslims and the Five Percenters.

WHITENESS

Despite the great success of artists like The Beastie Boys, Eminem, and Macklemore, white rappers are still a minority—albeit a very visible one—in rap music. Given the genre's close association with blackness, white rappers need to negotiate claims of authenticity, cultural appropriation, and privilege to succeed. Mickey Hess theorizes three ways that white rappers can find a way in to hip-hop culture: imitation, immersion, and inversion.[25]

Imitation is typically the least successful of these strategies, and the career of Vanilla Ice offers the clearest example. Armond White criticizes Ice for his blatant imitation of hip hop, positioning him in a long line of white artists that have appropriated black cultural forms, starting with blackface minstrelsy and moving through people like Paul Whiteman, Elvis Presley, and Pat Boone. Such appropriation, White writes, is a political act: "When 'smoothing over' a black sound occurs, it is a moralizing act, judging the ethnic traits and meanings of a sound inferior, unbeautiful, or bad, somehow in need of white correction."[26] This "smoothing over" undoubtedly contributed to Vanilla Ice's chart success: in 1990, "Ice Ice Baby" became the first rap song to top the *Billboard* Hot 100 chart. On the other hand, the "smoothing over" cost him his credibility as a rapper: Kajikawa observes that Vanilla Ice's failure was so spectacular that no new white rap artists were able to establish themselves until Eminem's rise almost ten years later.[27]

Despite the inroads that white artists have made into hip hop, artists still try to enter the genre via imitation. In the 2014s, Iggy Azalea hit the top of the *Billboard* charts with her single "Fancy," becoming only the fourth female rapper to land at number 1. Originally from Australia, Azalea moved to Miami as a teenager and spent time in Houston and Atlanta as well. Questions about authenticity have plagued Azalea since she came on the scene. In particular, her command of AAVE (see Chapter 3) is almost too good: Eve, Jean Grae, Jill Scott, and Azealia Banks have all been critical of her performance, suggesting that she is merely imitating or appropriating AAVE. A study of her lyrical performance by linguists suggests that she is actually "over-performing" the dialect to a degree that Eminem or any number of black rappers do not: Jean Grae called her performance "verbal blackface." The matter is complicated by the fact that when speaking, Azalea's Australian accent is still present, suggesting that her use of AAVE is "put on" for performance.[28]

The Beastie Boys offer a good example of **immersion**. Immersion suggests that the rappers are an authentic part of the culture, having authenticated themselves by studying and participating in hip hop for some time. Typically, their music does not call attention to their whiteness in any overt way and may even feature anti-racist themes, condemning racism and the institutions that support it. Being on the Def Jam label certainly lent The Beastie Boys some credibility. The song "Paul Revere" from their debut album demonstrates the ways in which The Beastie Boys subtly signify their whiteness without calling direct attention to it.

LISTENING GUIDE 9.3

Artist: The Beastie Boys
Song: "Paul Revere"
Album: *Licensed to Ill*
Record label: Def Jam
Year released: 1986
DJ or Producer: Rick Rubin and The Beastie Boys
Samples used: (none)

If "Paul Revere" were made into a movie, it would undoubtedly be a Western (a characteristically white genre). The song opens with Ad-Rock riding through the desert on his horse, being chased by the sheriff's posse, images that when taken together conjure a picture of the Wild West (or at the very least, situate this song outside of an urban environment, a strategy adopted by many white rappers). This is one way in which The Beastie Boys allude to their being white. Their exaggerated Brooklyn accents, coupled with their word choices, also reveal their whiteness. Ad-Rock recounts that MCA said "howdy," a word that is evocative of the American West and, by extension, whiteness.

The song can also be read as a history of The Beastie Boys. The opening of the song is similar to many stock "fairy tale" openings: "Now here's a little story I got to tell." In the first verse, Ad-Rock is "one lonely Beastie [. . .] All by myself without nobody." He meets up with MCA, and, in the third verse, the two of them meet Mike D.

Perhaps the most distinctive feature of this song is the background track, which was composed on a TR-808 drum machine, recorded to tape, and then played backward. Playing the loop backward gives the song its distinct "sucking" sound.

There are quite a few rap artists now who are accepted as part of the culture as a result of their immersion in it: G-Eazy, Mac Miller, Machine Gun Kelly, Eyedea, Yelawolf, Aesop Rock, and Sage Francis are other white MCs who rightfully earned their place in hip-hop culture.

The third strategy that Hess presents is **inversion**. Inversion involves making whiteness explicit, often through parody. Eminem used this strategy to catapult himself to stardom. Eminem's first album, *Infinite*, was largely imitative and met with limited success. As a battle rapper, Eminem earned his stripes by taking away his opponents' ammunition: recognizing that they would almost certainly call him out based on the color of his skin, Eminem started parodying his whiteness. This approach has been immortalized in the climactic battle scene of the movie *8 Mile*, in which Eminem's character B-Rabbit wins a battle with Papa Doc by owning up to his own past before exposing his competitor's lack of authenticity: Doc's real name is Clarence, he attended private school, and he lives at home with his (presumably) happily married parents. Eminem deals the final blow with the line "I'm a piece of fucking white trash, I say it proudly" and challenges Doc to "tell these people something they don't know about me."[29]

Hess writes that Eminem "inverts a standard rap narrative to position himself as a racial underdog." Eminem's whiteness was an obstacle to be overcome, just like his poverty. Hess also writes that Eminem recognizes the advantages his white privilege confers on him in terms of his "accessibility to white listeners."[30] Eminem establishes his authenticity by connecting with the poverty narrative that many black artists establish—the "white trash" line above is one of many examples. "White trash," however, evokes a very different kind of poverty than that experienced by black artists, conjuring images of trailer parks instead of housing projects, the suburbs instead of the city. In the hook for "White America," Eminem tacitly acknowledges that his audience reflects his whiteness ("I could be one of your kids"). In the first verse, he suggests that Dr. Dre (his producer and "sponsor") likely has as many white fans as Eminem has black fans. He addresses his privilege in the second verse, in which he observes: "Look at these eyes, baby blue, baby just like yourself/If they were brown, Shady'd lose, Shady sits on the shelf [. . .] Let's do the math: If I was black I would've sold half."

The *Source*

The *Source* has been one of the leading magazines of hip-hop culture since its founding in 1988. The magazine, which started as a one-page newsletter, was founded by two white Harvard undergraduates, David Mays and Jon Shecter. At the outset, it featured writing by those immersed in hip-hop culture: Jeff Chang writes that "It would epitomize hip hop's attitude—that b-boy stance [. . .] the barely secret joy of having something no army of parents, baby-boomer cultural critics, or grizzled rock journalists could ever really understand."[31] As the magazine grew, it began to reflect the increasing commercialization of hip hop, eventually losing the regional reports in favor of long-form interviews and political writing. While many accused it of selling out, it set the template for future hip-hop magazines like *Vibe* and *XXL*. It hosts an annual music awards show, and its five-mic album rating is considered by many to be the holy grail of hip hop: only forty-five albums have earned the honor.

Raymond "Benzino" Scott, a co-owner of the *Source*, did not approve of Eminem's success and sought to undermine him. In 2002, Benzino told MTV that Eminem was just another Vanilla Ice, "the hood ornament for the machine" that was attempting to whitewash hip hop. He claimed to have a tape on which Eminem used the N-word in a hateful way toward black women and threatened to release it. The two traded diss tracks back and forth, and the feud played out in print and on the radio. The *Source*'s credibility took a hit as a result of the beef—the magazine was supposed to be impartial and objective—Interscope (Eminem's record label) pulled its advertising, and Benzino eventually left his position. He has since admitted he was wrong, claiming that Eminem had as a much a right to rap as anyone else.

More recently, artists like Macklemore and Lil Dicky have put their whiteness front and center via inversion; however, the two artists approach their whiteness from very different angles. Macklemore acknowledges the privileges that whiteness confers on him, and he tends to apologize repeatedly for it. His song "White Privilege" offers a window into the issues that white artists face in the rap industry. In the hook, he raps that "hip hop started on a block that I've never been to/To counteract a struggle that I've never even been through."

As Macklemore began to achieve national mainstream airplay, he became increasingly conscious of his cultural appropriation. His 2012 album *The Heist*, as well as some of the singles on it, were nominated for—and won—several awards. After sweeping the rap categories at the Grammys in 2014 in an upset victory over Kendrick Lamar's *Good Kidd, M.A.A.D. City*, Macklemore texted Kendrick: "You got robbed. I wanted you to win. You should have. It's weird and it sucks that I robbed you." Macklemore posted the text message to his Instagram account so that his millions of followers could see his act of contrition. By doing so, Macklemore seems to acknowledge the role that white privilege played in his win; however, he ultimately did little to rectify the situation.

Lil Dicky is another unusual case: he is college-educated, comes from an upper-middle-class Jewish family, and believes that he has something unique to offer rap. On one level, his songs function as parodies of common rap tropes: in "$ave Dat Money," he embarks on a quest to film a typical rap video without paying for anything. To do so, he leverages white privilege in a way that black rappers could not. He knocks on doors in wealthy neighborhoods, asking residents whether he can use their home to shoot a rap video; he asks a car dealer whether he can "grab one of these McLarens for like fifteen minutes." Ramon Ramirez writes, "At the risk of being cynical, I don't believe the sweet, elderly white woman who ultimately lets Dicky film in her mansion answers the security buzzer if it's Rich Homie Quan at the door."[32] The track features guest spots by Fetty Wap and Rich Homie Quan—two of the biggest names in rap at the time—which offer Lil Dicky some credibility (in the same way that Dr. Dre acted as a "sponsor" for Eminem). Lil Dicky was also elected a member of the *XXL* "Freshman Fifteen" for 2016, an honor that recognizes his contributions to hip-hop culture. This song in particular, and Lil Dicky's output generally, also play to Jewish stereotypes about being thrifty and less than masculine.

LATINX AND NATIVE AMERICAN HIP HOP

While the experience of being black in America can be traced to being brought by force to the New World, the experience of Native Americans and Latinx communities can be understood in terms of being forcibly removed from their land. In the case of Native People, the conflict manifests itself in claims over tribal land and life on the reservation; in the case of the Latinx community, the conflict takes place in the realm of immigration law. These practices are among the many political systems of confinement that communities of color face in the United States, which will be addressed in more detail in the following chapters.

In 2016, Energy Transfer Partners began construction on the Dakota Access Pipeline, an oil pipeline that runs from North Dakota to Illinois. The pipeline was slated to run through a number of tribal lands, and the Native populations in the area strongly opposed the construction on two grounds: first, that it would harm the environment—drinking water in particular—and, second, that it would invade sacred land. The Standing Rock Sioux tribe, whose land lies on the border of North and South Dakota, sent water protectors to halt the construction. They were soon joined by members of tribes from around the country and other allies (most notably military veterans) in a protest that garnered international attention. Legal challenges and support from the international community slowed the construction, but in January 2017, President Donald Trump signed an executive order that put aside the legal challenges and advanced the construction of the pipeline.

Frank Waln, a Sicangu Lakota rapper who grew up on the Rosebud Reservation in South Dakota, is one of many Native hip-hop artists who spoke out against the pipeline. His 2017 song "Treaties" was written in response to Trump's executive order. Waln said in an interview that, as an indigenous rapper, it was important to him to let the voices of his ancestors speak through him: he samples not only work by other Native artists, but also news reports, speeches, and a Leonard Cohen song, "Nevermind."[33] We never actually hear him rap in this song; rather, we hear his arrangement and presentation of the voices of those who came before him into an audio collage that calls attention to the disregard that the United States has shown toward treaties with Native People: "since the founding of this country, the US government has made and broken over 500 treaties with various Indian tribes all across our nation," relates Kevin Gover (Director of the National Museum of the American Indian) at the beginning of the track and throughout.

When President Bill Clinton signed NAFTA (the North American Free Trade Agreement) into law in 1993, supporters hoped that the trade pact between the United States, Canada, and Mexico would create jobs and facilitate trade among the three countries. The agreement ultimately strengthened corporate farms in the United States, making it easier for them to undercut their Mexican counterparts and ultimately forcing those workers off their land and out of work. This led to a massive wave of emigration from Mexico to the United States and, in turn, an increasingly militarized border along the southern United States. As NAFTA removed barriers to trade, it erected barriers to human migration. Immigrants were criminalized—often referred to as "illegals"—and "illegal immigrant" quickly became synonymous with "Mexican." State and local governments began to pass laws that further targeted immigrant communities, like California's Proposition 187 (which denied non-citizens access to non-emergency public services) and Arizona's SB 1070 (which required residents to carry documentation with them and allowed the police to inquire about immigration status in the course of a lawful stop or arrest). The xenophobia reached a fever pitch during the Trump presidential campaign in 2016. Trump claimed that Mexicans were drug dealers and rapists; he pledged to build a wall along the border to stem the tide of immigration and put an end to the DACA (Deferred Action for Childhood Arrivals) program.

Mare Avertencia Lirika is a Zapotec (that is, indigenous to the Oaxaca region) rapper whose lyrics are informed by her experiences as a woman in post-NAFTA Mexico. As with the Native Americans discussed above, indigenous people like the Zapotec were leaders of the resistance to NAFTA. On her 2016 track "Bienvenidx," she welcomes listeners to the capitalist, neoliberal, heteropatriarchal hell that her country has become ("bienvenidas a este infierno, llamado sistema económico capitalista, neoliberal, a este heteropatriarcado."). She brings awareness to the broken promises of the colonizing forces for the current state of her homeland and chastises those who fell prey to the allure of capitalism, but the song ends with a call to action: "We have the option to put out the flames and build our own paradise, but we must have the desire to start, and start now." Mare is one of many artists—indigenous and immigrant—who are raising their voice to draw attention to the plight of the Latinx community. In the United States, Snow Tha Product in particular has also been an outspoken opponent of the Trump administration, and she is featured prominently on "Immigrants (We Get the Job Done)" from *The Hamilton Mixtape*.

WHY WHITE KIDS LOVE HIP HOP

In *Hip Hop: Beyond Beats and Rhymes*, Jadakiss tells Byron Hurt that, as far as record sales, "Beyond 700,000 [sold] it's all white people."[34] A widely circulated statistic suggests that roughly 70% of rap music is purchased by white people, many of whom reside in the suburbs.[35] In a 1992 interview, Ice-T opined that "Black kids buy the records, but white kids buy the cassette, the CD, the album, the tour jacket, the hats, everything. Black kids might just be buying the bootleg on the street."[36] Certainly there are economic reasons for this: middle-class white America has more disposable income with which to *buy* rap music: the statistic measures only sales, not general consumption. Tricia Rose indicates that such figures do not account for the circulation of bootlegs and mixtapes.[37] With the advent of the internet, sales figures are no longer an accurate measure of consumption: downloads and streams—both legal and illegal—undoubtedly skew the figures. If, as Perry, Cobb, and others claim, rap is primarily black music, what accounts for its popularity with white audiences? There are four interrelated ways to think about how white audiences engage with hip hop: mainstream hip hop reinforces the power dynamics of white supremacy; it is aligned with being cool; it provides a strategy for rebellion; and it offers an opportunity to dismantle racial barriers.[38]

As we have seen in various places throughout this book, rap music—mainstream rap in particular—reinforces many of the structures of white supremacist capitalist patriarchy through its repetition of negative stereotypes. For listeners who grew up in predominantly white suburban or rural communities and who may have had limited opportunities to interact with oppressed communities, hip-hop culture, as mediated through music, television, and film, might be their only "interaction" with the black community. This kind of cultural voyeurism is problematic because the images of black culture in hip hop are very much mediated images, and the interaction is one-sided. Rose refers to this phenomenon as "racial tourism"; Stanley Crouch and Kevin Powell call it a "cultural safari."[39] Jay-Z echoes these sentiments. In an interview with Kitwana, he likens hip hop to a movie: "You get to put on this pair of headphones, close your eyes and go through this movie without experiencing it for the most part. You get to go through this fantasy world, where the ultra, super hero guy who nobody could harm, has been through a tough situation and he came out great. Take the CD out. Take the headphones off and go shoot hoops. That's a very easy education."[40] Rose argues that by failing to address the social policies that give rise to the lifestyles depicted in most mainstream rap, artists and record labels are profiting from black suffering, thanks in part to "naive consumption across the color line."[41] For the most part, record labels avoid overt critiques of white supremacy because they are complicit in the system and would risk alienating white listeners and losing profits.

Black music and culture has historically been associated with coolness, and many young people choose to participate in hip hop as they formulate their identities. Mainstream white culture is normative and bland; to paraphrase bell hooks, rap music functions as a "spice" to liven it up.[42] Imani Perry observes the irony in this: "They [white rap consumers] long for rituals, rules, and codes, which they hope to purchase at the local mall in the rap section."[43]

Trying to capitalize on rap's coolness can easily devolve into imitation, as was the case with Vanilla Ice. Hess writes that the wigger—"a white person who aspires to African-American coolness and cultural cache by mimicking aspects of the speech and fashion style of black hip hop artists"—is among the most scorned figures in hip hop.[44] The term surfaced in the late 1980s as hip-hop culture—not just the music, but fashion as well—was becoming increasingly mainstream and available to white audiences. Its origins are clearly problematic, in that it evokes the N-word and, much like that epithet, "wigger" has been used both as an insult and as a term of endearment. Historian David Roediger presents evidence that the word may have originated in African-American culture. He observes that some African Americans have used the term to refer to whites who genuinely embrace the culture ("in contrast to 'wannabe' dabblers in the external trappings of rap"); in other cases, they use it dismissively, as is often the case when white people use it to refer to other white people.[45]

A scene near the end of Hurt's documentary features a blonde-haired, blue-eyed young white man from Columbus, Ohio, behind the wheel of an SUV—his father's car, he sheepishly admits. The man is in Daytona Beach, Florida, for BET's Spring Bling. As Fabolous's "Keepin' It Gangsta" plays on the radio, Hurt asks him how long he's been listening to hip hop: "Seven, eight years . . . since it started to come out in like, '91 or '92." When asked what draws him to hip hop, he praises the emotions, the beats, and the lyrics, mentioning that it's his "style." "You guys—colored people—could say that it's their music, but I can get down to it as much as they can." When Hurt calls him out on his use of "colored people," he quickly defends himself, saying he is "not racist at all."[46] And while that may be true, the ignorance of the culture that he displays—that hip hop started in the 1990s, his use of "colored people," and the sense of entitlement that he feels toward the music—reveals that he is simply imitating and borrowing superficially from the culture: he is precisely the naive listener that Rose describes.

One of the other appealing things about rap music is its status as forbidden fruit: parents, critics, religious leaders, and politicians have all heralded rap as the source of many social ills. The previous chapter mentioned Reverend Calvin Butts' campaign. Dan Quayle, who served as vice president under George H. W. Bush, called for Time Warner Records to pull Tupac's debut album, *2Pacalypse Now*, from the shelves after a copy of the album was found in a truck that was stolen by someone who murdered a police officer. The officer's family sued the label, claiming that the lyrics provoked "imminent lawless action." Conservative commentator Bill O'Reilly frequently made rap music a target on his show: he pressured Pepsi to drop its endorsement deal with Ludacris in 2002, criticized artists like Cam'ron, Lupe Fiasco, Lil Wayne, and Jay-Z for writing lyrics that he believed were damaging to the community, and even claimed that rap music was responsible for declining numbers of Christians in America. Claims such as this—that rap music causes violence, or sexism, or poverty—are impossible to substantiate; rather, it is more likely that the music is a symptom of the social, political, and economic policies that create the conditions. Placing the blame on hip hop ignores the role of white supremacy in enacting and enforcing those policies: we will explore these ideas more fully in Chapter 12.

Given the disdain that these public figures have for rap music, some youth look to rap music as means to defy authority. Kitwana notes that grunge served as the countercultural voice for many young white people in the early 1990s, but it disappeared almost as quickly as it peaked: Kurt Cobain, the lead singer of Nirvana, killed himself in 1994, an event that many believe hastened the genre's decline.[47] The same shifts in the music industry that led to grunge's popularity also pushed rap to the top of the charts (see Chapter 6), and, as grunge faded, many young people sought out hip hop for its political messages.

While it may be the case that many listeners engage with rap on a rather superficial level, there are those who embrace it as a way in to social justice. Bakari Kitwana suggests that young people identify with more than just the music: they identify with the broader culture that hip hop represents.[48] Two conditions distinguish this kind of engagement with hip hop from the three previously mentioned. First, listeners must be willing to look beyond the pleasure that brought them to hip hop in the first place.[49] As the young man above indicated, the beats and the lyrics are what bring people to hip hop, but, as Rose cautions, we must "beware the manipulation of the funk."[50] Second, an understanding of hip hop's history, the social, political, and economic conditions that gave rise to it, and the ways in which mainstream media use it as a tool for social control by commodifying black hypermasculinity need to be in place. Whether that knowledge is acquired through formal means (reading this book or many others written about hip hop) or informal means (immersion in hip-hop culture) is irrelevant. hooks warns that a perspective based in imperialist nostalgia—a longing for that which we were complicit in destroying—is unproductive. Rather, white allies must assert their role in the destruction and work toward dismantling the systems that led to the destruction in the first place. She writes, "mutual recognition of racism, its impact both on those who are dominated and those who dominate, is the only standpoint that makes possible an encounter between races that is not based on denial and fantasy."[51] Some early rap, particularly those groups with a strong political message, and a good bit of contemporary underground rap has done a lot to recognize the racism inherent in these systems. Kajikawa notes that for the most part, underground hip hop is colorblind as a result of its pushing back against the tenets of mainstream rap.[52] Anthony Kwame Harrison writes about how authentic engagement in the underground hip-hop scene yields alternative racial formations, in part because the genre inverts the standard race and class hierarchies found in the United States.[53] These alternative formations challenge the prevailing racial binary found in most contemporary mainstream rap. hooks argues that it's impossible to take Public Enemy seriously in songs like "Fight the Power" because PE is not linked to an organized movement, a sentiment echoed by Kevin Powell. While songs like that may sound an alarm, they accomplish little more than that. Powell notes that, unlike some current hip-hop protest songs—he is referring specifically to Jay-Z's song "Open Letter"—Public Enemy's message is directed outward at an audience, "an expression for all of us," not just an "individual expression."[54] Nonetheless, hip hop has been—and continues to be—a valuable tool for community organizing, a topic that will be covered in more depth in Chapter 12.

OUTRO

Names you should know:

- Omar Offendum
- The Himalayan Project
- Vanilla Ice
- Eminem

- Iggy Azalea
- Frank Waln
- Mare Avertencia Lirika

Terms you should know:

- Imitation
- Immersion

- Inversion

Questions for discussion/writing prompts:

1. Listen to "Pop Goes the Weasel" and "Gas Face" by 3rd Bass, a white rap group that was roughly contemporary with Vanilla Ice. How do Pete Nice and MC Serch negotiate their racial identity?

2. What are some elements of Southeast Asian, Muslim, or East Asian culture that hip hop has appropriated?

3. A number of underground Asian-American rappers, such as the Chinese-American Jin and Korean-American Dumbfoundead, use their music to address issues of race and representation. Choose a song by one of these artists—consider "Learning Chinese," or "Safe," respectively—and, using the strategies in this chapter, discuss how they deal with these issues.

Additional listening:

- "Complexion," Kendrick Lamar (feat. Rapsody)
- "Backpackers," Childish Gambino

Muslim rap:

- *Starwomen*, Poetic Pilgrimage
- "Ahmed," "Obama Nation," Low-Key
- *Islah*, Kevin Gates
- *All the Beauty in This Whole Life*, Brother Ali

Desi rap:

- "Blood Brothers," Karmacy
- *The Middle Passage*, The Himalayan Project

Native rap:

- "Stand Up/Stand N Rock," Taboo, et al.
- "Prayer Loop Song," Supaman
- "R.E.D.," Tribe Called Red

Latinx rap:

- "Immigrants (We Get the Job Done)," K'naan, Snow Tha Product, Riz MC, Residente
- "La Raza," Kid Frost
- "Bad Lil Bish," Raven Felix
- "Mexican Power," Proper Dos

Whiteness:

- "White America," Eminem
- "Before They Called You White," Brother Ali
- "White Privilege," Macklemore
- "Till I Die," Machine Gun Kelly
- "Professional Rapper," Lil Dicky

NOTES

1 Imani Perry, *Prophets of the Hood* (Durham, NC: Duke University Press, 2005), 10.
2 William Jelani Cobb, *To the Break of Dawn: A Freestyle on the Hip Hop Aesthetic* (New York: New York University Press, 2007), 7.
3 bell hooks, *We Real Cool: Black Men and Masculinity* (New York: Routledge, 2004), 151. Nelson George makes a similar claim, that the music was never "solely African-American created, owned, controlled, and consumed": see *Hip Hop America* (New York: Viking, 1998), 19. See also David Samuels, "The Rap on Rap: The 'Black Music' That Isn't Either" *New Republic* (November 11, 1991), 24–9. Reprinted in *That's the Joint! The Hip-Hop Studies Reader*. Ed. Murray Forman and Mark Anthony Neal (New York: Routledge, 2004), 147–53.
4 Charise L. Cheney, *Brothers Gonna Work It Out: Sexual Politics in the Golden Age of Rap Nationalism* (New York: New York University Press, 2005), chapters 1 and 2 in particular.
5 Michael Omi and Howard Winant, *Racial Formation in the United States*, 2nd ed. (New York: Routledge, 1994), 55.

6 Anthony Kwame Harrison offers a perspective on these competing theories of hip hop's racial dynamics in chapter 3 of *Hip Hop Underground: The Integrity and Ethics of Racial Identification* (Philadelphia: Temple University Press, 2009).

7 Loren Kajikawa, *Sounding Race in Rap Songs* (Berkeley: University of California Press, 2015), 5.

8 Kajikawa 6.

9 Kajikawa 10.

10 Justin A. Williams, *Rhymin' and Stealin': Musical Borrowing in Hip Hop* (Ann Arbor: University of Michigan Press, 2013), chapter 2.

11 Williams 47.

12 Williams 64–6. The article he cites is David Malley, "Digable Planets" *Rolling Stone Album Guide*: www.rollingstone.com/artists/digableplanets/biography.

13 Harrison, chapter 3.

14 Hisham Aidi, " 'Verily, There Is Only One Hip-Hop Umma': Islam, Cultural Protest and Urban Marginality" *Socialism and Democracy* 18 no. 2 (July–December 2004): 108–9.

15 Aidi 109. See also Cheney, chapter 5.

16 Su'ad Abdul Khabeer, *Muslim Cool: Race, Religion, and Hip Hop in the United States* (New York: New York University Press, 2016), 8–9.

17 Khabeer 8.

18 "Getting to Know Omar Offendum," www.youtube.com/watch?v=zdgJ3F8S_14.

19 "Getting to Know Omar Offendum."

20 Abouzeid Rania, "Syria's War, and Its Past, on a Street Called Straight" *New Yorker* (2013): www.newyorker.com/news/news-desk/syria-war-and-its-past-on-a-street-called-straight.

21 Nitasha Tamar Sharma, *Hip Hop Desis: South Asian Americans, Blackness, and a Global Race Consciousness* (Durham, NC: Duke University Press, 2010), introduction and chapter 1.

22 Sharma 2–3.

23 Sharma 28.

24 Kathy Iandoli, "Beats, Rhymes, and Death" *Vice* (November 13, 2012): www.vice.com/en_us/article/beats-rhymes-and-death-0000345-v19n11.

25 Mickey Hess, *Is Hip Hop Dead? The Past, Present, and Future of America's Most Wanted Music* (Westport, CT: Praeger, 2007), chapters 5 and 6.

26 Armond White, "Who Wants to See Ten Niggers Play Basketball?" in *Droppin' Science: Critical Essays on Rap Music and Hip Hop Culture*. Ed. William Eric Perkins (Philadelphia: Temple University Press, 1996), 199.

27 Kajikawa 124.

28 Jeff Guo, "How Iggy Azalea Mastered Her 'Blaccent' " *Washington Post* (January 4, 2016): www.washingtonpost.com/news/wonk/wp/2016/01/04/how-a-white-australian-rapper-mastered-her-blaccent.

29 Hess 126.

30 Hess 128.

31 Jeff Chang, *Can't Stop, Won't Stop: A History of the Hip-Hop Generation* (New York: St. Martin's, 2005), 412.

32 Ramon Ramirez, "Lil Dicky's '$ave Dat Money' Video Reveals an Ugly Truth about Hip-Hop and Race" *Daily Dot* (September 18, 2015): www.dailydot.com/via/lil-dicky-save-dat-money-fetty-wap.

33 "Frank Waln's New Single 'Treaties' Is a Call for Justice" *RPM (Revolutions Per Minute)* (February 7, 2017): http://rpm.fm/music/premiere-frank-waln-new-single-treaties-is-a-call-for-justice.

34 Byron Hurt, *Hip-Hop: Beyond Beats and Rhymes* (Northampton, MA: Media Education Foundation, 2006).

35 Bakari Kitwana challenges this statistic in chapter 2 of *Why White Kids Love Hip Hop: Wankstas, Wiggers, Wannabes, and the New Reality of Race in America* (New York: Basic Civitas Books, 2005).

36 Alan Light, "The Ice-T Interview" *Rolling Stone* (August 20, 1992): www.rollingstone.com/music/news/the-rolling-stone-interview-ice-t-19920820.

37 Tricia Rose, *Black Noise: Rap Music and Black Culture in Contemporary America* (Hanover, NH: Wesleyan University Press, 1994), 6–8.

38 See Kitwana, *White Kids*, introduction and chapter 1.

39 Tricia Rose, *The Hip Hop Wars* (New York: BasicCivitas, 2008), 224–5; Bakari Kitwana, "Zen and the Art of Transcending the Status Quo: The Reach from the Hood to the Suburbs," in *Jay-Z: Essays on Hip-Hop's Philosopher King*. Ed. Julius Bailey (Jefferson, NC: McFarland, 2011), 110.

40 Kitwana, "Zen," 110.

41 Rose, *Hip Hop Wars*, 224.

42 bell hooks, "Eating the Other: Desire and Resistance," in *Black Looks: Race and Representation* (Boston: South End Press, 1992), 14.

43 Perry 126.

44 Hess 140.

45 David R. Roediger, "Elvis, Wiggers, and Crossing over to Nonwhiteness," in *The Hip Hop Reader*. Ed. Tim Strode and Tim Wood (New York: Longman, 2008), 85–7.

46 Byron Hurt, *Hip-Hop: Beyond Beats and Rhymes* (Northampton, MA: Media Education Foundation).

47 Kitwana, *White Kids*, 28.

48 Kitwana, *White Kids*, xii.

49 hooks, "Eating the Other," 35–6.

50 Rose, *Hip Hop Wars*, 262–4.

51 hooks, "Eating the Other," 28.

52 Kajikawa 143, fn 1.

53 Harrison 2009.

54 Travis L. Gosa and Erik Nielson, "'There Are No Saviors': An Interview with Kevin Powell," *in The Hip-Hop and Obama Reader*. Ed. Travis L. Gosa and Erik Nielson (New York: Oxford University Press, 2015), 80; hooks, "Eating the Other," 33.

TIME LINE

1966 Huey Newton and Bobby Seale form the Black Panther Party for Self-Defense in Oakland, California.

1982 Grandmaster Flash & The Furious Five's song "The Message" is released.

—Afrika Bambaataa & The Soul Sonic Force release "Planet Rock."

1991 Tupac Shakur releases his debut album, *2Pacalypse Now*.

IN THIS CHAPTER, YOU WILL LEARN ABOUT

- The role and sound of the city in hip hop
- Hip hop's expression of confinement and mobility
- How groups of people construct space

CHAPTER 10

Listening to Space

OVERVIEW

This chapter considers the ways in which spaces are created, as well as the roles that these spaces play throughout hip hop's history. Following the work of Murray Forman, we will define "space" here as a set of repeated social practices. While the relationship among the topics in this chapter may initially seem disparate, all the topics represent a different way of constructing and thinking about spaces. In the first part, we consider the construction of the "'hood" or the "ghetto" as it appears in rap lyrics and throughout history. The Black Panther Party for Self-Defense emerged in the 1960s in order to defend the black community from the police, which they viewed as an occupying force. Street gangs in the Bronx, in Los Angeles, and elsewhere claimed turf and would defend it against others who tried to encroach. In some cases, these gangs evolved into hip-hop crews, and battles for turf moved to the dance floor or the microphone. The rise of the internet over the last two decades has seen the rise of virtual spaces, where artists and fans can connect in new ways and where traditional music industry practices have been subverted. The interplay between confinement and mobility is central to understanding rap music.

LISTENING TO THE CITY

The second verse of Ice-T's "Midnight" begins with driving directions: "We boned down Vernon, made a right on Normandie/Left on Florence, jettin' through the E.T.G.'s/Spun out on Vermont, made a left on Colden/Right on Hoover, E where we goin?" Ice-T's characteristic attention to detail allows listeners to trace the exact location of this late-night car chase through south-central Los Angeles: Vernon, Normandie, Florence, Vermont, Colden, and Hoover are all street names. The song gives us a very strong sense of **place**; that is, a specific geographical location. The reference to E.T.G. is a bit more obscure: E.T.G. refers to the Eight Tray Gangster Crips, an offshoot of the West Side Crips. Ice-T and his friends are in unfriendly territory, a **space** whose boundaries are defined by the members of the gang. When talking about hip hop, it is useful to distinguish between place and space. Place is an actual physical location: the Bronx, the Marcy Projects, Ice-T's route, or the intersection of Apple and Eagle Streets in Hollygrove, near Lil Wayne's childhood home. Space is socially constructed by a different, more abstract set of barriers: poverty, economic climate, and food deserts—among other things—enforce spaces. Unlike places, spaces can shift: gentrification is a clear example of this process. Rappers can create spaces in their lyrics as well: the generic image of the "inner city" and the more specific image of Wu-Tang's Shaolin (Staten Island) are two examples. One of the central dynamics of hip hop is the interplay between confinement and mobility, the ability to navigate place and space.[1]

William Jelani Cobb notes that both the mobility offered by the railroad and the metaphorical decision implied by the crossroads, both hallmarks of early blues, are replaced with a more static image in hip hop: the ghetto. He writes, "the relationship between blues and hip hop is the relationship between journeys and destinations."[2] The **ghetto** can be defined as a place where people are forced to live and where the prospects for leaving are often slim. The mechanisms for keeping residents trapped range from the political and economic to the use of force. Chapter 5 outlined the impact of politics in the South Bronx during the 1970s. Economically, **postindustrialization**—the after-effects of manufacturing industries moving out of a region—is another contributor to poverty. Often, laborers are left unemployed, with few opportunities available for unskilled workers.[3] **Redlining** kept residents of certain areas—which were often literally outlined in red on maps—from getting loans or mortgages. M. K. Asante, in his "Interview with the Ghetto," writes that the Federal Housing Administration (FHA) cautioned lenders against areas that exhibited "inharmonious racial groups" and that many largely black neighborhoods were zoned "industrial," which restricted development and improvement to the neighborhood.[4] Businesses that aim to profit from suffering—check-cashing establishments, fast-food restaurants, and liquor stores, among others—appear with greater frequency in the inner city and further keep the population at a disadvantage by discouraging saving and investing, hampering healthy eating habits, and facilitating substance abuse.

Historically, the Jewish ghettos in Europe leading up to the Second World War were walled off and patrolled by soldiers who were instructed to kill anyone who tried to leave. While the situation in the United States today might not appear as drastic as that in 1930s Europe, a strong argument could be made that police departments, particularly those with so-called "broken windows" or "stop-and-frisk" policies, are serving a similar function. The theory of broken-windows crime prevention argues that enforcing small crimes like littering and vandalism will ultimately prevent major crimes from taking place. This same philosophy led to "stop-and-frisk" laws, which gave the police authority to temporarily detain and search any person that they believed looked suspicious. Nearly 90% of those stopped were young black or Latino men. Very few were actually arrested, and, if they were charged, it was often with a simple misdemeanor. Mass incarceration (which we will examine in Chapter 12) continues the cycle of confinement. The use of stop-and-frisk by the New York City Police Department dropped dramatically from 2011 to 2015, in part due to pressure from a number of lawsuits. Talk of stop-and-frisk reappeared in the national news as part of Donald Trump's "tough on crime" presidential platform in 2016.

The ghetto, the 'hood, the projects, the block, and the corner are examples of socially constructed space and are central to hip hop. Building on the work of Lakoff and Johnson, Scott Crossley suggests that these terms are conceptual metaphors that help us understand complex ideas. Crossley observes that many of the metaphors used to describe the environments in which minority communities live (i.e., "crib," "block") have come to imply restriction as opposed to protection, and he believes that these metaphors have, in turn, contributed to "the general suspicion and disenfranchisement that many of the hip-hop generation have toward US power structures."[5] Thus, rap music not only reflects the characteristics implicit in these metaphorical spaces, but also helps define and redefine them. Crossley continues, noting that these metaphors synthesize an assortment of features that are more social than geographical: a general lack of available employment (and subsequent reliance on underground economies), materialism, views on gender and sexuality, and violence. The metaphors also imply communities as well. Both Murray Forman and Michael Eric Dyson make similar claims with respect to the "hood" or "ghetto." Not only do the terms denote a specific geographical region, but also they connote a community: in Dyson's words, "a bond established between those who suffer and struggle together who long for an exit from its [the ghetto's] horrible limits."[6]

As the urban renewal project began in the 1930s and 1940s, many of the homes that were destroyed—particularly in East Coast cities—were replaced with high-rise apartment buildings: given the scarcity of land area, the only direction in which to build was up. Mark Katz describes the *sound* of Afrika Bambaataa's home, the Bronx River Housing Projects: "a complex of nine fourteen-story buildings with more than three thousand residents. Standing in the courtyard is like standing at the bottom of a canyon, and the sounds emanating from the densely populated buildings can be all-enveloping."[7] DJs in the inner city, then, had to drown out their surroundings in order to get the crowd moving. Furthermore, these sound systems were a way of *claiming* territory: recall the fifty-five-gallon drum speakers from Chapter 5 that could be heard—felt—from ten blocks away.[8]

LISTENING GUIDE 10.1

Artist: Grandmaster Flash & The Furious Five
Song: "The Message"
Album: (single)
Record label: Sugar Hill
Year released: 1982
DJ or Producer: Written by Melle Mel and Duke Bootee; Reggie Griffin (synthesizer)
Samples used: (none)

TIME	MUSICAL CHARACTERISTICS	LYRICS	DESCRIPTION
0:00	Introduction (2 measures); cymbal roll leads into a synthesizer riff (8 measures)		
0:26	Refrain (x2) (2 measures) + 4 "extra" measures	"It's like a jungle sometimes/It makes me wonder how I keep from goin' under"	Melle Mel Spoken almost under his breath
0:45	Verse 1 (8 measures)	"Broken glass everywhere . . ."	
1:04	Hook (4 measures) + refrain	"Don't push me 'cause I'm close to the edge . . ."	The syncopation makes the lyrics sound like he's teetering on the edge.
1:18	Verse 2 (10 measures)	"Standin' on the front stoop . . ."	
1:42	Hook + refrain (x2)	"Don't push me 'cause I'm close to the edge . . ."	
2:01	Verse 3 (12 measures)	"My brother's doin' bad . . ."	Duke Bootee Note the excited tone near the end of the verse.

TIME	MUSICAL CHARACTERISTICS	LYRICS	DESCRIPTION
2:30	Hook + refrain	"Don't push me 'cause I'm close to the edge . . ."	
2:48	Verse 4 (16 measures)	"My son said, Daddy . . ."	
3:27	Hook + refrain	"Don't push me 'cause I'm close to the edge . . ."	Melle Mel
3:46	Verse 5 (28 measures)	"A child is born . . ."	The lyrical delivery sounds more desperate here and gets more intense as the verse unfolds.
4:54	Hook + refrain	"Don't push me 'cause I'm close to the edge . . ."	Menacing laughter after the chorus
5:13	Skit	"Yo, Mel—you see that girl over there?"	

Despite the billing, Grandmaster Flash and four of The Furious Five do not appear on the track until the skit at the end, when the group has a run-in with the police. The song was written and performed by Melle Mel and Duke Bootee, a studio musician at Sugar Hill Records, and the memorable synthesizer riff was added by Reggie Griffin, another studio musician.

"The Message" is significant because it was the first rap release that really drew attention to the conditions that the residents of the South Bronx (and no doubt other inner-city areas) experienced on a daily basis. Murray Forman argues that Grandmaster Flash's "The Message" almost single-handedly moved rap music from inside the clubs to outside on the streets, where it has remained for nearly four decades.[9] Thematically, the song is about systems of confinement:

- "Got no money to move out; I guess I got no choice"
- "I tried to get away, but I couldn't get far/Because a man with a tow truck repossessed my car"
- "Can't take the train to the job, there's a strike at the station"
- "Got sent up for an eight-year bid"

The song also addresses the sound of the city: the opening line, "Broken glass everywhere," is accompanied by the sound of shattering glass. The skit at the end includes the sound of a car horn, police sirens, and a scuffle between the band members and the police.

Conceptions of space are not necessarily tied to physical locations. Descriptions of the ghetto resonate in many ways with descriptions of black masculinity: both rely heavily on metaphors of containment. bell hooks writes: "In patriarchal culture, all males learn a role that restricts and confines. When race and class enter the picture, along with patriarchy, then black males endure the worst impositions of gendered masculine patriarchal identity."[10] At the beginning of *Beyond Beats and Rhymes*, Byron Hurt refers to masculinity as a box; Conrad Tiller, a pastor whom Hurt interviews, talks about it as a prison.[11] hooks argues that love has the power to set them free: "If black males were loved they could hope for more than a life locked down, caged, confined; they could imagine themselves beyond containment."[12]

THE BLACK PANTHER PARTY

In 1966 in Oakland, California, Huey Newton and Bobby Seale laid the groundwork for the **Black Panther Party for Self-Defense.** The BPP emerged in response to widespread acts of police harassment and aggression toward residents of Oakland. Inspired by both Marxist revolutionaries around the world and the Civil Rights movement in the American South (the Black Panther was the same logo used by the Lowndes County Freedom Organization, a black political party formed in 1965 in Alabama), the Panthers used the law to their advantage in an effort to put an end to police brutality. Dressed in distinctive leather jackets and berets and visibly armed with rifles and shotguns, the Panthers would observe the activities of the police and read suspects their rights. California was an open-carry state—and Oakland's gun laws, in particular, were very permissive—so the Panthers were permitted to carry guns. The image of the party thus stood in stark contrast to the images of nonviolent protest associated with Dr. Martin Luther King Jr. and his followers (though the Panthers eventually recruited Stokely Carmichael, the one-time head of the Student Nonviolent Coordinating Committee—SNCC—and founder of the Lowndes County Freedom Organization, to their cause). The aggressive tactics of the Panthers led the California State Legislature to tighten restrictions on the open carry of firearms, and the new law—the Mulford Act of 1967—was widely viewed as racially motivated.

In the context of the BPP, self-defense is more of a collective action than an individual one. The Panthers viewed the police as an occupying force, and their activities were directed at defending their communities against this occupying force. They believed that their situation had much in common with similar occupations in China, Cuba, and Vietnam, and they studied the work of Mao Tse-tung, Che Guevara, Frantz Fanon, and other revolutionaries for guidance. Robyn C. Spencer situates their philosophy in the context of other contemporary black nationalist organizations. The Panthers were inspired by former head of the NAACP Robert Williams, who believed in "meeting machine gun with machine gun, hand grenade with hand grenade"; in short, "whatever method in our possession" to protect the interests of the black community. Spencer contends that the Panthers' "radical edge was in conceiving African Americans within the American political contract, challenging the historic correlation of a constitutionally protected right to bear arms with white privilege."[13] The Panthers' knowledge of history and willingness to use it against the government is nowhere more apparent than in their Ten-Point Program.

The Ten-Point Program

The Black Panther Party's Ten-Point Program reads very much like a bill of rights for the African-American community: each of the points includes a statement of "What we want" and "What we believe." In short, the party wanted an end to racist government policies that continued to deprive them of basic human rights and freedoms on which America was presumably founded. The tenth point Signifies on the opening of the Declaration of Independence:

> When, in the course of human events, it becomes necessary for one people to dissolve the political bands which have connected them with another, and to assume, among the powers of the earth, the separate and equal station to which the laws of nature and nature's God entitle them, a decent respect to the opinions of mankind requires that they should declare the causes which impel them to the separation.
>
> We hold these truths to be self-evident, that all men are created equal; that they are endowed by their Creator with certain unalienable rights; that among these are life, liberty, and the pursuit of happiness.

By including the text of the Declaration verbatim (in a context that suggests the Bill of Rights), the BPP called attention to the hypocrisy of the governmental policies that they sought to have overturned.

Newton wanted the Ten-Point Program to be accessible to the "brothers on the block." Newton, Seale, and others repeatedly invoked the "block" metaphor. In a chapter of his autobiography *Revolutionary Suicide* titled "Brothers on the Block," Newton draws a clear distinction between the "brothers on the block" and the "system" and how he had to negotiate both spheres while he attended college. "In school, the 'system' was the teacher but on the block the system was everything that was not a positive part of the community."[14] People went to college to become part of the system, Newton observed, to earn money and move away. The block, on the other hand, was a space where people "struggled for survival."[15] Newton tried to bridge the divide by bringing philosophy and poetry to the block:

> I told them about the allegory of the cave from Plato's *Republic*, and they enjoyed it. In the cave allegory Plato describes the plight of the prisoners in a cave who receive their impression of the outside world from shadows projected on the wall by the fire at the mouth of the cave. [. . .] The allegory seemed very appropriate to our own situation in society. We, too, were in prison and needed to be liberated in order to distinguish between truth and the falsehoods imposed on us.
>
> The dudes on the block still thought I was "out of sight" and sometimes just plain crazy.[16]

Newton's conversations on the block also informed his schoolwork. His conversations on the block led him to study police science and law, which laid the groundwork for the Panthers' first interventions. To Newton, the block seems to provide a sense of authenticity—"keepin' it real"—that the system cannot, a belief that would come to pervade hip-hop culture as well. His recollection of these interactions shows how he was able to work simultaneously in two different spaces.

The BPP soon spread to other major cities. The charismatic Fred Hampton quickly became a leader in the Chicago arm of the party. Hampton worked with other revolutionary groups of all races and ethnicities to forge a coalition dedicated to freedom for all: this marked him as a serious threat, and on December 4, 1969, he was killed in his bed during an early-morning police raid. While the images spread by the media of the Panthers painted them as violent revolutionaries, this was far from the truth. One of the BPP's most important programs involved providing free breakfast to children. The party also championed health care for the community.

The activities of the BPP, as well as those of other activist groups, caught the attention of the Federal Bureau of Investigation (FBI), headed at that time by J. Edgar Hoover. At one point, Hoover stated publicly that the BPP presented the single greatest internal threat to national security. Hoover established a Counter-Intelligence Program, COINTELPRO, to monitor the activities of these groups. COINTELPRO had unprecedented surveillance capabilities, used spies to infiltrate the organizations, and forged letters from members to destabilize the leadership. In April of 1969, police in New York City arrested twenty-one Panthers, charging them with conspiracy to kill police officers and bomb several government buildings. Bail was set unreasonably high—$100,000 for each defendant—in a move that many viewed as an effort to keep the accused imprisoned. Many Hollywood celebrities came to the aid of the "**Panther 21**," as they were called, including Marlon Brando, Jane Fonda, and Leonard Bernstein. (The association between these stars and groups like the BPP was famously caricatured in Thomas Wolfe's essay "Radical Chic.") Among those arrested was Afeni Shakur—who, at the time, was pregnant with a son, Tupac.

While generally thought of as the face of West Coast rap, Tupac Shakur was actually born in New York and grew up in Baltimore before moving to the West Coast. Tupac's mother; his stepfather, Mtulu; his aunt, Assata; and his godfather, Geronimo Pratt, were all active members of the BPP. Thus Tupac grew up immersed in revolutionary ideology. One of the first soio tracks Tupac recorded was "Panther Power," which clearly outlines many of the beliefs of the party. The song predates his debut album, *2Pacalypse Now*, which includes another lesson in Panther power, albeit more subtly framed.

LISTENING GUIDE 10.2

Artist: Tupac Shakur
Song: "Violent"
Album: *2Pacalypse Now*
Record label: Death Row
Year released: 1991
DJ or Producer: Underground Railroad
Samples used: "Rebel without a Pause," Public Enemy

Against a reggae-inspired beat, the song opens with the lyrics "They claim that I'm violent/Just because I refuse to be silent," suggesting that Tupac's race inflects how people interpret his speech and lyrics. Hints of his Panther upbringing occur throughout the first verse, in which he criticizes the "hypocrites"—those who claim to abide by the rule of law; see the Ten-Point Program above—and point out that America (i.e., the government) has its own history of violence. State-sanctioned violence, however, is rarely subject to public critique, since it appears legitimate and natural. At the end of that verse, Tupac invokes a common rap metaphor: that his words are weapons. By establishing this metaphor, Tupac invites the listener to interpret the remaining verses as an extension of it. A line toward the end of the song, "We'll shoot 'em up with their own fuckin' weapons," resonates with the ways in which the Panthers worked inside the system, using the government's own language and laws against them.

In the second verse, Tupac details an encounter that he and his friend have with the police. The lyrical context suggests that the traffic stop was (another) case of racial profiling, perhaps a drug stop (they "Call me a dope man cause I rock dope beats," another metaphor). The police inform Tupac that he and his friend were out past curfew: curfew laws are among the political tactics that society can employ to construct a confining space. Tupac recalls that he had a choice to make: "I better make my mind up/Pick my nine [-millimeter pistol] up or hit the lineup." The line is important, given the criticisms of rap music as inherently violent. Tupac and his friend decide to comply with the officer's request but are nonetheless subjected to hostile treatment. The shooting match that closes the song—presumably before Tupac and his friend are gunned down by police—is thus an act of self-defense, not aggression on Tupac's part.

FROM THE BLACK SPADES TO THE ZULU NATION

Given the anarchy that prevailed in the South Bronx in the 1960s, street gangs formed as a way to protect neighborhood interests. In the early 1970s, the Bronx had more than 100 gangs, with membership totaling close to 11,000.[17] The two biggest gangs were the Black Spades, whose membership was predominantly black, and the Savage Skulls, whose membership was largely Puerto Rican. These gangs had divisions throughout the borough: Jeff Chang notes that there were almost fifty divisions of the Savage Skulls that reached out beyond the Bronx, past New York City and into New Jersey and Pennsylvania.[18] Gabriel Torres, Minister of Defense for the Young Lords Party (a mostly Puerto Rican gang in New York City) says that the gangs "sprouted up [. . .] as a defense for the particular communities."[19] Danny DeJesus, a member of the Savage Skulls, said, "Before they would go to the local police, the people would come to us to solve their problems."[20] The gangs also provided a system of social support for young people in communities where the education system was failing, unemployment was high, and social opportunities had been destroyed. Another Savage Skull, Tata, claimed, "That's the only way we can survive out here, because if we all go our own ways, one by one, we're gone."[21]

Afrika Bambaataa was the leader of the Black Spades. Bambaataa recognized the damaging effects that gang life was having on his community and acknowledged the power that art had to bring people together. Under his leadership, the Black Spades became the Organization, which then became the Zulu Nation. Bambaataa was inspired by a 1964 British film, *Zulu*, in which an African tribe valiantly stands up against a colonizing British force: the Zulu Nation, then, represented an effort to reclaim what had been taken from the residents of the South Bronx by white America. Rather than settle disputes with violence, the Zulu Nation encouraged rival groups to settle their arguments through competitive dancing, graffiti, and music.

Not unlike the gangs of the South Bronx, early hip-hop DJs had their own territories and crews that offered support and protection. Grandmaster Flash recounts: "Kool Herc had the West Side, Bam[baataa] had Bronx River, DJ Breakout had way uptown past Gun Hill. Myself, my area was like 138th Street, Cypress Avenue, up to Gun Hill, so that we all had our territories and we all had to respect each other."[22] Forman theorizes that the territories that Flash describes are attached as much to place as they are to space: they not only are defined geographically, but also are defined by repeated practices within those regions. As Forman notes, the respect that Flash speaks of has little to do with a particular DJ's skill and more to do with an acknowledgment of the boundaries of his territory.[23] Bambaataa played an important role in breaking down these barriers and encouraging the spread of hip hop beyond the Bronx, New York City, and even the country. He was one of the first rappers to travel and tour internationally, and his status as the "master of records" (see Chapter 5) could be seen as a metaphor for his global consciousness. "[W]hen you came to an Afrika Bambaataa party, you had to be progressive-minded and knew that you was going to hear some weird type stuff," Bambaataa recalls.[24]

LISTENING GUIDE 10.3

Artist: Afrika Bambaataa & The Soul Sonic Force
Song title: "Planet Rock"
Album title: (single)
Record label: Tommy Boy
Year released: 1982
DJ or Producer: Arthur Baker
Samples used: "Trans-Europe Express," "Numbers," Kraftwerk; "The Mexican," Babe Ruth; "Super Sporm," Captain Sky

"Planet Rock" is one of the most influential songs in rap's history. Many argue that it almost single-handedly laid the groundwork for Miami bass, Los Angeles' early electro-funk sound, and many genres of electronic dance music. The futuristic soundscape that provides the backdrop for the group's lyrics is the result of the Kraftwerk samples, the TR-808, and the Fairlight Musical Instrument. Kraftwerk was a pioneering German synthesizer-driven band. The Fairlight was one of the earliest computer musical instruments: it provides the big synth "hit" that appears on the first beat of every two measures. Bambaataa gets the party started, shouting out The Soul Sonic Force and the Zulu Nation with his robotic voice (his voice is altered with a vocoder). Like other early rap songs we have considered, the song emulates a party, with simulated crowd noises, call and response, and long breaks for dancing. The members of The Soul Sonic Force—Pow Wow, G.L.O.B.E., and Mr. Biggs—rhyme individually and in unison, and they relay syllables to one another.

Planet Rock is a metaphor for the disco, a place where people from diverse communities can come together. The song comes on the heels of the Afrofuturist aesthetic that emerged in the 1970s, spearheaded by writers like Octavia Butler and musicians like George Clinton and Sun Ra. Afrofuturism envisioned a space—both literal and figurative—in which the problems the black community was facing did not exist. Often, this space took shape not just in the future, but also on another planet.

Jeff Chang traces the origins of the Crips, one of the West Coast's largest and most well-known gangs, to the Los Angeles chapter of the Black Panther Party. When Bunchy Carter, the leader of the BPP in Southern California, was killed in 1969, and his bodyguard, "Geronimo" Pratt (who would later become Tupac's godfather) was arrested, Raymond Washington emerged as the next charismatic leader of the area's young people. The group he led was called the Baby Avenues, and they were well known for their violent actions. Although the exact origins of the name are unknown, the group eventually started calling themselves the Crips. The Bloods had their start in Compton, on Piru Street (Bloods are sometimes referred to as "Pirus"). As the gangs grew in size, they splintered into "sets," specific to particular neighborhoods (the Eight Tray Gangster Crips, the Rollin' 20 Crips, etc.). There was not only a rivalry between the Crips and the Bloods, but also often violent infighting among different Crip sets. Gang activity died down in the 1970s as the result of an industrial boom, but once the jobs left and crack hit the streets, the gangs reemerged. Chang estimates that there were 155 gangs, with approximately 30,000 members, in Los Angeles at the dawn of the 1980s.[25]

Gang life figured prominently in a lot of West Coast rap: "West Coast" and "gangsta rap" are practically synonymous. Many rappers were gang members and would represent their set, flash gang signs in videos or in concert, or recount stories of gang life, usually in the form of cautionary tales. Ice-T achieved some notoriety for doing the "C-Walk," or Crip Walk, on stage (although he claims that rapper WC did it first). The move is part of a Crip ritual but has become separated from the gang as more and more people—particularly those with no gang ties—treat it as a dance. In 1990, a posse cut by the West Coast Rap All-Stars (which featured Ice-T, J. J. Fad, Young MC, MC Hammer, and several members of N.W.A,) titled "We're All in the Same Gang" pleaded for an end to gang violence.

The word **posse** originally meant a group of armed men organized by the town sheriff to enforce the law. The hip-hop community co-opted the term to mean any group of people with a common affiliation. Many rappers have a posse that accompanies them in their free time, on tour, or even on stage. The Beastie Boys use the word repeatedly on their *Licensed to Ill Album* (perhaps as a nod to their whiteness by evoking the old West), even including a song titled "Posse in Effect"; N.W.A.'s first album was titled *N.W.A. and the Posse*; Sir Mix-A-Lot's first hit was "Posse on Broadway." In Chapter 3, we talked about "posse cuts," in which the song is the element that binds the artists together.

It is not uncommon for rappers to **shout out** their posses, mentioning their names and praising them. These shout-outs can take several forms. Sometimes rappers give shout-outs within a song, as in Busdriver's "Imaginary Places" (Chapter 6) or Master P's "I'm 'Bout That 'Bout That"

(Chapter 11). Shout-outs can sometimes take up an entire track (usually the last track on the album). Biz Markie's "To My Boys," Ice Cube's "I Gotta Say What Up!!!," Ice-T's "M.V.P.S.," and Eminem's "Square Dance" are examples of this. In "I Gotta Lotta Love," Ice-T shouts out the gangs of Los Angeles in the wake of 1992's gang truce. Shout-outs can also name places or—as product placement in rap has become increasingly lucrative—products. These shout-outs are typically spoken naturally, not rapped. When physical media was more dominant, one could find shout-outs on the album cover or in the booklet that came with the cassette or CD. As digital music has come to dominate, shout-outs may appear on websites or social media.

Not only have hip-hop crews emerged from gangs; in some instances, gangs have sprung up around rappers. Fans of the duo Insane Clown Posse (ICP) and other artists on their record label, Psychopathic Records, have grown into a group known as Juggalos. The name came into being during an ICP concert in 1994: following a performance of their song "The Juggla," ICP member Violent J called the audience members "Juggalos," and the crowd's reaction led to the name sticking. Many ICP fans are white, and most self-identify as "outsiders" or "outcasts"—subject positions that often appear in the duo's music—and are often stereotyped by outsiders as poor, racist, violent, and undereducated. These experiences form the basis for the creation of a community, much like the conditions faced by residents of the South Bronx and south-central Los Angeles.

Just like any culture, Juggalos have their own language and rituals. Juggalos sometimes refer to one another as "ninjas" and greet each other or express agreement with a "whoop whoop." They share a love of Faygo soda, are often seen with their faces painted in "corpse paint" (white face with black highlights around the eyes and mouth), and are expected to attend the annual Gathering of Juggalos. The Gathering spans several days, typically draws around 10,000 Juggalos, and features performances by Psychopathic Records artists as well as friends of the ICP: MC Hammer, Ice Cube, and other high-profile artists have played the festival. The festival includes wrestling matches—sponsored by the Juggalo Wrestling league—and a Miss Juggalet beauty pageant. For a brief period, the Juggalos even had their own social networking site, Juggalobook, where fans could connect and—rather than "like"—give a "whoop whoop" to someone else's status update.

Despite the widespread ridicule the group and their fans have faced—they have repeatedly earned "worst band," "worst album," or "worst song" honors from major media outlets—their album sales and the devotion of their fans are recognized as unique in hip-hop culture. DJ Paul of Three 6 Mafia told a reporter for *Vice*: "No rapper out, I don't give a shit who it is, could do what they did. They created a movement. [The Gathering of the Juggalos] has people sleeping in their cars or in the grass for three days straight. I can't think of another rapper who can do that. You gotta have more than some good songs and sold a [few] million records to do that. [They had a] a genius plan."[26] Even the FBI took notice, adding the Juggalos to a list of "Non-traditional hybrid gangs" in 2011.[27] It is possible that the Juggalos' affiliation with hip hop led the FBI to classify them as a gang; however, the report noted no significant activity beyond some anecdotal crimes. Although some of the crimes were violent, much of the violence depicted in ICP's music is cast as revenge fantasies against childhood abusers. On September 16, 2017, the Juggalos staged a march on Washington, DC, to protest the gang label and the adverse effects it was having on the community: Juggalos were losing jobs, being denied the ability to serve in the military, and losing custody of their children as a result of the gang label.

BEEF

Battles between hip-hop artists—not only rappers, but also DJs, break-dancers, and crews—have been around nearly as long as hip hop itself. We have already touched on several **beefs** in this book. In Chapter 1, we looked briefly at DJ battles; in Chapter 5, we examined the first major beef between MCs, the battle between Chief Rocker Busy Bee and Kool Moe Dee, as well as the so-called Roxanne Wars. Such beefs are battles for spatial control, whether that space be physical, ideological, or commercial. Afrika Bambaataa and the Zulu Nation are widely credited with using hip hop as a nonviolent way to settle these conflicts; however, beefs in rap still occasionally devolve into violence. The most well-known is undoubtedly the East Coast—West Coast beef between Bad Boy Records and Death Row Records, in the course of which The Notorious B.I.G. and Tupac Shakur were murdered. With the rise of social media, the nature of beef between rappers has changed.

In 1986, MC Shan and DJ Marley Marl, members of The Juice Crew, released a track titled "The Bridge," which tells the story of hip hop's origins in the Queensbridge housing projects. The record, which samples The Honey Drippers' song "Impeach the President," begins with the lines: "Ladies and gentlemen, we got MC Shan and Marley Marl in the house tonight. They just came from off tour, and they wanna tell you a little story about where they come from." The song continues, giving a short history of rap as Shan remembers it. There's a list of people and places, talk of parties in the park at night, and other elements that recall the discussion about hip hop in the Bronx earlier in this chapter. Most of the names that Shan mentions are unfamiliar to even the most knowledgeable fans of hip hop: perhaps they achieved very little status outside of the neighborhood.

LISTENING GUIDE 10.4

Artist: MC Shan
Song: "The Bridge"
Album: *Down by Law*
Record label: Juice
Year released: 1986
DJ or Producer: Marley Marl
Samples used: "Impeach the President," The Honey Drippers

Artist: Boogie Down Productions
Song: "South Bronx"
Album: *Criminal Minded*
Record label: B-Boy Records
Year released: 1986
DJ or Producer: Scott La Rock
Samples used: "Get Up Offa That Thing" and "Get Up, Get into It, Get Involved," "Funky Drummer," James Brown; "Smokin Cheeba-Cheeba," Harlem Underground Band

"The Bridge" begins with not only an allosonic quotation from "Impeach the President," but an autosonic quotation as well: Marley Marl samples the song's drums and speaks over them, "Ladies and gentlemen, we've got MC Shan and DJ Marley Marl in the house tonight," clearly alluding to the phrase that starts The Honey Drippers' track. Following the introduction, Marl scratches in what amounts to the song's hook: "The Bridge, Th-th-th-the Bridge." In the song, Shan describes the conditions under which hip hop emerged in his neighborhood. He refers to important figures (most of whom have now vanished into obscurity), landmarks, parties in the park, and shows in the clubs.

KRS-One, a member of the Boogie Down Productions (BDP) crew, "misheard" the opening of Shan's song—"You love to hear the story again and again/Of how it all got started way back

	A	broth-	er	who's		known		for	his		rap			
		Jab-	by	Jack										
1	e	&	a	2	e	&	a	3	e	&	a	4	e	&	a

K	R	S		One		is	the	hol-	der	of	a	boul-		der	
		Mon-	ey	fol-	der										
1	e	&	a	2	e	&	a	3	e	&	a	4	e	&	a

Figure 10.1 Comparison of a line from MC Shan's "The Bridge" with a line from BDP's "South Bronx"

when"—and believed that Shan was claiming that hip hop originated in Queensbridge. KRS-One and DJ Scott La Rock rushed to the studio to set the record straight: hip hop started in the South Bronx, and BDP wanted to make sure everyone knew that. They recorded "South Bronx" in two hours and got the record to DJ Red Alert, one of hip hop's earliest tastemakers.

BDP's response to "The Bridge" Signifies heavily on it. The opening of both songs is quite similar; the rhythm and content of the hook is similar, and the content is similar; however, the hip-hop pioneers that KRS-One mentions—"Coke La Rock, Kool Herc, and then Bam[baataa]," "a kid named [Grandmaster] Flash," and others—remain well-known names. KRS-One even acknowledges that he is "biting" Shan's style in the line "I only use this type of style when I choose it." There is one line in particular that accentuates the strong rhythmic similarity between Shan's and KRS-One's flow: it appears in Figure 10.1.

In both cases, the first line basically fills the bar, and the few syllables in the second line come after beat 1 and leave a lot of empty space at the end of the measure. While there is no doubt that the song is a response to Shan's record, it is important to note that nowhere in the song does KRS refer directly to Shan, Marl, or The Juice Crew.

Shan and his crew fired back with "Kill That Noise," which sampled the chorus of "South Bronx"; BDP responded with "The Bridge Is Over," which is based on a previously unreleased drum track by Marley Marl. Marl had inadvertently left a tape of drum sounds in the studio (in Queensbridge!) where BDP ended up recording their song, so they took advantage of it. This beef offers a very clear example of a turf war waged in song. In an interview for the documentary *Beef*, MC Shan boasts that he "battl[ed] a whole borough by himself."[28] Not only was there actual territory in dispute (Queensbridge and the South Bronx), but there were reputations at stake—both the artists' and the boroughs'—and a kind of sonic territory as well: in biting Shan's style, KRS-One effectively occupied it and demonstrated that he could come and go as he pleased.

Thirty years later, the beef resurfaced when MC Shan appeared on a radio show and presented a very different perspective than the one that has gone down in hip-hop history. He released a diss track aimed at KRS-One, and KRS responded swiftly with "S.H.A.N. (Still Huggin' a Nut)," a scathing takedown that shows that he is still a master craftsman. The battle here is no longer over turf, but recognition, and it was waged on a new frontier: the internet.

The rise of social media—not only networking sites like Facebook, Twitter, and Instagram, but also music services like Spotify, SoundCloud, and Bandcamp—have impacted the way rap beefs play out in recent years. The territory in question now is far more abstract, detached from physical location by virtue of the commercialization and subsequent globalization of hip-hop culture. On July 21, 2015, rapper Meek Mill tweeted "Stop comparing me to drake [*sic*] too . . . He don't write his own raps!" He then specifically accused Drake of using a ghost-writer for a verse that he contributed to "R.I.C.O.," a track on Mill's 2015 album *Dreams Worth More Than Money* (*DWMTM*): "and if I woulda knew, I woulda took it off the album." The beef attracted commentary from many other high-profile rappers and producers, including Rick Ross (a labelmate of Mill's), Lupe Fiasco (who argued on his Instagram page that ghostwriting is actually quite common), and Boi-1da. Later that week, Drake released a diss track aimed at Mill—"Charged Up"—on OVO Radio, which is broadcast on Beats 1, an Apple Music stream-ing station. Mill was slow to respond, and Drake released a second, more aggressive diss track on SoundCloud titled "Fired Up." YouTube videos of Mill (and his girlfriend, Nicki Minaj) dissing Drake in concert appeared. Mill took his time responding to Drake's disses and ended up releasing "Wanna Know" in August 2015, which many fans thought was too little too late.

SoundCloud rapper means different things to different people. To some, it's a derogatory reference to the legions of unskilled artists with weak beats that inhabit the music-streaming website, hoping to get noticed and make it big. However, some artists have used the platform in combination with other forms of social media to develop a substantial following that has led to lucrative national tours and, in some cases, record deals. Lil Uzi Vert, Lil Yachty, and Playboy Carti are among the pioneers of the style, which most often sounds like lo-fi (that is, made with substandard equipment, a kind of do-it-yourself aesthetic) trap music. More recently, Lil Pump, XXXTentacion, and Ski Mask the Slump God have been pushing the style toward a mix of psychedelia with the raw emotion of punk.

Some thirty years after the Bridge Wars, the internet has redefined the ways that rappers beef with one another. The internet era has also accelerated the pace that we expect these events to unfold. Social media gives fans more access to the artists they like, and vice versa. This access can be a blessing and a curse, as Mill found out. Hundreds of memes poking fun at Mill appeared. One fan even set up a GoFundMe page, hoping to raise $3,000 in order to underwrite Mill's response. Social media also plays an important role in the music's self-cri-tique. Regina Bradley discusses two incidents that took place in 2013: a leaked Rick Ross verse that proposed sex without consent, and a Lil Wayne verse in which he bragged about "beating the pussy up like Emmett Till." Both artists faced an immediate and severe social media backlash: Ross, despite repeated apologies, lost a major endorsement deal with Reebok as a result.[29]

HIP HOP SPREADS

In 1971, the *New York Times* ran an article about a young man best known as Taki 183: "Taki" was a nickname for Demetrius, and "183" was a reference to 183rd St., where he lived. Taki 183 worked as a messenger in New York City, and, as he traveled the city, he started "tagging" places he went with his tag, Taki 183. According to the article, graffiti was becoming a serious problem in New York City, and the cost of cleaning it was escalating.[30] Before too long, graf-fiti writers were sneaking into trainyards and painting giant murals, many of which included giant stylized tags (like the Blade car in Chapter 1). The subway cars provided the artists with a way to achieve fame outside of their neighborhood as the cars traveled throughout the city.

Philadelphia: The "Graffiti Capital of the World"

Less than a week after the *New York Times* published its interview with Taki 183 and bemoaned the growing problem of graffiti, the paper published another article that dubbed Philadelphia the "graffiti capital of the world." While New York usually receives the credit for being the birthplace of hip hop, at least one of the four elements (as we know it) originated in Philadelphia. As early as 1967, Cornbread, Cool Earl, and others were spray-painting their names around Philadelphia in large block letters that would become the hallmark of graffiti style.

New York City is predominantly a pedestrian culture; as such, much of the music was mixed to sound good on portable audio players like Walkmans, Discmans, and so-called boom boxes. Boom boxes were to pedestrian culture what aftermarket sound systems would become to car culture: a portable method of marking sonic space. Chuck D observes that a shift took place in New York City after people were being killed for their boom boxes: more personal audio playback devices like Walkmans became more popular, and their technological limitations shaped how music was produced.[31] Both boom boxes and Walkmans were combination radio and cassette players, and even the limitations of the cassette tape's frequency and dynamic ranges impacted the sound of early hip hop. Cassette tapes' audio quality was inferior to vinyl, but they were less expensive and portable. Most important, perhaps, was the ability to record and rerecord on them. Many early hip-hop radio shows, like Mr. Magic's Rap Attack, simply played recordings of live hip-hop performances (remember that the first rap singles—"songs"—were not released until 1979). As rap became increasingly popular through the 1980s, people would often copy tapes that they owned to give to friends or make **mixtapes** of their favorite songs to share. Dual-deck cassette players facilitated this process, even though it was technically illegal. Trading tapes like this certainly cut into record labels' profits, although it is impossible to know to what extent.

A **mixtape** is a compilation of favorite songs recorded onto a cassette tape. Early hip-hop artists like Kool Herc and Afrika Bambaataa would create mixtapes as promotional vehicles, to spread the word about upcoming shows, get new bookings, or gain radio airplay. These were often tapes of live shows, but they could have also been made privately. As compact-disc sales overtook cassette-tape sales in the early 1990s, and compact-disc recording technologies became less expensive (into the 2000s), the media of the mixtape changed. As the internet became faster and more accessible, mixtapes became playlists compiled by an individual. Sites like DatPiff and HotNewHipHop allow users to download mixtapes by current artists—usually for free. These mixtapes are still generally promotional, and they may feature a variety of artists working with a particular producer, perhaps, or comprise tracks that were left off of an album.

While political and economic forces conspired to keep residents of the inner city trapped on the block, hip hop was able to escape, and the automobile played an important role in spreading the music. In "Rapper's Delight," Big Bank Hank rhymes: "I'm gonna get a fly girl, gonna get some spank, and take off in a def OJ." Contrary to popular opinion, "OJ" refers to neither orange juice nor O. J. Simpson but rather a luxury-car service used by residents of the Bronx in the 1970s. The car services played an important role in the early days of rap, because drivers were often playing tapes made by the DJs. Kool Herc and Afrika Bambaataa discussed the phenomenon with Nelson George:

Bam: We were selling cassettes of your mixes that were really our first albums. We had luxury cabs like OJ and the Godfathers and Touch of Class that would buy our tapes.

Herc: How it worked was people would call for a car, and if they had a dope Herc tape, or a dope Bam tape, or a dope Flash tape, that particular customer might stay in the cab all day long. So these cab drivers were making extra money and at the same time they were advertising us.[32]

Much as tagging and painting subway cars was a way for graffiti artists to get their names out of their home territory, these car services helped get early rap music out of the Bronx and into the rest of the city.

Cars have played a role in popular music since the 1950s. Not only have cars been the subject of many songs, but also developments in the automotive industry influenced the direction of popular music. This is nowhere more apparent than in the case of Motown, whose founder Berry Gordy implemented much of what he learned working on an assembly line at the Lincoln-Mercury plant in Detroit to the production of popular music. Among Gordy's innovations were testing how his label's music would sound on car-radio systems, applying an assembly-line approach to the recording process, and implementing quality control.

As rap spread from New York City to Miami and the West Coast, the car became central to not just its consumption, but its production as well. Dr. Dre told journalist Brian Cross: "I make the shit for people to bump in their cars, I don't make it for clubs [. . .] The reason being is that you listen to music in your car more than anything. You in your car all the time, the first thing you do is turn on the radio, so that's how I figure. *When I do a mix, the first thing I do is go down and see how it sounds in the car.*"[33] Many have noted the strong relationship between the geography in Los Angeles and its car culture: roughly half of Los Angeles is devoted to roads and parking lots, and many trends in car culture, such as aftermarket audio, hot rods, and drive-ins, originated in the region.[34] Automobile customization is common and may include paint jobs, interior work, raising or lowering the car (via tires/rims, hydraulics, or other means), and aftermarket stereo equipment. The car thus mobilizes a personal listening space, and the size of that space is determined by the system's volume, sometimes even at the expense of sound clarity: as Williams notes, this music is meant to be *felt*.[35] The mobility of these spaces allows them to intersect with and challenge the sonic spaces of others, including the police. Robin D. G. Kelley paints a vivid picture of a hypothetical encounter: "Imagine a convertible Impala or a Suzuki pulling up alongside a 'black-and-white' [police car], pumping the revenge fantasy segment of Ice Cube's 'The Wrong Nigga to Fuck wit' from *Death Certificate*, which promises to break Chief Darryl [*sic*] Gates's 'spine like a jellyfish,' or Cypress Hill's 'Pigs' from *Cypress Hill*, vowing to turn 'pigs' into 'sausage.'"[36] Such acts can be understood politically, as we will see in Chapter 12.

With the rise of internet service providers like America Online—which facilitated e-mail and instant messaging—and, later, sites like Okayplayer, MySpace, and Napster, the production, consumption, and distribution of music underwent a sea change. Physical (and to some extent, economic) barriers to collaboration and production were essentially destroyed, making collaboration possible no matter where the artists were located. In 2004, North Carolina–based MC Phonte and Dutch producer Nicolay formed Foreign Exchange. The duo's album was composed almost entirely via e-mail and instant messenger. The Brooklynati project brought together artists from Brooklyn and Cincinnati who created an online virtual space whose name was a portmanteau of the two cities' names.[37] In 2007, Soulja Boy Tell 'Em translated the viral success of his "Crank Dat (Soulja Boy)" into a deal with Interscope Records.

In 1999, the peer-to-peer file-sharing service **Napster** shook the foundations of the music industry. Napster allowed users to share MP3 files freely among their libraries, with no money changing hands. Many artists were angered by the loss of revenue and sued: Metallica and Dr. Dre were among the first to charge Napster with copyright infringement. More legal trouble came from a team of major labels, led by A&M Records, who also sued. The service shut down in 2001 to address the litigation but was relaunched a year later with new security features in place as well as a subscription service. Not everyone was outraged by the service. Chuck D wrote in a *New York Times* op-ed that the benefits of Napster—including increased visibility for lesser-known artists—far outweighed the disadvantages.[38] Public Enemy was among the first groups to give away digital copies of its music online, and it launched the online radio station Rapstation.com in 1999. Cypress Hill and Limp Bizkit embarked on a tour that was sponsored by Napster. Napster inspired a host of other services, like LimeWire, Grokster, and Kazaa, and arguably laid the groundwork for iTunes and subsequent streaming services. The ease of file-sharing has resulted in more and more albums being leaked before their official release dates. This has led artists and labels to explore new ways of releasing music, such as the surprise release, exemplified by Beyoncé's 2013 release, *Beyoncé*.

Today, applications and websites like Spotify, Apple Music, Bandcamp, SoundCloud, and TIDAL enable artists to upload their own music with ease (and to profit from it). YouTube adds a video dimension to the music, while Facebook, Twitter, and other social networking sites make promotion easy. Artists can maintain control over their product without having to pay record labels. In the 2010s, two artists in particular have leveraged this technology to their advantage: Macklemore and Chance the Rapper. With "Thrift Shop," Macklemore and Ryan Lewis became the first independent artists in roughly twenty years (and only the second in history) to occupy the top spot on *Billboard*'s Hot 100. While they do have a distribution deal with a major label (Warner Bros.), their success was almost entirely due to social media promotion. The album on which "Thrift Shop" appears, *The Heist*, entered the *Billboard* album chart at number 2. Chance the Rapper has never sold a single album: he has released all of his music for free. Following the success of *Coloring Book* in 2016, the Recording Academy revised its Grammy Awards rules in order to make streaming-only albums (that is, albums that are not purchased) eligible for consideration. *Coloring Book* was nominated for seven Grammys and won three (Best New Artist, Best Rap Album, and Best Rap Performance) at the 2017 ceremony.

OUTRO

Names you should know:

- Huey Newton
- Bobby Seale
- The Black Panther Party
- The "Panther 21"
- Crips
- Bloods
- Boogie Down Productions (KRS-One, Scott La Rock)
- The Juice Crew (MC Shan, DJ Marley Marl)
- Insane Clown Posse
- Juggalos

Terms you should know:

- Place
- Space
- Redlining
- Postindustrial
- The Ten-Point Program
- Set

- Posse
- Shout-out
- Beef
- Mixtape
- Napster

Questions for discussion/writing prompts:

1. Loren Kajikawa writes that N.W.A. used "outlaw personae through first-person gangsta narratives" to develop "a sophisticated cultural hustle that allowed them to profit from the very system conspiring to contain them."[39] How would you interpret this statement in light of the themes of confinement and mobility presented in this chapter?

2. Research the artists and songs associated with some other high-profile beefs in hip hop. Examine how the songs Signify on one another. Some well-known feuds include N.W.A. vs. Ice Cube; Common vs. Ice Cube; Jay-Z vs. Nas; 50 Cent vs. Ja Rule; and Nicki Minaj vs. Remy Ma.

3. Consider the intersections of race and place. While "authentic" rap music represents "the streets," artists like Public Enemy, De La Soul, and Rakim hail from the suburbs but tend to situate their music in the city. White artists like Asher Roth and Lil Dicky highlight their suburban experiences in their music. In what ways are spaces racialized?

4. In 2007, New Orleans funk band Galactic released an album titled *From the Corner to the Block*, on which they collaborated with a number of well-known MCs. The MCs were asked to contribute a rhyme that addressed "the corner." Listen to the album and discuss how each rapper constructs "the corner."

Additional listening/viewing:

Listening to the city:

- "Once Upon a Time in the Projects," "It Was a Good Day," Ice Cube
- "Every Ghetto. . .," Lauryn Hill
- "The Corner" (remix), "On My Block," Scarface
- "Block Party," Jean Grae
- "A Tale of Two Cities," J. Cole
- "Get By," Talib Kweli
- "Waving Flag," K'Naan

The Black Panther Party:

- "Panther Power," Tupac Shakur
- "A Song for Assata," Common
- "Panthers," Dead Prez (feat. Common and The Last Poets)

Gangs:

- "Self Destruction," Stop the Violence Movement
- "All in the Same Gang," West Coast All-Stars
- "Juggalo Homies," "What Is a Juggalo?" "Miracles," Insane Clown Posse

Hip hop spreads:

- Reiss, Jon. *Bomb It*. New York: Docurama Films, 2008.
- *The World According to RZA*
- "Area Codes," Ludacris

NOTES

1 Murray Forman provides the most extensive treatment of hip hop, place, and space in *The 'Hood Comes First: Race, Space, and Place in Rap and Hip-Hop* (Middletown, CT: Wesleyan University Press, 2002).
2 William Jelani Cobb, *To the Break of Dawn: A Freestyle on the Hip Hop Aesthetic* (New York: New York University Press, 2007), 25.
3 Tricia Rose and Robin D. G. Kelley both explore the influence of the postindustrial city on hip hop's development, with Rose focusing on New York City and Kelley focusing on Los Angeles. See Rose, *Black Noise: Rap Music and Black Culture in Contemporary America* (Hanover, NH: Wesleyan University Press, 1994) and Kelley, "Kickin' Reality, Kickin' Ballistics: Gangsta Rap in Postindustrial Los Angeles," in *Droppin' Science: Critical Essays on Rap Music and Hip Hop Culture*. Ed. William Eric Perkins (Philadelphia: Temple University Press, 1996): 117–58.
4 M. K. Asante, *It's Bigger Than Hip Hop: The Rise of the Post-Hip-Hop Generation* (New York: St. Martin's Press, 2008), 39–41.
5 Scott Crossley, "Metaphorical Conceptions in Hip-Hop Music" *African American Review* 39 no. 4 (2005): 505.
6 Michael Eric Dyson, *Know What I Mean? Reflections on Hip-Hop* (New York: Basic Books, 2007), 11. Quoted in Mickey Hess, ed. *Hip Hop in America: A Regional Guide*. vol. 1 (Santa Barbara: Greenwood Press, 2010), xiii.
7 Mark Katz, *Groove Music* (New York: Oxford University Press, 2012), 39.
8 Katz 49.
9 Murray Forman, *The 'Hood Comes First: Race, Space, and Place in Rap and Hip-Hop* (Middletown, CT: Wesleyan University Press, 2002), 82–3. See also Loren Kajikawa, *Sounding Race in Rap Songs* (Berkeley: University of California Press, 2015), 58.
10 bell hooks, *We Real Cool: Black Men and Masculinity* (New York: Routledge, 2004), x.
11 Byron Hurt, *Hip-Hop: Beyond Beats and Rhymes* (Northampton, MA: Media Education Foundation).
12 hooks ix.
13 Robyn C. Spencer, *The Revolution Has Come: Black Power, Gender, and the Black Panther Party in Oakland* (Durham, NC: Duke University Press, 2016), 36–7.
14 Huey Newton, *Revolutionary Suicide* (New York: Harcourt Brace Jovanovich, 1973), 74.
15 Newton 75.
16 Newton 76.
17 Henry Chalfant and Rita Fecher, *Flyin' Cut Sleeves* (Pottstown, PA: MVD Visual, 2009).
18 Jeff Chang, *Can't Stop, Won't Stop: A History of the Hip-Hop Generation* (New York: St. Martin's, 2005), 44.
19 Chalfant and Fecher.
20 Chang 49.
21 Chang 49.
22 Quoted in Forman 69.
23 Forman 70.
24 Jim Fricke, *Yes Yes Y'all: The Experience Music Project Oral History of Hip-Hop's First Decade*. Ed. Charlie Ahearn and Experience Music Project (Cambridge, MA: Da Capo Press, 2002), 47–9.

25 Chang 311–14.

26 Mitchell Sunderland, "Tears of a Clown: The American Nightmare That Created the Insane Clown Posse" *Vice* (April 29, 2015): www.vice.com/en_us/article/tears-of-a-clown-insane-clown-posse-find-hope-after-a-life-of-struggle-and-trauma-456.

27 Federal Bureau of Investigation, "National Gang Threat Assessment" (2011): www.fbi.gov/stats-services/publications/2011-national-gang-threat-assessment. With the help of the ACLU, the Juggalos sued, arguing that the "gang" label encroached on their right to free expression. See Natasha Lennard, "The Juggalos Are Right: An FBI 'Gang' Label Does Matter" *Vice* (July 8, 2014): https://news.vice.com/article/the-juggalos-are-right-an-fbi-gang-label-does-matter.

28 Casey Suchan, *Beef* (Chatsworth, CA: QD3 Entertainment, Inc., 2003).

29 Regina N. Bradley, "Barbs and Kings: Explorations of Gender and Sexuality in Hip-Hop," in *The Cambridge Companion to Hip-Hop*. Ed. Justin A. Williams (Cambridge: Cambridge University Press, 2015), 181–2.

30 "'TAKI 183' Spawns Pen Pals," *New York Times* (July 21, 1971).

31 Mark Dery, "Public Enemy Confrontation" *Keyboard* (September 1990), 81–96. Reprinted in *That's the Joint! The Hip-Hop Studies Reader*. Ed. Murray Forman and Mark Anthony Neal (New York: Routledge, 2004), 413.

32 Nelson George, "Hip-Hop's Founding Fathers Speak the Truth" *Source* 50 (November 1993), 44–50. Reprinted in *That's the Joint! The Hip-Hop Studies Reader*. Ed. Murray Forman and Mark Anthony Neal (New York: Routledge, 2004), 51.

33 Cross, Brian, *It's Not about a Salary: Rap, Race, and Resistance in Los Angeles* (London: Verso, 1993), 197, quoted in Justin A. Williams, *Rhymin' and Stealin': Musical Borrowing in Hip Hop* (Ann Arbor: University of Michigan Press, 2013), 90.

34 Williams 91. See also Forman, *Represent*; Kajikawa chapter 3.

35 Williams 76–7.

36 Kelley 134.

37 Mickey Hess, "Introduction," in *Hip Hop in America: A Regional Guide*. 2 vols. Ed. Mickey Hess (Santa Barbara: Greenwood Press, 2010), vii–xxx.

38 Chuck D, "'Free' Music Can Free the Artist" *New York Times* (April 29, 2000).

39 Kajikawa 91.

TIME LINE

1986 2 Live Crew (Miami) releases its debut, . . . *Is What We Are.*

1988 N.W.A. (Los Angeles) release *Straight Outta Compton.*

1989 LaFace Records (Atlanta) is founded.

1990 Master P launches his label (Bay Area), No Limit Records. The label moved to New Orleans in 1995.

1991 Rodney King is pulled over by the police in Los Angeles and beaten. A year later, the officers are acquitted, and riots erupt throughout the city.

    —Geto Boys (Houston) release *We Can't Be Stopped.*

    —Cash Money Records (New Orleans) is founded.

1992 Dr. Dre (Los Angeles) releases *The Chronic.*

1993 The Coup (Bay Area) releases its debut album, *Kill My Landlord.*

2000 OutKast (Atlanta) releases *Stankonia.*

2004 Daddy Yankee (Puerto Rico) releases *Barrio Fino*, brining reggaeton to an international audience.

    —Mike Jones (Houston) releases *Who Is Mike Jones?*

2005 Young Jeezy (Atlanta) releases *Let's Get It: Thug Motivation 101.*

    —Hurricane Katrina devastates the Gulf Coast.

2006 E-40's (Bay Area) *My Ghetto Report Card* is released.

IN THIS CHAPTER, YOU WILL LEARN ABOUT

- Some American regional hip-hop scenes and styles
- How these scenes engage with the dynamics of confinement and mobility
- How these styles reflect the spaces in which they were created

CHAPTER 11

Listening to Regional Styles

OVERVIEW

Despite its strong regional affiliations, rap's boundaries are not as hard-and-fast as they appear. While "East Coast" is often used as a metonym for New York City, Philadelphia, Baltimore, and Washington, DC, all boast thriving and unique hip-hop scenes. Ice-T and Tupac, both of whom are synonymous with West Coast rap, were born on the East Coast. Public Enemy's Bomb Squad did the production on Ice Cube's *AmeriKKKa's Most Wanted*. Snoop Dogg's characteristic drawl has little to do with Long Beach and everything to do with Mississippi. Oakland and Atlanta developed a symbiotic relationship in the late 2000s: Bay Area legend Too $hort moved to Atlanta, and **crunk** mastermind Lil Jon produced one of E-40's most popular albums. These distinct styles characterized not just a particular place, but also a particular time: 1990s Houston rap sounds quite different from 2000s Houston rap. As regional scenes emerged into the national spotlight, they exerted their influence on other local scenes, thus transforming them.

MIAMI AND PUERTO RICO

Miami was the first city outside of New York to emerge with a distinct sound. The music had a much heavier bass sound, faster tempos, and raunchier lyrics. The bass sound played well on car stereos and in the clubs; the faster tempos mark the style as dance music; and the raunchy lyrics hearken back to the likes of Rudy Ray Moore and Richard Pryor. 2 Live Crew helped pioneer the **Miami bass** sound, which flourished in the late 1980s. 2 Live Crew's debut album, . . . *Is What We Are* (1986), was the first rap record by a group outside of New York City to be certified gold. The group's music led to legal troubles on several occasions (which only helped raise its visibility). As discussed in Chapter 1, Roy Orbison's agents sued the group over copyright infringement in 1991 for its parody of "Pretty Woman." Florida politicians led a charge against the group's sexual content, which culminated in the group members' arrest and a federal judge's ruling that the content of 2 Live Crew's third album, *As Nasty as They Wanna Be* (1989), was obscene. The ruling represented the first time in history that an album was ruled indecent, making it illegal to sell the album to minors. Support for the group came from many corners, including Harvard professor Henry Louis Gates Jr., Bruce Springsteen, and the American Civil Liberties Union. The ruling was later overturned and the members acquitted.

LISTENING GUIDE 11.1

Artist: 2 Live Crew
Song: "Throw the D"
Album: . . . *Is What We Are*
Record label: Skyywalker
Year released: 1986
DJ or Producer: Mr. Mixx
Samples used: "Dance to the Drummer's Beat," Herman Kelly & Life; "Planet Rock," Afrika Bambaataa; "Al-Naafiysh," Hashim; "Change the Beat," Beside

"Throw the D" was the single that put Skyywalker Records on the map, and it has all the characteristics of the Miami bass (sometimes called "booty bass") sound. The deep TR-808 kick drum anchors the rapid tempo, which clocks in around 125 beats per minute. Most other music around this time hovered around 90 beats per minute, with some Public Enemy tracks approaching 110. "Throw the D" bears the imprint of (among other things) "Planet Rock" by Afrika Bambaataa & The Soul Sonic Force, another up-tempo song with an 808 beat (see Chapter 10 for a listening guide). On the album version, DJ Mr. Mixx cuts in excerpts of "Planet Rock" (these are absent from the single) as well as the phrase "let's dance" from "Dance to the Drummer's Beat," and the famous "Ah" and "Fresh" samples from Beside's "Change the Beat."[1]

The rapid tempo complements Fresh Kid Ice's quick, staccato delivery, with hints of a Caribbean accent noticeable throughout (he was born in Port of Spain, Trinidad & Tobago). The lyrics are about a "brand-new dance," which was popular among the youth in Miami at the time, but it could easily be heard as a thinly veiled euphemism for sex—the moaning at the beginning of the single suggests as much. In the single version, Mr. Mixx punches in dirty words and bits of raunchy comedy by Rudy Ray Moore and others to support the ribald reading.

The Miami bass style was closely associated with strip clubs, and, given the large number of male lyrical subjects, performers, and producers, it is often blamed for the rampant misogyny that would come to pervade the next generation of rap music.[2]

Given its proximity to Miami, it is not surprising that Caribbean music styles historically have had a strong influence on the Miami sound. Conversely, once hip hop became established in south Florida, it began to influence the kinds of music being produced in the islands. While Miami bass music was a rather short-lived style, its influence reemerged through **reggaeton**, a genre with complex roots and diverse influences. Reggaeton can trace its origins to artists like El General, a Panamanian artist who was recording Jamaican dancehall music with Spanish lyrics, called "reggae en Español." Vico C, from Puerto Rico, was one of the first artists to rap almost entirely in Spanish (unlike Kid Frost, Mellow Man Ace, or Cypress Hill). Puerto Ricans DJ Playero, DJ Negro, and DJ Nelson added hip-hop beats to reggae en Español, and the music became popular in the barrios and clubs. Lyrically, many of the songs featured violence, drug use, and graphic sex, much like the music of 2 Live Crew. This new music—reggae en Español fused with rapping and hip-hop beats—came to be known as "underground" (which has a slightly different connotation here than it did in Chapter 6). By virtue of its many influences, Juan Flores has suggested that reggaeton might be the first truly transnational music.[3]

Barrio literally means "neighborhood," "district," or "ward"—any sort of official subdivision in a city. But like its English relatives, "'hood" and "ghetto," it has come to be affiliated with generally poor, working-class neighborhoods, and it can refer to the community of people that inhabit that geographical space as well.

Daddy Yankee brought reggaeton into mainstream American culture in 2004 with the release of *Barrio Fino*. The album was the first platinum-selling reggaeton record, and it earned many accolades from the music press. Sales of Latin albums increased dramatically, peaking in 2005 and declining rapidly thereafter.

LISTENING GUIDE 11.2

Artist: Daddy Yankee
Song: "Gasolina"
Album: *Barrio Fino*
Record label: Polydor
Year released: 2004
DJ or Producer: Luny Tunes
Samples used: "Dem Bow," Shabba Ranks

TIME	MUSICAL CHARACTERISTICS	LYRICS	DESCRIPTION
0:00	Electronic sounds imitating Spanish flamenco guitar (rapid rhythm, half-step relationship)	"Jo! Jo!" "Dad-dy Yan-kee" on last two measures	Introduction (8 measures)
0:10	Daddy Yankee starts rapping Bass drum divisions get louder	"Zumbale mambo pa' que mis gatas prendan los motores" (repeated)	Intro cont'd (8 measures)
0:20	"Dem Bow" rhythm kicks in	"Mamita, yo sé que tú no te me vas a quitar."	Verse 1 (8 measures)
0:29	Call and response (male + female) After 8 measures, the snare sound changes		Hook (16 measures)
0:48	Original snare sound returns		Verse 2 (16 measures)
1:09	"Dem Bow" beat drops out for 8 measures; bass drum fill gradually gets louder and brings it back in	(reminiscent of the introduction, with "Jo!")	Hook (16 measures)
1:29			Verse 3 (16 measures)
1:50	Engine starting sound effects		Bridge
1:52	8 measures w/o Dem Bow (sung)		
2:02	Dem Bow returns		
2:12	Daddy Yankee starts rapping Bass drum divisions get louder	"Zumbale mambo pa' que mis gatas prendan los motores" (repeated)	Intro cont'd (8 measures)
2:21			Verse 1 repeated; hook repeated; music continues; ends abruptly

Daddy Yankee's hit "Gasolina" epitomizes the transnational origins of reggaeton. In a close reading of the song, Wayne Marshall unpacks the many musical influences that shape the track, in an

	1	e	&	a	2	e	&	a	3	e	&	a	4	e	&	a
Snare					X								X			
Kick drum	X								X							

Figure 11.1 The "Dem Bow" beat

effort to reveal its transnational composition. He describes the frantic opening figure as "a riff befitting a bullfight": it features the marching rhythm and the half-step motion that evoke matadors and bullfights, as heard in compositions like "España Cañí" by Pascual Marquina Narro.[4]

The **dembow** beat is at the heart of most reggaeton songs. It is often transliterated as *boom-ch-boom-chick*, and appears above as Figure 11.1. The pattern juxtaposes a 3+3+2 division over the four beats of the measure, and, as Marshall notes, the pattern is common to a number of Caribbean musical styles, including calypso, salsa, and son.[5] The beat originates in a song by Jamaican reggae artist Shabba Ranks called "Dem Bow" (1991). While Bobby "Digital" Dixon was the producer on that song, the dembow as it appears was actually an arrangement of Dixon's beat done by Steely and Clevie, dancehall producers who were working in New York City at the time. Luny Tunes, the producers on "Gasolina," consists of Francisco Saldaña (Luny) and Víctor Cabrera (Tunes), who were born in the Boston area but of Dominican heritage. The duo has worked on tracks for many of the top reggaeton artists, including Don Omar, Tego Calderón, and Ivy Queen. In "Gasolina," they synthesize diverse musical elements and manage to vary the dembow while preserving its identity: for example, the alternating snare sounds (most notable in the hook) function not only to propel the song forward and add variety, but also to recall hip hop's sampling practice in which two different samples might be spliced next to each other.[6]

In addition to evoking Caribbean musics and recalling Spanish influences (via colonialism), the song also demonstrates strong ties to rap and related forms of electronic dance music, which are associated with the United States. Marshall notes that the builds in the bass drum, for instance (as in the end of the introduction, from around 0:12 to 0:19) as well as the breaks (where all the instruments except the percussion drop out, like 1:09), are characteristic of techno music and not reflective of any of the more traditional Caribbean musics from which reggaeton draws.

Despite falling off the scene for a period, Miami has made a comeback as a hip-hop center in the 2010s with artists like Pitbull, Flo Rida, and Rick Ross (whose debut album was titled *Port of Miami*), and radio personality and producer DJ Khaled.

LOS ANGELES

In the early 1980s, Los Angeles suffered from two related problems: gangs and crack cocaine. Both flourished as a result of the deindustrialization that swept the city: the conditions in south-central Los Angeles mirrored very closely those in the South Bronx.[7] The two main gangs on the West Coast were the Bloods and the Crips (see Chapter 10). In contrast to New York City and Chicago—the only two cities in the country larger than Los Angeles—the Los Angeles Police Department was severely understaffed. As a result, Daryl Gates, who served as chief of police from 1978 to 1992, pioneered many innovative but aggressive police tactics. Under his leadership, the first SWAT teams in the nation came into existence as a way to deal with increasingly violent and well-armed criminals. SWAT teams used heavy weapons and paramilitary tactics in their operations, laying the groundwork for the militarization of contemporary police forces. The D.A.R.E. (Drug Abuse Resistance Education) program was intended to help curb the drug problem that Los Angeles was facing.

The LAPD's aggressive policing tactics resulted in further devastation of the neighbor-hoods. In order to gain the advantage of surprise, police would often stage their raids very early in the morning and would act swiftly and violently. This allowed them to gain entry before the suspects were able to dispose of evidence (drugs were often flushed down the toilet and guns hidden away). Their approach was epitomized by the "batterram," a tank that had a 14-foot battering ram attached to it, which they would use to break down doors of suspected drug houses. Compton rapper Toddy Tee immortalized the tactic in his 1985 single "Batter-ram." In the same way that Grandmaster Flash & The Furious Five's song "The Message" gave listeners a window into the devastation of the South Bronx, Toddy Tee's song represented a departure from the electro-rap style that dominated the clubs in Los Angeles and paved the way for gangsta rap.

Ice-T's song "6 in the Mornin'" (1986) was the first well-known gangsta-rap song. While the genre is typically identified with the West Coast, New Jersey native Ice-T credits Phil-adelphia rapper Schoolly D's "P.S.K. (What Does It Mean?)" as the inspiration behind his gritty urban travelogue. When gangsta rap first emerged in the late 1980s, one aspect of the genre that concerned critics was the style's reliance on first-person narratives. This perspec-tive implied that the rappers actually participated in the activities they were describing. Brian Turner, the president of Priority Records—the label that signed N.W.A.—said of the group:

> What impressed me about N.W.A. and Eazy-E was that these guys lived the things they talk about. All I was hearing on the news was the perspective of the police and outsiders—you never get the perspective of the actual guy they're talking about. When I saw what these guys wrote, it really hit me that their side of the story was important to tell.[8]

Robin D. G. Kelley suggests that the use of first-person perspective enables rappers to recount how they function in relation to conditions not of their own creation.[9] Furthermore, many rappers—Ice-T perhaps chief among them—made their gang affiliations clear. MC Ren (of N.W.A.), X-Raided, Kurupt, and Snoop Dogg were Crips; DJ Quik, Suge Knight, B-Real, and Sen Dog were Bloods. While not an official member, Ice-T identified with the Crips: he called some of the first lyrics he wrote "Crip Rhymes."

N.W.A. was the brainchild of Eazy-E, a drug dealer who used his earnings to start Ruthless Records and bankroll a rap group. The group comprised Eazy-E, Dr. Dre, Ice Cube, and others. Their songs shaped the emerging gangsta-rap genre and helped establish the West Coast's rap identity. Their most famous song, "Fuck tha Police," became the soundtrack to the Los Angeles riots in 1992.[10]

LISTENING GUIDE 11.3

Artist: N.W.A.
Song: "Fuck tha Police"
Album: *Straight Outta Compton*
Record label: Priority
Year released: 1988
DJ or Producer: Dr. Dre
Samples used: "It's My Thing," Marva Whitney; "The Boogie Back," Roy Ayers Ubiquity; "Funky Drummer," James Brown; "Feel Good," Fancy; "Get Me Back on Time, Engine #9," Wilson Pickett

N.W.A.'s anthem called attention to the rampant police misconduct that residents of south-central Los Angeles had been experiencing. The song is staged as a trial, with each member of the group acting as a "prosecuting attorney." After the spoken introduction, which sets the stage, Ice Cube begins his verse (0:30) by stating that the police target members of his community simply because of their skin color.

Three skits separate the hook from the verses. In the final skit (5:13), Dr. Dre (the judge) announces the verdict, calling the cop (among other things) "redneck" and "chickenshit," two terms that originate in the American South. These language choices highlight the migration patterns not only of the black community in Los Angeles, but also of the police officers. William Parker, who was chief of police from 1950 to 1966, recruited military veterans, particularly those from the South, who were likely to subscribe to his racist policing strategies. The LAPD's racism even caught the attention of the Ku Klux Klan, a white supremacist organization, who tried to recruit members in 1991.

On March 3, 1991, Rodney King was pulled over by the LAPD and brutally beaten. The beating was captured on videotape and eventually broadcast all around the country. It is important to note that, in contrast to the ubiquity of cameras today, the recording of the incident was unusual for its time; the beating, sadly, was not. Ice Cube told MTV: "It's been happening to us for years. It's just we didn't have a camcorder every time it happened."[11] Four police officers were charged with use of excessive force but were acquitted. The acquittal sparked a week of riots in Los Angeles in 1992, which resulted in 55 dead, 2,000 injured, and nearly a billion dollars in property damage.

Two weeks after the Rodney King beating, the death of Latasha Harlins added fuel to the fire. Harlins was a 15-year-old black girl who was shot by Soon Ja Du, a Korean shopkeeper who believed Harlins was shoplifting. Du was convicted of voluntary manslaughter and fined but did not serve any prison time. The shooting represented a peak in escalating tensions between South Central's black community and its growing Korean population, and much of this anger was released during the riots. Ice Cube included a song called "Black Korea" on his album *Death Certificate*, his second solo album since leaving N.W.A. in late 1989. The track called for violence against the Korean community in the aftermath of Harlins' death. The song begins with an excerpt of a scene from Spike Lee's film *Do the Right Thing*, which portrays an interaction between the main character, Radio Raheem, and two Korean shopkeepers. In the space of about forty-five seconds, Cube conflates Chinese and Korean and uses "Oriental" and "chop-suey ass" as blanket insults against them: all of this occurs in the midst of other lines throughout the album that are directed at the Asian community. As Chang points out, Cube (and many others in the black and Asian communities) fell victim to the media narratives of racial divide, failing to recognize that both groups were really the victims of a failing economic system. In addition, despite their "minority" status, the black community is considerably larger and wields more power than the Korean community.[12]

Suge Knight

Marion "Suge" Knight and his friends helped Dr. Dre separate from N.W.A. by allegedly threatening Jerry Heller—the group's manager—and Eazy-E with baseball bats. Knight and Dre, along with The D.O.C. (who was also affiliated with N.W.A.), formed Death Row Records in 1991. The label released

Dre's *Chronic* in 1992 and Snoop Doggy Dogg's debut, *Doggystyle*, in 1993, both of which went multi-platinum. Tupac Shakur, Lady of Rage, and MC Hammer were also signed to the label, and Tupac's high-profile beef with The Notorious B.I.G. made Death Row into a household name: Knight was in the car with Tupac the night that he was killed. Knight is known for his strong-arm tactics and has a long arrest record. He allegedly dangled Vanilla Ice from a balcony by his ankles to collect royalties he was owed from the success of "Ice Ice Baby." Death Row went bankrupt in 2006. In 2015, Knight landed in prison after his involvement in a hit-and-run accident that left one person dead and another injured.

When Dr. Dre and D.O.C. split with N.W.A. in 1991, they teamed up with Suge Knight to form Death Row Records. The label released Dre's *Chronic* in 1992, and the G-Funk sound took the rap universe by storm: Shea Serrano contends that the album "made California the most important place in rap," wresting the title from New York City for the first time in history.[13] Among its contributions, the album introduced a young Snoop Doggy Dogg to the world. It spent twenty-seven weeks on the *Billboard* charts, peaking at number 2; has consistently placed in the top ten on many "best of" lists; and won Dre a Grammy—his first—for "Let Me Ride."[14]

The laid-back, cruising sound of G-Funk matched the (momentarily) peaceful atmosphere that resulted from the end of the riots, the gang truce, and improved relations between the black and Korean communities. Inspired by George Clinton and Parliament's funk style (P-Funk), G-Funk is characterized by a slow tempo, thinner percussion, and soaring synthesizers—which were unusual in rap production for the time—over a funky bass line, all of which combine to make a rather thick texture.[15] Dre hired studio musicians to recreate the sounds of his favorite breaks: this allowed him to micromanage the "samples" to a degree that would not have been possible had he just taken them from a recording. In contrast to the more chaotic sounds of his N.W.A. productions, G-Funk presents a more melodic approach: Kajikawa observes that the synthesizer melodies create units of two and four bars, which contrasts with rap's tendency to repeat a single bar over and over (which contributes to the "frantic" sound of N.W.A.'s production, or that of the Bomb Squad, for instance).[16] Musical features aside, this is clearly gangsta rap: the misogyny and violence that were hallmarks of N.W.A.'s style are still present, but the message is delivered with a kind of nonchalance that makes it even more concerning.

LISTENING GUIDE 11.4

Artist: Dr. Dre (feat. Snoop Doggy Dogg)
Song: "Nuthin' But a G Thang"
Album: *The Chronic*
Record label: Death Row
Year released: 1992
DJ or Producer: Dr. Dre
Samples used: "I Wanna Do Something Freaky to You," Leon Haywood

"Nuthin' But a G Thang" is the quintessential G-Funk track, with Dre's laid-back production supporting Snoop's "Calabama drawl."[17] The song kicks off with the rattle of a vibraslap and a tambourine marking subdivisions of the beat. The high-pitched synthesizer follows, replicating melodies that were played by a string ensemble on Haywood's original track. As Snoop begins to rap the first verse (0:10), a two-bar long melodic bass line enters for support. The vibraslap, which sounds again at the beginning of the first verse, articulates the beginning of each four-measure group. The hook begins at 1:07, when Snoop and Dre are accompanied by a different synth melody. Dre's verse follows at 1:15.

Unlike much gangsta rap, which explores themes of confinement, G-Funk imbued the genre with a newfound sense of mobility. This was music that was clearly designed to be listened to in an automobile.[18] The video features Dre, Snoop, and their friends driving around south-central Los Angeles in their customized cars, at one point passing a police officer on a motorcycle, who does not give chase, but appears to wave back at the passing cars (2:53). This is a marked difference from songs like "Straight Outta Compton" and "Fuck the Police," in which the police are enemies whose job it is to keep Dre and his companions from leaving the neighborhood.

N.W.A.'s brash gangsta style would influence rappers like Houston's Geto Boys, while Dr. Dre's smooth G-Funk would shape the sound of rap around the country for years to come.

HOUSTON

Nelson George notes that 2 Live Crew, N.W.A., and Geto Boys were all composed of black male artists, signed by black entrepreneurs, and distributed independently (at least at first). These three groups, representing three different parts of the country, each pushed boundaries in their own way. George contends that they represented what the *black* community was interested in at the time, and he also asserts that they laid the groundwork for the misogyny that would come to characterize mainstream hip hop.[19]

Houston's Geto Boys were the first important rap act to come from Texas. The group came together in 1986 and shuffled through several different members before arriving at the lineup known for *Geto Boys* (1990), *We Can't Be Stopped* (1991), and *Resurrection* (1996). The group's name, of course, situates them in the general space of the ghetto, but their sound and language choices specify the location, specifically Houston's Fifth Ward. Houston is divided into six wards, and the fifth ward is located in the northeast part of the city. Their earliest material mimicked the style of Run-D.M.C., but Bushwick Bill recalls thinking that "we should talk about southern stuff, instead of trying to pretend we were from the East or West Coast. We should deal with the situations that were all around us."[20] What set Geto Boys apart from their peers were their excessively graphic tales of paranoia, murder, and even necrophilia. This pessimistic realism became a hallmark of Houston's rap scene.[21] As such, Geto Boys were no strangers to controversy: their second album, *Grip It! On That Other Level*, caught the ear of Rick Rubin, who remixed and rerecorded some of the tracks to reissue on his Def American label. Def American's distributor, Geffen, refused to release the album, in large part due to the tracks "Mind of a Lunatic" and "Assassins." Rubin and Geffen parted ways, and Rubin was able to distribute the album through WEA. In addition to the Parental Advisory sticker, the album was released with another sticker that claimed: "Def American Recordings is opposed to censorship. Our manufacturer and distributor, however, do not condone or endorse the content of this recording, which they find violent, sexist, racist and indecent."

Rap-A-Lot Records

Rap-A-Lot Records was founded in 1986 by J Prince. The label launched the careers of Geto Boys, as well as Bun B and Pimp C (who would go on to form UGK), and Devin the Dude. The label pioneered the horror-rap style that came to be associated with Houston. Despite offers from major labels, Prince continued to work independently, releasing dozens of records that caught national attention. The strength of Prince's label enabled him to sell big numbers locally, thus making the case for national distribution easy. Geto Boys' *Grip It!* sold 500,000 copies, which demonstrates the reach of Houston's independent hip-hop scene.

Geto Boys' "Mind Playin' Tricks on Me" is characteristic of Houston rap in the early 1990s. It was unique for its time for its portrayal of the mental state of a gangsta. The song examines confinement from a variety of perspectives.

LISTENING GUIDE 11.5

Artist: Geto Boys
Song: "Mind Playing Tricks on Me"
Album: *We Can't Be Stopped*
Record label: Rap-A-Lot
Year released: 1991
DJ or Producer: Scarface
Samples used: "Hung Up on My Baby," Isaac Hayes; "The Jam," Graham Central Station

The Isaac Hayes sample, which forms the bedrock of this track, appeared on the soundtrack to a blax-ploitation film titled *The Three Tough Guys* (1974), which starred Hayes. The movie's title is no doubt also a reference to the three tough guys who compose Geto Boys. The smooth R&B—perhaps more blues than rhythm—track seems almost at odds with the subject matter of the song, tempering the extreme violence of the lyrics and projecting a sense of sadness or loneliness.

"Mind Playing Tricks on Me" is much like other first-person gangsta-rap narratives that use that perspective to demonstrate individual responses to deteriorating social and economic situations. This song adds another level to that interaction: the confining conditions often lead to violence and crime, which, in turn, lead to a paranoid state of mind like those described in the song. The track starts with a brief passage spoken by Scarface, who describes the confining space of his room: the spoken pas-sage is identical to one of his verses in "Mind of a Lunatic" and sounds almost like a false start. The confinement described in this song is not only physical (the four walls) and political (the ghetto and the underground economy) but mental as well. His paranoia has him paralyzed: nightmares keep him from sleeping, and he is in constant fear that he is being watched. In the third verse, Scarface says that he is looking for "an exit out the business." He confesses that he's considered suicide, but even that would not relieve him of his burden: he has a son to care for, and knowing that his son would be fatherless keeps Scarface alive.

Songs like this work to uncover the complex interactions that perpetuate cycles of poverty, crime, incarceration, and death. Serrano suggests that this song, with its vivid descriptions of the rapper's mental states, laid the groundwork for similarly violent, paranoid tracks like Cypress Hill's "Insane in the Brain," The Notorious B.I.G.'s "Suicidal Thoughts," Eminem's "Kim," and Immortal Technique's "Dance with the Devil."[22] In the last few years, the taboos around mental health issues are increas-ingly falling away in hip hop, with artists like Jay-Z, Kid Cudi, and Logic admitting that they've been to therapy. Kodak Black's song "Can I," Kendrick Lamar's "I," and Logic's "1-800-273-8255" (which happens to be the number for the National Suicide Prevention Lifeline) relay their struggles with depression, anxiety, and other issues.

Few styles are as evocative of a specific place as **chopped and screwed** is to Houston. DJ Screw pioneered the remix technique in the early 1990s, ultimately releasing hundreds of mixtapes. The technique involves slowing the record down considerably (to a tempo of around 60 bpm), running the voices through various effects, creating echoes by using two copies of the record on two turntables, and chopping up the lyrics and rearranging them. The overall effect of chopped and screwed music is supposed to mimic the experience of being high on syrup. While the style was popular in Texas, it did not achieve national visibility until about 2005, roughly five years after DJ Screw's death at the age of 29.

Syrup (aka "sizzurp," "lean," or "purple drank"), properly known as liquid codeine or promethazine, was the drug of choice for many Houston rappers in the 2000s. Its use dates back to the 1960s, but it was popularized by DJ Screw, who referred to it often in his mixtapes. To make it more palatable, the drug is often combined with a sweet soft drink or sugary candy. In large doses, it produces numbness, lethargy, and drowsiness, and it is addictive. An overdose can cause respiratory or cardiac arrest: the drug is suspected in the deaths of several rappers, including DJ Screw, Big Moe, and Pimp C.

DJ Michael "5000" Watts carried on DJ Screw's legacy and founded Swishahouse Records in 1997. The label featured Slim Thug, Paul Wall, Chamillionaire, and Mike Jones. Many of the releases were available with chopped and screwed remixes, most of which were prepared by Watts. "Still Tippin'" by Mike Jones (featuring Slim Thug and Paul Wall) almost single-handedly put Houston rap back on the national radar in 2004.[23]

LISTENING GUIDE 11.6

Artist: Mike Jones (feat. Slim Thug and Paul Wall)
Song: "Still Tippin'"
Album: *Who Is Mike Jones?*
Record label: Jive/Warner Bros.
Year released: 2004
DJ or Producer: Salih Williams
Samples used: "William Tell" overture, Gioacchino Rossini

"Still Tippin'" originally appeared in 2002: it was built on a freestyle by Slim Thug, featured Chamillionaire, and was produced by Bigg Tyme. The version that became a hit appeared on a Swishahouse mixtape, *The Day All Hell Broke Loose 2*, before its release as the first single from Mike Jones' debut album. Paul Wall replaced Chamillionaire, and Salih Williams handled production on the hit version.

The song describes a Houston that is very different from that described by Geto Boys. Paranoia and violence have been replaced with cruising and sipping on lean, and the laid-back tempo of the song reflects both activities. Car culture figures prominently in the song: the title of the song refers to using hydraulics to raise one side of the car higher than the other. The hook refers to a particular style of spoked rim with Vogue tires (Vogue invented the whitewall tire and released a version with a gold stripe as well). In the first verse, Slim Thug continues to describe his car as he cruises around the city, drinking barre (another name for promethazine).

Mike Jones takes the second verse and continues with the automotive references, including his wood-grain steering wheel and "candy" paint job. Jones had a unique marketing strategy, which involved saying his name as often as possible—"Mike Jones! Who?"—and distributing T-shirts and other materials with his phone number on them (the phone number had a 281 area code, locating him in Houston). He also mentions "Who is Mike Jones comin'" in his verse, letting his fans know that an album is on the way. The relentless self-promotion worked, and the album sold nearly 200,000 copies in the first week. It also led to the mainstream success of other Swishahouse artists, including Slim Thug, Paul Wall, and Chamillionaire.

In addition to launching the careers of other Houston artists, "Still Tippin'" helped bring Houston's hip-hop culture to a national audience. Candy paint, lean, and grills (gold and bejeweled items worn over the teeth) became popular, as did the chopped and screwed style that was associated with the city. Listen to the chopped and screwed remix of this song and compare it with the original: what are the differences? What elements remain intact, and which are altered or missing?

OAKLAND AND THE BAY AREA

Bay Area hip hop is characterized by a strong emphasis on funk and a connection to revolutionary politics.[24] The pioneering funk band Sly & The Family Stone came from the Vallejo neighborhood, the same area where Mac Dre was born and **hyphy** (pronounced "hi-fee") came to be in the early 2000s. Bay Area radio stations featured Rickey Vincent's funk program and Davey D's hip-hop show. As the birthplace of the Black Panther Party, and home to the famously liberal University of California at Berkeley, political action has long been a fact of life in the Bay Area. This characteristic blend of funk and politics can be seen in the album cover for Funkadelic's *Uncle Jam Wants You*, which Signified on a well-known image of Huey Newton.

Oakland's revolutionary legacy found its voice in hip hop with artists like Tupac Shakur, Del the Funky Homosapien (Ice Cube's cousin), and The Coup. Boots Riley, the lead rapper and producer of The Coup, has a long history in activism, and his community involvement is apparent in the group's music. The Coup's debut album, 1993's *Kill My Landlord*, met with great critical acclaim, but gangsta rap's rise to prominence in the early 1990s pushed political rap to the side, and the album only had moderate commercial success.

LISTENING GUIDE 11.7

Artist: The Coup (feat. Elements of Change)
Song: "Kill My Landlord"
Album: *Kill My Landlord*
Record label: Wild Pitch/EMI
Year released: 1993
DJ or Producer: Boots Riley
Samples used: "Last Night Changed It All," Esther Williams; "Backdoor Man," The Doors; "Never Let 'Em Say," Ballin' Jack

In contrast to Public Enemy's chaotic, in-your-face style of political music, The Coup's music is much more laid-back. The beat is clearly funk-inspired, and Riley's delivery is far more mellow than Chuck D's. The song begins with a reference to Karl Marx's *Communist Manifesto*, and references to other revolutionary groups and figures (Che Guevara, Mao Tse-tung, Kwame N'krumah, H. Rap Brown, and Geronimo Pratt) pervade the rest of the song.

The lyrics are openly critical of the government, the police, the media, and the whitewashing of American history. Riley criticizes cuts to welfare, former president Bush's immigration policies, and the COINTELPRO operation that undermined the Black Panther Party and other revolutionary organizations. The revolutionary nature of their music has led to increased interactions with police. Riley raps that "we never had no funk/Until you found out our joints are revolutionary" (1:27), a sentiment that echoes the opening lines of Tupac's "Violent" (discussed in the previous chapter): "They claim that I'm violent/Just 'cause I refuse to be silent." The government and the media try to blame social problems on black-on-black crime, or crack, but The Coup argues that 400 years of slavery, lynching, and exploitation ("Told the streets were paved with gold/Whoever paved that shit got minimum wage too"; 1:53) are the root cause of problems in the black community.

Bay Area legend Too $hort essentially created the figure of the mack in hip hop. He got his start by selling his "Freaky Tales" tapes in the parking lot of the stadium after Oakland Raiders games (as did MC Hammer, another Oakland native). $hort mixed bawdy lyrics with funk beats and laid the groundwork for the next generation of Bay Area rappers. Shock G was born in New York City, worked as a DJ in Florida, and eventually moved to Oakland, lured by the strong funk culture there. Shock G and his group, Digital Underground, worked to incorporate the sound of George Clinton and Parliament-Funkadelic into rap years before the sound became nationally known via Dr. Dre's G-Funk style. (Shock G's most important contribution to hip hop, however, may have been mentoring a young Tupac Shakur, who had moved from Baltimore to the Bay Area and got his start as a dancer with Digital Underground.)

Sideshows have been a unique part of Oakland life since the 1980s. Part car show and part street party, they represent an effort by the black community to reclaim public space in a city that was rapidly undergoing transformation. Then-mayor Jerry Brown was trying to revitalize the city and turn it from postindustrial ruin into a tourist attraction: as is often the case, this meant marginalizing the poor and people of color. Many gathering places, like hip-hop clubs, were shut down, leaving Oakland's youth with nowhere to go. The sideshows first occupied parking lots of abandoned shopping centers in East Oakland, before police began cracking down on them, at which point they took to the street. Police enforcement efforts escalated—spectators could be arrested and cars impounded—and there have even been attempts to ban sideshows. Despite all of this, the sideshows continued unabated and, in fact, began to draw in young people from outside the area.

At a sideshow, people bring out their "scrapers"—typically American cars like Buicks and Pontiacs that feature brightly colored paint jobs and 20-inch or bigger rims—to go cruising, spin donuts, "ghost ride the whip" (getting out and walking alongside or standing atop a still-running car), and "gas-brake dip" (a way to simulate the up-and-down motion of hydraulics). Some sideshows include hundreds of cars. Music has always been an integral part of the sideshow, offering drivers a chance to show off their sound systems and even "choreograph" driving routines to the beat.

While they predate hyphy by about ten years, sideshows became emblematic of the culture. E-40's hyphy anthem "Tell Me When to Go" encapsulates the hyphy movement in song.

LISTENING GUIDE 11.8

Artist: E-40 (feat. Keak da Sneak)
Song: "Tell Me When to Go"
Album: *My Ghetto Report Card*
Record label: Reprise
Year released: 2006
DJ or Producer: Lil Jon
Samples used: "I'm Doing Fine," Moodyman; "Dumb Girl," Run-D.M.C.

E-40's "Tell Me When to Go" is an anthem of the hyphy movement. The sparse, up-tempo beat, comprising little more than a bass drum and the occasional sound effect (sampled from "I'm Doing Fine"), lends itself to dancing. The song also relies heavily on call and response, heard initially in the hook, as a way to encourage audience participation. The bridge also features call and response and functions as a kind of hyphy how-to: E-40 tells listeners to "Put your stunna shades on" (cheap, oversized sunglasses), ghost ride, and make a "thizz face" (a puckered look after taking ecstasy, hyphy's drug of choice), among other things. On the surface, it appears that hyphy is a culture accessible to all; however, E-40's language choices might suggest otherwise.

The repeated "dumb dumb dumb" is sampled from Run-D.M.C.'s song "Dumb Girl." In hyphy, going "dumb" or "stupid" involves doing any kind of extreme activity associated with the movement, like ghost riding. The hyphy movement is about "letting go," through dance, music, cars, and drugs. The use of terms like "dumb," "stupid," or "retarded" has been criticized by those in the field of disability studies as being ableist; that is, the terms reinforce discrimination against those with disabilities. Moya Bailey contends that, while these behaviors are attention-seeking and transgressive—two characteristics that are essential to hip-hop culture—associating them with slurs directed at those with disabilities reinforces the perception of abnormality or the stigma that society attaches to the disabled. Furthermore, even having the ability to "go" dumb or stupid reflects a kind of ableist privilege.[25]

Hyphy forged a regional identity for Oakland and the Bay Area in the 2000s, and it created a bond with a city on the other side of the country, Atlanta—hence Keak da Sneak's line "From the Bay to the A" in "Tell Me When to Go." Too $hort moved to Atlanta in 1994, and the mastermind of crunk, Lil Jon, produced E-40's *My Ghetto Report Card*.

NEW ORLEANS

No city in America defines itself in terms of its musical legacy more than New Orleans. New Orleans is a melting pot of musical cultures, the birthplace of jazz, and an important contributor to the world of rap. A 1989 single by Gregory D and Mannie Fresh called "Buck Jump Time" was the first song to blend the city's musical traditions—brass bands and second lining—with hip hop.[26] Many neighborhoods in New Orleans have brass bands that march through the area on a regular basis. Those who follow the band are known as the "second line"; they do dances like the Buck Jump, make noise, and generally add to the party atmosphere. "Buck Jump Time" features the syncopated bass line that characterizes brass-band music, accompanied by a fast, cowbell-heavy 808 beat and horn punctuation. The hook features a call and response between Gregory D and the "crowd," in which he shouts out a list of housing projects in the city: Roni Sarig writes that, locally, the song was known as "The Project Rap."[27]

Not long after "Buck Jump Time," MC T. Tucker and DJ Irv released "Where Dey At?" (1991), a song that served as the foundation for the first distinctly New Orleans subgenre, **bounce**. The style is characterized by a moderate tempo, 808 drums, and high-pitched piano or similar sounds, which are often referred to as the "bones" or the "bells."[28] The lyrics lack any kind of narrative structure and do little more than repeat a handful of catchy phrases, some of which were well-known clichés in New Orleans specifically ("Where dey at?") or hip hop in general ("The nigga you love to hate," the title of an Ice Cube song). This repetition remained a characteristic of the style, with artists repeating the names of dances, housing projects, or other short phrases, in a flow that approaches the sung style.[29] The subject matter, lack of narrative, and otherwise simplistic structures of the music left bounce open to criticism; however, it could be argued that the music was intended for dancing and that lyrical sophistication would have taken away from its enjoyment in those contexts. On the other hand, Nadia Ellis writes that this repetition was evident from the beginning of the genre, and it represents a kind of political statement, tying it to experiences of confinement in the housing projects of New Orleans.[30] A guest appearance on a local single titled "Bounce (for the Juvenile)" launched the career of Juvenile, who would help bring bounce to a national audience.

Rap in New Orleans is most closely associated with two record labels: Master P's No Limit Records and Cash Money Records. Although he was born and raised in New Orleans, Master P moved to the Bay Area (Richmond, specifically) to join his mother after a knee injury derailed a promising basketball career. At the time, Too $hort and others were raising that region's visibility in the hip-hop world. P's empire started with a record store, **No Limit Records**, that he opened in 1989. A year after studying the industry and connecting with Bay Area artists, he launched his own record label (which shared the store's name) and used it to release his debut album, 1991's *Get Away Clean*. At the start, many of the artists on his roster were members of his family, including Silkk the Shocker and C-Murder (his brothers) and Sonya C (his wife). As No Limit's reputation grew, and as artists from the "**Third Coast**" (the South) were gaining popularity, P returned to New Orleans in search of talent emerging there. He signed Magnolia Slim (who would change his name to Soulja Slim), Mia X, KLC, Mystikal, and Serv-On. P moved No Limit to New Orleans in 1995, heralding the return with one of his best-known tracks, "I'm 'Bout It, 'Bout It."

LISTENING GUIDE 11.9

Artist: Master P (feat. Mia X)
Song: "I'm 'Bout It, 'Bout It"
Album: *True*
Record label: No Limit
Year released: 1995
DJ or Producer: KLC (Beats By The Pound)
Samples used: (none)

TRU (The Real Untouchables) comprised Master P and his brothers: at one time, the crew included his wife and a handful of other New Orleans rappers—P mentions them all by name in the hook. The beat is considerably slower than a typical bounce track, and the thick, bass-heavy synthesizers are clearly influenced by Dr. Dre's G-Funk. Even Master P's down-and-dirty flow bears the imprint of some West

Coast MCs. Sonically and lyrically, then, the song encapsulates the relationship between the Bay Area and New Orleans.

In a spoken introduction, P assures listeners that he would never forget where he's from, a sentiment that is expanded in the first verse, in which he references his journey from Richmond back to New Orleans and shouts out his neighborhood, the Third Ward Calliope projects. Note his pronunciation of "Calliope": the word is typically pronounced "kuh-LIE-oh-pee," but in New Orleans, it is often pronounced "KAL-lee-ope," or shortened to "KAL-lee-oh." P references other wards in New Orleans later in the first verse, as does Mia X in her verse. Mia also refers to New Orleans' nickname, the Crescent City; its location below sea level; gris-gris (Voodoo amulets); and étouffée, a popular Cajun/Creole dish.

Cash Money Records was founded in 1991 by brothers Bryan ("Baby"; "Birdman") and Ronald ("Slim") Williams. Their early releases were bounce-oriented tracks, but the sound began to evolve when they brought on Mannie Fresh as their producer: their beats and lyrics began to gravitate toward gangsta rap. The label's most famous artist, Lil Wayne, started his affiliation with the label when he was in his early teens: his 1999 debut, *Tha Block Is Hot*, shared space in *Billboard*'s top 20 with labelmate Juvenile's *400 Degrees* as well as releases by two other Cash Money artists, including B.G.'s *Chopper City in the Ghetto*, which introduced the words "bling bling" into the vocabulary of the nation. Eventually, Cash Money ran into trouble as the label's artists began to question their compensation: Juvenile and B.G. left in 2001; Mannie Fresh left in 2005; Bow Wow, in 2012; and Tyga, in 2014. More recently, Lil Wayne has accused Birdman of stalling the release of *Tha Carter V*, calling himself a "prisoner" of the label. In early 2015, Wayne sued for $51 million and asked to separate Young Money Entertainment from Cash Money.

Young Money Entertainment is a label founded by Lil Wayne in 2005 as a subsidiary of Cash Money Records. The label enjoyed considerable success in the 2010s with albums from its small but high-profile roster, which includes Wayne, Drake, and Nicki Minaj and formerly featured Curren$y, DJ Khaled, and Tyga.

Late in the summer of 2005, Hurricane Katrina battered the Gulf states. New Orleans, much of which lies below sea level, was woefully unprepared for the devastation that the storm wrought, and the poor communities—those who could not afford to leave the area—were hit hardest. Government at all levels was widely critiqued not only for the slow, inadequate response, but also for its failure to create and maintain the kind of infrastructure that would have at least minimized if not prevented the resulting human suffering. People's perceptions of the lack of government response to Katrina significantly shaped the 2008 presidential election.

During a telethon to raise funds for those affected by the disaster, Kanye West called attention to the differences in media representations of race, going off the teleprompter script, eventually concluding his tirade by saying, "George Bush doesn't care about black people," before the cameras cut away. This was one of the most high-profile accusations of racism in the immediate aftermath of the hurricane, a theme that pervades many rap songs written in the aftermath of the hurricane. A number of artists released songs that addressed Katrina, including Jay-Z's "Minority Report," Lil Wayne's "Tie My Hands," Juvenile's "What's

Happening?" Public Enemy's "Hell No We Ain't Alright," and The Legendary K.O.'s "George Bush Doesn't Care about Black People." Mos Def weighed in with "Dollar Day," a song that borrowed from one of Juvenile's New Orleans party anthems, "Nolia Clap."

LISTENING GUIDE 11.10

Artist: UTP (Juvenile, Skip, and Wacko)
Song: "Nolia Clap"
Album: *The Beginning of the End*
Record label: Rap-A-Lot
Year released: 2004
DJ or Producer: Donald XL Robertson

Artist: Mos Def
Song: "Dollar Day"
Album: *True Magic*
Record label: Geffen
Year released: 2005 (as a single); album in 2006
DJ or Producer: Donald XL Robertson (see above)
Samples used: "Nolia Clap" (see above)

Compare and contrast Juvenile's "Nolia Clap" with Mos Def's "Dollar Day." Consider the following questions:

1. What does "Nolia" mean in the title of the first song? What does "Dollar Day" mean in the title of the second song?
2. How does Juvenile's song construct New Orleans (how do we know that's where it's set)?
3. Why do you think Mos Def chose to use the same beat as UTP?
4. Describe the difference in voice between the two songs.

As the rap community came together figuratively to support those affected by the disaster, the devastation forced many New Orleans–based rappers to relocate. This led to a sudden spread of the New Orleans sound around the country, with many relocating to nearby urban centers like Miami, Houston, and Atlanta. Atlanta's T.I. and Mississippi's David Banner used their celebrity to raise money for those affected. Mississippi, of course, was also hit hard in the storm; however, much of the media attention was focused on New Orleans. Banner's concert was one of the largest hip-hop fundraising events in history. The HBO television series *Treme*, which premiered in 2010, featured New Orleans musicians of all genres prominently throughout its run. Among those featured in the program were Big Freedia, who quickly gained mainstream popularity, resurrected bounce and was among those who popularized **twerking**, a dance associated with bounce that involves squatting low and rapidly shaking your hips.

ATLANTA

Atlanta is one of the biggest transportation hubs on the East Coast. It boasts the largest airport in the country, and many major highways pass through it. The regional headquarters for major record labels and music publishing houses are located in Atlanta, making it an ideal destination for someone looking to break into the industry. The city's rich black history and a strong black middle class also draw people to the city. Many rappers associated with the Atlanta hip-hop scene are not originally from the city: OutKast's Big Boi came from Savannah, Georgia; Ludacris moved from Champaign, Illinois; and Too $hort, from the Bay Area.[31]

Atlanta's early rap music was very much Miami-influenced, which is not surprising, given the relative proximity of the two cities. As rap scenes grew in Houston and Los Angeles (the latter of which influenced the former), Atlanta's sound began to shift away from booty bass toward the gangsta narratives. In the early 1990s, a distinctly Atlanta sound was beginning to coalesce as the result of a few high-profile releases from a local label with national clout—LaFace Records, started in 1989 by two music industry veterans, L.A. Reid and Kenneth "Babyface" Edmonds, in partnership with Arista Records. LaFace had its first big success with TLC, a trio that blended R&B with New Jack Swing. The group's debut, *Ooooooohhh . . . On the TLC Tip* came out in 1992, preceded by its first single, "Ain't 2 Proud 2 Beg."

Arrested Development's debut album, *3 Years, 5 Months and 2 Days in the Life of . . . ,* appeared about a month after TLC's album. Its lead single was "Tennessee," a song that in many ways epitomized the rural Southern way of life. The song, cast as a prayer, encapsulates themes of spirituality, migration, slavery, and lynching, using the past as a means of understanding contemporary issues faced by the black community. Musically, it draws inspiration from the Native Tongues movement, with traces of New Jack Swing. The video trades images of the city for images of the rural South. The song won a Grammy for Best Rap Performance by a Duo or Group in 1993, and the group won Best New Artist, showing early signs that rap's center was moving to the South. The more sophisticated sounds of OutKast's *Southernplayalisticadillacmuzik* (1994) and Goodie Mob's *Soul Food* (1995) helped LaFace cement the South's dominance of hip hop in the 1990s, an argument buttressed by successful releases by Miami, Houston, and New Orleans-based artists, as discussed earlier in this chapter. At the 1995 *Source* awards—as the fires of the Bad Boy–Death Row, East Coast–West Coast feud were being stoked—the audience booed the bestowal of Best New Artist to OutKast. In a short but significant acceptance speech, André 3000 said: "But it's like this, though . . . I'm tired of folks—you know what I'm sayin'—closed minded folks. It's like we got a demo tape and don't nobody wanna hear it. But it's like this. The South got somethin' to say. That's all I got to say."

LISTENING GUIDE 11.11

Artist: OutKast
Song title: "B.O.B. (Bombs Over Baghdad)"
Album title: *Stankonia*
Record label: LaFace
Year released: 2000
DJ or Producer: Earthtone III
Samples used: (none)

"B.O.B." was the lead single from the duo's fourth album. While it did not achieve much in the way of chart success, it was a groundbreaking song for many reasons. The tempo is a blistering 155 bpm, much faster than just about anything that had come before it. The beat is inspired by drum-and-bass electronic dance music and juxtaposed with a Jimi Hendrix–inspired guitar part, organ, and gospel choir. While others have rapped just as fast (or faster), the impression of André 3000 and Big Boi keeping up with the rapid beat made the song a standout performance.

Like some of the other artists detailed in this chapter, OutKast paints a complex picture of life in the ghetto, one that goes beyond the drugs and violence and examines the everyday realities of and choices faced by people who live there. In the first verse, André 3000 uses a fence as a metaphor for confines of the ghetto, saying it is "too high to jump" and "too low to dig." He juxtaposes his new responsibilities as a father (listen to "Ms. Jackson" on the same album for a nuanced perspective on this part of his life) with his old life as a hustler: "gold grill and a baby mama/Black Cadillac and a pack of Pampers." In the last few lines of the verse, he relates the toll that his lifestyle takes: "Thoughts at a thousand miles per hour/Hello, ghetto, let your brain breathe." The lines also refer to the speed of the song, turning its breakneck tempo into a kind of metaphor as well, while the "let your brain breathe" line signals the end of his verse and ushers in the hook. In verse 2, Big Boi offers a similar perspective, juggling family life with hustling. He encourages listeners to get out of the drug trade, buy a laptop, and "make a fat diamond out of dusty coal."

André 3000 claims that he overheard the phrase "bombs over Baghdad" in a news report, and he worked it into a song because he liked the way it sounded. The title has led many commentators to speculate on a connection between the song and US involvement in the Middle East: the first Gulf War, which took place from 1990 to 1991, and the invasions of Iraq and Afghanistan that took place after the September 11, 2001, attacks on the United States. But the song was released well after the former and before the latter; the duo claims that the song is not directly related to the attacks.

Crunk came to dominate Atlanta's sound in the mid-2000s. Pioneered by Lil Jon, a producer who enjoyed the high energy of punk shows and DJed around town, crunk revitalized Atlanta's shrinking bass scene by fusing high-energy tracks with deep, booming bass. Much like bounce, crunk abandoned narrative structures almost entirely in favor of short, memorable chants. Lil Jon and his crew, The East Side Boyz, along with the Yin Yang Twins, popularized the style, which is best exemplified by their collaboration "Get Low" (2002). While trap music would quickly bury crunk, Lil Jon stayed in the public eye, shifting his talents to the Bay Area's emerging hyphy scene.

Atlanta's status as an East Coast transit hub makes it ideal for drug trafficking. Locals began referring to houses—often abandoned—where drugs are made, bought, and sold as **"traps."** Lyrically, trap music tends to detail life in the drug trade, although the content has broadened to include other kinds of hustles as the genre has evolved. The flow tends to be in compound meter (that is, the beat is divided into three equal parts). The beats sound ominous, featuring deep bass notes, rapid hi-hats, and very often lush synthesizer harmonies filling out the texture. While T.I. claims to have named the style with his second album, 2003's *Trap Muzik*, Young Jeezy's 2005 debut, *Let's Get It: Thug Motivation 101*, is widely considered to be the album that buried crunk and brought trap into the mainstream.

LISTENING GUIDE 11.12

Artist: Young Jeezy
Song: "Thug Motivation 101"
Album: *Let's Get It: Thug Motivation 101*
Record label: CTE/Def Jam

Year released: 2005
DJ or Producer: Shawty Redd
Samples used: (none)

This song contains the seeds of the sound that would come to characterize Atlanta's rap scene in the 2010s, including artists like Future, Migos, and 2 Chainz. The basic trap music texture is there: persistent hi-hat, deep 808 kick drum, and synthesizers in the middle. Young Jeezy's flow comes across as rough, with many of the lyrics mumbled and moving in and out of the beat. Throughout, Jeezy punctuates the texture with various ad-libs like "yeah," "ha-haaaa," "damn," and "aaaaay."[32]

The song is a rags-to-riches tale about his days as a drug dealer: Jeezy presents himself as an example of the virtues of hard work: "I used to hit the kitchen lights: cockroaches everywhere/Hit the kitchen lights now, it's marble floors everywhere." He recounts his days cooking cocaine in the kitchen, earning money to take care of his friends and family. By the end of the verse, he has become the trap Donald Trump. He boasts about his work ethic in the hook as well: "pies" refers to the shape of crack cocaine ("white") when it is removed from the pan.

Jeezy's experiences are authenticated by his involvement with the Black Mafia Family (BMF), which was one of the largest drug-trafficking operations in the country, and Big Meech, the kingpin. Meech ran a record label, BMF Records, that helped many Atlanta-based artists, including Jeezy, grow their careers. While there was only ever one artist officially signed to the label—a rapper named Bleu DaVinci—Meech booked shows and funded video shoots.

Jeezy paved the way for a host of Atlanta artists, including Gucci Mane, Migos, Future, Lil Yachty, 21 Savage, and Young Thug. As the genre evolved, tempos slowed down and more and more effects were added to the voice, the end result of which is a disembodied, drugged-out sound.

OUTRO

Names you should know:

- 2 Live Crew
- Daddy Yankee
- N.W.A.
- Dr. Dre
- Suge Knight
- Death Row Records
- Snoop Doggy Dogg
- Rap-A-Lot Records
- Geto Boys
- DJ Screw
- Swishahouse Records

- Mike Jones
- The Coup
- E-40
- Master P
- No Limit Records
- Cash Money Records
- Juvenile
- Mos Def
- LaFace Records
- OutKast
- Young Jeezy

Terms you should know:

- Miami Bass
- Dembow

- G-Funk
- Reggaeton

- Chopped and screwed
- Syrup (lean, purple drank)
- Hyphy
- Sideshow
- Bounce

- Third Coast
- Twerking
- Crunk
- Trap

Questions for discussion/writing prompts:

1. Throughout this chapter, we have considered how various regional styles have migrated around the country, inflecting the sound of other local scenes. Trace the migration of one of these scenes and its influence on other regional rap styles.

2. In this chapter, we have only surveyed a few of hip hop's many regional styles. Choose another region, find some artists closely associated with it, and describe its sound. Some possibilities are Chicago, Kansas City (Missouri), Baltimore, Memphis, and Detroit.

3. The track "International Player's Anthem (I Choose You)" by Houston's UGK features Atlanta's OutKast, with production from Memphis' Three 6 Mafia. How does the sound of each region manifest itself in this track?

4. Use social media to research an artist in your area: find their website, Facebook, or Twitter accounts; listen to their music on YouTube, SoundCloud, Bandcamp, or Spotify, and write an album review as if you were writing for a local newspaper or music blog.

Additional listening/viewing:

Miami:

- "Take It to the House," Trick Daddy
- "My Neck, My Back," Khia
- "Hustlin'," Rick Ross
- "Welcome to Miami," Pitbull

Reggaeton:

- Reynolds, Tom. *Straight Outta Puerto Rico: Reggaeton's Rough Road to Glory*. Santa Monica, CA: Xenon Pictures, 2008.
- *King of Kings*, Don Omar
- "Te He Querido, Te He Llorado" and "La Mala," Ivy Queen
- "Oye Mi Canto," N.O.R.E.

Los Angeles:

- Lowe, Richard, and Martin Torgoff. *Planet Rock: The Story of Hip Hop and the Crack Generation*. New York: Prodigious Media, 2011.
- "Dial-A-Freak," Uncle Jamm's Army
- "Supersonic," J. J. Fad
- "Who Got the Camera," Ice Cube
- "Midnight," Ice-T

Houston:

- "One Day," UGK
- "On My Block," Scarface
- "Ridin' Dirty," Chamillionaire

Bay Area:

- "The Humpty Dance," Digital Underground
- "Changes," Tupac Shakur
- "Blow the Whistle," Too $hort
- "Recognize," Suga T
- "I Got 5 on It," The Luniz

New Orleans:

- Lessin, Tia, and Carl Deal. *Trouble the Water*. New York: Zeitgeist Films, 2009.
- "Drag Rap (Triggaman)," Showboys
- "A Milli," Lil Wayne
- "Shake Ya Ass," Mystikal

Atlanta:

- "Tennessee," Arrested Development
- "Waterfalls," TLC
- *Soul Food*, Goodie Mob
- *Word of Mouf*, Ludacris
- "Stilettos (Pumps)," Crime Mob

NOTES

1 Mark Katz discusses the significance of these samples in early hip hop in *Groove Music* (New York: Oxford University Press, 2012), 89–93.
2 Matt Miller, "Tropic of Bass," in *Hip Hop in America: A Regional Guide*. 2 vols. Ed. Mickey Hess (Santa Barbara: Greenwood Press, 2010), 594. See also Nelson George, *Hip Hop America* (New York: Viking, 1998), 190. Miller points out that, despite the male-dominated nature of the music, women comprised a significant portion of the audience and were "an important minority in the ranks of its artists."
3 Juan Flores, "Foreword: What's All the Noise About?" in *Reggaeton*. Ed. Raquel Z. Rivera, Wayne Marshall, and Deborah Pacini Hernandez (Durham, NC: Duke University Press, 2009), x.
4 Wayne Marshall, "From Music Negra to Reggaeton Latino: The Cultural Politics of Nation, Migration, and Commercialization," in *Reggaeton*. Ed. Raquel Z. Rivera, Wayne Marshall, and Deborah Pacini Hernandez (Durham, NC: Duke University Press, 2009), 19–20.
5 Marshall 23.
6 Marshall 21; see also fn. 46 on p. 71.
7 Robin D. G. Kelley, "Kickin' Reality, Kickin' Ballistics: Gangsta Rap in Postindustrial Los Angeles," in *Droppin' Science: Critical Essays on Rap Music and Hip Hop Culture*. Ed. William Eric Perkins (Philadelphia: Temple University Press, 1996), 122–3.
8 Alex Henderson, "Active Indies" *Billboard* (December 24, 1988), R-16. Quoted in Reebee Garofalo and Steven Waksman, *Rockin' Out: Popular Music in the U.S.A.* (Upper Saddle River, NJ: Prentice Hall, 2011), 347.
9 Kelley 124.

10 Mark Ford, *Uprising: Hip Hop and the L.A. Riots* (Santa Monica: Creature Films, 2012).

11 Quoted in Kelley 118.

12 Jeff Chang, *Can't Stop, Won't Stop: A History of the Hip-Hop Generation* (New York: St. Martin's, 2005), 346–53.

13 Shea Serrano, *The Rap Yearbook: The Most Important Rap Song from Every Year since 1979, Discussed, Debated, and Deconstructed*. Ed. Arturo Torres and Ice-T (New York: Abrams Image, 2015), 89.

14 Serrano 90–1.

15 Justin A. Williams, *Rhymin' and Stealin': Musical Borrowing in Hip Hop* (Ann Arbor: University of Michigan Press, 2013), 84–5.

16 Loren Kajikawa, *Sounding Race in Rap Songs* (Berkeley: University of California Press, 2015), 104.

17 Kajikawa 114.

18 See Williams chapter 3 and Kajikawa chapter 3.

19 George 190.

20 Brian Coleman, *Liner Notes for Hip-Hop Junkies*. vol. 1 (New York: Villard, 2005), 222.

21 Jamie Lynch, "The Long, Hot Grind: How Houston Engineered an Industry of Independence," in *Hip Hop in America: A Regional Guide*. 2 vols. Ed. Mickey Hess (Santa Barbara: Greenwood Press, 2010), 432–6.

22 Serrano 85–6.

23 Serrano 163.

24 George Ciccariello-Maher and Jeff St. Andrews, "Between Macks and Panthers: Hip Hop in Oakland and San Francisco," in *Hip Hop in America: A Regional Guide*. 2 vols. Ed. Mickey Hess (Santa Barbara: Greenwood Press, 2010), 257–86.

25 Moya Bailey, "'The Illest': Disability as Metaphor in Hip Hop," in *Blackness and Disability: Critical Examinations and Cultural Interventions*. Ed. Christopher Bell (East Lansing: Michigan State University Press, 2011). The Black Eyed Peas, who got their start as a rap group in Los Angeles, were widely criticized for their song "Let's Get Retarded," which used that word in a similar fashion. The group released an edited version of the single as "Let's Get It Started."

26 Roni Sarig, *Third Coast: OutKast, Timbaland, and How Hip-Hop Became a Southern Thing* (Cambridge, MA: Da Capo Press, 2007), 253.

27 Sarig 254.

28 Matt Miller, *Bounce: Rap Music and Local Identity in New Orleans* (Amherst: University of Massachusetts Press, 2012), 79.

29 Miller, *Bounce*, 90–6.

30 Nadia Ellis, "New Orleans and Kingston: A Beginning, A Recurrence" *Journal of Popular Music Studies* 27 no. 4 (December 2015): 387–407.

31 Matt Miller, "'The Sound of Money': Atlanta, Crossroads of the Dirty South," in *Hip Hop in America: A Regional Guide*. 2 vols. Ed. Mickey Hess (Santa Barbara: Greenwood Press, 2010), 470.

32 Alyssa Woods examines Young Jeezy's vocal delivery in "Vocal Practices and Identity in Rap: A Case Study of Young Jeezy's 'Soul Survivor'," in *Pop-Culture Pedagogy in the Music Classroom*. Ed. Nicole Biamonte (Lanham, MD: Scarecrow Press, 2011), 265–80.

TIME LINE

1971 President Richard Nixon declares drug abuse "public enemy number one" and launches "the War on Drugs."

1992 Ice-T faces backlash for his song "Cop Killer" and is ultimately dropped by his record label, Warner Brothers.

1993 Cypress Hill releases its second album, *Black Sunday*.

2004 Immortal Technique releases *Revolutionary, Vol. 2*.

2011 Jay-Z and Kanye West release the collaboration *Watch the Throne*.

2012 Killer Mike releases *R.A.P. Music*.

—Trayvon Martin is shot and killed by George Zimmerman, a citizen who felt threatened by his presence. The incident was a catalyst for the Black Lives Matter movement.

IN THIS CHAPTER, YOU WILL LEARN ABOUT

- The racial politics of noise and rap music
- Relationships between rap music and the criminal justice system
- Rap music as protest and community organizing

CHAPTER 12

Listening to Politics

OVERVIEW

"Politics" is a word with many different connotations. When most people think of politics, they think of government, a formal structure in which those in power make and enforce laws. But the term "politics" can also refer to less formal power relations that we encounter in our daily lives—"office politics," for instance. A theme that runs throughout this chapter is the ways in which race is politicized. Since its inception, hip hop has always engaged with politics, both formally and informally. Rappers have championed one political candidate over another, critiqued systems and institutions, or provided a voice to those otherwise voiceless. Government and media have attacked rap music, accused it of promoting violence and drug use, shut down concerts, and toughened copyright laws in response to concerns about sampling. Despite this, hip hop remains a powerful organizing force in the community, as seen in the words and actions of a new generation of artists.

THE POLITICS OF NOISE

The definition of noise is political, and some would argue that the dividing line between music (or pleasant sounds generally) and noise corresponds to the line that separates white America from black. Philosopher Richard Shusterman suggests that the aesthetics of rap music are contrary to what people typically value in Western art: ideals like originality, single-authorship, and universality. The aesthetics of hip hop, he argues, are fundamentally postmodern: they sample preexisting materials, value collaboration, speak to a specific place and time, and embrace mass-media technologies. Shusterman argues that challenging rap on aesthetic grounds provides the (largely white) middle class with leverage as they "compete for the same mass-media channels of cultural transmission, and who have a need to assert their sociocultural (and ultimately political) superiority over black America."[1] The sentiment is mirrored by the number of radio stations that, in the 1980s and '90s, used taglines like "All the best music—and no rap" to attract listeners.[2] Thus, what constitutes noise is determined by hegemonic forces—hooks' imperialist white supremacist capitalist patriarchy—and efforts to criticize or silence rap on aesthetic grounds can often be seen as racially motivated. Furthermore, many critics tend to subscribe to the belief that rap music *causes* social problems rather than reflects them. These efforts to silence rap take three main forms: censorship of lyrical content based on literal readings, criticism on aesthetic grounds, and policing of hip-hop venues.

2 Live Crew was the first rap group to face censorship in the public sphere, and Geto Boys dealt with it around the same time: both groups' legal troubles were surveyed in the previous chapter. Encounters between rap artists and government agencies became increasingly visible as gangsta rap began to dominate the airwaves in the early 1990s. N.W.A.'s "Fuck tha Police," which was released in 1988, broadcast the acts of police brutality that residents of south-central Los Angeles were subjected to on a regular basis. The song caught the attention of many police departments around the country, the FBI, and the Secret Service. The FBI sent a letter to the group's label, Ruthless Records, which made the Bureau's position on the song clear. The letter concluded with the director stating that his views "reflect the opinion of the entire law enforcement community." While the letter was not directly a call for censorship, the implication was certainly strong. The song had been banned by radio stations and record stores around the country. Some police departments refused to provide security for N.W.A. concerts; others would, but only if there was an assurance that "Fuck tha Police" was not on the set list.

The PMRC

The Parents Music Resource Center (PMRC) was formed in 1985 by Tipper Gore to make parents more aware of questionable content in popular music. On the heels of Senate hearings, the group sought to warn parents of drug-related, sexual, and violent content by labeling albums with a "parental advisory" sticker. While the group's early targets were popular music and heavy metal, it did not take long for their attention to turn to rap music. Ice-T's 1987 album *Rhyme Pays* was the first rap album to bear the sticker. Rappers like Ice-T and Eminem have called out Gore and the PMRC in their songs ("Freedom of Speech" and "White America," respectively). Many stores, like Walmart and Sam's Club, refused to carry albums that bore the sticker. The sticker persists, and it has been added to recent releases by Drake, Lil Wayne, and other contemporary artists; however, the rise of streaming services has rendered it all but obsolete.

In 1992, Ice-T released an album with his hardcore band, Body Count, that featured a song called "Cop Killer." The song was met with an immediate backlash from police unions and was condemned by Congress, the vice president, and the president. The mounting pressure on Warner Brothers, his label, led Ice-T to remove the song from the album and ultimately resulted in the record company terminating his contract. It is important to note that "Cop Killer" was a *hardcore* song, a genre that grew out of punk and has much in common with heavy metal in terms of expressing white male anger. Barry Shank argues that the mixing of gangsta-rap content with a musical style that was identified as white allowed the white community to empathize with the kind of black anger that fueled the Los Angeles riots and that this mixed racial coding is what ultimately led to the record's censorship. Shank contends that the song creates a confrontation between the two prevailing views about the riots: some believed that rap music caused the violence, while others argued that rap simply reflected the violence created by stifling social, political, and economic conditions.[3] Shank argues that the backlash against the song can be seen as racially motivated, and he demonstrates this by surveying a number of songs by white artists that promote violence against police (like Eric Clapton's version of Bob Marley's "I Shot the Sheriff"). A study conducted by psychologist Carrie B. Fried further illuminates this phenomenon. Fried took a set of song lyrics by the Kingston Trio (a famous folk group from the late 1950s), told participants that they were lyrics to a folk song, a country song or a rap song, and asked them to rate how offensive or dangerous the lyrics were. The participants overwhelmingly said that the "rap" version was more objectionable, leading Fried to believe that racism played a role in their interpretation.[4]

Jennifer Lynn Stoever developed the concept of the "sonic color line" to examine the ways in which sounds are culturally coded with racial information. Before embarking on the historical roots of the subject, Stoever presents a tragic contemporary manifestation of her theory, the death of Jordan Davis. Seventeen-year-old Davis and three of his friends were in a car at a gas station, listening to rap. Michael Dunn, a 47-year-old white man, asked them to turn down the "rap-crap," and when they refused, he fired ten shots into the car, killing Davis. As outlined in Chapter 10, car stereos provide a way for listeners to claim territory by creating mobile listening spaces: Stoever writes that, by shooting Davis, Dunn "marked his aural territory" as well.[5] Dunn's perception of the "noise" emanating from the car that Davis and his friends were occupying shows the ways in which sound can be politicized: noise, argues Stoever, has become attached to the bodies of people of color.[6]

The sonic color line extends to lyrics as well. In the last decade, rap lyrics have increasingly been used as evidence in criminal trials. In 2008, Vonte Skinner was convicted of attempted murder in New Jersey. The police found notebooks in his car that were filled with violent lyrics written years before the crime, and they played an important role in convicting him: prosecutors argued that they provided evidence of prior violent tendencies. The Supreme Court of New Jersey reversed the ruling in 2014, allowing lyrics to be entered as evidence only if there was a direct connection to the crime in question. A Virginia rapper, Antwain Steward, was arrested and charged with murder in 2014 after detectives read lyrics that he wrote, which, they believed, constituted a confession to the crime. Although his lyrics were not used against him in court, they clearly led to his implication in the crime.

The first-person narratives of graphic violence common to mainstream rap have contributed to an image of young black men as prone to violence. Lyrics have been used as evidence in criminal trials since the early 1990s: in virtually all cases, rap lyrics have been examined—Stoia, Adams, and Drakulich write that in only one case in the United States and one case in Canada were lyrics from a genre other than rap put forth as evidence.[7] Prosecutors have used rap lyrics as evidence of prior violent tendencies, as a kind of written confession, or as evidence of a direct threat.[8] Using rap lyrics in this way requires those involved in the case to interpret the lyrics literally. Throughout this book, we have considered several strategies that rappers use to distance themselves from their subject matter and to call attention to the systems that give rise to their circumstances; however, these strategies tend to be overlooked, given the kinds of images that have been mainstreamed in conjunction with rap's reputation for "keeping it real." In the ruling that overturned Skinner's conviction, Justice Jaynee LaVecchia wrote that reading lyrics risks "poisoning the jury" and that the lyrics should be interpreted as artistic product: "One would not presume that Bob Marley, who wrote the well-known song 'I Shot the Sheriff,' actually shot a sheriff, or that Edgar Allan Poe buried a man beneath his floorboards, as depicted in his short story 'The Tell-Tale Heart,' simply because of their respective artistic endeavors on those subjects. [Skinner's] lyrics should receive no different treatment."[9]

Keepin' It Real

Members of the hip-hop community often talk about "keepin' it real," which means being true not just to oneself, but also to the fundamentals of hip-hop culture. Today, keepin' it real often means conforming to the media stereotypes of what a rapper should be like: a young, black male who engages in violent, misogynist behavior and who talks about life "on the streets." As we have seen, this is far from reality for most people, rappers included. Nonetheless, the posturing of many mainstream rappers works to create the illusion of authenticity. This authenticity becomes problematic, as lyrics are taken at face value rather than in the context of systemic racism or media influence.

Violence has been associated with hip-hop shows from the beginning: the strength of the security detail at Bambaataa's shows was well known by attendees, and one thing MC Shan and KRS-One did agree on as they traded barbs in the Bridge Wars was that people were getting shot at shows. It was largely a result of the rise of hip hop that metal detectors and certain dress codes (no Timberlands, no gang colors, etc.) came to be at clubs.[10] Police departments in New York City, Los Angeles, Miami, and other major metropolitan areas have "hip-hop task forces" that are responsible for surveilling the music industry.[11] Historically, cities have enforced ordinances that have limited the ability of clubs to host shows in general and hip-hop shows in particular, believing that keeping youth—particularly those who were associated with music that was perceived as violent—off the streets would keep the crime rate down. In Oakland, licensed venues are required to submit their monthly event calendars to the Oakland Police Department's Special Event Unit for review. A 2017 article in the *East Bay Express* indicated that venues that promoted hip-hop shows were subject to more intensive scrutiny than other venues and that the costs to provide police security were prohibitively high, approaching $5,000 per event. Proprietors of clubs that did not typically host rap shows said that the enforcement of special-events regulations was generally lax and that they were rarely required to pay additional police-security fees. One club, New Karibbean City, has a late-night clause in its permit, allowing it to operate until 4:00 a.m. on weekends, as long as no rap shows are booked on the extended nights.[12] Policies such as this are clearly discriminatory and emerge from the widespread belief that rap music causes violence.[13] They deprive local and traveling artists of income, forcing them either to rebook in a nearby city like San Francisco or to skip the Bay Area altogether.

The ways in which rap music sounds race are subject to political sanctions when those in power believe that the music, its producers, or its consumers have crossed the sonic color line. The consequences of these sanctions drive a wedge further into America's racial disparities.

THE WAR ON DRUGS

Alcohol and drugs have always been a part of hip-hop culture: they are addressed in hundreds of songs; rappers name themselves after famous drug kingpins (i.e., Scarface, Noreaga, Nas' alter ego Escobar, and Rick Ross); and many rappers either advertise for prominent alcoholic beverages (like Ice Cube's ads for St. Ides malt liquor or Biggie's endorsement of Moet and Alizé) or have their own brands (like Diddy's Ciroc vodka). These substances tend to be featured in rap music in four main ways: as a part of the artist's past, as a metaphor, as a problem facing the community, or as a way to escape or cope—a pleasure-seeking behavior. Biggie's "Ten Crack Commandments" relays lessons learned during his days as a drug dealer, and songs like Rick Ross' "Hustlin'" and Clipse's "Grinding'" recall their time as pushers. Ice-T's "Pusherman" uses drugs as a metaphor for the rap game, while Chance the Rapper uses drugs as a metaphor for love in "Same Drugs." Hip hop's rise to national visibility began around the same time as the crack epidemic was spreading in American cities, and many rappers call attention to the negative impacts of drugs on their communities. Melle Mel's "White Lines

(Don't Do It)" and N.W.A.'s "Dopeman" warn of the dangers of the drug trade. Geto Boys' "City under Siege" and Immortal Technique's "Peruvian Cocaine" take a broader perspective, moving beyond the street dealers to implicate the government and law enforcement. Cypress Hill's "Hits from the Bong" and Gravediggaz' "Defective Trip (Trippin')" celebrate the pleasures of being intoxicated.[14]

As we saw in Chapter 5, rap music came into being as a result of politics, chiefly the desperate situation of New York City in the 1970s and the reign of Robert Moses. Politics at the national level would also become a shaping force in hip-hop culture. Richard Nixon, who served as president from 1969 until his resignation in 1974, launched the **War on Drugs**, a program initially focused on treatment and prevention of drug abuse. As reelection became a consideration, the administration was forced to shift the narrative from one of treatment to one of prosecution, and drug use became increasingly criminalized. This shift would be amplified by Nixon's successors, particularly Ronald Reagan, who served as president from 1981 to 1989, and First Lady Nancy Reagan, whose "Just Say No" campaign aimed to steer young people away from drugs.

Drug laws disproportionately target and affect communities of color. Five times as many whites use drugs in comparison to African Americans, yet African Americans are ten times more likely to be incarcerated for drug-related offenses. Roughly 12% of African Americans admit to using drugs, but African Americans comprise 38% of those arrested for drug offenses and 58% of those serving time in state prison for those offenses.[15] In 1986, Congress passed the Anti-Drug Abuse Act, which changed the sentencing guidelines for those convicted of drug-related offenses. The bill called for mandatory minimum sentences, which restricted judges' discretion on sentencing. The law also distinguished between powder cocaine and crack—crack is basically powder cocaine cooked with water and baking soda—and set a 100:1 sentencing ratio for the two drugs. A person in possession of 1 gram of crack cocaine would receive the same sentence as a person in possession of 100 grams of powder cocaine. With the media increasingly portraying crack as an "inner-city" (read: black) problem, it is no surprise that these sentencing guidelines had devastating effects on communities of color. In 2010, Congress passed the Fair Sentencing Act—lowering the sentencing proportion to 18:1, which, while certainly an improvement, still reflects the inequity.

Cypress Hill was the first group to vocally and repeatedly advocate for the legalization of marijuana for recreational and medicinal purposes, which would drastically reduce the number of people arrested for low-level drug offenses. Historically the drug had been associated with Latino communities, and enforcement policies could be seen a means of controlling that population. Jeffrey O. G. Ogbar writes that half of the American population has admitted to using marijuana at least once, as have US presidents Bill Clinton, George W. Bush, and Barack Obama. Despite this, more than 15 million people have been incarcerated for marijuana use since 1975.[16] Cypress Hill's eponymous first album, released in 1991, comprised mostly standard gangsta-rap fare, with little discussion of marijuana. Their second album, 1993's *Black Sunday*, turned them into celebrity advocates for legalizing the drug. The album included songs that dealt with all aspects of being high: the pleasure ("I Wanna Get High" and "Hits from the Bong"), the paranoia ("Insane in the Membrane"), and a plea for legalization ("Legalize It"). The album's liner notes even included a fact sheet about marijuana. The album debuted at number 1 on the *Billboard* Hot 200 and had the highest first-week sales of any rap album to date. Since then, the group has lobbied vocally for the legalization of marijuana, making it the focal point of many subsequent releases. Their work paved the way for other pro-pot artists like Snoop Doggy Dogg and Dr. Dre, whose album title *The Chronic* is an overt reference to the drug. In 2014, Colorado and Washington became the first states to decriminalize marijuana, and many other states have followed suit.

Immortal Technique's posse cut "Peruvian Cocaine" tells the stories of all who are impacted by the drug trade, from those who harvest the crops to those in positions of government authority. The song emphasizes the danger and the hypocrisy that are often overlooked in conversations about the War on Drugs.

LISTENING GUIDE 12.1

Artist: Immortal Technique (feat. Pumpkinhead, Diabolic, Tonedeff, Poison Pen, Loucifer, and C-Rayz Wallz)
Song: "Peruvian Cocaine"
Album: *Revolutionary, Vol. 2*
Record label: Viper Records
Year released: 2004
DJ or Producer: Southpaw
Samples used: The soundtrack to *Scarface*, Giorgio Moroder; dialogue from *New Jack City*

The movie *Scarface* functions as a thread throughout the song: the song's opening dialogue comes from it, as does the musical sample. Just as the movie does, Immortal Technique and his guests paint a complex picture of the global drug industry, including who profits from it and how, as well as who it harms.

In this song, each artist raps a verse from the perspective of someone involved in the drug supply chain:

- Verse 1: Immortal Technique as a laborer in the fields of Bolivia (Immortal Technique was actually born in Peru and raised in Harlem.)
- Verse 2: Pumpkinhead as a field boss
- Verse 3: Diabolic as a Peruvian dictator
- Verse 4: Tonedeff as a CIA (Central Intelligence Agency) agent
- Verse 5: Poison Pen as a low-level drug dealer
- Verse 6: Loucifer as a police officer
- Verse 7: C-Rayz Wallz as a prison inmate

The different backgrounds of each character are highlighted by their language choices and their tone of voice. Spanish dialogue is sprinkled throughout; Pumpkinhead's flow is more relaxed than Immortal Technique's, indicative of the power dynamic between them. Tonedeff's delivery is very square and comes off as a parody of whiteness, which contrasts with Poison Pen's stylized gangsta delivery (which evokes Ice Cube and his protégé Yo-Yo). C-Rayz Wallz brings the two sides of the story together in the last verse. Street-level dealers may think that they are making money, but those in positions of power—the government and law enforcement—are really the ones profiting from the drug trade ("We control blocks, they lock countries and own companies/We had nice cars and sneaker money").

The song closes with a sample from the 1991 movie *New Jack City*, which examines the impact of drugs on inner-city communities. Wesley Snipes' character, the drug kingpin Nino Brown, delivers the speech as part of his testimony (Incidentally, Brown's gang is the Cash Money Brothers, and the apartment building that they deal from is the Carter: the movie inspired the name Cash Money Records and Lil Wayne's string of albums *Tha Carter*).

The conditions that Immortal Technique lays out in this song parallel the activities associated with some high-profile South American dictators, most notably Panama's Manuel Noriega and Bolivia's Luis García Meza Tejada. Noriega worked for years as a CIA informant while trafficking drugs, laundering money, and rigging elections in his favor before the United States ousted him from power in 1989. García Meza staged a military coup in 1980—known as the "Cocaine Coup"—and began a short but brutal reign. International condemnation of his drug-trafficking activities and strong criminal ties ultimately forced him to resign in 1981.

Trap music once again brought drug culture back into mainstream rap in the 2010s. As the style evolved, the music became less about dealing drugs and more about taking them. The drugs of choice changed: "molly" (MDMA), Percocet, and Xanax (an antidepressant) replaced crack. The shift represents a move from the negative connotations of crack—the underground economy, addiction and death, and racially motivated penalties—to an association of drugs with pleasure and leisure. Songs like Future's "Mask Off" and Migos' "Designer Drugs" simulate the high they produce through slow, bass-heavy beats and multiple effects (like autotune and delay) on the vocals. While these songs are often seen as celebrating the pleasure of drugs, their roots in trap music suggest that drugs are still part of the underground economy and used by many as a coping mechanism.

ABSENT FATHERS, SINGLE MOTHERS

In 1965, Daniel Patrick Moynihan, an aide in the US Department of Labor, wrote a report titled *The Negro Family: A Case for National Action*, more commonly known as the **Moynihan Report**. In the report, Moynihan argued that the dissolution of the black family was in large part to blame for the poor conditions in America's inner cities. Following "three centuries of sometimes unimaginable mistreatment," black families, he asserted, were in grave danger.[17] Moynihan believed that reinforcing patriarchy via government-funded jobs and guaranteed minimum income would do more to advance the cause of black families than any pending civil-rights legislation. In what is perhaps the most frequently quoted phrase from the document, Moynihan suggests that "most Negro youth are in *danger* of being caught up in the tangle of pathology that affects their world."[18] Moynihan's report was very progressive for its time, and it was rather sympathetic to the plight of black families; however, the actual report was not widely circulated, and as bits and pieces of the report leaked out, the initial intentions were grossly misrepresented. Ultimately, the report became a tool for reinforcing structural racism—the "tangle of pathology"—in the communities it originally tried to help. The report came to be seen as an indictment of the absent father and the matriarchal family structure (which, in hindsight, is sexist, as Coates points out).[19] These views persist even today: conservative pundits like Bill O'Reilly and CNN's Don Lemon have repeatedly inveighed against the dissolution of the black family and the lack of male role models. The absent-father trope appears repeatedly in hip hop (as in the Malcolm X paradigm presented in Chapter 2). Lupe Fiasco's song "He Say She Say" uses an innovative structure to illuminate the issues.

LISTENING GUIDE 12.2

Artist: Lupe Fiasco (feat. Gemini and Sarah Green)
Song: "He Say She Say"
Album: *Food and Liquor*
Record label: Atlantic
Year released: 2006
DJ or Producer: Soundtrakk
Samples used: "The Last One to Be Loved," Burt Bacharach

"He Say She Say" is a plea to an absent father to take a more active role in his son's life. The verse outlines the "tangle of pathology" that the Moynihan Report warns against:

In essence, the Negro community has been forced into a matriarchal structure which, because it is so out of line with the rest of the American society, seriously retards the progress of the group as a whole, and imposes a crushing burden on the Negro male and, in consequence, on a great many Negro women as well.[20]

In the verse, we get a sense of the absent father's impact on the promising young man's life—the beginning of the "crushing burden": his grades begin to falter, he starts getting in fights, and he begins to turn to alcohol. The effects on the mother are apparent, too: it sounds as though she tries to downplay the stress the situation is causing ("Some days it ain't sunny but it ain't so hard"). The son also recognizes the strain on his mother: "Mommy, that ain't your job, to be a man."

The two verses are virtually identical, differentiated by only a few changes in pronouns: verse 1 presents the mother's point of view, and verse 2 presents the son's. The opening line of each verse, "She said to him . . ." and "So he said to him . . ." indicates that both perspectives are relayed through a narrator: we never learn the identity of the narrator. The three-way conversation among the mother, son, and father lends itself to a typical three-verse song structure. One could argue that the absence of a third verse takes away the listener's chance to hear the father's perspective, but it is possible to interpret the interplay of voices in the hook as a conversation between the mother and father. It is not clear why the father is not a part of the boy's life: reading work by Michelle Alexander, Coates, and others would lead us to believe that he may be under correctional control; however, the lyrics give us reason to believe that the father made a choice not to be around.

The video offers one possible interpretation, but certainly not the only plausible one. The first verse consists of a close-up shot of the mother lip-synching to Fiasco's lyrics, with images of the angry father and the son periodically interspersed. The second verse is a close-up shot of the son lip-synching the lyrics. During the chorus, the camera pans around the interior of a house, occasionally including a shot of one of the characters.

The decades following the Moynihan Report saw a radical change in the way that America viewed incarceration. Prison was once seen as an opportunity to rehabilitate criminals; over the second half of the twentieth century, prison became a place to keep offenders out of society and punish them for their crimes. Drug offenders went from people who needed help to people who were dangerous and needed to be locked up. From 1970 to 2000, the prison population in the United States increased from 300,000 to 2.2 million, many of whom were people of color charged with low-level drug offenses.[21] In 2008, people of color comprised 58% of the prison population, despite being only 25% of the country's population.[22] Those who serve their time are, in many cases, still subject to what Michelle Alexander calls "correctional control": they are unable to vote, have difficulty getting a job, and may be on parole. All of these factors make it more likely that they will end up in prison again: more than two-thirds of offenders reenter the prison system within three years of release.[23]

Coates writes that by the end of the twentieth century, more black men had served time in prison than had gone to college or served in the military.[24] Nelson George called prison "not a cruel punishment but a rite of passage for many that helped define one's entry into manhood. And what being a man meant could be perversely shaped by imprisonment."[25] Many rappers have spent time in prison and have chronicled their experiences in their lyrics. Several artists have even recorded albums from behind bars. Robin D. G. Kelley interprets such tracks in terms of what Michel Foucault calls the "counter-discourse of prisoners," the idea that what the prisoners have to say about their situation is more important than how society at large constructs ideas about delinquency.[26] Kelley suggests that while many rappers take a "scared straight" approach to prison—making an effort to warn their comrades about the horrors of incarceration—they also illustrate the ways in which people's behaviors are influenced or dictated by their circumstances.[27]

Throughout this book, we have explored ways that rap music reflects place and space, as well as the individual's relationship to space and place, and the music of these artists is no exception. Mac Dre's "Back N Da Hood" hardly glamorizes the time he spent in prison: he paints a rather dreary picture of life on "the inside," one made more authentic by the sound of his voice.

LISTENING GUIDE 12.3

Artist: Mac Dre
Song: "Back N Da Hood"
Album: *Back N Da Hood*
Record label: Strictly Business/Thizz
Year released: 1992
DJ or Producer: Khayree
Samples used: (none)

Mac Dre recorded this entire EP over the phone while he was incarcerated in the Fresno County Jail, awaiting trial for a charge of conspiracy to commit robbery, and in the Lompoc Federal Penitentiary, where he served a five-year sentence. The Vallejo police were monitoring Dre's lyrics and those of his Romper Room crew for clues that might have connected them to a string of strong-arm robberies in the area.

The track begins with a ringing phone; there follows a conversation between the operator and (presumably) Khayree, the producer. This opening sets the scene, establishes Dre's authenticity, and offers an explanation for the poor quality of the vocal recording that follows. Landline telephones drastically limit the frequency range of audio signals transmitted through them, offering a range of roughly 300 to 3,300 Hertz (Hz; a measure of frequency—pitch—in cycles per second). An average human can hear frequencies in the range of 20 to 20,000 Hz (for comparison, middle C on the piano vibrates at about 263 Hz; the highest note on a piano vibrates at about 4,200 Hz and the lowest at about 27 Hz). The frequency limitations give the audio track its distinct quality and effectively "sound" Dre's incarceration.

Dre paints a very unappealing picture of prison life: he cannot sleep, in part because his cellmate is snoring; he misses women, drugs, and his friends. Later in the song, he criticizes the system for keeping him locked up on "punk-ass charges," perhaps alluding to the fact that his profile as a rapper—and, by extension, his race—was the main reason for prosecutors' dragging the case out. He does recognize a positive side to his incarceration: keeping his name in the news helped sell records—Dre even thanks Detective Nichelman for his boosting his popularity. Dre was not afraid to call out him out by name, which hip-hop historian Davey D. says was unusual at the time: even releases by N.W.A. and Public Enemy only make generic references. In an earlier song, "Punk Police," Dre had taken aim at the Vallejo Police Department and a Detective David McGraw.[28] Mentioning names like this lends Dre's vocal track an even greater sense of authenticity.

Persistent policies of mass incarceration, a holdover from the failed War on Drugs, continue to destroy families, a problem that has recently been exacerbated by the rise of privately owned, for-profit prisons. A report by the ACLU indicates that from 1990 to 2009, the number of inmates housed in for-profit prisons grew by approximately 1,600%.[29] As government budgets grew tighter, corporations like CCA (Corrections Corporation of America) and GEO Group offered the opportunity for communities to outsource their correctional facilities. Since these organizations were *for*-profit, they had strong incentives to keep costs low in order to maximize profits. To that end, many of the contracts that CCA and GEO entered into with the cities require a minimum number of inmates in order for the contract to remain in force (in some cases, the figure is around 90% of capacity). The prisons will typically house only low-level, low-risk offenders: high-risk inmates (who may be violent or require significant medical care) are too expensive. These strictures provide strong incentive for arresting and convicting people of petty crimes and for imposing lengthier sentences.

Alexander calls mass incarceration "the New Jim Crow" and argues persuasively that these policies are simply a continuation of slavery, sharecropping, and the Jim Crow laws that were enacted in the 1890s.[30] Kanye West summarizes many of the points made so far in this chapter in his song "New Slaves": "Meanwhile the DEA [Drug Enforcement Agency] teamed up with the CCA/They tryin' to lock niggas up, they tryin' to make new slaves."

HIP HOP AND OBAMA

Bakari Kitwana was the first to discuss in detail the "**hip-hop generation**," which comprises individuals born between 1965 and 1984. The generation is characterized by young people who grew up with hip-hop culture. The Civil Rights movement was largely behind them, economies and media are shaped by forces of globalization, and while segregation is no longer legal, policies such as the War on Drugs and mass incarceration continue to divide the population along race and class lines.[31] M. K. Asante describes a "post-hip-hop generation" that is attempting to carve out an identity for themselves that challenges the tenets of commercial hip hop, while Jeffrey O. G. Ogbar proposes a second hip-hop generation, hip-hop millennials, that includes those born between 1982 and 2000, combining all of these groups into the "long hip hop generation."[32] The mobilization of the long hip-hop generation in the 2000s played a significant role in the election of Barack Obama as the nation's first black president in 2008, and rap music and musicians played an important role in this mobilization. Rappers like Jay-Z, Ludacris, Lil Wayne, and Young Jeezy publicly supported Obama; others like Diddy organized "get out the vote" efforts.

Obama's association with hip hop was an asset and a liability. While the hip-hop generation played an important role in getting him elected, Jay-Z said that he made an effort to keep his distance: "I didn't want the association with rappers and gangsta rappers to hinder anything that he was doing," he says. "I came when I was needed; I didn't make any comments in the press, go too far or put my picture with Obama on MySpace, Twitter, none of that."[33] In 2011, First Lady Michelle Obama invited Common to the White House as part of a poetry reading, and his appearance was widely criticized by conservatives, despite the fact that he is widely viewed in hip-hop circles as a conscious rapper, not a gangsta rapper.

Following Obama's election to the presidency, many believed that America had finally entered a **post-racial** age; that is, the inequalities among racial groups had disappeared.[34] In a speech to the Democratic National Convention in 2008, Jay-Z told the audience: "You can be anything you want to be in the world. Black people are no longer left out of the American dream."[35] Obama never made race a central focus of his campaign; however, his performance—or, more accurately, performances—of race helped him appeal to a broad swath of the American people. Once in office, few of his initiatives and policies directly addressed the needs of the black community.[36] To many, he was simply another establishment politician who could turn on "hip-hop swagger" as needed.

Jay-Z's claim about the American dream spoke to his own lifestyle. In 2011, he and Kanye West released *Watch the Throne*, an album that literally defined **luxury rap**. While it was not uncommon for rappers to tout their material successes, both Jay-Z and Kanye were at a level well above most of the hip-hop community at the time. The album's gilded packaging—designed by Riccardo Tisci, creative director at Givenchy—belied its musical contents: most of the lyrics dealt with a lifestyle that was accessible only to the wealthiest 1% of the population.[37] On one hand, this aesthetic was in line with the many rags-to-riches stories found in rap; on the other, the kind of luxuries that Jay-Z and Kanye were boasting about were well out of reach to most of their audience (and many of their industry peers as well). Songs like "Niggas in Paris" and "Otis" celebrate excessive wealth but frame it in terms of racial stereotypes of poverty.

LISTENING GUIDE 12.4

Artist: Jay-Z and Kanye West (feat. Otis Redding)
Song: "Otis"
Album: *Watch the Throne*
Record label: Roc-A-Fella
Year released: 2011
DJ or Producer: Kanye West
Samples used: "Try a Little Tenderness," Otis Redding

Otis Redding is a legendary soul singer who was killed in a plane crash in 1967. While there are frequent requests for his samples, few are approved: that Kanye was able to get permission to use it speaks to the power he wields in the music industry (Kanye is known for his use of soul samples; he previously used a Redding sample in "Gone" from *Late Registration*). According to Redding's daughter, Karla Redding-Andrews, Jay-Z and Kanye offered to have Otis listed as a featured artist on the track, and she agreed.

The lyrics are full of references to high-end luxury items: Hublots and Rolexes ("Rollies") watches, some of which sell for upward of $100,000; multiple Mercedes; private jets (G450); and travel abroad. Jay-Z raps about a trip to Cuba, which at the time was technically illegal, but his wealth afforded him the opportunity not only to travel there, but also to have a cigar with Cuban leader Fidel Castro. In the fourth verse (Kanye's second verse), he coins the term "luxury rap": "Couture-level flow is never going on sale/Luxury rap, the Hermes of verses."

The video reinforces ideas of high-end conspicuous capitalism as a manifestation of the American dream. The video is full of patriotic imagery: the American flag, and even the "white T-shirt, jeans, and baseball cap" look that Jay-Z and Kanye sport. The car at the center of the video is a Maybach, a high-end luxury car manufactured by Mercedes that appears frequently in rap songs (Rick Ross' record label is Maybach Music). The inclusion of the car itself would have been enough to justify their wealth—a base-model Maybach starts at around $200,000—but in the video, the car is cut to pieces and reassembled. This act clearly indicates that money is no object to the duo, as they joyride around an abandoned lot in the chopped-up car.

All of these elements—the album cover, the sample, the lyrics, and the video—combine to form an image of extreme wealth. The American dream that Jay-Z referred to in his speech to the Democratic National Convention is achievable to some; the kind of luxury represented in this video is accessible to very few.

Obama did receive widespread praise for much of what he accomplished—he was easily reelected to a second term—but many were also critical of that which he failed to accomplish, particularly in terms of aiding underprivileged and oppressed communities. People were deported in record numbers during his tenure in office, the prison at Guantanamo Bay remained open, and little effort was made to end the War on Drugs. In the preface to a conversation with Cornel West, Christa Buschendorf opined, "The ascendancy of Barack Obama could easily dampen Black prophetic fire," the kind of charismatic leadership exhibited by Malcolm X, Martin Luther King Jr., Fred Hampton, and others. Such a dampening would "render critiques of the American system as acts of Black disloyalty" and produce "a new sleepwalking in Black America in the name of the Obama success."[38] While hip hop clearly helped Obama get elected, it also did not hesitate to criticize him. Artists like Killer Mike, Immortal Technique, Boots Riley (of The Coup), and Lupe Fiasco were among those openly critical of Obama's failures. Fiasco's was probably the most high-profile statement: in his 2011 song "Words I Never Said," he called Obama the country's "biggest terrorist," a term loaded with cultural, political, and racial implications. Fiasco also rhymed that "Gaza Strip was getting bombed/Obama didn't say shit/That's why I ain't vote for him." Fiasco's song is one of many that show rap music's increasing distaste for Obama.

On his 2012 album *R.A.P. Music*, Killer Mike included a track that compared Obama with one of his predecessors, Ronald Reagan. In an interview, Mike argues that he did not make the comparison: "Barack Obama tied him and Ronald Reagan together. Barack Obama compares himself to Reagan." According to Mike, all the candidates in the 2012 election compared themselves to Reagan.[39]

LISTENING GUIDE 12.5

Artist: Killer Mike
Song: "Reagan"
Album: *R.A.P. Music*
Record label: Williams Street Records
Year released: 2012
DJ or Producer: El-P
Samples used: (none)

In this song, Killer Mike details the ways in which Reagan's policies adversely affected the black community. Autosonic quotations from Reagan's speeches placed on either side of the first verse highlight the hypocrisy of his administration. The first verse could be understood as an indictment of the kind of materialism espoused by Jay-Z and Kanye West in "Otis." The second verse addresses many of the topics outlined in this chapter: the War on Drugs, mass incarceration, private prisons, racial profiling, and police brutality. Mike states that these policies that originated with Reagan have persisted through the Bush, Clinton, and Obama presidencies: they are all "talking head[s], telling lies on teleprompters." The "teleprompter" line underscores a perceived lack of authenticity in what the politicians claim and strengthens Mike's claim that they are all complicit in a system of oppression.

Despite the Obama administration's lack of attention to disadvantaged communities of color, Mike still encouraged people to vote for him: "Because, his image can help you, in your household, it can help you in the real world and you can profit from it. [But] I'm saying that you also should be demanding of him an African-American jobs program by saying we're not gonna go vote."[40] Killer Mike and producer El-P would team up to form Run the Jewels, one of the most acclaimed hip-hop acts of the 2010s. During the 2016 election, Mike became a vocal supporter of Bernie Sanders, one of the Democratic nominees for president.

journalist and community activist Kevin Powell, who supported Obama, observes that no one person can solve all the problems facing the country and that putting so much faith in Obama was bound to lead to disappointment. Obama is but one part of a large, complex system. Powell uses the term "straitjacketed" to describe Obama's relationship with these systems, and suggests that mainstream rappers are also straitjacketed: while they might want to share progressive ideologies through their lyrics, they are also subject to commercial pressures that dictate what will and will not sell.[41]

Hamilton

Hamilton: An American Musical, written by Lin-Manuel Miranda, uses rap to tell the story of Alexander Hamilton and the "founding fathers" of the United States. Based on a biography of Hamilton written by Ron Chernow, the musical has been one of the hottest tickets on Broadway since its debut in 2015. The show won Grammy awards and received a record sixteen Tony nominations (it won eleven of them). It also earned Miranda the Pulitzer prize for Drama and MacArthur Genius grant. Despite the critical acclaim and commercial success, the show has met with some criticism. While the cast consists mainly of people of color, they are portraying white men and women, many of whom were slave owners. In relaying the story of the white contributions to the formation of the United States, the show also marginalizes the actual contributions by people of color to the birth of the nation. When the *Wall Street Journal* asked Daveed Diggs, who played Thomas Jefferson, how it felt to portray a white slave owner, Diggs avoided the question entirely.

In 2016, *The Hamilton Mixtape* was released. The album featured songs from the musical, performed by a who's who of rap music, including The Roots, Nas, Busta Rhymes, Snow Tha Product, Alicia Keys, and Wiz Khalifa. *Hamilton* was not the first hip-hop musical, however: it was preceded by *In the Heights* (1999) and *Bring It On* (2012)—both of which were by Miranda and enjoyed modest success—and *Holler if You Hear Me* (2014), a musical based on the life of Tupac Shakur that starred Saul Williams.

#BLACKLIVESMATTER

Mainstream rap music perpetuates negative stereotypes of the black community. These stereotypes prove dangerous as they become more deeply entrenched in our society, supported by like images across media types. The last few years have seen an increase in the attention paid to the deaths of people of color at the hands of police and vigilantes. The increased attention and ensuing outrage is a result of the more widespread use of cameras—by both law enforcement and citizens—and the ability of social networking sites like Facebook, YouTube, and Twitter to spread information and mobilize people rapidly. Social media has helped give rise to the Black Lives Matter movement, which galvanized a nationwide response to these killings.

In February 2012, 17-year-old Trayvon Martin was shot and killed by George Zimmerman, a neighborhood watch captain who believed Martin looked suspicious. Zimmerman invoked Florida's so-called "stand your ground" law, which allows citizens to use force to defend themselves without retreating first, thus blurring the line between an aggression and self-defense. The #BlackLivesMatter hashtag originated in the wake of Martin's shooting and helped bring attention to the alarming number of people of color who have been killed as the result of excessive use of force by law enforcement or as the result of the stereotyping of black youth as violent criminals. On August 9, 2014, in Ferguson, Missouri (just outside of St. Louis), 18-year-old Michael Brown was shot and killed by police officer Darren Wilson. Brown and a friend, Dorian Johnson, were suspected of stealing cigarillos from a convenience store before they were confronted by Wilson. Wilson claims that Brown charged toward him, and Wilson fired a dozen bullets at the teenager, claiming that he feared for his life. Eyewitness accounts were conflicting, with some agreeing with Wilson's account and others saying that Brown had his hands up in surrender. "Hands up, don't shoot" became a rallying cry of the protestors after Brown's death. On November 24, the St. Louis County prosecutor announced that the grand jury would not indict Wilson for the shooting. Protests and unrest followed this announcement, not just in Ferguson, but in major cities around the country, and it was during this unrest that "#BlackLivesMatter" came into national consciousness, with tens of thousands of tweets bearing the hashtag.[42]

As the movement gained steam, a formal Black Lives Matter organization coalesced, led by Alicia Garza, Opal Tometi, and Patrisse Cullors. The group, which has chapters around the country and internationally, is committed to fighting the many manifestations of state violence, including police brutality; the undue burden placed on black women as a result of "a relentless assault on their children and our families"; mass incarceration; LGBTQ, immigration, and disability rights; and the role of black girls as "negotiating chips during times of conflict and war."[43] The intersectionality evolved from previous movements, many of which were largely patriarchal, or at least presented as such.

From the outset, hip hop has played an important role in the movement. Hip hop has the power to raise awareness, create a sense of community, and challenge dominant media narratives. A number of hip-hop artists, such as Talib Kweli, J. Cole, The Game, Jasiri X, and Tef Poe, have contributed their voices to the Black Lives Matter movement. Talib Kweli went to Ferguson soon after Brown was shot. He participated in actions on the ground, helped raise more than $100,000 for the Ferguson Legal Defense Fund, and sparred with CNN's Don Lemon on national television. Kweli criticized the media for presenting only one perspective, arguing that what he witnessed as a participant deviated from the media's narrative of events. Kweli frequently used Twitter to combat false narratives, present counter narratives, and promote the fundraising efforts. While Powell suggested that many mainstream rap artists may be straitjacketed and unable to speak out on controversial issues, two releases by prominent artists prove otherwise. J. Cole's "Be Free," one of the first songs to be released in the wake of Brown's death, expresses the pain of the struggle and allows listeners to grieve. In it, J. Cole displays a kind of vulnerability not typically seen in mainstream hip hop (but that is common to his music; see Chapter 2). Cole performed the song on *Late Night with David Letterman* in December 2014. His performance conveys not only grief, but also a kind of exhaustion, expressed through his posture and his behind-the-beat delivery, particularly in the hook. The performance brought Cole's message—and the concerns of the black community—to a wide audience, one that might not typically be exposed to his viewpoint.

The Game brought stars of the mainstream hip-hop community in a visible way on his posse cut "Don't Shoot," the title of which was taken from the "Hands up, don't shoot" chant. The track features close to a dozen rappers from all around the country, including DJ Khaled, 2 Chainz, Diddy, Rick Ross, Curren$y, Wale, and Swiss Beatz. Songs like this are part of a long tradition in hip hop (and popular music generally) of bringing a diverse group of artists in support of a shared cause—it has its roots in tracks like Stop the Violence Movement's "Self Destruction" and West Coast Rap All-Stars' "We're All in the Same Gang"—and money raised through sales of the track went to the Mike Brown Defense Fund. At ten verses, the song is a bit unwieldy, and it is perhaps not as nuanced as some of the other tracks discussed in the chapter: Diddy takes an opportunity to plug his Ciroc vodka and to remind listeners that he produced Biggie; Rick Ross reiterates his catchphrase, "I'm a boss." Nonetheless, it could function as a way in to a deeper conversation for listeners who may more readily relate to mainstream rappers whom they know. Several artists criticize the media attention given to the "Ice Bucket Challenge," a viral fundraiser organized by the ALS Society (Amyotrophic Lateral Sclerosis, also known as Lou Gehrig's Disease), at the expense of attention to the killing of Michael Brown. The song includes references to Emmett Till, Ezell Ford, and Trayvon Martin as well, all victims of racially motivated violence.

Both Powell and bell hooks argue that political rap music is ineffectual unless it is tied to a movement.[44] While that may be true of the songs mentioned above, artists like Pittsburgh's Jasiri X and St. Louis' Tef Poe are not only skilled rappers, but also dedicated community organizers and activists. While their names may not be as well known as J. Cole or The Game, they work to affect change from a grassroots level, working daily in their own communities, out of the national spotlight.[45] Jasiri X launched his One Hood foundation in 2006 to educate young people on how to interpret media critically. Tef Poe cofounded HandsUpUnited, a St. Louis–based organization that sponsors a Books and Breakfast program, a tech institute for young people of color, and a food pantry, among other community-based programs. The qualities that lead to successful grassroots organizing are virtually identical to those that lead to success as an underground rap artist. William Wimsatt, an author and organizer, claims: "If you can make a demo tape, you can make a voter guide. If you can organize a party, you can organize a voting drive."[46]

LISTENING GUIDE 12.6

Artist: Jasiri X
Song: "Trayvon"
Album: (single)
Record label: (self-released)
Year released: 2012
DJ or Producer: 88-Keys, Mike Dean, Kanye West
Samples used: "No Church in the Wild," Jay-Z and Kanye West/88-Keys

Sampling Jay-Z and Kanye's luxury-rap track forces a comparison between the kinds of images commonly found in mainstream rap (and, in this case, exaggerated) and the reality of what many in the black community—Trayvon Martin, for example—encounter on a daily basis.

The first verse of Jasiri X's song sets the scene and begins to recreate the events that led to Trayvon Martin's death. Throughout the song, Jasiri points to the problems that arise from stereotyping of black men: "Some people have an ingrown hate for your family" in the first verse and in the second verse "Who's this nigga walking in my/Neighborhood, he fits all the specifics/of criminal statistics he looks suspicious/911, what's your emergency/A black man's walking through my 'hood purposely." Jasiri X ends the song by saying that "only white lives are protected," a line that resonates with the phrase "black lives matter."

LISTENING GUIDE 12.7

Artist: Tef Poe (feat. Dharma Jean)
Song: "Say Her Name"
Album: *War Machine III*
Record label: Footklan
Year released: 2015

DJ or Producer: Duke Rellington
Samples used: (none)

Poe casts "Say Her Name" as an elegiac love song to the women who have been killed by police. Women have been a driving force of the BLM movement and have also been the victims of police brutality, but their stories are often overshadowed by those of their male counterparts. This should not be surprising, given the patriarchal nature of American society and the characterization of black men as excessively violent, a perception often used to justify such shootings. Poe takes a jab at the misogyny that contributes to this atmosphere, writing in a brief vignette in which a woman rebukes him for referring to her as a "bitch." In the song, Poe justifies violent retaliation as long as "they keep killing us all." He indicates that "they" are not just white men but that black men are guilty too.

The plot of the video involves a young black woman being pulled over by the police, and it ends with her body being dragged away. Throughout the video, still photos of black women who have been killed by police appear on screen, along with their names (written as hashtags), dates, and headlines that illustrate the injustices that have characterized the cases. Later in the song, Poe recites their names in a dark twist on shout-outs. In the end, he dedicates the song to his nieces, establishing a personal connection to the epidemic.

In response to Trayvon Martin's death, Obama empathized, "If I had a son, he would look like Trayvon." William Jelani Cobb called Obama's responses to the killings a genre of their own: expressing condolences and calling for peace. Cobb questions whether the unpunished deaths of these young black men during the term of America's first black president is simply irony or whether it is an indication that "American democracy has reached the limits of its elasticity—that the symbolic empowerment of individuals, while the great many remain citizen-outsiders, is the best that we can hope for."[47] Cole, Jasiri X, and Poe have all been outspoken in their criticism of Obama, whose response to these killings was rather mild. Cole's appraisal of Obama's actions mirrors Kevin Powell's, that no one person can be a savior. Tef Poe, on the other hand, called Ferguson "Obama's Katrina" in his song "War Cry" and offered a critique of the president's response in an open letter to the *Riverfront Times*:

> The police attacked us for taking to the streets to resist police brutality, and our beloved black president seemingly endorsed it. I'm sure you will say this isn't the case, but as a young black man in America I speak for a large demographic of us that has long awaited our black president to speak in a direct tone while condemning our murders. From our perspective, the statement you made on Ferguson completely played into the racist connotations that we are violent, uneducated, welfare-recipient looters. [. . .]
>
> When an assault rifle is aimed at your face over nothing more than a refusal to move, you don't feel like the American experience is one that includes you. When the president your generation selected does not condemn these attacks, you suddenly begin to believe that this system is a fraudulent hoax—and the joke is on you.[48]

As the movement continues to grow and spread, it remains to be seen how large a role hip hop will play in shaping it. With the election of Donald Trump, hate crimes have spiked across the country, and people from many different backgrounds have responded by mobilizing to protest and enact change. Hip hop will no doubt continue to be on the vanguard of that social change.

OUTRO

Names you should know:

- The Parents Music Resource Center (PMRC)
- Cypress Hill
- Immortal Technique
- Lupe Fiasco

- Mac Dre
- Killer Mike
- Tef Poe
- Jasiri X

Terms you should know:

- Sonic color line
- The War on Drugs
- The Moynihan Report
- The hip-hop generation

- Post-racial
- Luxury rap
- #BlackLivesMatter

Questions for discussion/writing prompts:

1. Lupe Fiasco's "He Say She Say" is the beginning of an extended story that continues on his next album, *The Cool* (2007). The saga centers on Michael Young History, spanning "The Coolest," "Gotta Eat," "The Die," "Superstar," and "The Cool." Trace the story through one or more of these songs, and interpret it through the material in this chapter.

2. Visit the Black Lives Matter website (blacklivesmatter.com) and read about the organization's mission. How can hip hop help advance the mission? How might it run contrary to the mission?

3. In what ways are rappers political leaders?

Additional listening/viewing:

Hip hop and politics:
- "Jesse," Grandmaster Flash & The Furious Five
- "Politics as Usual," Ludacris
- "Obama Nation," Lowkey
- "Fuck Donald Trump," YG

War on Drugs:
- "White Lines (Don't Do It)," Grandmaster Flash & The Furious Five
- "Night of the Living Baseheads," Public Enemy
- "Water," The Roots
- "Swimming Pools (Drank)," Kendrick Lamar

Absent fathers:
- "Dear Mama," Tupac Shakur
- "Follow My Life," Obie Trice

Mass incarceration:

- DuVernay, Ava. *13*th. Sherman Oaks, CA: Kandoo Films, 2016.
- Jarecki, Eugene. *The House I Live In*. New York: Virgil Films, 2013.
- *Ridin' Dirty*, UGK
- "Deuce Five to Life," X-Raided
- "What Your Life Like," Beanie Sigel
- "Prisoner I & II," Lupe Fiasco

#Blacklivesmatter

- "Alright," Kendrick Lamar
- "Hands Up," Vince Staples
- "White Privilege II," Macklemore
- "Early," Run the Jewels

NOTES

1 Richard Shusterman, "The Fine Art of Rap" *New Literary History* 22 no. 3 (1991): 613–4.
2 J. D. Considine, "Fear of a Rap Planet" *Musician* (February 1992): 34–43, 92. Reprinted in *The Pop, Rock, and Soul Reader*. Ed. David Brackett (New York: Oxford University Press, 2005), 408–13
3 Barry Shank, "Fears of the White Unconscious: Music, Race, and Identification in the Censorship of 'Cop Killer'" *Radical History Review* 66 (Fall 1996): 124–45. These two divergent views form the core of Tricia Rose's *The Hip Hop Wars* (New York: BasicCivitas, 2008). See also *The Google Versus Debate: Hip Hop on Trial*, Intelligence Squared (June 26, 2012): www.intelligencesquared.com/events/versus-hip-hop.
4 Carrie B. Fried, "Bad Rap for Rap: Bias in Reactions to Music Lyrics" *Journal of Applied Social Psychology* 26 no. 23 (1996): 2135–46 and "Who's Afraid of Rap: Differential Reactions to Music Lyrics" *Journal of Applied Social Psychology* 29 no. 4 (1999): 705–21. Adam Dunbar, Charis E. Kubrin, and Nicholas Schurich successfully replicated the experiment in "The Threatening Nature of 'Rap' Music" *Psychology, Public Policy, and Law* 22 (2016): 280–92.
5 Jennifer Lynn Stoever, *The Sonic Color Line: Race and the Cultural Politics of Listening*. New York: New York University Press, 2016), 2.
6 Stoever 13.
7 Nicholas Stoia, Kyle Adams, and Kevin Drakulich, "Rap Lyrics as Evidence: What Can Music Theory Tell Us?" *Race and Justice* (2017): 4.
8 Erik Nielson and Charles E. Kubrin, "Rap Lyrics on Trial" *New York Times* (January 13, 2014).
9 Victoria M. Walker, "A State Court Says Rap Lyrics Can't Be Used as Evidence in a Criminal Trial" *Code Switch* (NPR). 2014.
10 For more on policing of rap venues, see Tricia Rose, *Black Noise: Rap Music and Black Culture in Contemporary America* (Hanover, NH: Wesleyan University Press, 1994), 124–45.
11 See, for instance, Derrick Parker, *Notorious C.O.P.: The Inside Story of the Tupac, Biggie, and Jam Master Jay Investigations from NYPD's First 'Hip-Hop Cop'* (New York: St. Martin's, 2006).
12 Sam Lefebvre, "Blacklisted: How the Oakland Police Department Discriminates against Rappers and Music Venues" *East Bay Express* (April 26, 2017).
13 Tricia Rose refutes this argument in chapter 1 of *The Hip Hop Wars*.
14 Two articles by Denise Herd trace the changing representations of alcohol and drugs in rap music. See "Changes in the Prevalence of Alcohol in Rap Music Lyrics 1979–2009" *Substance Use & Misuse* 49 no. 3 (February 2014): 333–42 and "Changes in Drug Use Prevalence in Rap Music Songs, 1979–1997" *Addiction Research and Theory* 16 no. 2 (April 2008): 167–80.
15 NAACP, "Criminal Justice Fact Sheet": www.naacp.org/criminal-justice-fact-sheet.

16 Jeffrey O. G. Ogbar, "Message from the Grassroots: Hip Hop Activism, Millennials, and the Race for the White House," in *The Hip Hop and Obama Reader*. Ed. Travis L. Gosa and Erik Nielson (New York: Oxford University Press, 2015), 47.

17 Ta-Nehisi Coates, "The Black Family in the Age of Mass Incarceration" *Atlantic* 316 no. 3 (October 2015): 63. See also Michelle Alexander, *The New Jim Crow: Mass Incarceration in the Age of Colorblindness*. Rev. ed. (New York: The New Press, 2012).

18 Coates 63.

19 Coates 80.

20 Quoted in Coates 63.

21 Coates 64.

22 NAACP.

23 Matthew R. Durose, Alexia D. Cooper, and Howard N. Snyder, "Recidivism of Prisoners Released in 30 States in 2005: Patterns from 2005 to 2010—Update" *Bureau of Justice Statistics* (April 22, 2014): www.bjs.gov/index.cfm?ty=pbdetail&iid=4986.

24 Coates 74.

25 Nelson George, *Hip Hop America* (New York: Viking, 1998), 44.

26 Robin D. G. Kelley, "Kickin' Reality, Kickin' Ballistics: Gangsta Rap in Postindustrial Los Angeles," in *Droppin' Science: Critical Essays on Rap Music and Hip Hop Culture*. Ed. William Eric Perkins (Philadelphia: Temple University Press, 1996), 135.

27 Kelley 135.

28 Dean Van Nguyen, "Vallejo Rapper Mac Dre Pioneered the Hyphy Movement" *Wax Poetics* 53 (2014): www.waxpoetics.com/blog/features/articles/bay-area-boss-mac-dre.

29 David Shapiro, *Banking on Bondage: Private Prisons and Mass Incarceration* (New York: American Civil Liberties Union, 2011): www.aclu.org/banking-bondage-private-prisons-and-mass-incarceration.

30 Alexander 2010.

31 Bakari Kitwana, *The Hip Hop Generation* (New York: Basic Civitas Books, 2005), chapter 1.

32 Molefi K. Asante, *It's Bigger Than Hip-Hop: The Rise of the Post-Hip-Hop Generation* (New York: St. Martin's Press, 2008), chapter 1; Ogbar 31–3.

33 Malik Meer, "Jay-Z: The Magna Carter" *Guardian* (August 28, 2009): www.theguardian.com/music/2009/aug/29/carter-jaz-z-hip-hop.

34 These claims appear to apply largely in the case of the black/white racial binary and do not seem to include other minority and oppressed groups.

35 Quoted in Travis L. Gosa and Erik Nielson, "Introduction," in *The Hip Hop and Obama Reader*. Ed. Travis L. Gosa and Erik Nielson (New York: Oxford University Press, 2015), 5.

36 Gosa and Nielson 6–8.

37 Occupy Wall Street was in its formative stages at this point. Among its most important achievements was popularizing the wealth gap in America via the slogan "We are the 99%," implying that 1% of the population controlled most of the wealth in the country.

38 Cornel West, *Black Prophetic Fire: In Dialogue with and Edited by Christa Buschendorf*. Ed. Christa Buschendorf (Boston: Beacon Press, 2014), 11.

39 Paul Arnold, "Killer Mike Explains His Comparison of Barack Obama to Ronald Reagan, His Brotherly Bond with El-P" *HipHopDX* (May 21, 2012): http://hiphopdx.com/interviews/id.1896/title.killer-mike-explains-his-comparison-of-barack-obama-to-ronald-reagan-his-brotherly-bond-with-el-p.

40 Paul Arnold.

41 Travis L. Gosa and Erik Nielson, " 'There Are No Saviors': An Interview with Kevin Powell," in *The Hip Hop and Obama Reader*. Ed. Travis L. Gosa and Erik Nielson (New York: Oxford University Press, 2015), 70–87.

42 Deen Freelon, Charlton D. McIlwain, and Meredith D. Clark, *Beyond the Hashtags: #Ferguson, #Blacklivesmatter, and the Online Struggle for Offline Justice* (Washington, DC: Center for Media and Social Impact, 2016): http://cmsimpact.org/resource/beyond-hashtags-ferguson-blacklivesmatter-online-struggle-offline-justice.

43 "Guiding Principles | Black Lives Matter": http://blacklivesmatter.com/guiding-principles.

44 Powell 79; bell hooks, *Eating the Other: Desire and Resistance* (Albany: State University of New York Press, 1998), 375.

45 Kitwana 55.

46 Quoted in Ogbar 40.

47 William Jelani Cobb, "Chronicle of a Riot Foretold in Ferguson" *New Yorker* (November 25, 2014): www.newyorker.com/news/daily-comment/chronicle-ferguson-riot-michael-brown.

48 Tef Poe, "Dear Mr. President: A Letter from Tef Poe" *Riverfront Times* (December 1, 2014): www.riverfronttimes.com/musicblog/2014/12/01/dear-mr-president-a-letter-from-tef-poe.

Appendix: Time Line

1948 Construction begins on the Cross Bronx Expressway, which devastates the South Bronx and displaces thousands of residents.

1964 Clarence 13X splits from the Nation of Islam and forms the Five-Percent Nation. The beliefs of the Five-Percent Nation will pervade East Coast hip-hop culture in the late 1980s and early 1990s.

1965 Malcolm X is assassinated at the Audubon Ballroom in New York City. The ballroom will later become an important early hip-hop venue.

Daniel Patrick Moynihan, an aide in the US Department of Labor, issues his report *The Negro Family: A Case for National Action*.

1966 Huey Newton and Bobby Seale form the Black Panther Party for Self-Defense in Oakland, California.

1968 Martin Luther King Jr. is assassinated at a hotel in Memphis, Tennessee.

1970 James Brown releases "Funky Drummer," which will become one of the most frequently sampled breaks in rap.

The Last Poets release their eponymous debut album.

Gil Scott-Heron releases *Small Talk at 125th and Lenox*.

1971 A graffiti artist whose tag is "Taki 183" is profiled by *The New York Times*, bringing tagging and graffiti into the public eye.

1973 Clive Campbell, also known as DJ Kool Herc, discovers the power of the break beat at a party that he and his sister have hosted in the basement of their apartment building.

1974 Rudy Ray Moore releases the movie *Dolemite*.

1975 MCs come on the scene to support the DJs. Important early figures include Coke La Rock (Kool Herc's MC) and Chief Rocker Busy Bee Starski.

1977 In summer, a citywide blackout cripples New York City. Widespread looting ensues, and thousands of turntables are among the stolen goods, resulting in a DJ boom around the city.

The Rock Steady Crew, one of the earliest and most influential break dance crews, forms in New York City.

1979 Chic's "Good Times" tops *Billboard*'s R&B and pop charts.

Sugar Hill Records releases the single "Rapper's Delight." Although it is not the first rap single, it paves the way for rappers to make it on records.

Mr. Magic launches his radio show on WHBI in Newark, New Jersey.

1980   Kurtis Blow becomes the first rap artist to sign with a major record label, Mercury. His debut single, "The Breaks," becomes the third single (in any style) in history to sell more than 500,000 copies.

Roland introduces the TR-808 drum machine.

1981   Blondie releases "Rapture," the first song with rapping in it to reach number 1 on the *Billboard* charts.

The first record to showcase the talents of a DJ, "Grandmaster Flash on the Wheels of Steel," is released.

1982   Kool Moe Dee battles Busy Bee at Harlem World. Moe Dee wins the battle and almost single-handedly changes the craft of MCing.

Grandmaster Flash & The Furious Five release "The Message."

MC Sweet's *Gospel Beat: Jesus Christ*, widely considered the first Christian rap album, is released.

1982   Afrika Bambaataa & The Soul Sonic Force release their single "Planet Rock."

The film *Wild Style* is released.

The first international hip-hop tour, which featured Afrika Bambaataa and the Rock Steady Crew, is launched.

1983   Herbie Hancock's "Rockit," an instrumental jazz track that features Grandmixer D.ST on the turntables, brings scratching to the mainstream.

1984   Run-D.M.C. release their eponymous first album. Their single "Rock Box" is the first rap video to air on MTV.

Russell Simmons and Rick Rubin launch Def Jam Records, the first single from which is "It's Yours" by T La Rock and Jazzy Jay.

KDAY in Los Angeles becomes the first all-rap radio station.

1985   Philadelphia rapper Schoolly D releases "P.S.K. (What Does It Mean?)," regarded by many as the first gangsta-rap track.

Tipper Gore convenes the Parents Music Resource Council (PMRC), the group responsible for the "Parental Advisory" stickers.

1986   Run-D.M.C. becomes the first rap group to go platinum with *Raising Hell*, the album that includes the collaboration with Aerosmith, "Walk This Way."

Uptown Records, the label that will give rise to New Jack Swing, is founded.

The Bridge Wars between MC Shan and DJ Marley Marl (of the Juice Crew) and Boogie Down Productions (KRS-One and Scott La Rock).

The Beastie Boys—the first successful white rappers—release their debut, *Licensed to Ill*, on Def Jam.

Ice-T releases "6 'N the Mornin,'" which will become the template for West Coast gangsta rap.

1987   Eric B & Rakim release *Paid in Full*.

1988   *To: MTV Raps* debuts.

DJ Jazzy Jeff & The Fresh Prince win the first rap Grammy award, but they boycott the ceremony because the segment is not scheduled to air on television.

N.W.A. release the gangsta-rap landmark *Straight Outta Compton.*

Public Enemy releases *It Takes a Nation of Millions to Hold Us Back.*

Ice-T's *Power* is the first rap album to have a Parental Advisory sticker on it.

MC Lyte becomes the first female MC to sign with a major label and releases her debut, *Lyte as a Rock.*

1989   De La Soul's *3 Feet High and Rising* and The Beastie Boys' *Paul's Boutique* are released; along with PE's *It Takes a Nation . . .* they are considered the pinnacle of sample-based hip hop.

Queen Latifah releases her debut, *All Hail the Queen.*

—The Good Life Café in Crenshaw, California, starts hosting open-mic nights that will eventually become Project Blowed.

1990   Miami's 2 Live Crew releases *As Nasty as They Wanna Be.* The album lands the group in legal trouble, facing charges of copyright infringement and obscenity.

The sitcom *The Fresh Prince of Bel-Air* premieres, starring Will Smith and launching his acting career.

Houston rap emerges on the scene with the release of Geto Boys' self-titled debut.

Japanese rappers Scha Dara Parr release their debut album.

Master P founds No Limit Records.

1991   Rodney King is pulled from his car and beaten by a group of Los Angeles police officers. The beating is caught on film and aired widely.

Suge Knight and Dr. Dre launch Death Row Records in Los Angeles.

The landmark case *Biz Markie vs. Gilbert O'Sullivan* shapes the future of sampling.

Billboard begins using SoundScan to track music-sales data more accurately. Within months, the data reveal that country, rap, metal, and grunge dominate the charts.

Brian and Ronald Williams start Cash Money Records in New Orleans.

1992   After the police officers who beat Rodney King are tried and acquitted, riots break out around Los Angeles.

Dr. Dre releases *The Chronic,* which introduces the world to Snoop Doggy Dogg and the laid-back G-Funk sound that will come to characterize West Coast rap.

Atlanta-based Arrested Development releases the single "Tennessee."

1993   Scha Dara Paar appear on De La Soul's "Long Island Wildin'."

Vibe magazine, cofounded by music legend Quincy Jones as an alternative to the *Source,* starts regular publication.

1994   OutKast releases *Southernplayalisticadillacmuzik,* which, along with Goodie Mob's *Soul Food* (1995), will put Atlanta on the hip-hop map.

The Supreme Court rules in favor of 2 Live Crew in *Campbell vs. Acuff-Rose,* granting that the group's use of Roy Orbison's "Pretty Woman" constitutes a parody and is protected under the fair-use doctrine.

1995   Members of the Minneapolis-based Headshots crew, comprising producer Anthony "Ant" Davis, rappers Sean "Slug" Daley and Musab Saad, and CEO Brent "Siddiq" Sayers found Rhymesayers Records.

At the Source Awards, OutKast wins Best New Artist, solidifying the South's claim, while Suge Knight disses Puff Daddy on stage, igniting the East Coast–West Coast hip-hop feud.

1996   Tupac Shakur is shot and killed in Las Vegas.

1997   Notorious B.I.G. is shot and killed after leaving the Soul Train Awards in Los Angeles; his second album, *Ready to Die*, is released soon after.

1999   Eminem releases the Dr. Dre–produced *Slim Shady LP*, which catapults him to fame as one of the most skilled rappers in the game.

Lauryn Hill is nominated for ten Grammy awards for *The Miseducation of Lauryn Hill*; she wins five, including Album of the Year.

2001   Jay-Z and Nas trade diss tracks in an effort to claim the title "King of New York."

The first CD turntables appear.

2003   Eminem is the first rapper to win an Oscar, for the song "Lose Yourself," featured in the autobiographical film *8 Mile*.

50 Cent releases his debut, *Get Rich or Die Trying*.

2004   Reggaeton goes mainstream as Daddy Yankee releases *Barrio Fino*.

Foreign Exchange, a group consisting of North Carolina–based MC Phonte and Dutch producer Nicolay, release *Connected*. The album was composed almost entirely via e-mail and instant messenger. Nicolay also collaborated with Kay, a Houston-based rapper.

2005   Kanye West says, "George Bush doesn't care about black people," on a nationally televised program to raise money for victims of Hurricane Katrina.

2006   Three 6 Mafia's song "It's Hard out There for a Pimp," from the movie *Hustle and Flow*, wins an Oscar for Best Original Song and is the first rap song to be performed at the Academy Awards.

2008   Barack Obama becomes the first black president of the United States.

2012   Macklemore releases "Same Love" in support of a same-sex marriage ballot initiative in his home state of Washington.

Frank Ocean, a member of the Odd Future collective, announces he had a relationship with a man on his Tumblr page.

Le1f's "Wut" becomes a viral hit.

2014   Houston radio station KROI-FM 92.1 becomes Boom 92, the country's first classic hip-hop station.

Lecrae's *Anomaly* is the first album to top *Billboard*'s Hot 200 and gospel charts in the same week.

Eighteen-year-old Michael Brown is shot and killed by police officer Darren Wilson in Ferguson, Missouri. The decision not to indict Wilson catalyzes the Black Lives Matter movement.

Le1f performs the song "Wut" on *Late Night with David Letterman*, marking the first time an openly gay rapper performs on late-night television.

2015 The music-industry drama *Empire* debuts on Fox

Kendrick Lamar releases *To Pimp a Butterfly*, which debuted at #1 on the *Billboard* charts and would go on to win half a dozen Grammys.

The musical *Hamilton* by Lin-Manuel Miranda opens on Broadway.

2016 N.W.A. is inducted into the Rock and Roll Hall of Fame.

Drake releases *Views*, which topped the *Billboard* charts for ten weeks, selling millions of copies, and earning Drake Grammy awards for "Hotline Bling."

Young M.A. releases her first single, "Ooouuu," which became a viral sensation.

Chance the Rapper releases his third album, *Coloring Book*. It would go on to win Best Rap Album at the 2016 Grammys, becoming the first streaming-only album to win a Grammy.

A Tribe Called Quest releases their first album in nearly two decades, *We Got It From Here . . . Thank You 4 Your Service*, just months after the death of Phife Dawg.

2017 Future releases *FUTURE* and *HNDRXX* in the span of two weeks, making him the first artist to debut at #1 on the *Billboard* charts in two consecutive weeks.

Nicki Minaj breaks Aretha Franklin's record as she places her 76th single on the *Billboard* Hot 100.

Data analytics firm Nielsen (owners of SoundScan) reports that, for the first time, rap music overtakes rock music as the most popular genre in the United States.

Cardi B, formerly of *Love & Hip Hop: New York*, releases the single "Bodak Yellow," which reaches #1 on the *Billboard* charts, making her the first solo female artist to reach the top spot since Lauryn Hill in 1998.

LL Cool J becomes the first rap artist to be honored at the Kennedy Center Honors.

Glossary

A cappella: Voice alone, with no musical accompaniment. (Chapter 1)

Ad-lib: Grunts, moans, yelps, or other noises that are easily identifiable as belonging to a particular artist. (Chapter 3)

African-American Vernacular English (AAVE): The dialect heard in many rap songs. It is often construed in terms of deviation from "standard" English. (Chapter 3)

Alliteration: Repetition of a sound (consonant or vowel) at the beginning of words. (Chapter 2)

Allosonic quotation: Incorporates the artist's previous material by rerecording it or performing it live. (Chapter 6)

(Auto)biography: A genre of rap that relates the story of an individual or group. (Chapter 2)

Autosonic quotation: Quotes the artist's previous material by means of digital or analog sampling. (Chapter 6)

Autotune: A metonym for any kind of technology used to correct pitch in real time. (Chapter 3)

B-side: The song on the other side of a hit single (the A-side). (Chapter 6)

Backpack rap: A colloquial term for underground rap in which the focus is on lyrical skill. (Chapter 6)

Bar (or measure): A unit of **meter** comprising two, three, or four **beats**. (Chapter 1)

Beat: 1) The musical track that supports a rapper's rhyming; 2) A regularly recurring pulse in music. (Chapter 1)

Beat box: Using the voice to imitate the sounds of drums, other percussion instruments, and **turntable** techniques. (Chapter 3)

Beef: A dispute, typically settled musically. In recent years, beefs have played out on social media. (Chapter 10)

Black Arts movement: A movement launched by Amiri Baraka to reclaim African aesthetics in art. It emerged in the wake of Malcolm X's assassination and Stokely Carmichael's call for black power. (Chapter 4)

Black Lives Matter: A movement that emerged in 2012 to call attention to police brutality in the black community. It grew to embrace other forms of systemic oppression as well. (Chapter 12)

Boom Bap: A production style characterized by a particular bass-snare drum (boom-BAP) pattern, popular in the 1990s. (Chapter 1)

Bounce: A style associated with New Orleans, characterized by a moderate **tempo**, 808 drums, high-pitched piano or similar sounds, and repeated chanting of short phrases. (Chapter 11)

Break (or break beat): The part of a song in which nearly all the instruments drop out except for the percussion. Looping the break is the fundamental aesthetic of rap music. (Chapter 1)

Bridge: A unit of musical form that is not a **verse** or a **chorus**, often provided for contrast. (Chapter 1)

Cadence: The speed at which the rapper delivers text; can be thought of in terms of syllables per minute. (Chapter 3)

Chopped and screwed: A style of remix most closely associated with Houston and DJ Screw, who would slow records down and rearrange the material in them to simulate the effects of being on **syrup**. (Chapter 11)

Chronological: A form of narrative that arranges events in some kind of temporal order. (Chapter 2)

Codes: Sonic and visual elements that are understood as unique identifiers of a particular style or genre. (Chapter 6)

Commercialization: How an object is bought and sold. (Chapter 6)

Commodification: The process by which an idea (or something otherwise not traditionally commercial) is transformed into something that can be bought or sold. (Chapter 6)

Common measure: A poetic device that features alternating lines of eight and six syllables, with rhymes at the end of the six-syllable lines. (Chapter 6)

Consonance: Repetition of a consonant sound appearing within a group of words. (Chapter 2)

Crossfader: A sliding lever on a mixer that determines the amount of input from the left and right **turntables**. (Chapter 1)

Crunk: An Atlanta-based style with similar musical characteristics to **bounce**. (Chapter 11)

Dembow: A rhythmic formula characteristic of **reggaeton**. The pattern juxtaposes a 3+3+2 division over the four beats of the measure and is often written as *boom-ch-boom-chick*. (Chapter 11)

Dialogic: Defining one term of a binary opposition with respect to the other term. (Chapter 7)

Digging in the crates: The practice of a DJ looking for records to play. (Chapter 5)

Disco: A style of dance music that emerged among marginalized communities in the 1970s. It had a strong influence on the early days of hip hop. (Chapter 4)

Diss: A genre of rap in which the rapper insults an opponent. (Chapter 2)

The dozens: Trading insults, typically in the form of "Your mama" jokes, until one party abandons the game. (Chapter 4)

Effusive style: A style of flow that more closely mirrors natural speech (in contrast to **sung style**). (Chapter 3)

End rhyme: When words at the end of two lines rhyme. (Chapter 2)

Epistolary: A song or story told in the form of letters. (Chapter 2)

Feature: A verse contributed to a song by a guest artist. (Chapter 2)

Flow: One of the fundamental aesthetics of hip-hop culture; most often refers to the combination of lyrics and musical **rhythm**. (Chapter 3)

Fly Girl: A female MC who embraces her sexuality and independence. (Chapter 7)

Form: The arrangement of verses, hooks, and other musical components, like **intros**, outros, and **bridges**. (Chapter 1)

Four pillars of hip hop: Break dancing (b-boying), writing (graffiti), MCing, and DJing, according to Afrika Bambaataa. Bambaataa later added a fifth element, knowledge of the culture. (Chapter 5)

Funk: A musical style characterized by repetition of a groove, with the rhythmic emphasis on beat 1. The **rhythm** is driven by the percussive use of all instruments, not just the drums. (Chapter 1)

G-Funk: A style of production most closely associated with Dr. Dre and West Coast rap. It features laid-back grooves and melodic **synthesizers** and is rooted in the sounds of Parliament-Funkadelic. (Chapter 1)

Griot: A West African oral historian. (Chapter 4)

Hashtag rap: A method of constructing similes that replaces "like" or "as" with a space, which is understood to function like a hashtag in social media. "Hashtags" can also alert the listener to a rapper's "unstated" feelings. (Chapter 2)

Heteronormative: A belief that male and female are the only two genders and that heterosexuality is the normalized way to express sexuality. (Chapter 7)

Hip-hop generation: Comprises individuals born between 1965 and 1984, who grew up after the Civil Rights movement and for whom hip hop was always a presence in their lives. (Chapter 12)

HomoHop: A collective of queer hip-hop artists that emerged in the Bay Area in the early 1990s. (Chapter 7)

Hook (or chorus): A larger unit of musical form that typically features the same music and the same lyrics with each repetition. (Chapter 1)

Hypermasculinity: An exaggerated display of qualities typically considered masculine, such as strength, aggression, and violence. (Chapter 7)

Hyphy: Music associated with sideshow culture in Oakland. It often features call and response and is well suited for dancing. (Chapter 11)

Imitation: Engaging with hip-hop culture simply through empty appropriation. (Chapter 9)

Immersion: Becoming an authentic part of hip-hop culture by studying and participating in it for some time. (Chapter 9)

Intentional fallacy: The belief that there is some true meaning in a work of art and that we can decipher that meaning if we know the author's intentions when he or she created the work. (Chapter 2)

Internal rhyme: When words within a line rhyme. (Chapter 2)

Intersectionality: An understanding that people can be subject to more than one form of oppression simultaneously. (Chapter 7)

Intertextuality: A belief that texts (songs, lyrics, sounds) have no inherent meaning but instead develop meaning through their relationships with other texts. (Chapter 2)

Intro/outro: The beginning or ending material of a song that is not a verse or chorus. (Chapter 1)

Inversion: An identification strategy in which artists take material that might be "used against them" (i.e., race, ethnicity, sexuality) and parody it in order to earn a way in to hip-hop culture. (Chapter 9)

Layering: One of the fundamental aesthetics of hip hop, it involves juxtaposing musical sounds either simultaneously or sequentially. (Chapter 1)

Listening subject: An idealized listener to a song; the intended audience; the person the song is addressed to. (Chapter 2)

Luxury rap: Rap about extreme wealth that has little connection to "the streets." (Chapter 12)

Lyric: A kind of narrative that evokes a feeling, rather than unfolding in time. (Chapter 2)

Metaphor: A direct comparison between two otherwise dissimilar objects. (Chapter 2)

Meter: The grouping of **beats** into regularly recurring patterns of strong and weak. Meter can be duple (two beats per **bar**), triple (three beats per bar), or quadruple (four beats per bar), and it can be simple (the beat is divisible by two) or compound (the beat is divisible by three). (Chapter 1)

Miami bass: A style of music popular in Miami in the 1990s, featuring booming bass, fast **tempos**, and often raunchy lyrics. (Chapter 11)

Mixer: A device that allows the DJ to blend the sounds of two or more **turntables** or other audio devices (like drum machines and **synthesizers**). (Chapter 1)

Mixtape: A compilation recording, first distributed on cassette tapes but now made available on the internet. Mixtapes are typically free and used as promotional material. (Chapter 10)

Moynihan Report: Officially called *The Negro Family: A Case for National Action*, Moynihan's report almost single-handedly created the stereotype of the single mother and absent father in the black community and diagnosed this family structure as "pathological." (Chapter 12)

Multisyllabic rhyme: A device in which at least two consecutive syllables in a word rhyme. (Chapter 2)

Napster: A music file-sharing service that launched in 1999. The ability to share files without paying for them angered some in the music industry and paved the way for music-streaming services. (Chapter 10)

Narrative: The ways in which stories are told. (Chapter 2)

New Jack Swing: A popular musical style in the 1990s pioneered by Teddy Riley and Uptown Records, featuring rapid **tempos**, synthesized **beats**, and a strong snare on the backbeat. The aesthetic inspired films and fashion as well. (Chapter 1)

Nommo: The power of the word. A **griot's** words were thought to be capable of effecting change in the world. (Chapter 4)

Panther 21: Members of the Black Panther Party who were arrested in New York, accused of conspiracy to kill police officers and plotting to bomb government buildings. Tupac's mother, Afeni Shakur, was among the twenty-one. (Chapter 10).

Party: A genre of rap that is meant to be danced to, usually with lighter subject matter. (Chapter 2)

Peer reference: Referencing rappers, historically important DJs, or break-dancing crews in a song or video. (Chapter 6)

Percussion-effusive: A style of rap delivery in which the voice is used as a percussion instrument. (Chapter 3)

Personification: Ascribing human characteristics to an inanimate object. (Chapter 2)

Place: A specific, physical, geographical location. (Chapter 10)

Posse: In hip hop, any group of people with a common affiliation. (Chapter 10)

Posse cut: A song that features several artists, often from different labels, with each contributing a verse. (Chapter 3)

Postindustrial: The economic after-effects of manufacturing industries moving out of a region. (Chapter 10)

Post-racial: A belief that the inequalities among racial groups had disappeared as a result of the appearance of equal opportunity. (Chapter 12)

Producer: One who creates **beats**, usually with electronic instruments as opposed to **turntables**. (Chapter 1)

Punch phrase: Cutting in a brief segment of another record by quickly moving the **crossfader** over and back again. (Chapter 1)

Pun/punch line: A play on like-sounding words, often used to humorous effect. (Chapter 2)

Queen Mother: A female rapper who typically projects an Afrocentric appearance and takes the role of a nurturing caregiver. (Chapter 7)

Reality: A genre of rap that purportedly relays gritty tales of street life. (Chapter 2)

Redlining: Denying people loans or other services based on their residing in a "bad" area. (Chapter 10)

Refrain: A short, repeated phrase of text. (Chapter 4)

Reggaeton: A genre that emerged from Puerto Rico in the 1990s, fusing hip hop with reggae en Español. (Chapter 11)

Rhythm: Any combination or division of **beats**. (Chapter 1)

Rupture: Any interruption of the **flow**. (Chapter 3)

Sampler: A digital musical instrument capable of recording, storing, and altering the recorded sound. (Chapter 1)

Sampling: The act of digitally extracting a sound or a component of a sound.

Scratching: Moving a record back and forth with your hand to create percussive effects. (Chapter 1)

Sequencer/drum machine: An electronic musical instrument used to arrange different sounds—sampled and synthesized—into a particular order, which can then be looped repeatedly. Roland's TR-808 is one of the most commonly used sequencers in early rap. (Chapter 1)

Set: A local unit of a gang. (Chapter 10)

Shout-out: The mention of a name of a friend, peer, loved one, group, or product in a song. (Chapter 10)

Sideshow: Part car show and part street party, sideshows represent an effort by the black community to reclaim public space in Oakland, California. (Chapter 11)

Signifyin(g): A way of using language that involves misdirection and layered meanings. (Chapter 4)

Simile: An implied comparison that uses the word "like" or "as." (Chapter 2)

Sista with Attitude: A female MC who adopts postures typically considered masculine. (Chapter 7)

Slant rhyme: Sometimes called "near" or "half" rhyme, it occurs when the consonants but not the vowels, or the vowels but not the consonants, sound similar. (Chapter 2)

Sonic color line: A series of cultural practices through which race is made audible. (Chapter 12)

Sonic signature: The unique sonic identifier of a producer that emerges from a combination of the instruments ("real" or digital) that the producer uses, the kinds of samples he or she prefers, the overall sound quality of the final product, and name shout-outs. (Chapter 1)

SoundCloud rapper: A rapper who uses the popular music streaming site SoundCloud in an effort to launch his or her career. Sometimes used as a pejorative. (Chapter 10).

SoundScan: A point-of-sale technology adopted by *Billboard* in 1991 to tabulate more accurate record-sales data. (Chapter 6)

Space: A territory—often associated with a place—that is constructed through repeated practices. (Chapter 10)

Speech-effusive: A style of rap delivery that most closely approximates natural speech. (Chapter 3)

Stylisitic allusion: Imitating earlier styles of rap music, the flow of a particular artist, or older technological equipment. (Chapter 6)

Subjectivity: Subjectivity addresses who is telling the story and who is listening to the story. The subjects can be real or hypothetical. (Chapter 2)

Sung style: A style of rap delivery associated with the old school, characterized by clear line breaks marked with end rhymes, as well as a gradual drop in pitch over the course of the line. (Chapter 3)

Supreme Alphabet: A method of interpreting texts, similar to an acronym, used by the Five-Percent Nation. (Chapter 8)

Supreme Mathematics: A numerological system of unlocking truths and correspondences in the universe, used by the Five-Percent Nation. (Chapter 8)

Swing: An uneven division of the **beat**—a long-short feel—that results from grouping the first two subdivisions in a compound **meter**. (Chapter 1)

Syncopation: Creating the effect of an accent on weak parts of the **beat**. (Chapter 2)

Synthesizer: An electronic musical instrument that uses analog or digital technology to mimic conventional sounds, most often musical instruments. (Chapter 1)

Syrup (lean, purple drank): Properly known as liquid codeine or promethazine, and was the drug of choice for many Houston rappers in the early 2000s. (Chapter 11)

Tempo: The relative speed of the **beat**. (Chapter 1)

Ten-Point Program: A document drafted by the Black Panther Party that detailed the organization's goals, modeled on the Bill of Rights. (Chapter 10)

Third Coast: A nickname for the American South that challenges the East Coast–West Coast binary that often characterizes rap. (Chapter 11)

Toasting (note: two different meanings)/talk over: 1)A epic tale, often passed down as oral tradition in the black community; 2) In Jamaican culture, talking in rhyme over a record that is playing. (Chapter 4)

Transformative rhyme: When words that do not rhyme at all are pronounced in such a way that a rhyme is forced. (Chapter 2)

Trap: 1) A house, usually abandoned, in which drugs are made and sold (Chapter 11); 2) A particular style of music popular in the 2000s characterized by slower **tempos**, deep bass, and rapid hi-hat figures. (Chapter 1)

Turntable: Another name for a record player. (Chapter 1)

Turntablist: A term used to describe DJs who make music to be listened to, not danced to. (Chapter 1)

Twerking: A dance associated with **bounce** that involves squatting low and rapidly shaking your hips. (Chapter 11)

Underground: A term used for rap music that is outside of the mainstream commercial channels. (Chapter 6)

Verse: A large unit of musical form consisting of multiple **bars**. Typically the music stays the same in each verse, but the lyrics change. (Chapter 1)

Versioning: Making different pressings of the same record: one might have no vocal track; another might have the instrumental levels mixed differently. (Chapter 4)

Virtuosity: Exhibiting the highest level of skill. (Chapter 6)

War on Drugs: An effort to curb drug use and abuse in the United States launched by Richard Nixon and perpetuated by subsequent leaders. The War on Drugs devastated certain communities as a result of its treatment of drug use as a crime, racially biased laws, and aggressive police tactics. (Chapter 12)

Bibliography

This bibliography includes what I consider the canonical texts of rap and hip-hop scholarship; it is not intended to be exhaustive. Some of the books appear in the endnotes; others are not referenced directly in this text but are worth exploring by any fan or scholar of rap music. They would also be useful adjunct texts for a class on rap music.

Bradley, Adam. *Book of Rhymes: The Poetics of Hip-Hop*. New York: Basic Civitas Books, 2009.

Bradley, Adam, and Andrew DuBois. *Anthology of Rap*. New Haven, CT: Yale University Press, 2010.

Chang, Jeff. *Can't Stop Won't Stop: A History of the Hip-Hop Generation*. New York: Picador, 2005.

Charnas, Dan. *The Big Payback: The History of the Business of Hip-Hop*. New York: New American Library, 2010.

Cobb, William Jelani. *To the Break of Dawn: A Freestyle on the Hip Hop Aesthetic*. New York: New York University Press, 2007.

Coleman, Brian. *Check the Technique: Liner Notes for Hip Hop Junkies*. 2 vols. New York: Villard Books, 2007, 2015.

Edwards, Paul. *How to Rap: The Art and Science of the Hip-Hop MC*. Chicago: Chicago Review Press, 2009.

Forman, Murray. *The 'Hood Comes First: Race, Space, and Place in Rap and Hip-Hop*. Middletown, CT: Wesleyan University Press, 2002.

Forman, Murray, and Mark Anthony Neal, eds. *That's the Joint! The Hip-Hop Studies Reader*. 2nd ed. New York: Routledge, 2012.

George, Nelson. *Hip Hop America*. New York: Penguin Books, 1998.

Kajikawa, Loren. *Sounding Race in Rap Songs*. Berkeley: University of California Press, 2015.

Katz, Mark. *Groove Music: The Art and Culture of the Hip-Hop DJ*. New York: Oxford University Press, 2012.

Keyes, Cheryl. *Rap Music and Street Consciousness*. Urbana and Chicago: University of Illinois Press, 2002.

Krims, Adam. *Rap Music and the Poetics of Identity*. Cambridge: Cambridge University Press, 2000.

Light, Alan. *The Vibe History of Hip Hop*. New York: Three Rivers Press, 1999.

Perkins, Willam Eric, ed. *Droppin' Science: Critical Essays on Rap Music and Hip Hop Culture*. Philadelphia: Temple University Press, 1996.

Perry, Imani. *Prophets of the Hood: Politics and Poetics in Hip Hop*. Durham, NC: Duke University Press, 2004.

Potter, Russell A. *Spectacular Vernaculars: Hip-Hop and the Politics of Postmodernism*. New York: State University of New York Press, 1995.

Rose, Tricia. *Black Noise: Rap Music and Black Culture in Contemporary America*.

Rose, Tricia. *The Hip Hop Wars: What We Talk about When We Talk about Hip Hop—And Why It Matters*. New York: Basic Books, 2008.

Schloss, Joseph. *Making Beats: The Art of Sample-Based Hip-Hop*. Middletown, CT: Wesleyan University Press, 2004.

Toop, David. *The Rap Attack: African Jive to New York Hip-Hop*. Boston: South End Press, 1984.

Williams, Justin, ed. *The Cambridge Companion to Hip-Hop*. Cambridge: Cambridge University Press, 2015.

Williams, Justin. *Rhymin' and Stealin': Musical Borrowing in Hip-Hop*. Ann Arbor: University of Michigan Press, 2012.

Credits

"Follow the Leader" by Eric B. and Rakim

Words and Music by Eric Barrier, Rakim and Bob James Copyright (c) 1988 EMI Blackwood Music Inc., Eric B. & Rakim Music and Remidi Music All Rights on behalf of EMI Blackwood Music Inc. and Eric B. & Rakim Music Administered by Sony/ATV Music Publishing LLC, 424 Church Street, Suite 1200, Nashville, TN 37219 International Copyright Secured All Rights ReservedReprinted by Permission of Hal Leonard LLC.

"Lost Ones" by J. Cole

Words and Music by Jermaine Cole Copyright (c) 2011 SONGS OF UNIVERSAL, INC. All Rights Reserved Used by Permission Reprinted by Permission of Hal Leonard LLC.

"Monster" by Nicki Minaj

Words and Music by SHAWN CARTER, KANYE WEST, MIKE DEAN, PATRICK REYNOLDS, ONIKA MARAJ, JUSTIN VERNON, MALIK JONES and WILLIAM ROBERTS. Copyright © 2010 WB MUSIC CORP., CARTER BOYS MUSIC, PLEASE GIMME MY PUBLISHING INC., STILL N THE WATER PUBLISHING, HARAJUKU BARBIE MUSIC, JABRIEL IZ MYNE, 4 BLUNTS LIT AT ONCE PUBLISHING and COPYRIGHT CONTROL. All Rights on behalf of itself and CARTER BOYS MUSIC Administered by WB MUSIC CORP. All Rights Reserved. Used By Permission of ALFRED MUSIC.

Words and Music by Kanye West, Mike Dean, William Roberts, Shawn Carter, Onika Maraj, Justin Vernon, Malik Yusef Jones, Patrick Reynolds, Ben Broffman, Daniel Lynas and Harley Wertheimer. Copyright (c) 2010 EMI Blackwood Music Inc., Please Gimme My Publishing Inc., Sony/ATV Songs LLC, 4 Blunts Lit At Once, First N Gold Publishing, Carter Boys Music, Papa George Music, Money Mack Music, Harajuku Barbie Music, Plain Pat What Up Publishing, Universal Music Corp. and Jabriel Iz Myne. All Rights on behalf of EMI Blackwood Music Inc., Please Gimme My Publishing Inc., Sony/ATV Songs LLC and 4 Blunts Lit At Once Administered by Sony/ATV Music Publishing LLC, 424 Church Street, Suite 1200, Nashville, TN 37219. All Rights on behalf of First N Gold Publishing Administered by Songs Of Kobalt MusicAll Rights on behalf of Carter Boys Music and Papa George Music Administered by WB Music Corp. All Rights on behalf of April Base Publishing Administered by BMG Rights Management (US) LLCAll Rights on behalf of Money Mack Music, Harajuku Barbie Music, Jabriel Iz Myne, Plain Pat What Up Publishing and

Songs Of Universal, Inc. Administered by Universal Music Corp. International Copyright Secured All Rights Reserved Reprinted by Permission of Hal Leonard LLC.

"The Breaks" by Kurtis Blow
Words and Music by James B. Moore, Lawrence Smith, Kurt Walker, Robert Ford, and Russell Simmons. Used courtesy of Music Management, Neutral Gray Music and Funk Groove Music.

"Wake Up! (Reprise in the Sunshine)" by Brand Nubian
Words and Music by Maxwell Dixon, Lorenzo Deschalus and Derek Murphy Copyright (c) 2001 UNIVERSAL MUSIC CORP. All Rights Reserved Used by PermissionReprinted by Permission of Hal Leonard LLC.

"Rapper's Delight" by Sugar Hill Gang
Words and Music by BERNARD EDWARDS and NILE RODGERS. Copyright © 1979 BERNARD'S OTHER MUSIC and SONY SONGS, INC. All Rights For BERNARD'S OTHER MUSIC Administered by WARNER-TAMERLANE PUBLISHING CORP. All Rights Reserved. Used By Permission of ALFRED MUSIC.

Words and Music by Nile Rodgers and Bernard EdwardsCopyright (c) 1979 Sony/ATV Music Publishing LLC and Bernard's Other MusicAll Rights on behalf of Sony/ATV Music Publishing LLC Administered by Sony/ATV Music Publishing LLC, 424 Church Street, Suite 1200, Nashville, TN 37219 International Copyright Secured All Rights Reserved Reprinted by Permission of Hal Leonard LLC.

"The Message" by Grandmaster Flash
Words and Music by Edward Fletcher, Clifton Chase, Sylvia Robinson and Melvin Glover-Copyright (c) 1982 SUGAR HILL MUSIC PUBLISHING LTD. and TWENTY NINE BLACK MUSIC All Rights Controlled and Administered by SONGS OF UNIVERSAL, INC.All Rights Reserved Used by PermissionReprinted by Permission of Hal Leonard LLC.

"I Need Love" by LL Cool J
Words and Music by JAMES TODD SMITH, STEVEN ETTINGER, DARRYL PIERCE and DWAYNE SIMON. Copyright © 1995 WB MUSIC CORP., LL COOL J MUSIC, UNIVERSAL MUSIC PUBLISHING GROUP and DEF JAM MUSIC, INC. All Rights on behalf of Itself and LL COOL J MUSIC Administered by WB MUSIC CORP. All Rights Reserved. Used By Permission of ALFRED MUSIC.

Words and Music by James Todd Smith, Dwayne Simon, Bobby Ervin, Darryl Pierce and Steven Ettinger Copyright (c) 1987, 1995 UNIVERSAL MUSIC CORP. and LL COOL J MUSIC All Rights Reserved Used by PermissionReprinted by Permission of Hal Leonard LLC.

"Queen Bitch" by Lil' Kim
Words and Music by KIMBERLY JONES, CARLOS BROADY, NASHIEM MYRICK. Copyright © 1997 UNDEAS MUSIC (BMI), NOTORIOUS K.I.M. MUSIC (BMI), NASH MACK MUSIC (ASCAP) and 6TH OF JULY MUSIC (NS). All Rights on Behalf of UNDEAS MUSIC and NOTORIOUS K.I.M. MUSIC Administered by WARNER-TAMERLANE PUBLISHING CORP. All Rights Reserved. Used By Permission of ALFRED MUSIC.

Carlos Broady, Kimberly Jones, Nashiem Myrick, © Copyright 1996. Six July Publishing/BMI (admin. By ClearBox Rights)/Nashmack Publishing/ASCAP/Warner-Tamerlane Publishing Corp/BMI. All rights reserved. Used by permission.

"Blazin' Mics" by T-Bone
Used by permission of Rene Sotomayor and Fun Attic Music. © 2002 All Rights Reserved.
"Roxanne, Roxanne"
UTFO
"Roxanne's Revenge"
Roxanne Shante

Index